# THE TEXTS OF THE WHITE YAJURVEDA

# THE TEXTS OF THE WHITE YAJURVEDA

**Translated with a Pupular Commentary**

by

## RALPH T. H. GRIFFITH

GYAN

*Published by*

Gyan Publishing House
5, Ansari Road
Daryaganj, New Delhi-110002
Phone: 011-47034999, 9811692060
E-mail: books@gyanbooks.com

*Distribution Network*
gyanbooks.com
India, USA, Canada, UK, Australia, France



ISBN : 978-81-212-2982-1 (HB)
First Published, 1899

2nd Impression 2021

*Printed at:* Gyan Press, Delhi.



**The Texts of the White Yajurveda**
Author: Ralph T. H. Griffith

# THE TEXTS OF

# THE WHITE YAJURVEDA

## TRANSLATED WITH A POPULAR COMMENTARY

BY

RALPH T. H. GRIFFITH,

FORMERLY PRINCIPAL OF BENARES COLLEGE, AND SOMETIME DIRECTOR OF PUBLIC INSTRUCTION, NORTH-WEST PROVINCES AND OUDH.

BENARES:

PRINTED AND PUBLISHED BY E. J. LAZARUS AND CO.

1899.

# CONTENTS.

## BOOK III.



## BOOK IV.

## BOOK IX.

## BOOK XIII.

## BOOK XVI.



## BOOK XVII.

## BOOK XX.

# PREFACE.

THE YAJURVEDA—derived from the roots *yaj*, to sacrifice or worship, and *vid*, to know,—is the Knowledge of Sacrifice or Sacrificial Texts and Formulas as distinguished from the Ṛigveda or Knowledge of Recited Praise, the Sâmaveda or Knowledge of Chanted Hymns, and the Atharva or Brahmaveda which is the Knowledge of Prayer, Charm, and Spells. Though ranking second in the Indian enumeration of the Vedas and containing much that is of very ancient origin, its compilation in its present form, exhibiting as it does the almost complete development of castes and mixt castes and considerable advance in arts and sciences, trades, handicrafts and occupations, is evidently of later date than that even of the Atharva. The Saṃhitâ or Collection of its hymns, texts, and formulas, constituting the hymn-book and prayer-book of the Adhvaryu priests as distinguished from the Hotar, the Udgâtar, and the Brahman, the special priests, respectively, of the three other Vedas, owes its origin to the increasing multiformity and complication of the Indian ritual and the recognized insufficiency of the simple and unsystematically arranged Collection of Ṛigveda Hymns to meet the requirements of the performers of various essentially important rites and ceremonies.

The Yajurveda, owing to a schism among its earliest teachers and their followers, was divided into two distinct Saṃhitâs or Collections called—probably from the names of the Ṛishis or inspired Seers who are respectively their reputed compilers—the Taittirîya and the Vâjasaneya or Vâjasaneyi; the former and older being known also by the title Kṛishṇa or Black—probably from its dark or obscure appearance, the collection of sacrificial texts and formulas being perplexingly intermingled with the Brâhmaṇa or exegetical portion which explains them and teaches their ritual application—, and the latter being called Ṣukla or White, the revised, systematic and clear collection, containing the texts and formulas by themselves with a totally distinct Brâhmaṇa, the Ṣatapatha, as an appendix. In the two divisions, besides these essential points of difference, are found occasional verbal and orthoepic variations which are generally of little importance. The order of rites and ceremonies is substantially identical, but the White contains a few more texts than the Black.

The Saṃhitâ of the White Yajurveda consists of forty Adhyâyas or Books containing, with frequent repetitions of the same text, about two thousand verses. A large portion of these are Ṛichas or Strophes borrowed—frequently with variations—from the Ṛigveda, and sometimes from the Atharva: these, of course, are metrical. Nearly equal in quantity are the Yajus texts or sacrificial formulas—the most characteristic portion, from which the Veda derives its name—composed in measured prose 'which rises now and then,' as Professor Weber observes, 'to a true rhythmical swing,' and long passages, such as the lists of victims to be tied up and dedicated at the Aṣvamedha and the Purushamedha, which are necessarily in the simplest prose.

For further information with regard to this Veda the reader should consult Professor Weber's History of Indian Literature (English Translation by John Mann and Theodor Zachariae: Trübner's Oriental Series); Professor Max Müller's History of Ancient Sanskrit Literature; Professor J. Eggeling's Introduction, Vol. XII. of the Sacred Books of the East, or, for a briefer account, Mrs. Manning's Ancient and Mediaeval India, Vol. I. pp. 107—109.

My translation follows the fine edition of the White Yajurveda or Vâjasaneyi-Sanhitâ, in the two recensions—the Mâdhyandina and the Kâṇva—, with Mahîdhara's Commentary, the Vedadipa, or Lamp of Knowledge, written towards the close of the sixteenth century, published under the patronage of the Honourable Court of Directors of the East India Company in 1849 at Berlin by Dr. Albrecht Weber, at that time Docent of the Sanskrit language at that University. This excellent edition consisting of three Parts the latter two of which contain the Ṣatapatha-Brâhmaṇa in the Mâdhyandina recension with extracts from the Commentaries of Sâyaṇa, Harisvâmin, and Dvivedaganga, and the Ṣrautra-Sûtra of Kâtyâyana with extracts from the Commentaries of Karka and Yâjñikadeva, has not been reprinted and is now practically unobtainable. In India the text of the Mâdhyandina recension with Mahidhara's Commentary has been issued in a cheap form at Calcutta by Pandit Jîbânanda Vidyâsâgara, B. A., Superintendent of the Free Sanskrit College, of which a second edition appeared in 1892; and a lithographed edition of the text with a Hindî translation of Mahidhara's Commentary was published in 1874, at Besma in the North-Western Provinces, by Râjâ Giriprasâdavarman of that place. A cheap edition of the text, in unbound MS. form, has been published at Bombay.

No separate translation of the whole Saṃhitâ or Collection of Texts and Formulas has appeared in any European language. It was Professor Weber's intention, as signified in his History of Indian Literature, to bring out a translation giving the ceremonial belonging to each verse, together with a full glossary, but 'this promise has not been fulfilled, owing to the pressure of other labours.' This scholar had previously published a Latin translation, with annotations in the same language, of Books IX. and X. in his Vâjasaneya-Sanhitae Specimen (Breslau, 1846), and more recently a German version of Book XVI. in Indische Studien II. pp. 14 ff., and of the list of men and women to be dedicated at the Purushamedha in his treatise on Human Ṣacrifice among Indians of the Vedic Age reprinted in his Indische Streifen I. pp. 76-84. Of Book XL. as an Upanishad there are several translations into English.

Moreover, nearly the whole of the first eighteen Books has been incorporated—dissected and explained clause by clause—in the first nine Books of the Ṣatapatha-Brâhmaṇa; and an admirable translation of this vast work by Professor Julius Eggeling is now nearly completed in the Sacred Books of the East, four volumes (XII, XXVI., XLI., XLIII. of that series) having already appeared, and the concluding volume (XLV) being in the press. From this translation—which, but for its bulk and costliness would make half of my work superfluous—and from Professor Eggeling's annotations, I have derived the greatest assistance, and most gratefully record my obligations.

All that I have attempted to do is to give a faithful translation, to the best of my ability, of the texts and sacrificial formulas of the Veda, with just sufficient commentary, chiefly from Mahîdhara, to make them intelligible. Much additional information may be found in Professor A. Hillebrandt's Ritual-Litteratur, Vedische Opfer und Zauber (Grundriss der Indo-Arischen Philologie und Altertumskunde), Strassburg: 1897; and further minute details of the various sacrifices, rites and ceremonies are given in the Ṣatapatha-Brâhmaṇa as already mentioned, and in various articles, referred to in my notes, by Professor A. Weber, the great authority on the Yajurveda and all that is connected with it.

R. T. H. GRIFFITH.

KOTAGIRI, NILGIRIS:

*May, 1899.*

# THE TEXTS OF THE WHITE YAJURVEDA
## OR VÂJASANEYA-SAṂHITÂ.

## BOOK THE FIRST.

THEE for food. Thee for vigour. Ye are breezes.

To noblest work God Savitar impel you. Inviolable! swell his share for Indra.

No thief, no evil-minded man shall master you rich in offspring, free from pain and sickness.

Be constant, numerous to this lord of cattle. Guard thou the cattle of the Sacrificer.

---

Books I. and II. contain the texts and formulas required at the New and Full Moon sacrifices, the regular performance of which is obligatory on the Brâhmanical householder during thirty years from his Agnyâdhâna or ceremonial establishment of his own sacrificial fires; or, according to some authorities, during his whole remaining life. Each of these sacrifices usually requires two days for its performance, the work of the first day consisting in introductory ceremonies such as the preparation of the Âhavanîya and Dakshiṇâgni, or Eastern and Southern fire-places, for the reception of fire from the Western fire-place, the Gârhapatya or Householder's hearth; the solemn taking of the *vrata* or vow of fasting and abstention during the sacrifice; and the performance by the sacrificer of the evening Agnihotra or burnt oblation of milk. On this day also, the day before the appearance of the New or the Full Moon, the Adhvaryu priest, who performs the practical part of the sacrifice, cuts a branch from a Parṇa or Palâṣa tree (Butea Frondosa), or from a Ṣamî tree (Acacia Suma), trims it and uses it as a switch to drive the calves away from the cows whose milk is to form part of the offerings of the next day's special ceremony.

1 *Thee:* 'I cut' understood. The Palâṣa branch is addressed by the Adhvaryu. *For food:* as instrumental in obtaining the seasonable rain and the good harvest which will result from the sacrifice. *Thee for vigour:* 'I cut or trim,' in order to obtain the bodily strength which a sufficiency of food may be expected to bring. *Ye:* the Adhvaryu touches and addresses the calves. *Breezes:* as the winds purify the ground, so do ye with your droppings which are used for smearing, and so cleansing, the floors of houses; or, perhaps, meaning 'intruders,' preventing the milking of the cows; or, free to wander where you will, and then to return home. The following lines contain a benediction on the cows. *Noblest work:* the sacrifice, in which their milk is the most important element. *Savitar:* the Sun-God as the great vivifier and stimulator. *No thief, etc:* cf. R. V. VI. 28. 7. *Guard thou:* the Adhvaryu addresses the sacred branch which he hides on the eastern side of the Âhavanîya or of the Gârhapatya house.

2 Strainer of Vasu art thou. Thou art heaven. Earth art thou. Thou art Mâtarisvan's caldron.
Thou art the All-container. Stand thou firmly, secure by Law Supreme, and do not totter. Nor be thy Lord of Sacrifice unsteady.

3 Thou art the strainer, hundred-streamed, of Vasu. Thou art the strainer, thousand-streamed, of Vasu.
May Savitar the God with Vasu's strainer, thousand-streamed, rightly cleansing, purify thee.

4 Which didst thou milk? This is the cow Visvâyu. This Visvakarman. This is Visvadhâyas.
Thee, Indra's share, with Soma do I curdle. Be thou protector of the oblation, Vishnu.

5 I will observe the vow, Lord of Vows, Agni! May I have strength therefor. Success attend me.
Now into truth from untruth do I enter.

6 Who is it that unites thee? He unites thee. For what doth he yoke thee? For that he yokes thee.
You two for work, you two for its completion.

---

2 *Strainer of Vasu:* cleanser, purifier, of the sacrifice; *vasu* meaning originally good, kind, wealthy. This *pavitram* or strainer, made of two or three blades of Kusa grass or Darbha (Poa Cynosuroides), used at religious ceremonies, is fastened with this formula on the hidden Palâsa or Samî branch (verse 1). *Thou art heaven:* he puts the *sthâlî* or cooking-pot on the Gârhapatya fire, and addresses it. He calls it heaven because as an implement of sacrifice it aids in producing rain. *Earth:* as being made of clay. *Mâtarisvan's caldron:* a fanciful expression for the atmosphere or mid-region of air, Mâtarisvan being here identified with Vâyu the Wind-God. *Lord of Sacrifice:* the *yajamâna* or householder who institutes and takes part in the sacrifice. The strainer is then put on the cooking-pot, and addressed.

3 *Purify thee:* the milk which is to be used in the Agnihotra sacrifice.

4 *Which didst thou milk?:* this is properly part of verse 3. In reply to this question, thrice repeated, of the Adhvaryu, the milker (who may be any one above the rank of a Sûdra) mentions the ordinary name of each of the three cows, and the Adhvaryu gives her a sacrificial name, thereby imparting to her the virtues and powers which the name signifies. *Visvâyu:* All-life-containing. *Visvakarman:* All-effecting. *Visvadhâyas:* All-supporting. *Thee:* the milk which is now removed from the fire. The mixture is then covered over with a vessel not made of earth, and entrusted to the guardianship of Vishnu or the sacrifice.

5 Spoken by the sacrificer who with his wife is about to take the prescribed *vrata* or vow of abstinence from certain food and enjoyment during the performance of the ceremonies. *Lord of Vows:* Agni is said to be the Gods' *Vratapati*, Lord or Keeper of vows. *Truth:* reality, godhead. *Untruth:* unreality, perishable humanity; that is, 'I attain to a divine body and am no longer a mere man.' He is thus bound to speak nothing but the truth.

6 *Unites thee?:* places the vessel containing the water, which has been formally brought forward, by the side of the Âhavanîya fire? The question

7 Scorched are the fiends, scorched the malignant beings. Burnt out are fiends, burnt out malignant beings.
Throughout the spacious middle air I travel.

8 Thou art the yoke. Injure thou him who injures. Harm him who harm us. Harm the man we injure.
Thou art the Gods' best carrier, bound most firmly, filled fullest, welcomest, Gods' best invoker.

9 Thou art unbent, receiver of oblations. Stand firmly in thy place and do not totter.
Nor be thy Lord of sacrifice unsteady.
Let Vishṇu mount thee. To the wind lie open. The demons are expelled. Let the five grasp it.

10 By impulse of God Savitar I take thee with arms of Aşvins, with the hands of Pûshan,
Thee dear to Agni, dear to Agni-Soma.

11 Thee for abundance, not for evil spirit. May mine eye look upon the light of heaven.

---

is asked by the Adhvaryu. *For what?* or For whom? *For that:* or For him: *kasmai,* like Latin cui, being either masculine or neuter. The meaning of the questions is ambiguous, the interrogative pronoun *ka,* Who?, in all its cases being also regarded as a name of Prajâpati, Lord of Creatures. See The Hymns of the Ṛigveda, X. 121. *You two:* the ladle used in offering the Agnihotras, and the winnowing-basket with which chaff and grain are separated. *Work:* the sacrifice. The words 'I take' are understood.

7 *Scorched:* the ladle and winnowing-basket are heated, to symbolize the expulsion of malignant spirits who infest the air, after which the Adhvaryu is free to move in all directions.

8 The Adhvaryu addresses the yoke (*dhur*) of the cart which contains the grain and other elements of sacrifice. *Injure: dhûrva.* The play on the word is lost in translation. *Bound most firmly: sasnitamam;* or, in accordance with the etymology of the word, best provider, most liberal giver.

9 He addresses the cart. *Vishṇu:* the sacrifice. *Lie open:* he addresses the rice. *The five:* his fingers, with which, when he has mounted the cart, he touches the rice.

10 *By impulse: prasave. Savitar:* the Impeller and Vivifier. *Aşvins:* twin Light-Gods, heralds of Dawn, who are the Adhvaryus of the Gods. *Pûshan:* a solar Deity who destributes their respective portions to the Gods. *Thee:* the rice. Agni aud the dual Deity Agni-Soma are mentioned because an unaddressed oblation would cause doubt and contention among the Gods.

The offering to Agni at a Full Moon sacrifice is a rice-cake presented on eight potsherds, and that to Agni-Soma one on eleven.

11 *Thee:* the remainder of the rice; 'I leave' being understood. *For abundance:* or, according to Mahîdhara, for future oblation. *For evil spirit: arâtaye;* or, with Mahîdhara, for non-oblation. *Light:* comprehending, according to Mahîdhara, sacrifice, day, Gods, and Sun. *Those with doors:* houses, especially the house of the Sacrificer. *Throughout, etc.* see I. 7. *Navel:* or centre. *Aditi's lap:* the bosom of infinite Earth.

May those with doors stand on the earth securely. Throughout the spacious middle air I travel.

Upon the navel of the earth I place thee, on Aditi's lap. Protect the oblation, Agni !

12 Ye two are strainers that belong to Vishṇu. By Savitar's impulse, with this flawless strainer I purify you with the rays of Sûrya.

Bright Waters, flowing forward, foremost drinkers, lead forward now this sacrifice, lead forward the Sacrifice's Lord, the God-devoted Lord of the Sacrifice, the liberal giver.

13 Indra elected you in fight with Vṛitra: in fight with Vṛitra you elected Indra.

By over-sprinkling are ye consecrated. I sprinkle thee agreeable to Agni. I sprinkle thee welcome to Agni-Soma.

Pure for the work divine be ye, and holy, pure for the sacrifice to Gods. Whatever of yours the impure have by their touch polluted, hereby I cleanse for you from all defilement.

14 Giver art thou of happiness. Rejected are fiends, rejected are malignant beings.

Aditi's skin art thou. May Aditi receive thee. A wooden stone art thou. Thou art a broad-based stone. May the skin of Aditi receive thee.

15 Body of Agni art thou, the releaser of speech. I seize thee for the Gods' enjoyment.

A mighty stone art thou, formed out of timber.

---

12 *Strainers:* he makes two (see I. 2), and addresses them. *Vishṇu:* the sacrifice. *Flawless strainer:* the wind. *You:* the sacrificial waters. *Foremost drinkers:* of the Soma with which they are mingled.

13 *Elected:* mixed with Soma, to inspirit him. *Vṛitra:* the cloud-demon who obstructs and withholds the rain. The root of the word is *vṛi*, to encompass, also, to choose; hence the play on the words *avṛiṇīta*, he elected, *avṛiṇīdhvam*, ye elected, and *Vṛitra*. Cf. R. V. III. 34. 3, vṛitram avṛiṇot, he (Indra) encompassed Vṛitra the Encompasser. *Thee:* the oblation. *Be ye:* the sacrificial vessels which he purifies by sprinkling.

14 *Giver, etc.:* he addresses the black-antelope's skin—'one of the symbols of Brâhmanical worship and civilization.' See Sacred Books of the East, XII. p. 23 note. It is spread under the wooden mortar in which the rice is husked and pounded, to prevent any loss of the sacred offerings. *Rejected:* more literally, 'shaken off,' by shaking the skin as it falls to the ground. *Aditi:* Earth.

*Wooden stone:* the mortar is addressed, made of wood but representing the pressing-stones with which Soma juice is extracted.

15 *Thou:* the rice-oblations poured into the mortar. *Releaser of speech:* of the voice of the priest which hitherto has been restrained. *Great wooden stone:* the pestle is addressed. *Havishkṛit:* oblation-preparer; the Sacrificer, his wife, or another.

Make ready for the Deities this oblation: with careful preparation make it ready.

Havishkṛit, come! Havishkṛit, come! Havishkṛit, come!

16 Thou art a cock whose tongue is sweet with honey. Call to us hither sap and manly vigour.

May we with thee in every fight be victors. Rain-grown art thou. May the rain-grown receive thee.

Cleared off are fiends, cleared off are evil beings. Expelled are fiends. May Vâyu separate you. May Savitar the God, the golden-handed, with flawless hand unto himself receive you.

17 Bold art thou. Cast away the Corpse-consumer. Drive off the fire that eats raw flesh, O Agni.

That which makes offerings to the Gods bring hither.

Firm art thou. Make earth firm. For the foe's slaughter I set thee on, devoted to the priesthood, devoted to the nobles and the kinsmen.

18 Agni, do thou accept our holy service.

Keeper art thou: make firm the Air's mid-region. For the foe's death I set thee on, devoted to priesthood and nobility and kinsmen.

Thou art a stay: uphold the sky securely. For the foe's death, etc.

I set thee on for sake of all the regions. Formers of layers are ye, and heap-formers. With Bhṛigus' and Angirases' heat be heated.

---

16 *Thou:* the sacrificial implement, a peg or wedge, with which the pressing-stones are beaten, is addressed. *Cock:* on account of the noise it makes. *Sweet:* to the Gods, as announcing the preparation of sacrifice. *Rain-grown:* the winnowing-basket, made of reeds and strong grass that grow rapidly in the rainy season, is addressed. *Thee:* the husked rice, grown also in the Rains, which is poured into the winnowing-basket. *Cleared off:* together with the fallen husks. *Vâyu:* the wind. *You:* the husked and unhusked grain. *Flawless:* letting no grains fall through separated fingers. *Receive you:* the husked grain.

17 *Thou:* the poker or fire-shovel of Palâsa wood is addressed. *Corpse-consumer:* the fire of the funeral pile. *That eats raw flesh:* domestic fire for cooking meat. These two forms of fire are excluded, and the sacrificial fire is to remain. *Firm art thou:* the potsherd on which the oblation is to be cooked is addressed. *The kinsmen:* of the Sacrificer.

18 *Keeper:* a second potsherd is addressed. *Stay:* a third potsherd is addressed. *I set thee on:* he addresses a fourth potsherd which he puts on the fire. *Ye:* the remaining potsherds, which he covers with live coals. *Bhṛigus and Angirases:* ancient priestly families, most intimately connected with the worship of Agni.

19 Giver of happiness art thou. Rejected are fiends, rejected are malignant beings. Aditi's skin art thou. May Aditi receive thee.

Bowl, rock art thou. May Aditi's skin receive thee.

Thou art the sky's supporting pillar.

Bowl from the rock art thou. The rock receive thee.

20 Grain art thou. Please the Gods. Thee for in-breathing. For out-breath thee. Thee for diffusive breathing. May I impart to life a long extension.

May Savitar the God, the golden-handed, with flawless hand unto himself receive you.

Thee for the eye. Juice art thou of the Great Ones.

21 By impulse of God Savitar I strew thee, with arms of Asvins, with the hands of Pûshan.

With plants let waters, plants with sap be mingled. United be the rich ones with the moving. The sweet ones and the sweet be joined together.

22 For generation's sake I join thee. This is Agni's. This Agni-Soma's. Thee for food.

Thou art the caldron, life of all that liveth. Spread thyself widely forth, thou, widely spreading. So may thy Lord of sacrifice spread widely.

Thy skin let Agni harm not. In highest heaven let the God Savitar bake thee.

23 Fear not. Shrink not. Let not the sacrifice be languid, not languid be the Sacrificer's offspring.

For Trita thee. For Dvita thee. For Ekata thee.

---

19 *Giver, etc.*: the black-antelope's skin is again addressed. See I. 14. *Bowl, rock*: the nether pressing-stone now placed on the skin. *Bowl from the rock*: the upper and smaller stone regarded as the offspring of the nether stone.

20 *Grain*: the rice now poured on the nether stone is addressed. *Please*: *dhinuhi*, imperative of *dhi* from which Mahîdhara derives *dhânyam*, grain. *In-breathing, etc.*: three of the five or more vital airs. *Life*: of the sacrificer. *May Savitar, etc.*: repeated from I. 16. *Thee*: 'I look at' understood. *For the eye*: that the sacrificer's sight may be strengthened. *Thou*: the clarified sacrificial butter. *Great Ones*: the cows.

21 *Thee*: the ground rice which is now poured into a vessel which contains the two strainers (I. 12). *Plants*: the rice. *Rich ones*: the waters with which the flour is mixed. *The moving*: the plants, the rice.

22 *For generation's sake*: that children may be born to the Sacrificer. The mixture of rice and water is addressed. *This*: the dough is divided, one lump or cake for Agni and one for the dual deity, Agni-Soma. *Thee*: the clarified butter. *For food*: as in I. 1. *Caldron*: the rice-cake is likened to the caldron used at the Pravargya ceremony, introductory to the Soma Sacrifice. See Sacred Books of the East, XII. p. 44, note. *Agni*: the fire on which the cake is put.

23 *Fear not*: my touch. He addresses the cake and touches it. *Trita*

24 By impulse of God Savitar I take thee, with arms of Aṣvins, with the hands of Pûshan, thee who for Gods performest sacred service.

Indra's right arm art thou: sharp with a thousand spikes, a hundred edges. The keen-edged Wind art thou, the foeman's slayer.

25 O Earth, whereon men serve the Gods with worship, let me not do thy plant's root any damage.

Go to the pen, the cowstall. Heaven rain for thee.

On this earth's farthest end, God Savitar, bind him, with hundred fetters bind the man who hates us and whom we hate. Thence do not thou realease him.

26 May I drive Araru away from Earth, the seat of men's oblations to the Gods. Go to the pen . . . . . release him (as in verse 25).

O Araru, thou shalt not soar to heaven. Let not thy drop mount upward to the sky.

Go to the pen . . . . . . release him (as in verse 25).

27 I with the metre Gâyatrî enclose thee. I lay the Trishṭup metre round about thee. With Jagatî metre I confine and gird thee.

---

=τρίτος third; an ancient Vedic Deity, perhaps Agni in his third or lightning form. *Dvita* and *Ekata*, formed analogically from *dvi*, two, and *eka*, one, are Brâhmanical figments, and are said to be Trita's brothers. See Macdonell, Vedic Mythology, pp. 67-69. According to Mahîdhara the three are Agni's brothers. *Thee*: 'I pour out' understood; the water with which the cooking-vessel has been rinsed.

24 *Thee:* the *sphya*, a wooden implement shaped like a sword, used for stirring the boiled rice, drawing lines on the ground, and other sacrificial purposes. *Thousand spikes:* like, and representing in its power, the thunderbolt of Indra. *Foeman's slayer*: destroyer of Asuras or fiends and of those who hate and interrupt sacrifices.

25 *O Earth, etc.:* with this formula the Adhvaryu throws the *sphya* on a clump of grass placed between him and the altar. *Go to the pen, etc.*: be not wasted; mix with the droppings of the cows. He addresses the earth raised up by the *sphya*. *Rain for thee:* he addresses the altar. *Earth's farthest end*: that is, Naraka or hell. With this formula the loose soil is thrown upon the rubbish-heap.

26 The *sphya* is thrown a second time. *Araru*: a certain Asura or fiend. See R. V. X. 99. 10; A. V. VI. 46. 1. *Thy drop*: earth, or the altar in the shape of the earth, is addressed, while the *sphya* is thrown a third time. The *drop* is earth's life sustaining moisture which must not mount upward and be lost.

27 The names of the three chief Vedic metres are given to the three lines drawn with the *sphya* on three sides of the altar. *Thee:* Vishṇu, that is, the sacrifice. *Sprung from good soil*: the Vedi or altar is addressed.

Sprung from good soil art thou, and bliss-bestowing. Pleasant art thou, and a fair seat to rest on. Thou hast both strengthening food and drink in plenty.

28 Before the cruel foe's secret departure, Mighty One, raising high earth, life-bestower, which to the Moon they lifted by oblations, that earth the sages still point out and worship.

Deposit in its place the sprinkling-water. Thou art the slayer of the man who hates us.

29 Scorched are the demons, scorched the evil beings. Burnt out are fiends, burnt out malignant creatures.

Unsharpened, thou art slayer of the foemen. Thee, rich in food, I cleanse for the food's kindling.

Scorched . . . . . creatures (as above).

Thee rich in food, I cleanse for the food's kindling.

30 A zone for Aditi art thou. Pervader of Vishṇu art thou. For great strength I take thee. I look upon thee with an eye uninjured.

Thou art the tongue of Agni. Good invoker of Gods be thou at every holy station, at every sacrificial text I utter.

31 By Savitar's impulsion do I cleanse thee, with flawless strainer, with the rays of Sûrya.

By Savitar's impulsion do I cleanse you, with flawless strainer, with the rays of Sûrya.

Light art thou ; thou art splendid ; thou art Amrit. Thou, truly, art the Gods' beloved station, inviolable means of holy worship.

---

28 *The cruel foe's:* probably the demon Araru is meant. *Mighty One:* Vishṇu, or the sacrifice, is addressed. *Point out:* in the spots of the Moon. *Deposit:* the Âgnidhra or Fire-kindling priest is addressed. *Its place:* the altar. *Thou:* the water, which is called on to aid in defending the sacrifice from interruption.

29 *Scorched, etc.:* the formula is repeated from I. 7. The *sruva* or dipping-spoon is symbolically heated. *I cleanse:* by wiping it with sacred grass. *For the food's kindling:* with sacrificial butter. With this formula he cleanses the *sruk* or offering-spoon.

30 The Adhvaryu girds the Sacrificer's wife with a triple cord of Muñja grass (Saccharum Munja), and initiates her as her husband's associate in the ceremony. *Aditi:* Earth, represented by the Sacrificer's wife. *Pervader:* the southward end of the girdle is addressed. *Vishṇu:* the Sacrifice. *I:* the matron speaks as she looks down on the pot of sacrificial butter which the Adhvaryu places before her.

31 The Adhvaryu speaks. *Thee:* the clarified butter. *You:* the sprinkling waters. *Thou:* the butter. *Amrit:* nectar, the drink of the Gods; or, immortal. *Beloved station:* 'favourite resort (or, dainty)': Eggeling.

# BOOK THE SECOND.

THOU art a black-buck dwelling in the covert. I sprinkle thee agreeable to Agni.

Thou art the altar. Thee welcome to the sacred grass I sprinkle.

Thou art the sacred covering-grass. I sprinkle thee grateful to the sacrificial ladles.

2 Thou art what giveth Aditi her moisture. Thou art the hair-tuft on the head of Vishṇu. I spread thee, wool-soft, good for Gods to sit on.

Hail to the Earth's Lord! To the World's Lord Hail! Hail to the Lord of Beings!

3 For safety of this all let the Gandharva Viṣvâvasu lay thee round as a protection. Thou art the Sacrificer's guard, thou, Agni, lauded and worthy to receive laudation.

Indra's right arm art thou. For safety.........laudation.

For safety of This All, with firm law, northward let Mitra-Varuṇa lay thee round as keeper. Thou art the Sacrificer's guard......laudation.

4 Thee, Sage, who offerest to Gods their banquet, we will enkindle till thou shinest brightly, thee mighty in the sacrifice, O Agni.

---

1 *Thou:* the Adhvaryu addresses the fuel placed on the altar, as he unties and sprinkles it. *Black-buck:* sacrifice in the shape of a black deer: Mahîdhara. *Altar:* which he sprinkles. *Sacred grass:* the Barhis or sacrificial grass with which the altar is covered.

2 *Thou:* the remainder of the water, which he pours on the roots of the grass. *Aditi:* the earth. *Hair-tuft:* this formula is addressed to the Prastara, a tied-up bunch of grass put upon the sacred grass which covers the altar. *Thee:* the sacred grass. *Hail! etc.:* the fire is enclosed with three fenders or fencing sticks. Any part of the oblation that falls outside these sticks is offered to Agni's three brothers who are here called respectively Earth's Lord, World's Lord, and Lord of Beings.

3 Here begins the ceremony of laying the *paridhis* or enclosing-sticks, made of Palâṣa or other sacred wood, round the sacrificial fire. *Viṣvâvasu:* Lord of all Treasure (see R. V. X. 85. 21; 139. 4, 5.), chief of the Gandharvas, a class of celestial beings closely connected with light and the aerial waters. *Thee:* the first enclosing-stick, placed on the west side of the fire. *Indra's arm:* the second stick, placed on the south side. The third stick is laid on the north side. *Mitra-Varuṇa:* Mitra (the Friend) is the Irânian Mithra and identified with the Sun. Varuṇa (Encompasser), originally the starry heaven, is the chief Vedic deity next to Indra.

4 A *samidh* or kindling-stick is applied to light the fire. *Thee:* the Âhavanîya fire.

5 Thou art a kindler. From the east let Sûrya keep thee secure from every imprecation.

You are the arms of Savitar. I spread thee as soft as wool, good for the Gods to sit on. On thee sit Vasus, Rudras, and Âdityas!

6 Thou who art called Juhû art rich in fatness. On this dear seat, with the dear home, be seated.

Thou, Upabhṛit by name, art rich in fatness. On this...... be seated.

Thou who art called Dhruvâ, art rich in fatness. On this, etc.

In the Law's lap they have sat down in safety.

Guard these. Guard thou the Sacrifice, O Vishṇu. Keep thou the Sacrifice's Lord in safety.

7 O Agni, Winner of the Spoil, I cleanse thee, thee who wilt hasten to the spoil, Spoil-winner.

Obeisance to the Gods! Svadhâ to Fathers! Be both of you easy for me to handle.

8 May I to-day offer Gods unspilt butter. Let me not with my foot offend thee, Vishṇu.

Agni, may I approach thy shade abounding in store of riches. Thou art Vishṇu's mansion.

Hence Indra wrought his deed of manly vigour. The sacrifice stood firmly elevated.

---

5 *Thou:* a second kindling-stick is applied and addressed. *From the east:* as it is protected by enclosing-sticks on the three other sides. *Sûrya:* the Sun-God, the expeller of evil spirits who would disturb the sacrifice. *You:* two blades of grass laid cross-wise on the grass which covers the altar. *Thee:* the Prastara (II. 2), which he unties and spreads. *Vasus:* a group of deities eight in number, associated with Indra, and, in later texts, with Agni. *Rudras:* a group of deities, sons of Rudra, eleven or thirty-three in number. *Âdityas:* sons of Aditi, a class of Gods of whom Varuṇa is chief. Six are enumerated in R. V. II. 27. 1. In R. V. IX. 114. 3 they are said to be seven in number, and in R. V. X. 72. 8 eight.

6 The Adhvaryu addresses and takes hold of three offering-spoons or ladles made of different sorts of wood, the Juhû, the Upabhṛit, and the Dhruvâ, which he lays down in order, the first on the Prastara and the others on the Barhis or altar-grass beneath it. *The Law's lap:* the bosom of sacrifice. *Vishṇu:* the sacrifice.

7 *Spoil:* or food, according to Mahîdhara. *I cleanse:* he trims the fire. *Svadhâ:* the prescribed sacrificial exclamation or prayer on presenting an oblation to the Fathers, Manes or Spirits of deceased ancestors. The word means also the food offered to them. *Both of you:* the offering spoons called Juhû and Upabhṛit.

8 *With my foot:* he must step to the south side of the altar with the left foot in advance of the right, and return with the right foot before the left. *Vishṇu:* the personified Sacrifice. *Shade:* shelter; place of refuge. *Hence:* starting from this place of sacrifice. *His deed;* the slaughter of the drought-demon Vṛitra. *Firmly elevated;* securely established and uninterrupted after Indra's victory.

9 O Agni, undertake the Hotar's office, take on thyself the duty of an envoy.

Heaven and Earth guard thee! Guard thou Earth and Heaven. May Indra be, by this presented butter, maker to Gods of fair oblation. Svâhâ! Let light combine with light.

10 Indra bestow on me that Indra-power! May wealth in full abundance gather round us. Let blessings wait on us, yea, real blessings.

Our Mother, Earth, hath been invited hither. May Earth, our Mother, in return invite us. I, through my Kindlership, am Agni. Svâhâ!

11 The Father Heaven hath been invited hither. May Heaven the Father in return invite us.

By impulse of God Savitar I receive thee with arms of Aṣvins, with the hands of Pûshan. I feed upon thee with the mouth of Agni.

12 God Savitar, this sacrifice of thine have they proclaimed unto Bṛihaspati the Brahman Priest.

Therefore protect the sacrifice, protect the sacrifice's lord, protect thou me.

13 The butter's rapid flow delight his spirit! Bṛihaspati extend this act of worship. May he restore the sacrifice uninjured. Here let all Gods rejoice. Oᴍ! Step thou forward.

14 This is the stick for kindling thee, O Agni. By means of this grow strong and swell to greatness. May we too grow in strength and swell to greatness.

O Agni, thou who winnest food, I cleanse thee, thee who hast hastened to the food, Food-winner.

---

*Hotar's:* sacrificer's or invoker's; he is the chief priest with whom the Adhvaryu is associated. *Envoy:* messenger to the Gods to whom he bears oblations. *Svâhâ!:* a sacrificial exclamation: Ave! Hail! Benedictio sit! *Light combine:* the butter in the Juhû with that in the Dhruvâ, which he now mixes.

10 *That Indra-power:* the great power which I hope for. The formula is muttered by the Sacrificer. *May wealth, etc.:* taken from R. V. 1. 98. 3. *Earth:* Pṛithivî; the broad, expansive one.

11 *Father Heaven:* or Heaven-Father; Dyaushpitâ (Dyauḥ pitṛi) = Ζεὺς πατήρ, Jupiter; the Universal Father, the Consort of Earth. *I receive thee:* said by the Brahman or directing priest as he takes his allotted portion of the oblation.

12 *Bṛihaspati:* Lord of Prayer; the Brahman Priest of the Gods, and the representative and impersonation of human priesthood.

13 Oᴍ: the sacred mystical syllable; yea; so be it; Amen. *Step thou forward:* the Brahman's answer to the Adhvaryu.

14 The kindling-stick is consecrated by the Hotar. *Food:* or spoil, wealth, the prize.

15 After the victory of Agni-Soma may I obtain the victory. By impulse of sacrificial food I speed me onward.

May Agni-Soma drive off him who hates us, drive off the man whom we detest. By impulse of sacrificial food away I drive him.

After the victory of Indra-Agni may I obtain the victory. By impulse of sacrificial food I speed me forward.

May Indra-Agni . . . . . I drive him.

16 For Vasus thee. For Rudras thee. Thee for Âdityas.

Be, Heaven and Earth, accordant with each other. With rain may Mitra-Varuṇa assist thee.

May the birds go, licking what is anointed.

Go to the Maruts' speckled mares. Go, having become a speckled cow thyself, to heaven, and from that place bring the rain for us hither.

Thou art the eye's guard: guard mine eye, O Agni.

17 The stick which thou, God Agni, laidest round thee, what time thou wast kept hidden by the Paṇis, this do I bring to thee for thine enjoyment. May it remain with thee and ne'er be fruitless.

Approach, ye two, the place which Agni loveth.

18 The residue ye have to be your portion, mighty by food, ye Gods, ye who are stationed on the grass-bunch, and to be laid as fences.

All ye, applauding this my speech, be seated on this grass-bunch and there be joyful. Svâhâ! Vâṭ!

---

15 The formula is recited by the Sacrificer as he separates the Juhû and the Upabhṛit spoons and moves the former eastward. *Victory:* their undisturbed appropriation of the rice-cake offered to the dual Deity at the Full Moon sacrifice. *Indra-Agni*: as in the case of Agni-Soma, but the formula is to be used at the New Moon sacrifice.

16 With the first three formulas the Adhvaryu anoints the three enclosing-sticks in the order in which they were laid down. *Thee:* 'I anoint' being understood. *Accordant:* in producing rain. *Mitra-Varuṇa:* who are especially Rain-Gods (see R. V. V. 63 and 69). *Birds:* the metres Gâyatrî and others, according to Mahîdhara. *What is anointed:* the Prastara. According to the Śatapatha-Brâhmaṇa, the formula is: 'May (the Gods) eat, licking the anointed bird (the Prastara).' See Sacred Books of the East, XII. p. 242 *Speckled mares:* which convey the Maruts, the Gods of storm and rain. *Speckled cow:* representing the Earth.

17 *The stick:* the Adhvaryu throws the western enclosing-stick on the fire. *Paṇis:* demons of darkness who steal the Gods' cows, the rays of light, and hide them in caverns. *Ye two:* the remaining sticks which are now thrown into the fire.

18 *The residue:* of the sacrificial butter. *Ye Gods: Viṣve devâḥ*, the Viṣvedevas or All-Gods. *Grass-bunch:* the Prastara. *Fences:* that is, representatives of the enclosing-sticks. *Svâhâ:* All hail! *Vâṭ:* a sacrificial exclamation on making an offering of clarified butter, meaning, probably, Take, or carry (to the Gods).

19 Rich in oil are ye. Guard the two yoke-fellows. Ye two are full of grace, to grace conduct me.

Glory to thee, O Sacrifice, and increase! Stand firm in my auspicious, righteous worship.

20 O Agni of unweakened strength, far-reaching, protect me from the lightning-flash, protect me from bondage. from defect in sacrificing, from food injurious to health protect me.

Make thou the food that feeds us free from poison in the home good to sit in. Svâhâ! Vâṭ!

Hail to the Lord of close embracements, Agni! Hail to Sarasvatî enriched with glory!

21 Veda art thou, whereby, O godlike Veda, thou hast become for Deities their Veda: thereby mayst thou become for me a Veda.

O Deities, ye knowers of the Pathway, walk on the pathway having known the Pathway.

God, Lord of Spirit, hail! bestow upon the Wind this sacrifice.

22 Blest be the Grass with sacred food and butter. Let Indra be united with the Âdityas, the Vasus, Maruts, and the Viṣvedevas. Let Svâhâ-offerings rise to heavenly ether.

---

19 *Ye:* the Juhû and Upabhṛit spoons. *Yoke-fellows:* the two oxen who draw the cart containing the sacrificial elements.

20 *O Agni:* he grasps the two spoons, the *sruk* or Juhû and the *sruva*. *In the home good to sit in:* Mahîdhara alternatively supplies, 'establish me.' *Lord of close embracements:* oblation is offered to Agni as a God who presides over the production of children, and to Sarasvatî or Vâk, Goddess of Speech and Eloquence, who will make them famous.

21 The Matron, the Sacrificer's wife, unties the Veda, the tied-up bunch of sacred grass used for various purposes in sacrifice, passed from one priest to another, and handed to the Sacrificer, and to his wife when she recites a text or formula, as she does in this place. *Their Veda:* (from *vid*, to know, or obtain) their knower, or finder. *For me a Veda:* a finder, or obtainer. *O Deities:* he addresses all the invited Gods. *Pathway:* the sacrifice. *Walk on the pathway:* go your several ways; the formula of dismissing the Gods who are present at the sacrifice. *Lord of Spirit:* Genius of man's spiritual power and life; the Moon, according to Mahîdhara, or Parameṣvara the Supreme Lord. *The Wind:* representative of the New or Full Moon sacrifice. *This sacrifice:* special sacrifice, which is to be established in, or united with, the other.

22 *The Grass:* the Barhis or altar grass. Mahîdhara explains the verse differently: Together with Âdityas, Vasus, Maruts, and Viṣvedevas, thoroughly may Indra anoint the Grass with butter like to *havis* (sacred food). *Svâhâ-offerings:* duly consecrated oblations. *Heavenly ether:* the Sun in heaven.

23 Who liberates thee from the yoke? He frees thee. For whom? For him he looses thee. For plenty.

Thou art the Râkshasas' allotted portion.

24 We have combined with lustre, vigour, bodies; we have united with the blessèd spirit. May Tvashṭar, bounteous giver, grant us riches, and clear each fault and blemish from the body.

25 By Jagatî metre in the sky strode Vishṇu. Therefrom excluded is the man who hates us and whom we detest.

By Trishṭup metre in the air strode Vishṇu. Therefrom, etc.

By Gâyatrî upon the earth strode Vishṇu. Therefrom, etc.

From this food. From this resting-place excluded.

We have reached heaven. We have combined with lustre.

26 Thou, noblest ray of light, art Self-existent. Giver art thou of splendour. Give me splendour.

I move along the path that Sûrya travels.

27 Agni, may I become a good householder, through thee, Home-master, O Householder Agni. Mayst thou become an excellent Householder through me the master of the house, O Agni.

Through hundred winters may our household matters—not like a one-ox car—be smoothly managed.

I move along the path that Sûrya travels.

28 I have performed the vow, Lord of Vows, Agni! Full power was mine, and it has proved successful.

Now am I he I truly am, no other.

---

23 He pours on the altar the holy water which has been brought forward (*praṇîtâ*) for the ceremony by the Adhvaryu from the Gârhapatya house. *Who?:* or Ka. See I. 6. *Thee:* the holy water. *He:* Prajâpati. *Plenty:* the prosperity of the Sacrificer. *Thou:* the refuse of the rice, which is strewn on the rice-cake potsherd, under the black-buck's skin, as the allotted share of the Râkshasas or fierce and malicious demons.

24 The Adhvaryu, having gone round the fire, pours out a full vessel of water which the Sacrificer catches with both hands hollowed and placed together, and recites the text. *Bodies:* limbs and members fit for the performance of religious duties, or, perhaps, our wives and sons. *Tvashṭar:* the divine Artificer, developer and shaper of the forms of living beings.

25 He makes the three ceremonial Vishṇu-strides in imitation of that solar deity's strides through the three divisions of the world. *By Jagatî:* supernatural powers are attributed to the Vedic metres as representations of effectual prayers.

26 *Thou:* the Sun, to which he looks.

27 *Hundred winters:* regarded as the natural duration of human life. See The Hymns of the Ṛigveda, and The Hymns of the Atharva-veda, Index. *I move:* he turns from left to right.

28 Having completed the vow, the Sacrificer discharges himself of further obligations. *He I truly am:* a man, not a semi-divine being as I was while performing the vow. See I. 5 and note.

29 To Agni Hail! who bears gifts due to Sages. To Soma Hail! accompanied by Fathers.

Expelled are Asuras and fiends who sate upon the covering grass.

30 The Asuras, attracted by oblation, who roam at will assuming varied figures, from this our world may Agni drive them, whether they clothe themselves in large or little bodies.

31 O Fathers, here enjoy yourselves. Come hither, like bulls, come each to his allotted portion.

The Fathers have enjoyed themselves, and hither, like bulls, come each to his allotted portion.

32 Obeisance to your genial sap, O Fathers! Fathers, obeisance unto you for Ardour! Fathers, obeisance unto you for Svadhâ! Obeisance unto you for Life, O Fathers!

Fathers, to you obeisance for the Awful! Fathers, obeisance unto you for Passion! O Fathers, unto you be adoration.

Bestow upon us houses, O ye Fathers. Of what is ours, O Fathers, will we give you. With this your raiment clothe yourselves, O Fathers.

33 Fathers, bestow on me a babe, a boy enwreathed with lotuses, so that there may be here a man.

---

29 The following are texts for the Piṇḍapitṛiyajña, the monthly ancestral sacrifice or offering of obsequial cakes to the Fathers or Manes as part of the New and Full Moon sacrifices. *To Agni:* part of the oblation is presented to him as the general receiver of all sacrificial offerings. *Sages:* a special class of Manes. *To Soma:* as especially connected with the Fathers. See R. V. VIII. 48. 13; A. V. XVIII. 4. 72, 73; Macdonell, Vedic Mythology, p. 109. *Expelled:* he draws a line of demarcation from north to south.

30 He lays down a firebrand to keep the fiends at a distance. *Varied figures:* even the forms of departed ancestors. *Large or little bodies:* this is Mahîdhara's explanation of the doubtful words *parâpuraḥ* and *nipuraḥ*.

32 Obeisance is offered to the Fathers six times in accordance with the seasons of the year. *Your genial sap:* the fresh juices of trees and plants in Spring. *Ardour:* the Summer. *Life:* the vivifying water of the Rains. *Svadhâ:* or, viands; the food offered to the Fathers, representing fruitful Autumn. *The Awful:* the cold Winter. *Passion:* the chilling Dewy Season which kills the plants, Similarly it was the belief of the Old Northmen that their dead patriarchs had the power of sending good seasons. See Corpus Poeticum Boreale, II. 414, 418. *Houses:* wives and families. *Raiment:* threads, or wool, or hairs from the Sacrificer's chest, placed on each obsequial cake.

33 The matron who wishes for a son eats the middlemost of the three cakes and recites this formula.

34 Bearers of vigour and immortal fatness, milk and sweet beverage and foaming liquor, ye are a freshening draught. Delight my Fathers.

---

34 He addresses the waters which he pours on the cakes. *Immortal fatness:* imperishable *ghṛitam*, ghī, or clarified butter which goes to the Gods. According to Mahīdhara, *amṛitam* here means destroyer or banisher of all disease and death. *Sweet beverage: kīlāla;* a kind of Metheglin. *Foaming beverage: parisrut;* a sort of beer.

# BOOK THE THIRD.

SERVE Agni with the kindling-brand, with drops of butter wake the Guest.
In him pay offerings to the Gods.

2 To Agni Jâtavedas, to the flame, the well-enkindled God,
Offer thick sacrificial oil.

3 Thee, such, O Angiras, with brands and sacred oil we magnify,
O very brilliant, Youthfullest.

4 Rich in oblations, dropping oil, to thee, sweet Agni, let them go.
Accept with favour these my brands.

5 Earth ! Ether ! Sky !
Like heaven in plenty and like earth in compass ! Upon thy back, Earth, place of sacrificing to Gods, for gain of food I lay food-eating Agni.

6 This spotted Bull hath come and sat before the Mother and before
The Father, mounting up to heaven.

---

This Book contains formulas for the Agnihotra or morning and evening burnt-oblation of milk which is obligatory on the householder during (with some exception) the whole of his life, and for the Four-monthly sacrifices at the beginning of the three chief seasons, Spring, Rains, and Autumn.

1 This verse and the following contain texts for the Agnyâdhâna, the ceremonial laying-down or establishment of his own sacrificial fires by the young householder. *Guest:* Agni who is constantly maintained in mens' houses.

2 *Jâtavedas:* knower of (all) beings ; Omniscient. The text is taken from R. V. V. 5. 1.

3 *Angiras:* Agni, as the chief messenger to the Gods. *Youthfullest:* youngest of Gods, as being perpetually reproduced at sacrifice. *Them:* the three kindling-sticks of Asvattha wood, anointed with sacrificial butter, which are put on the fire with the texts 1, 3, 4 respectively.

5 *Earth ! Ether ! Sky:* he lays down the Âhavaniya-fire on the place prepared for it, with this solemn sacrificial exclamation which is said to comprehend the Universe, the aid of which the sacrificer thus obtains. Or, according to Mahîdhara, the three words refer to the respective creation of priests, nobles, and people ; or self, human beings, and lower animals. *Like heaven etc:* 'May I become' understood. *In plenty:* in the number of its stars. So numerous may my sons and cattle be. *Like earth:* so may I spread with my offspring, or be the refuge of living creatures.

6 With the recitation of this and the two following verses, which form Hymn 189 of Book X. of the Ṛigveda, he offers worship to Agni and lays down the Dakshinâgni or Southern Fire. *Spotted Bull:* the Sun, here represented by Agni. *The Mother:* Earth. *The Father:* the Sky.

7 As expiration from his breath his radiance penetrates within:
The Bull shines out through all the sky.

8 He rules supreme through thirty realms. Song is bestowed upon the Bird
Throughout the days at break of morn.

9 Agni is light, and light is Agni. Hail!
Sûrya is light, and light is Sûrya. Hail!
Agni is splendour, light is splendour. Hail!
Sûrya is splendour, light is splendour. Hail!
Light is Sûrya, Sûrya is light. Hail!

10 Accordant with bright Savitar and Night with Indra at her side,
May Agni, being pleased, enjoy. All-hail!

11 Approaching sacrifice, may we pronounce a text to Agni who
Heareth us even when afar.

12 Agni is head and height of heaven, the Master of the earth is he:
He quickeneth the waters' seed.

13 You two will I invoke, O Indra-Agni, will please you both together with oblation.
Givers, you twain, of vigorous strength and riches, you twain do I invoke for gain of vigour.

14 This is thine ordered place of birth whence, sprung to life, thou shonest forth.
Knowing this, Agni, rise thou up and cause our riches to increase.

15 Here by ordainers was this God appointed first Invoker, best at worship, to be praised at rites,
Whom Apnavâna and the Bhṛigus caused to shine, bright-coloured in the wood, spreading to every house.

---

8 *Thirty realms:* all the divisions of the world, the number being used indefinitely. *The Bird:* or the winged One; the Sun, his morning *song* representing prayer.

9 Here begin the formulas of the Agnihotra, or morning and evening oblations of burnt milk. *Agni:* formula to accompany the evening oblation. *Sûrya:* formula to be employed in making the morning offering.

12 Taken from R. V. VIII. 44. 16. *The waters' seed:* as lightning, Agni impregnátes the waters of the air.

14 *This:* the Gârhapatya fire. The verse is taken from R. V. III. 29. 10.

15 Taken from R. V. IV. 7. 1. *Ordainers:* regulators of sacrifice, the ancient fire-priests. *Apnavâna:* an ancient Ṛishi, connected with the priestly family of the Bhṛigus and the earliest worship of Agni. Cf. R. V. VIII. 91. 4.

16 After his ancient splendour they, the bold, have drawn the bright milk from
The Sage who wins a thousand gifts.

17 Thou, Agni, art our bodies' guard. Guard thou my body.
Giver of life art thou, O Agni. Give me life.
Giver of splendour art thou, Agni. Give me splendour.
All that is wanting in my body, Agni, supply for me.

18 Enkindled we enkindle thee through hundred winters, thee the bright;
We healthy, thee who givest health; we strong, thee author of our strength;
We, never injured, Agni, thee uninjured injurer of foes.
O rich in shining lights, may I in safety rich the end of thee.

19 Thou hast attained, O Agni, to the splendour of Sûrya, to the eulogy of Ṛishis, and to the habitation which thou lovest.
May I attain to lengthened life, to splendour, to offspring and abundant store of riches.

20 Ye are food, may I enjoy your food. Ye are might, may I enjoy your might. Ye are energy, may I enjoy your energy. Ye are abundant riches, may I enjoy your abundant riches.

21 Sport, wealthy ones, in this abode, this fold, this spot, this dwelling-place.
Remain just here, and go not hence.

22 Composed art thou of every form and colour. With sap and ownership of kine approach me.
To thee, dispeller of the night, O Agni, day by day with prayer,
Bringing thee reverence, we come;

---

16 Taken from R. V. IX. 54. 1. In the original hymn *the bold* are the Soma-pressers, and *the sage* is Soma. Here Mahîdhara, to suit the sacrificial occasion, explains the words as 'milkers' and 'cow.'

18 *Enkindled:* brightened or made illustrious by thy favour. *Hundred winters:* implying a prayer for life extended to that period. *Shining lights:* Moon and stars; he addresses Night.

19 *Splendour of Sûrya:* at night, when the setting Sun has entered the Âhavanîya fire. *Habitation:* or dainty offering.

20 He approaches the cow that has been milked for the oblation. *Ye:* thou and the other cows. *Food:* in the shape of milk and butter.

22 *Thou:* he touches and addresses the cow. *To thee:* he approaches the Gârhapatya fire and reverences it. This text and verses 23, 24 are taken from R. V. I. 1. 7-9.

23 Ruler of sacrifices, guard of Law eternal, radiant One,
Increasing in thine own abode.

24 Be to us easy of approach, even as a father to his son:
Agni, be with us for our weal.

25 O Agni, be our nearest Friend; be thou a kind deliverer and gracious Friend.
Excellent Agni, come thou nigh to us, and give us wealth most splendidly renowned.

26 To thee then, O most bright, O radiant God, we come with prayer for happiness for our friends.
So hear us, listen to this call of ours, and keep us far from every evil man.

27 O Iḍâ, come, O Aditi, come hither. Come hither, much-desired! From you may I obtain my heart's desire.

28 O Brahmaṇaspati, make him who presses Soma glorious,
Even Kakshîvân Auṣija.

29 The rich, the healer of disease, who findeth wealth, increaseth store,
The prompt,—may he be with us still.

30 Let not the foeman's curse, let not a mortal's treachery fall on us:
Preserve us, Brahmaṇaspati!

31 Great, heavenly, unassailable, ours be the favour of the Three,
Aryaman, Mitra, Varuṇa.

32 For over them, neither at home nor upon pathways perilous,
The evil-minded foe hath power.

33 For they, the Sons of Aditi, bestow eternal light upon
A mortal man that he may live.

---

23 *Law eternal:* the order of the universe, or, specially, established sacrifice.

25 This and the following verse make up Hymn 24 of R. V. V., the two halves of 26, transposed, forming verses 3 and 4.

27 He approaches and addresses the cow. *Iḍâ:* or Iḷâ, Nourishment personified; here a symbolical name of the cow as representing plenty. *Aditi:* here and elsewhere a sacrificial name of the cow.

28 This verse and the two following are taken from R. V. I. 18. 1-3. *Brahmaṇaspati:*—Bṛihaspati; Lord of prayer, or Guardian of the Veda, the special deity and prototype of the Brâhmans and the priestly community, and Purohita or tribal Priest of the Gods. *Kakshîvân:* called Auṣija or son of Uṣij, a renowned Ṛishi, the seer of several hymns of the Ṛigveda. *Glorious:* or clear of voice.

29 *The rich, etc.:* Brahmaṇaspati.

31 This verse and the two following form, with a variation in 33, Hymn 185 of Book X. of the Ṛigveda. *Aryaman:* the name of one of the Âdityas, commonly invoked with Mitra and Varuṇa.

34 Ne'er art thou fruitless, Indra, ne'er dost thou forsake thy worshipper.
But now, O Liberal Lord, thy bounty as a God is ever poured forth more and more.

35 May we attain that excellent glory of Savitar the God:
So may he stimulate our prayers.

36 May thine inviolable car wherewith thou guardest worshippers
Come near to us from every side.

37 Earth! Ether! Sky! May I be rich in offspring, well-manned with men and opulent with riches. Friendly to men! do thou protect my offspring. Worthy of praise! do thou protect my cattle.
O pointed One, protect the food that feeds me.

38 We have approached the Omniscient, best finder-out of wealth for us. Splendour and strength bestow on us, O Agni, thou Imperial Lord.

39 Lord of the Home, this Agni Gârhapatya is best at finding riches for our children.
Splendour and strength bestow on us, O Agni, Master of the Home.

40 Rich, furtherer of plenty is this Agni, Master of the Herd.
Splendour and strength bestow on us, O Agni, Master of the Herd.

41 Fear not, nor tremble thou, O House. To thee who bearest strength we come.

---

34 Indra, as Deity of the sacrifice, is associated with Agni. The verse is taken from R. V., Vâlakhilya, 3. 7.

35 Taken from R. V. III. 62. 10. This stanza is the Sâvitrî, the Gâyatrî *par excellence*, 'the celebrated verse of the Vedas which forms part of the daily devotions of the Brahmans. and was first made known to English readers by Sir William Jones's translation of a paraphrastic interpretation: he renders it, Let us adore the supremacy of that divine sun who illuminates all, from whom all proceed, to whom all must return, whom we invoke to direct our understandings aright in our progress towards his holy seat.' Wilson. See Rigveda Sanhitâ, Vol. III. p. 111. *Prayers:* or, thoughts.

36 Addressed to Agni *Come near to:* or, encompass.

37 *Earth! etc.:* see III. 5. *Friendly to men:* he approaches and addresses the Gârhapatya fire. *Pointed One:* flame of the fire.

38 He approaches the Âhavanîya fire. *The Omniscient:* Agni.

40 *Master of the Herd: purîshya;* the original meaning of *purîsha* is rubbish, loose soil, manure, and is used symbolically for the cattle which produce the manure.

41—43 Formulas to be used by the householder on approaching the Dakshina fire on departing from and returning to his house. *Fear not:* in the master's absence.

I, bearing strength, intelligent and happy, come to thee, House, rejoicing in my spirit.

42 The home on which the wanderer thinks, where cheerfulness and joy abound—
We call the Home to welcome us. May it know us who know it well.

43 Here have the cows been called to us, the goats and sheep have been called near,
And in our home we have addressed the meath that sweeteneth our food.
I come to thee for safety and for quiet. May joy be ours, felicity, and blessing.

44 We invocate the Maruts, the voracious, eaters of their foes,
Delighting in their mess of meal.

45 We expiate by sacrifice each sinful act that we have done,
Whether in village or the wild, in company or corporeal sense. Svâhâ!

46 Let us not here contend with Gods, O Indra, for, Fierce One! here is thine own sacred portion,
Thine, Mighty One, whose friends, the bounteous Maruts, his song who pours oblation, streamlike, honours.

47 The skilful workers have performed their work with voice that gives delight.
Having performed the work for Gods, go, ye companions, to your home.

48 O ever-moving Cleansing Bath, thou movest gliding on thy way.

---

42 *Meath: kîlâla;* a sweet beverage, the nature of which is uncertain.

44 Formulas follow for the three Four-monthly sacrifices at the beginning of Spring, the Rains, and Autumn. The Sacrificer's wife is first called upon to confess her infidelities, if she has been guilty of any, and to declare the name or names of her lover or lovers. After confession, or declaration of innocence, she is made to recite the text. *Eaters:* consumers, destroyers. The correctness of this traditional interpretation is doubtful. See Prof. Oldenberg, Vedic Hymns, Part II. p. 14 *Mess of meal:* a sort of gruel or porridge.

45 Spoken by the Sacrificer's wife, or by her and her husband. *In village:* by oppression. *The wild:* by cruelty to wild animals. *In company:* by contemptuous behaviour. *Corporeal sense:* by abuse of the tongue or other unruly member.

46 Taken from R. V. I. 173. 12. Spoken by the Sacrificer.

47 Spoken by the Matron. *Skilful workers:* priests.

48 The Avabhritha, or Purificatory Baptism in a stream of fresh water, is performed by the Sacrificer and his wife. *Who loudly roars:* the terrible fiend.

With Gods may I wash out the sin that I have sinned against the Gods, with men the sin against mankind.
Preserve me safe from injury, O God, from him who loudly roars.

49 Full, fly away, O spoon, and filled completely fly thou back to us.
O Śatakratu, let us twain barter, like goods, our food and strength.

50 Give me, I give thee gifts : bestow on me, and I bestow on thee.
To me present thy merchandize, and I to thee will give my wares.

51 Well have they eaten and regaled : the friends have risen and passed away.
The sages, luminous in themselves, have praised thee with their latest hymn.
Now, Indra, yoke thy two Bay Steeds.

52 Thee will we reverence, thee, O Lord of Bounty, who art fair to see.
Thus praised, according to our wish come now with richly-laden car. Now, Indra, yoke thy two Bay Steeds.

53 We call the spirit hither with a hero-celebrating strain,
Yea, with the Fathers' holy hymns.

54 The spirit comes to us again for wisdom, energy, and life,
That we may long behold the Sun.

55 O Fathers, may the Heavenly Folk give us the spirit once again,
That we may be with those who live.

---

49 Here begin the formulas for the presentation of the Sâkamedha offerings on the full moon of Kârttika (October-November). The Adhvaryu officiates. *Full :* of the boiled rice to be offered to Indra. *Spoon :* the ladle called *darvi*. *Filled completely :* with blessings in return. *Śatakratu :* Lord of a Hundred Powers; or sacrifices, according to the Commentators. *Barter:* cf. A. V. III. 15. 1: I stir and animate the merchant Indra. *Food and strength :* the sacred food purchasing strength for the worshipper.

50 *Give me, etc. : dehi me, dadâmi te ;* do ut des : the fundamental principle underlying sacrifice. According to Mahîdhara, line 1 is spoken by Indra and line 2 by the Sacrificer.

51, 52 Taken from R. V. I. 82. 2, 3. Food is offered to the Fathers, and Indra is addressed. *They . . . . the friends :* the Fathers. See II. 31.

53—56 Taken from R. V. X. 57, 3—6. *The spirit :* the mind or thought of the worshippers which in paying obeisance to the Fathers has, as it were, gone to the world of the Departed and is now invited to return to earth. In the original hymn the application is different, the spirit of a deceased man being recalled. See Max Müller, Royal Asiatic Society's Journal, 1866. pp. 449 and 458. *Strain : stomena :* the R. V. has *somena*, with Soma.

56 O Soma, with the spirit still within us, blest with progeny,
May we be busied in thy law.

57 O Rudra, this is thine allotted portion. With Ambikâ thy sister kindly take it. This, Rudra, is thy share, the rat thy victim.

58 We have contented Rudra, yea, put off Tryambaka the God,
That he may make us wealthier, may make us yet more prosperous, may make us vigorous to act.

59 Thou art a healing medicine, a balm for cow and horse and man, a happiness to ram and ewe.

60 Tryambaka we worship, sweet augmenter of prosperity.
As from its stem a cucumber, may I be freed from bonds of death, not reft of immortality.
We worship him, Tryambaka, the husband-finder, sweet to smell.
As from its stem a cucumber, hence and not thence may I be loosed.

61 This, Rudra, is thy food: with this depart beyond the Mûjavâns.
With bow unstrung, with mufled staff, clothed in a garment made of skin, gracious, not harming us, depart.

62 May Jamadagni's triple life, the triple life of Kaṣyapa,
The triple life of Deities—may that same triple life be ours.

---

56 *O Soma:* as being closely connected with the Fathers.

57 Rudra, the fierce Tempest-God, destroyer of men and cattle is to be propitiated. *This:* a rice-cake. There is to be one cake for each living son and servant of the Sacrificer, and one over for future additions, and these cakes are all to be on one potsherd. *Ambikâ:* the personification of Autumn with which Rudra kills. *The rat:* the supernumerary cake is to be buried in the earth thrown up by a rat or vole, and this symbolic sacrifice will satisfy Rudra and induce him to spare other animals.

58 *Tryambaka:* a name of Rudra as having three wives, sisters, or mothers, or Triocular, the Three-eyed God, as Ṣiva is represented in later literature.

59 *Thou:* Rudra in his gentle mood.

60 Spoken by the girls of the Sacrificer's family as they walk round the altar. The first two lines are taken from R. V. VII. 59. 12. *Husband-finder:* more usually a title of Aryaman. See A. V. XIV. 1. 17. *Hence and not thence:* from my father's house and not from my future husband's. Cf. R. V. X. 85. 25.

61 *Thy food:* provisions for thy journey; the remains of the rice-cakes packed in two baskets at the end of a pole and fastened on a tree, post, bamboo, or ant-hill. See Muir, Original Sanskrit Texts, II. 352. *Mûjavâns:* apparently a hill-tribe in the North-west.

62 Jamadagni and Kaṣyapa were ancient Vedic Ṛishis. See The Hymns of the Ṛigveda, Index.

63 Gracious, thy name; the thunder is thy father. Obeisance be to thee: forbear to harm me.

I shave thee for long life, for food to feed thee, for progeny, for riches in abundance, for noble children, for heroic vigour.

---

63 The Sacrificer's head and beard are shaved. *Gracious:* the razor is addressed. *Thunder:* the *vajra* or thunderbolt, made of iron like the razor. *I shave thee:* the Adhvaryu speaks, using the word *nivartayâmi* (cause thee to be turned round) the technical term to be employed at this sacrificial all-round shaving.

## BOOK THE FOURTH.

We have reached this earth's place of sacrificing, the place wherein all Deities delighted.
Crossing by Rik, by Sâman, and by Yajus, may we rejoice in food and growth of riches.
Gracious to me be these Celestial Waters!
Protect me, Plant. O Knife, forbear to harm him.

2 The Mother Floods shall make us bright and shining, cleansers of holy oil, with oil shall cleanse us.
For, Goddesses, they bear off all defilement. I rise up from them purified and brightened.
The form of Consecration and of Fervour art thou. I put thee on, the kind and blissful, maintaining an agreeable appearance.

3 The Great Ones' milk art thou. Giver of splendour art thou: bestow on me the gift of splendour.
Pupil art thou of Vṛitra's eye. The giver of eyes art thou. Give me the gift of vision.

4 Purify me the Lord of Thought! Purify me the Lord of Speech! Purify me God Savitar with perfect strainer, with the beams of Sûrya!

---

Books IV.—VIII. contain formulas for the Soma sacrifice in general.

1 *Place of sacrificing:* which has been carefully selected and prepared with shed, hall, etc. The Sacrificer recites the formula, holding in his hand the *araṇis* or two pieces of the wooden fire-drill, and grasping the chief post of the sacrificial hall. *Ṛik, Sâman, Yajus:* by means of the verse of praise, the chanted psalm, and the sacrificial formula. *Waters:* to be used in the Apsu-Dîkshâ or Consecration Ceremony by water or baptism. He moistens his right whisker for shaving. *Plant:* a blade of Kusa grass placed on his whisker. *Knife*: the razor, which is said to be a *svadhiti*, or thunderbolt. See III. 63. *Him:* the Sacrificer.

2 The first two lines are taken from R. V. X. 17. 10. The Sacrificers bathe in the consecrating waters. *Defilement:* the stain of sin as well as bodily impurity. *I rise up:* he steps out of the water. *Thee:* the linen garment prescribed for the occasion. *Fervour:* ardour, religious zeal, penance, or austere devotion.

3 *Great Ones' milk:* product of the cows; the fresh butter with which he is anointed from head to foot. *Pupil art thou:* the Adhvaryu anoints his eye with collyrium. It is said in the Taittirîya-Saṃhitâ, VI. 1. 5 that Vritra's eye-ball, when Indra conquered him, fell away and became ointment.

*Lord of Thought:* Prajâpati, Lord of Creatures. *Lord of Speech:* the same deity, or Bṛihaspati Lord of Prayer. *Perfect strainer:* or purifier, Vâyu the wind. *Lord of the strainer:* or of the means of purification, the Sacrificer who has gone through the ceremony. The meaning is, May I be able to accomplish the sacrifice in accordance with my preconceived wishes.

Of thee, Lord of the Strainer! who art by the strainer purified,

With what desire I purify myself, may I accomplish it.

5 We come to you for precious wealth, O Gods, as sacrifice proceeds.

O Gods, we call on you to give blessings that wait on sacrifice.

6 Svâhâ! from mind the sacrifice. Svâhâ! from spacious firmament.

Svâhâ! from Dyaus and Pṛithivî. Svâhâ! from Wind I seize. Svâhâ!

7 To Resolution, Motive, Agni, Svâhâ! All-hail to Wisdom, and to Mind, and Agni!

All-hail to Consecration, Fervour, Agni! Hail to Sarasvatî, Pûshan, and Agni!

Ye vast, divine, all-beneficial Waters, ye Heaven and Earth and spacious Air between them,

Let us adore Bṛihaspati with oblation. All-hail!

8 May every mortal man elect the friendship of the guiding God.

Each one solicits him for wealth: let him seek fame to prosper him.

9 Ṛik's, Sâman's counterparts are ye. I touch you. Protect me till the sacrifice be ended.

Thou art a place of refuge. Give me refuge. Obeisance unto thee! Forbear to harm me.

10 Strength of Angirases art thou. Wool-soft, bestow thou strength on me.

Thou art the garment-knot of Soma. Vishṇu's refuge art thou, the Sacrificer's refuge.

---

6 *Svâhâ:* Ave! All-hail! *The sacrifice:* 'I grasp, or take hold of' being understood. Various bendings of fingers and final closing of the hands are prescribed *Dyaus and Pṛithivî:* Heaven and Earth.

7 These formulas, with the oblations which they accompany, are specially called Audgrabhaṇa or Uplifting, because they raise the Sacrificer to heaven. *Resolution:* the intention or purpose of sacrificing.

8 Taken from R. V. V. 50. 1. *Guiding God:* Savitar, the Impeller and Leader.

9 Two black-antelope skins, tacked together and stretched on the ground for consecration purposes, are addressed and touched. *Counterparts:* in full accord, as used in sacred ceremonies, with the recited verses and chanted hymns of sacrifice. The white on the skins resembles the Ṛik, and the black the Sâman. *Thou art,* etc.: he kneels with his right knee on the skin.

10 He binds on and addresses a girdle of two plaited strands of hemp and one of Muñja grass. *Angirases:* descendants of Angiras, a semi-divine

Thou art the womb of Indra. Make the crops produce abundant grain.

Stand up erect, O Tree. Protect me from harm until this sacrifice be ended.

11 Prepare ye vow-food. Agni is the Brahman, Agni is sacrifice, the tree is holy.

For aid we meditate divine Intelligence, most merciful,

Free-giver, bringing worship. May it guide us gently, as we would.

Favour us Gods, mind-born, endowed with mind and intellectual might! All-hail to them! May they be our protectors.

12 Waters that we have drunk! become refreshing, become auspicious draughts within our belly.

Free from all sin and malady and sickness, may they be pleasant to our taste, divine Ones, immortal, strengtheners of eternal Order.

13 This is thy sacrificial form.

Not offspring, waters I discharge. Freeing from sin and consecrate by Svâhâ enter ye the earth. Be thou united with the earth.

14 O Agni, watch thou well. May we take joy in most refreshing sleep.

Protect us with unceasing care. From slumber waken us again.

---

patriarchal Ṛishi. See Index to The Hymns of the Ṛigveda. *Garment-knot:* the meeting ends of the cloth worn round the body; 'tuck': Eggeling. *Of Soma:* belonging to Soma after the consecration of the wearer, and to the Fathers before that ceremony. *Vishṇu's:* the Sacrificer's. *The womb of Indra:* he addresses a black-buck's horn which he ties to the fringe of his garment. See the legend. Sacred Books of the East. XXVI. 30—33. Mahîdhara gives a somewhat similar legend, from the Taittirîya-Saṃhitâ, ascribing Indra's birth to the union of Yajña (Sacrifice) with Dakshiṇâ Sacrificial Guerdon) instead of Vâk (Speech). *Make the crops:* he draws a line with the horn on the ground. *O Tree:* a staff of Udumbara (Ficus Glomerata) wood which the Adhvaryu gives to the Sacrificer.

11 *Vow-food:* or fast-food, chiefly milk which the attendants prepare. The Sacrificer pronounces this formula thrice. *The Brahman:* (neuter) the priesthood, or, according to Mahîdhara, the three Vedas. *The tree:* the Khadira (Acacia Catechu) and other trees whose wood is used for sacrificial purposes. *For aid:* to help us in the performance of the sacrifice.

12 Recited after drinking the milk.

13 *This, etc.:* *micturiens*, he takes up with the horn a lump of earth or something similar, and addresses embodied sacrifice: This earth is thy sacrificial form. *i. e.* place meet for worship. *Ye:* the waters of which he relieves himself. *Be thou:* he throws down the lump of earth.

14 With a prayer to the Guardian Agni he goes to sleep.

15 Thought hath returned to me, and life; my breath and soul have come again.

Our bodies' guard, unscathed, Vaiṣvânara Agni preserve us from misfortune and dishonour.

16 Thou, Agni, art the guardian God of sacred vows among mankind, thou meet for praise at holy rites.

Grant this much, Soma! bring yet more. God Savitar who giveth wealth hath given treasure unto us.

17 This is thy form, O Bright One, this thy lustre. Combine with this thy form and go to splendour.

Impetuous art thou, upheld by mind, and Vishṇu loveth thee.

18 Moved by thine impulse who hast true impulsion, may I obtain a prop to stay my body.

Pure art thou, glistering art thou, immortal, dear to all the Gods.

19 Thought art thou, mind, intelligence, the Guerdon, royal, worshipful, Aditi with a double head. Succeed for us in going forth, succeed for us in thy return. May Mitra bind thee by the foot. May Pûshan guard thy pathways for Indra whose eye is over all.

---

15 Uttered on awaking. *Vaiṣvânara:* All-men's; friendly or dear to all Âryan men.

16 The first two lines are taken from R. V. VIII. 11. 1. *Grant etc.:* this formula is to be used when a gift has been offered to him after his consecration.

17 This is the formula for the Hiraṇyavatî-Âhuti or Offering with Gold. Having poured the butter left in the dhruvâ ladle into the juhû, he throws on the butter a piece of gold tied with Darbha grass. *This* (1): the butter. *This* (2): the gold which is identified with light. So in old Northern poetry gold is called the gleam of Ocean; the fire of Oran (a Scottish stream); the sun of the deep. See Corpus Poeticum Boreale, II. p. 468. *Impetuous: vegayuktâ* is Mahîdhara's explanation of *jûḥ*. According to the Ṣatapatha-Brâhmaṇa, the meaning is 'singer of praises.' Vâk or Speech is addressed. *Vishṇu:* Sacrifice; or Soma.

18 *Thine:* Vâk's, as represented by the cow which is to be given in exchange for the Soma required for the sacrifice. *Pure art thou:* he addresses the piece of gold which he takes up.

19 The Adhvaryu addresses the Soma-purchasing cow. *Guerdon:* priestly fee, consisting chiefly of a cow or cows. *Aditi:* regarded as the Cosmic Cow. See R. V. IX. 96. 15. *With double head:* as mistress of the *prâyaṇîya* (introductory) and *udayanîya* (concluding) libations; or facing both ways, regarded as Vâk or Speech. *In going forth:* to procure the Soma. *Bind thee:* to prevent wandering and loss. *Pûshan:* as the guide of travellers and guardian of ways.

20 Thy mother give thee leave to go, thy father, thine own brother, and thy friend of the same herd with thee!
Go thou, O Goddess, to the God. To Soma go for Indra's sake.
May Rudra turn thee back. Return safely with Soma as thy friend.

21 Thou art a Vasvî, thou art Aditi, thou art an Âdityâ, thou art a Rudrâ, thou art a Chandrâ.
Bṛihaspati vouchsafe thee rest and comfort! Rudra with Vasus looks on thee with favour.

22 On Aditi's head I sprinkle thee, on the earth's place of sacrifice.
Footstep of Iḍâ art thou, filled with fatness. Hail!
Rejoice in us. Thy kinship is in us. In thee are riches. Mine be riches! Let us not be deprived of abundant riches. Thine, thine are riches.

23 I with my thought have commerced with divine far-sighted Dakshiṇâ.
Steal not my life. I will not thine. May I, O Goddess, in thy sight find for myself a hero son.

24 Tell Soma this for me: This is thy share allied with Gâyatrî.
For me say this to Soma: This is thine allotted Trishṭup share.
Tell Soma this for me: This is thy share allied with Jagatî.
Tell Soma this for me: Win thou sole lordship of the metres' names.
Ours art thou: pure thy juice for draught. Let separators pick thee out.

---

20 *Rudra:* as Lord of Cattle.

21 *Vasvî:* a female Vasu. See II. 5. *Âdityâ:* a daughter of Aditi; a female Âditya. *Rudrâ:* a female Rudra. *Chandrâ:* a female Moon; bright as the Moon-God.

22 *Aditi's head:* the surface of the earth. *Thee:* an oblation of clarified butter. *Footstep of Iḍâ:* he addresses the footprint of the cow identified with Iḍâ, a Goddess of Devotion, the daughter of Manu or man thinking on and worshipping the Gods. *In thee are riches:* he gives the impressed earth to the Sacrificer. *Mine:* the Sacrificer replies. *Let us not:* the Adhvaryu speaks for himself and others. *Thine, thine:* *totoḥ* for *tvayi tvayi;* spoken by the matron, to whom also the impressed earth has been given

23 Spoken by the matron, on whom the cow has been made to look. *Dakshiṇâ:* or Guerdon, the Soma-cow. See verse 19.

24 Spoken by the Sacrificer to the Adhvaryu. *With Gâyatrî:* this and the two other metres being used, respectively, at the morning, noon, and evening Soma-pressings. *Ours art thou:* the Soma-plant is addressed. *Pick thee:* selecting the parts that are fit for sacrificial use.

25 I sing my song of praise to him, Savitar, God between the Bowls, strong with the wisdom of the wise, of true impulsion, wealth-giver, the well-belovèd thoughtful Sage.

To him at whose impulsion shone aloft in heaven the splendid light.

Most wise, the Golden-handed hath measured the sky with skilled design.

For living creatures, thee. Let living creatures breathe after thee. Breathe after living creatures.

26 Thee who art pure, with what is pure I purchase, the bright with bright, immortal with immortal.

The Sacrificer keep thy cow. Let thy gold pieces be with us.

Fervour's form art thou, and Prajâpati's nature. With the most noble animal art thou purchased. May I increase with thousandfold abundance.

27 As friend, the giver of good friends, approach us!

Take thou thy seat on the right thigh of Indra, yearning on yearning, pleasing on the pleasing.

Anghâri, Svâna, Bhrâja, and Bambhâri, O Hasta, and Suhasta and Kṛiṣânu,

These are your prices for the Soma purchase. Keep them securely, let them never fail you.

28 Keep me, O Agni, from unrighteous conduct: make me a sharer in the path of goodness.

---

25 *The Bowls:* heaven and earth, so called from their hemispherical appearance. But see Hillebrandt, Vedische Mythologie, I. p. 177, and Ludwig, Ueber die Neuesten Arbeiten auf dem Gebiete der Ṛgvedaforschung, p. 87. *For living creatures, thee:* I tie thee (Soma) up in the wrapper, the ends of which are brought together, for the good of living creatures who will be benefited by the sacrifice.

26 *Thee:* the Soma *What is pure:* gold brought for the purchase. *The Sacrificer:* spoken by the Adhvaryu. The cow given in exchange for the Soma is now given back, and the gold pieces are similarly returned; the bargaining here being only a form, and the price of the Soma having probably been settled beforehand. See Sacred Books of the East, XXVI. 71; Haug's Aitareya-Brâhmaṇam, II. 59, note 2. *Fervour's form:* the Sacrificer addresses a she-goat, said to have sprung from the Fervour or Austere Devotion of Prajâpati, which has been placed looking westward. *Prajâpati's nature:* dear to the Gods as Prajâpati the Lord of Creatures; or because she produces young three times a year, hence also called *most noble* or most excellent

27 He gives the she-goat to the Soma-seller and takes the Soma with his right hand in exchange, reciting the formula. *Approach us:* O Soma. *Indra:* the Sacrificer (endowed during the ceremony with the attributes of Indra) on whose bared thigh the Soma is placed. *Anghâri, etc.:* the names of the seven Guardians of the celestial Soma, purchased from them by the Gods. Kṛiṣânu is frequently mentioned in the Ṛigveda. *These:* the articles given to the Soma-seller.

28 Recited by the Sacrificer. *Immortals:* especially Soma.

I, following Immortals, have arisen with longer life, with a good life before me.

29 Now have we entered on the path that leads to bliss without a foe,
The path whereon a man escapes all enemies and gathers wealth.

30 The skin of Aditi art thou. Sit on the lap of Aditi.
The Bull hath propped the sky and air's mid-region, the compass of the broad earth hath he measured.
He, King Supreme, approached all living creatures. Truly all these are Varuṇa's ordinances.

31 Over the woods the air hath he extended, put milk in kine and vigorous speed in horses,
Set intellect in hearts and fire in houses, Sûrya in heaven and Soma on the mountain.

32 Ascend the eye of Sûrya, mount the pupil set in Agni's eye
Where, radiant through the Wise One, thou speedest along with dappled steeds.

33 Approach, ye oxen, fit to bear the yoke; be yoked without a tear.
Slaying no man, urging the Brahman forward, go happily to the Sacrificer's dwelling.

34 Lord of the World, thou art my gracious helper: move forward on thy way to all the stations.
Let not opponents, let not robbers find thee, let not malignant wolves await thy coming.
Fly thou away having become a falcon. Go to the dwelling of the Sacrificer. That is the special place for us to rest in.

---

29 He puts the Soma on his head and goes towards the cart in which the Soma has been brought, reciting the text taken, with one variation, from R. V. VI. 51. 16.

30 The antelope-skin is spread in the Soma cart by the Adhvaryu who recites the formula. *Skin of Aditi:* See I. 14. *Sit:* O Soma. *The Bull:* the mighty Varuṇa, here meaning Soma. The text is taken, with alteration of two words, from R. V. VIII. 42. 1. *Approached:* 'pervades:' Mahîdhara; 'hath taken his seat over:' Eggeling. *Living creatures:* or, worlds.

31 He wraps the Soma in a cloth, reciting the texts taken from R. V. V. 85. 2.

32 He addresses the antelope-skin which he hangs up in front of the Soma-cart. *Wise One:* the All-knowing Sun. The skin, representing the Sun and Agni, will keep off evil spirits.

33 *Ye oxen:* the pair that draw the Soma-cart. *The Brahman:* the priest, or the sacrifice. *Happily:* or, safely, uninjured by evil spirits.

34 Spoken by the Sacrificer. *Lord of the World:* Soma is addressed. *Stations:* the Patnisâlâ or Matron's Hall, the Havirdhâna or Oblation-Store, and other places in the sacrificial enclosure.

35 Do homage unto Varuṇa's and Mitra's eye: offer this solemn worship to the Mighty God,
Who seeth far away, the Ensign born of Gods. Sing praises unto Sûrya, to the Son of Dyaus.

36 Thou art a prop for Varuṇa to rest on. Ye are the pins that strengthen Varuṇa's pillar.
Thou art the lawful seat where Varuṇa sitteth. Sit on the lawful seat where Varuṇa sitteth.

37 Such of thy glories as with poured oblations men honour, may they all invest our worship.
Wealth-giver, furtherer with troops of heroes, sparing the brave, come, Soma, to our houses.

---

35 The Sacrificer recites the text taken from R V. X. 37. 1. *Varuṇa's and Mitra's eye:* Sûrya, the Sun represented by the Soma. *Dyaus:* Zeus, Heaven or Sky personified.

36 *Thou:* the prop that supports the pole of the cart, which has now become the support of Varuṇa represented by the Soma. *Ye:* two wooden pegs that keep the prop steady. *The lawful seat:* he addresses the seat or throne on which Soma is placed, the antelope-skin having been spread over it. Varuṇa is represented by Soma throughout the verse.

37 The Sacrificer recites the text taken from R. V. I. 91. 19, as Soma is brought into the sacrificial hall. *Glories:* powers; Eggeling.

## BOOK THE FIFTH.

BODY of Agni art thou. Thee for Vishṇu. Body of Soma art thou. Thee for Vishṇu. Thou art the Guest's Reception. Thee for Vishṇu. Thee for the Soma-bringing Falcon. Thee for Vishṇu. Thee for the giver of abundance, Agni. Thee for Vishṇu.

2 Birth-place art thou of Agni. Ye are sprinklers. Thou art Urvaṣi. Thou art Âyu. Thou art Purûravas.

I rub and churn thee with Gâyatrî metre. I rub and churn thee with the Trishṭup metre. I rub and churn thee with the Jagatî metre.

3 Be ye for us one-minded, be one-thoughted, free from spot and stain.

Harm not the sacrifice, harm not the sacrifice's lord. Be kind to us this day, Omniscient Ones!

4 Preserver from the curse, Son of the Ṛishis, Agni is active having entered Agni.

Here for us kindly with fair worship offer oblation to the Gods with care unceasing. Svâhâ!

5 For him who flies around and rushes onward I take thee, for Tanûnapât the mighty, the very strong, of all-surpassing vigour.

---

Verses 1—4 contain formulas for the Âtithya or Ceremonial Reception and Entertainment of Soma when introduced into the sacrificial hall.

1 The Adhvaryu takes the *havis* or sacrificial food, that is, the elements of oblation, from the cart, and addresses it with the formula. *Thou:* the sacred food. *Vishṇu:* meaning, according to Mahîdhara, Soma the pervader of the sacrifice. *Thee:* 'I take' understood. *Falcon:* that brought the Soma from heaven. See R. V. IV. 27.

2 *Thou:* a piece of wood forming the lower part of the fire-drill, in which the spark is produced by rapid friction. *Sprinklers:* or, stallions, males. Two blades of Kuṣa grass, placed on the fire-drill, are addressed. *Thou:* the lower piece of the drill. *Urvaṣî:* a celebrated Apsaras or celestial nymph. *Âyu:* the butter in the pan is said to be Âyu the son of Urvaṣî. *Purûravas:* the human husband of Urvaṣî and father of Âyu. The upper piece of the drill is addressed as it is placed on the lower piece. The clarified butter, or sacrifice, is the child produced by the union. For the legend of Urvaṣî and Purûravas, see R. V. X. 95 (The Hymns of The Rigveda, Vol. II. (2nd ed.) pp. 527—530), and Max Müller, Chips from a German Workshop, Vol. IV. (new ed.) pp. 107—114. *Thee:* Agni, the fire. *With Gâyatrî, etc.:* while verses in these metres are recited.

3 *Ye:* the Âhavanîya fire and the newly-kindled fire which is thrown on it. *Omniscient One:* *jâtavedasau;* 'ye knowers of beings:' Eggeling.

4 *Son of the Ṛishis:* produced in sacrifice by the priests.

5 Here follow formulas for the Tânûnaptra, a ceremony in which Tanûnapât, usually Agni (Son of Himself, born from other fire), here Vâyu the

Strength of the Gods, inviolate, inviolable still art thou, the strength that turns the curse away, uncursed and never to be cursed.

May I go straight to truth. Place me in comfort.

6 O Agni, Guardian of the Vow, O Guardian of the Vow, in thee

Whatever form there is of thine, may that same form be here on me: on thee be every form of mine.

O Lord of Vows, let our vows be united. May Dîkshâ's Lord allow my Consecration, may holy Fervour's Lord approve my Fervour.

7 May every stalk of thine wax full and strengthen for Indra Ekadhanavid, God Soma!

May Indra grow in strength for thee: for Indra mayest thou grow strong.

Increase us friends with strength and mental vigour. May all prosperity be thine, God Soma. May I attain the solemn Soma-pressing.

May longed-for wealth come forth for strength and fortune. Let there be truth for those whose speech is truthful. To Heaven and Earth be adoration offered.

8 That noblest body which is thine, O Agni, laid in the lowest deep, encased in iron, hath chased the awful word, the word of terror. Svâhâ!

That noblest . . . . . . encased in silver, etc. Svâhâ!

That noblest . . . . with gold around it, etc. Svâhâ!

---

Wind-God, is invoked, and the sacrificial butter is touched by sacrificer and priests as a form of adjuration or bond of friendship. *Who flies, etc.:* Vâyu. *Thee:* the sacrificial butter. *Go straight to truth:* faithfully keep the promise which I am making. *Place me in comfort:* according to Mahîdhara, establish me in the fair path, the performance of sacrifice.

6 Formulas for a kind of minor Consecration. The Sacrificer exchanges persons with, and becomes, Agni. *Dîkshâ's Lord:* Soma, Lord of Consecration. *Fervour:* or Penance.

7 The priests perform the Âpyâyana, the sprinkling of the Soma with water to make it swell. *Ekadhanavid:* according to Mahîdhara, receiver or finder of the one chief prize, *i. e.* Soma; or, knower of the Ekadhanas, pitchers which hold the water which is to be mixed with the Soma.

8 Formulas for the Upasads (services or sieges; Milton's 'beseeching and besieging'), offerings of butter to Agni, Soma, and Vishṇu thrice daily for three days or more. According to the legend, the Asuras or rebel demons, having been defeated in battle by the Gods, made three castles, one of iron on earth, one of silver in mid-air, and one of gold in the sky. Agni, at the Gods' request, in the form of the Upasad deity entered and burnt them and they became the three bodies of Agni mentioned in the text. *T awful word:* the threats of the Asuras.

9 For me thou art the home of the afflicted. For me thou art the gathering-place of riches. Protect me from the woe of destitution.

Protect me from the state of perturbation.

May Agni know thee, he whose name is Nabhas. Go, Agni, Angiras, with the name of Âyu.

Thou whom this earth containeth, down I lay thee with each inviolate holy name thou bearest.

Thou whom the second earth, etc. Thou whom the third earth, etc.

Thee, further, for the Gods' delight.

10 A foe-subduing lioness art thou: be fitted for the Gods.

A foe-subduing lioness art thou: be purified for Gods.

A foe-subduing lioness art thou: adorn thyself for Gods.

11 Indra's shout guard thee in the front with Vasus. The Wise One guard thee from the rear with Rudras. The Thought-swift guard thee on the right with Fathers. The Omnific guard thee, leftward, with Âdityas.

This heated water I eject and banish from the sacrifice.

12 Thou art a lioness. All-hail! Thou art a lioness winning Âdityas. All-hail!

Thou art a lioness winning Brâhmans and Nobles. All-hail!

Thou art a lioness that wins fair offspring, win abundant wealth. All-hail!

A lioness art thou. Bring the Gods hither for him who offers sacrifice. All-hail!

To living creatures, thee.

---

9 The lines of the altar and of the pit from which earth is to be dug out for its construction are now marked out. *Thou:* the earth. *Thee:* the earth dug out of the pit. *Nabhas:* or, Vapour. *Âyu:* Life, said to be a name of Agni. Before this address to Agni, the Adhvaryu throws the Sphya or wooden sword to the place where the pit is to be dug. *Thou whom:* O Agni, who art in this loose dug earth which I scatter on the place where the high altar is to be. *Second. . . . third:* the ceremony and he formula are repeated with these substitutions for 'this.' *Thee, further:* he takes up earth a fourth time.

10 He sets apart the earth required for the high altar, addresses and sprinkles it.

11 *Indra's shout:* as God of Battles. *The Wise One:* Varuna, the moral Governor of the world, from whom no secrets are hid. *The Thought-swift:* Yama, God of the Departed. *The Omnific:* Visvakarman, an abstract deity representing the Supreme God as Creator of all things. *Heated water:* after having sprinkled waters on four sides he pours away the rest outside the altar place.

12 With four invocations he pours butter on the four corners of the altar place, and with the fifth on the centre. *Thee:* the offering-ladle. 'I raise' understood.

13 Firm art thou, steady thou the earth. Firm-seated art thou, steady thou the air.
Movelessly set art thou, steady the sky. Agni's completion art thou.

14 The priests of him the lofty Priest well-skilled in hymns harness their spirits, yea harness their holy thoughts.
He only knowing works assigns their priestly tasks. Yea, lofty is the praise of Savitar the God. All-hail!

15 Forth through This All strode Vishṇu: thrice his foot he planted, and the whole was gathered in his footstep's dust. All-hail!

16 Rich in sweet food be ye, and rich in milch-kine, with fertile pastures, fain to do men service.
Both these worlds, Vishṇu, hast thou stayed asunder, and firmly fixed the earth with pegs around it.

17 Heard by the Gods, ye twain, to Gods proclaim it.
Go eastward, O ye twain, proclaiming worship. Swerve ye not: bear the sacrifice straight upward.
To your own cow-pen speak, ye godlike dwellings.
Speak not away my life, speak not away my children.
On the earth's summit here may ye be joyful.

---

13 He encloses the centre or navel of the altar place with sticks of Pitudâru (Pinus Deodara). With three invocations he addresses, respectively, the middle stick, the southern, and the northern. *Completion:* or equipment; *purîsha:* all that is required to make Agni complete, bdellium (guggulu), sweet-scented reed-grass, and the tufts that have grown between the horns of a ram.

14 The Commentator gives rules for the construction of Havirdhânas or sheds for the carts that bring Soma and other elements of sacrifice, of the Sadas or Priests' shed, of the Soma-pressing place, and of the Dhishṇyas or side-altars or hearths. *The priests:* an offering of butter, taken up in four ladlings, is made to Savitar with recitation of this text from R. V. V. 81. 1. *Knowing works:* skilled in the rules which regulate religious functions.

15 Having laid a piece of gold in the right-hand track of the right-hand cart he makes an offering with this text from R. V. I. 22. 17. *Thrice:* on earth, in the air, in the sky.

16 *Ye:* the offering ladle and the pot or saucer of sacrificial butter which the Pratiprasthâtar or assistant priest takes up, and having laid a piece of gold in the left-hand track of the left-hand cart makes an oblation with the text taken from R. V. VII. 99. 3, the first line of which appears to be, originally, Vishṇu's benediction on heaven and earth when he parted and supported them. *Pegs:* such as those used for stretching a woven cloth or a skin. In later literature the word means also 'rays,' sunbeams. 'With beams of light didst thou hold fast the earth on all sides': Eggeling.

17 *Ye:* the Matron addresses the two axle-pins, which she anoints with the remains of the butter. *Straight upward:* to the Gods. *Cow-pen:* signifying wealth in cattle to the Sacrificer. *Dwellings:* the house-like carts. *Speak not away:* destroy not with ill-omened creaking. *Earth's summit:* the high sacrificial ground. *Be joyful:* in your rest.

18 Now will I tell the mighty deeds of Vishṇu, of him who measured out the earthly regions.
Who propped the highest place of congregation, thrice setting down his foot and widely striding.
For Vishṇu thee.
19 Either from heaven or from the earth, O Vishṇu, or, Vishṇu, from the vast wide air's mid-region,
Fill both thy hands full with abundant riches, and from the right and from the left bestow them.
For Vishṇu thee.
20 For this his mighty deed is Vishṇu lauded, like some wild beast, dread, prowling, mountain-roaming,
He within whose three wide-extended paces all living creatures have their habitation.
21 Thou art the frontlet for the brow of Vishṇu. Ye are the corners of the mouth of Vishṇu. Thou art the needle for the work of Vishṇu. Thou art the firmly-fastened knot of Vishṇu. To Vishṇu thou belongest. Thee for Vishṇu.
22 By impulse of God Savitars I take thee with arms of Aṣvins and with hands of Pûshan.
Thou art a woman. Here I cut the necks of Râkshasas away.
Mighty art thou, mighty the sound thou makest. Utter thy mighty-sounding voice to Indra:
23 Fiend-killing, charm-destroying voice of Vishṇu.
Here I cast out that charm of magic power which stranger or housemate for me hath buried.

---

18 The Adhvaryu puts up a wooden prop to support the pole of the right-hand or southward cart, and recites the text taken from R. V. I. 154. 1. *Thee:* 'I support' understood.

19 Similarly the Pratiprasthâtar supports the left-hand or northward cart, reciting the text from Atharva-veda, VII. 26. 8.

20 The Sacrificer, after touching the middle reed-mat of the cart-shed, recites the text from R. V. I. 154. 2. *Paces:* see verse 18.

21 *Thou:* he addresses a post on which is a wreath of Darbha grass. *Ye:* the ends of the band of grass. *Needle:* 'sewer': Eggeling. This is a wooden peg used in stitching together the folding doors ('hurdles': Eggeling) of the cart-shed. *Knot:* he ties the string in a knot. *Thou belongest:* he touches the completed shed. *Thee:* 'I touch' understood.

22 Formulas to accompany the preparation of the Uparavas or sound-holes made in the earth to increase the noise of the pressing or pounding of the Soma. *Thee:* a wooden digging instrument, a trowel or short spade. *Woman:* connected as a helper with the men who manage the ceremony. Moreover, the word *abhri*, spade, is feminine. *Here:* he draws outlines of the holes. *Râkshasas:* the malignant fiends who would mar or obstruct the sacrifice. *Mighty:* he addresses each hole that he has dug. *Utter:* when thou art made use of at the Soma pounding.

23 *Of Vishṇu:* belonging to him as guardian of the sacrifice. *Charm of magic power:* *valaga*, a collection of bones, nails, hair, etc., tied up in a

Here I cast out the charm of magic power buried for me by equal or unequal.
Here I cast out the charm that hath been buried for me by non-relation or relation.
I cast the charm of magic out.

24 Self-ruler art thou, conquering foes. Ruler for ever art thou, killing enemies.
Men's ruler art thou, slaying fiends. All ruler, killing foes, art thou.

25 I sprinkle you whom Vishṇu owns, killers of fiends and evil charms.
I lay down you whom Vishṇu loves, killers of fiends and wicked charms.
I scatter you whom Vishṇu loves, killers of fiends and wicked charms.
You two whom Vishṇu loves, who kill fiends and ill charms do I lay down.
You two whom Vishṇu loves, who kill fiends and ill charms I compass round.
To Vishṇu thou belongest. Ye are Vishṇu's.

26 By impulse of God Savitar I take thee with arms of Aṣvins, with the hands of Pûshan.
Thou art a woman. Here I cut the necks of Râkshasas away.
Barley art thou. Bar off from us our haters, bar our enemies.
Thee for heaven, thee for earth, thee for air's region.
Pure be the worlds, the Fathers' dwelling-places. Thou art the habitation of the Fathers.

---

piece of old matting or cloth, and buried arm-deep in the ground to injure enemies. See The Hymns of the Atharva-veda, X. 1. 18. and note. The digger of these sound-holes dislodges by his act any such charms as have been buried there, and recites a formula as he throws up the earth from each hole.

24 By way of benediction the Sacrificer touches and addresses each of the completed holes, with a formula for each.

25 He sprinkles lustral water over the holes. *I lay down:* two pressing-boards, one on each of two pits. *I scatter:* blades of Darbha grass. *You two:* the pressing-boards. *I compass round:* with earth to keep them steady. *Thou:* the skin used in the Soma-pressing process. *Ye:* the five pressing-stones which belong to Vishṇu as guardian of the sacrifice.

26 Formulas for putting up a branch or post of Udumbara (Ficus Glomerata) in the centre of the Sadas or shed where the priests sit. *By impulse, etc.:* two lines repeated from verse 22. He throws barley into the sprinkling-water. *Barley: yava. Bar off: yavaya.* There is a play on the words. *Thee for heaven:* he sprinkles the top of the branch. *For earth:* the bottom. *For air's region:* the middle. *Pure be the worlds:* he pours the remaining water into the hole made for the branch. *Thou:* a layer of Darbha grass which he strews in the hole.

27 Prop heaven, fill full the air, on earth stand firmly. Dyutâna, offspring of the Maruts, plant thee !, Mitra and Varuṇa with firm upholding.

I close thee in, thou winner of the Brâhmans, winner of Nobles and abundant riches.

Strengthen the Brâhmans, strengthen thou the Nobles, strengthen our vital power, strengthen our offspring.

28 Firm-set art thou. Firm be this Sacrificer within this home with offspring and with cattle.

O Heaven and Earth, be ye filled full of fatness.

Indra's mat art thou, shelter of all people.

29 Lover of song, may these our songs encompass thee on every side;

Strengthening thee of lengthened life, may they be dear delights to thee.

30 Thou art the needle for the work of Indra. Thou art the firmly fastened knot of Indra. Indra's art thou. Thou art the Viṣvedevas'.

31 All-present art thou, carrying off. Oblation-bearing priest art thou.

Thou art the Swift, the Very Wise. Tutha art thou, who knoweth all.

32 Thou art the yearning one, the sage. Anghâri, Bambhâri art thou.

---

27 He raises and addresses the branch or post. *Dyutâna:* the name of a Vedic Ṛishi, seer of R. V. VIII. 85. It is said to mean Vâyu, the son or attendant of the Storm-Gods. *I close thee in:* with earth put round it.

28 *Thou:* the Udumbara post, which he (the Sacrificer) touches. *O Heaven and Earth:* he pours clarified butter on the forked top of the post. *Indra's mat:* of grass, to thatch the Sadas or Priests' shed. *All people:* the Sacrificer and the officiating priests.

29 After enclosing the shed with mats, he addresses Indra as Lord of the Sadas with the text taken from R. V. I. 10. 12.

30 *Thou:* he addresses the rope with which the mats are fastened. *Needle:* 'Sewer': Eggeling. See verse 21. *Thou art Indra's:* he addresses the enclosed Sadas. *Viṣvedevas':* belonging to the All-Gods. See II. 18.

31 and 32 contain formulas for the consecration of the eight Dhishṇyas, side-altars or hearths, each of which is addressed in turn: (1) the Âgnîdhriya or hearth of the Âgnîdhra or Fire-kindler (*carrying off,* meaning 'bearing oblations to the Gods'); (2) the Hotar's hearth; (3) the hearth of the Maitrâvaruṇa or first Assistant of the Hotar; (4) the hearth of the Brâhmaṇâchhaṇsi (*Tutha* meaning 'Brahman priest,' who knows how priestly fees are to be distributed).

32 (5) The hearth of the Potar or Cleansing Priest is addressed as *the yearning one;* (6) the hearth of the Neshṭar, the priest who leads forward the Sacrificer's wife, is addressed by the names of Anghâri and

Aid-seeker art thou, worshipping. Cleanser art thou, the cleansing-place. Kṛiśânu, Sovran Lord, art thou.

Thou art the Pavamâna of the assembly. Thou art the welkin ever moving forward. Swept clean art thou, preparer of oblations. Thou art the seat of Law, heaven's light and lustre.

33 A sea art thou of all-embracing compass. Aja art thou, who hath one foot to bear him. Thou art the Dragon of the Depths of ocean. Speech art thou, thou the Sadas, thou art Indra's. Doors of the sacrifice, do not distress me!

Lord, Ruler of the pathways, lead me onward. In this God-reaching path may I be happy.

34 Look ye upon me with the eye of Mitra.

O Agnis, ye, receivers of oblations, are by a lauded name lauded together. Protect me, Agnis! with your glittering army. Fill me with riches, Agnis! be my keepers. To you be adoration. Do not harm me.

35 Thou art a light that wears all forms and figures, serving the general host of Gods as Kindler.

---

Bambhâri, two of the guardians of the celestial Soma. See IV. 27; (7) the hearth of the Achhâvâka or Inviting Priest is addressed as *Aid-seeker*; (8) the Mârjâlîya hearth on which the sacrificial vessels are cleaned is addressed as *Cleanser*. After the completion of the Dhishṇyas the Âhavanîya fire is pointed at and addressed as Kṛiśânu, the chief guardian of the Celestial Soma. *The Pavamâna:* the Adhvaryu addresses the Bahishpavamâna place, the place where a morning Stotra or hymn of praise is sung outside the Vedi or altar *Assembly:* of priests. *Welkin:* the pit from which the earth for the altar and Dhishṇyas is taken is likened to the sky with openings between clouds. *Moving forward:* or, perhaps, precipitous, shelving downward. According to Mahîdhara, circumambulated by the priests. *Swept clean:* the slaughtering-place is addressed. *Seat of Law:* the Udumbara post, where Sâmans are chanted at sacrifice.

33 *A sea:* the seat of the Brahman priest, to which all Gods resort and where the Brahman of fathomless knowledge sits. *Aja:* the fire at the door of the Prâchînavaṃśa hall (the hall whose supporting beam is turned eastward) is addressed. Aja Ekapâd, or the One-footed Unborn, is perhaps the Sun or Lightning. See The Hymns of the Ṛigveda, VI. 50. 14, and Macdonell, Vedic Mythology, pp. 73, 74. *Dragon of the Depths:* Ahi Budhnya, frequently associated with Aja-Ekapâd, is a deity of the atmospheric ocean. See The Hymns of the Ṛigveda, Index, and Macdonell, Vedic Mythology, pp. 72, 73. The Gârhapatya fire is thus addressed. *Speech:* the Sadas or shed in which the priests perform religious duties with spoken words. *Doors, etc.:* that is, let me pass in and out without stumbling. *Ruler of the pathways:* the Sun is addressed. *God-reaching path:* sacrifice.

34 *Look ye:* the priests are addressed. *Mitra:* or, of a friend. *Agnis:* the fires of the Dhishṇyas. *Glittering: raudreṇa;* or, Rudra-like, awful, destructive of enemies.

35 With the text, he takes clarified butter mixed with sour curds. *Thou:* the clotted butter. *Kindler:* 'for,' says Mahîdhara,' 'the Gods are illuminated or brightened when they have enjoyed the sacrificial butter.'

Thou, Soma, wilt withhold thy wide protection from body-wounding hatreds shown by others. All-hail!
Let the Swift graciously enjoy the butter. All-hail!

36 By goodly paths lead us to riches, Agni, thou God who knowest every sacred duty.
Remove the sin that makes us stray and wander: most ample adoration will we bring thee.

37 Wide room and comfort may this Agni give us, and go before us cleaving down our foemen.
May he win booty in the fight for booty: May he quell foes in his triumphant onset.

38 O Vishṇu, stride thou widely forth, give ample room for our abode.
Drink butter, homed in butter! Still speed on the sacrifice's lord. All-hail!

39 To thee, God Savitar, belongs this Soma. Guard him securely: let not demons harm thee.
Now hast thou joined the Gods as God, God Soma: men have I joined here through abundant riches.
All-hail! from Varuṇa's noose am I delivered.

40 O Agni, Guardian of the Vow, O Guardian of the Vow, on me whatever form of thine hath been, may that same form be upon thee. Whatever form of mine hath been on thee, may that be here on me.
O Lord of Vows, our vows have been accomplished. Dîkshâ's Lord hath approved my Consecration, and holy Fervour's Lord allowed my Fervour.

41 O Vishṇu, stride thou widely forth, make ample room for our abode.
Drink butter, homed in butter! Still speed on the sacrifice's lord. All-hail!

---

*Thou, Soma:* with this formula he offers an oblation. *Let the Swift:* he offers to Soma a second time.

36 The Sacrificer recites the text taken from R. V. 1. 189. 1.

37 The Adhvaryu lays the fire on the Âgnîdhra hearth, and in its shed puts down the pressing-stones, the Soma-trough, and the Soma vessels, and offers oblation with the text.

38 He offers oblation in the Âhavanîya fire with the text.

39 He spreads the black-antelope skin in the right-hand or southward cart, and lays the Soma thereon with the text. *Delivered:* handing over the Soma has secured me from danger of punishment by Varuṇa.

40 He lays a kindling-stick on the Âhavanîya fire. *O Agni, etc.:* repeated from verse 6.

41 Formulas for the preparation of the Yûpa or Sacrificial Stake. The ceremony begins with an offering and a verse (repeated from 38) to Vishṇu, as he is the sacrifice and the stake belongs to him.

42 I have passed others, not approached to others. On the near side of those that were more distant, and farther than the nearer have I found thee.

So, for the worship of the Gods, with gladness we welcome thee God, Sovran of the Forest! Let the Gods welcome thee for the Gods' service. For Vishṇu thee. Plant, guard! Axe, do not harm it!

43 Graze not the sky. Harm not mid-air. Be in accordance with the earth.

For this well-sharpened axe hath led thee forth to great felicity.

Hence, with a hundred branches, God, Lord of the Forest, grow thou up.

May we grow spreading with a hundred branches.

---

42 He them takes the rest of the butter and goes with the carpenter to the wood in search of a suitable tree, a Palâśa, Khadira, Vilva (Aegle Marmelos or Bel), or the like. When he has found it he recites the verse expressing the trouble he has taken. *Others:* other trees. *Sovran of the Forest: vanaspati;* a large tree; the technical name of the Sacrificial Stake regarded as a form of Agni. *For Vishṇu thee:* he touches it with the dipping-spoon. *Plant!:* a blade of Kuśa-grass which he puts where the first cut will be made.

43 He addresses the tree as it falls, and as it, as well as the axe, is a thunderbolt, entreats it to spare the three worlds. *To great felicity:* as bearing a most important part in sacrifice. *Hence:* from this stump.

## BOOK THE SIXTH.

By impulse of God Savitar I take thee with arms of Asvins, with the hands of Pûshan. Thou art a woman. Here I cut the necks of Râkshasas away. Barley art thou. Bar off from us our haters, bar our enemies.

Thee for heaven, thee for earth, thee for the welkin. Pure be the worlds, the Fathers' dwelling-places. Thou art the habitation of the Fathers.

2 Thou art a leader, easy, to Unnetars, of access. Know this. It will stand upon thee.

Savitar, God, anoint thee with sweet butter. Thee for the plants laden with goodly fruitage!

Thou with thy top hast touched the sky, hast with thy middle filled the air, and steadied with thy base the earth.

3 Those seats of thine which we desire to visit, where there are many-horned and nimble oxen,

There, of a truth, was mightily imprinted the loftiest step of widely-striding Vishṇu.

I close thee in, the winner of the Brâhmans, winner of Nobles and abundant riches.

Strengthen the Brâhmans, strengthen thou the Nobles, strengthen our vital power, strengthen our offspring.

4 Look ye on Vishṇu's works, whereby the Friend of Indra, close-allied,

Hath let his holy ways be seen.

---

The Sacrificial Stake, which may be of any length from five cubits to seventeen or even more, is then brought to the enclosure and erected with the following formulas.

1 The formula is the same as that for the erection of the Udumbara post. See V. 26. *Thee:* the spade.

2 *Thou:* The first chip cut from the stake and thrown into the hole in which the stake is to stand. *Leader:* introducer of the stake into its receptacle. *Unnetars:* priests who pour the Soma juice into the cups. *Know this:* that the stake will stand on thee. *Savitar, etc.:* he anoints the stake. *Thee for the plants:* he anoints the cap or wooden top-ring and fastens it on the stake, that rice and other plants may thrive and be productive. *Thou with thy top:* the stake is erected.

3 He fixes the stake in the hole with the text which is a modification of R. V. I. 154. 6. *Oxen:* the stars with their ever-twinkling rays. Cf. R. V. I. 105. 10.

4 The Sacrificer touches the stake and recites the verse taken from R. V. I. 22. 19. *Let . . . be seen:* Mahîdhara takes *paspaśe* as from *spaśh*, to bind: 'bound on himself.' According to Sâyana, the meaning is *anutishṭhati*, performs.

5 The princes evermore behold that loftiest place where Vishṇu is,
Laid as it were an eye in heaven.

6 Thou art invested. Heavenly hosts invest thee! Riches of men invest this Sacrificer!
Heaven's son art thou. This is thine earthly station. Thine is the beast whose home is in the forest.

7 Encourager art thou. The hosts of heaven have come to yearning Gods, the best conductors.
God Tvashṭar, make the wealth of cattle quiet. Delightful to the taste be thine oblations.

8 Joy, wealthy ones! Bṛihaspati, save our riches.
I bind thee with the noose of holy Order, thou offering to the Gods. Bold be the Slayer.

9 By impulse of God Savitar I bind thee, with arms of Asvins and with hands of Pûshan, thee welcome unto Agni and to Soma.
Thee for the waters, thee for plants. Thy mother grant thee permission, and thy father, brother born of one dam, thy friend, thy herd-companion. I sprinkle thee welcome to Agni-Soma.

10 Drinker art thou of water. May the Waters, the Goddesses, add sweetness to the oblation prepared for Gods, even though already sweetened.

---

5 He looks up to the cap of the stake. *Princes:* the wealthy institutors of sacrifice.

6 *Thou art invested:* he girdles the stake with a triple band of Kusa grass. *Heaven's son:* he addresses a chip of the stake which he inserts under the girdle of grass. The chip is cut from the stake which is produced from rain which comes from heaven. *Thine:* the stake is addressed.

7 Formulas for binding and slaughtering the victim. *Encourager:* he takes up and addresses some grass which, as a companion, encourages and guards him in his work. He touches the victim with the grass and recites the text. *Hosts of heaven:* the sacrificial animals which have consented to be immolated to the Gods. *Conductors:* of the Sacrificer, to heaven. *Tvashṭar:* as creator and lord of cattle. *Thine oblation:* he addresses the victim.

*Wealthy Ones:* the cows rich in milk. *I bind:* he puts a noose round the victim. *Bold be the Slayer:* this is Mahîdhara's explanation of 'dharshâ mânushaḥ,' which seems rather to mean, as Prof. Eggeling observes, 'be bold: I am (or he, the slaughterer is) a man.' 'Dare, being human,' addressed to the Immolator, would seem to give the meaning.

9 He binds the victim to the stake with the following formulas. *Thee:* 'I sprinkle' understood. *Waters . . . . plants:* rain and grass, to which the victim owes its existence. *Mother . . . father:* Earth and Heaven, according to Mahîdhara. *Grant thee permission:* consent to thy sacrifice.

10 *Drinker:* he holds lustral water under its mouth. *May the Waters:* he sprinkles the victim's chest and belly. *Thy breath:* he anoints the ani-

Thy breath join wind, thy limbs those meet for worship, the sacrifice's lord the boon he prays for.

11 Balmed, both of you, with butter, guard the cattle. Grant, Rich! the Sacrificer's prayer. Approach thou.
Meeting with heavenly Wind, from air's mid-region. Be thou united with this offering's body.
O Great One, lead the sacrifice's master on to a sacrifice of loftier order. All-hail to Gods! To Gods All-hail!

12 Become no serpent, thou, become no viper. To thee, O widely-spread, be adoration.
Advance, unhindered, on thy way. To rivers of butter move along the paths of Order.

13 Bear the oblation to the Gods, ye Waters celestial and pure and well-provided. May we become providers well-provided.

14 I cleanse thy voice, thy breath, thine eye, thine ear, thy navel, and thy feet, thy sexual organ, and thy rump.

15 Let thy mind, voice, and breath increase in fulness, thine eye be fuller, and thine ear grow stronger.
Whatever there is in thee sore or wounded, may that be filled for thee, cleansed and united.
Blest be the days. Plant, guard! Axe, do not harm him.

16 Thou art the demons' share. Expelled are demons. Here I tread down; here I repel the demons; here lead the demons into lowest darkness.

---

mal's forehead, shoulder and loins. *Join wind:* like to like. *Meet for worship:* the Gods, or sacrifices offered to them.

11 *Both:* a chip from the stake and the whittle or slaughtering-knife with which he touches the victim's forehead. *Cattle:* honorific plural, the victim. *Rich!:* the Goddess of Speech, Vâk. *Approach:* and inspire the Sacrificer. *From air's, etc.:* 'Guard him' understood. *O Great One:* or, O Rain-born; he addresses a blade of grass thrown down behind the Şâmitra or Slaughtering-place. *All-hail!:* Some Gods, says Mahîdhara, have Svâhâ or All-hail! before them and some have it after them.

12 He throws the victim's halter into the pit. *Serpent . . . viper:* a snake is called the Rope with Fangs. See A. V. IV. 3. 2; XIX. 47. 8. *To thee:* the Matron, bringing water for washing feet, recites the text. *O widely-spread:* the sacrifice.

14 The Matron wipes each organ of the animal as she recites the appropriate clause of the text. In the original, *şundhâmi*, 'I cleanse,' is repeated as each organ is named.

15 The Adhvaryu and the Sacrificer sprinkle all the members of the victim and recite the text. *Plant:* a blade of grass laid upon the victim when turned over on its back. *Axe:* here meaning the slaughtering-knife.

16 *Thou:* the lower part of the blade of grass which he has smeared with blood. *Ye two:* sticks, called vapâşrapanîs, on which the omentum or caul when extracted from the victim, is wrapped for roasting. *O Vâyu:* the Adhvaryu throws the upper part of the grass-stalk into the Âhavanîya fire.

Invest, ye two, the heaven and earth with fatness.
O Vâyu, eagerly enjoy the droppings. Let Agni eagerly enjoy the butter. All-hail!
Go, both of you, by Svâhâ consecrated, to Ûrdhvanabhas, offspring of the Maruts.

17 Ye Waters, wash away this stain and whatsoever taint be here,
Each sinful act that I have done, and every harmless curse of mine.
May Waters rid me of that guilt, and Pavamâna set me free.

18 Be they united, with the Mind thy mind, and with the Breath thy breath.
Thou quiverest. Let Agni make thee ready. Waters have washed together all thy juices.
Thee for the Wind's rush, for the speed of Pûshan. From heated vapour may it reel and totter,—the disconcerted hatred of our foemen.

19 Ye drinkers-up of fatness, drink the fatness; drink up the gravy, drinkers of the gravy! Thou art the oblation of the air's mid-region. All-hail!
The regions, the fore-regions, the by-regions, the intermediate and the upper regions,—to all the regions Hail!

20 In every limb is Indra's out-breath seated, in every limb is Indra's in-breath settled.
God Tvashṭar, let thine ample forms be blended, that what wears different shapes may be one-fashioned.
To please thee let thy friends, mother and father, joy over thee as to the Gods thou goest.

---

*Butter:* which is poured on the omentum. *Both of you:* the roasting-sticks which are thrown into the fire. *Ûrdhvanabhas:* He who is in the cloud on high; Vâyu.

17 The priests, the Sacrificer, and his wife purify themselves at the pit with the text which is found also in A. V. VII. 89. 3. Cf. R. V. I. 23. 22; X. 9. 8. *Pavamâna:* he who flows clear, or blows to purify; Soma, or Vâyu.

18 The Adhvaryu sprinkles the victim's heart with clotted butter. *Mind:* = heart; let thy heart be united with the heart of the Gods, and thy breath with theirs. *Thou quiverest:* he takes up the vasâ or melted fat and pieces of cooked meat. *Agni:* the fire. *Thee:* 'I take' understood. *Pûshan:* the Sun. *Heated vapour:* the wind.

19 *Ye drinkers:* the All-Gods, to whom the oblation is offered. *The gravy:* the vasâ. See verse 18. *Thou:* the gravy. *The regions, etc.:* I have borrowed Prof. Eggeling's translation of the words used to designate the intermediate points.

20 He touches the remains of the victim as he recites the text. The purpose of this part of the ceremony is to re-unite the separated portions and to re-animate the body for life in heaven.

21 Go to the sea. All-hail! Go to the air. All-hail! Go to God Savitar. All-hail!
Go thou to Mitra-Varuṇa. All-hail! Go thou to Day and Night. All-hail!
Go to the Metres. All-hail! Go to Heaven and Earth. All-hail! Go to the sacrifice. All-hail! Go to Soma. All-hail! Go to the heavenly ether. All-hail! Go to Vaiṣvânara Agni. All-hail! Bestow upon me mind and heart.
Thy smoke mount to the sky, to heaven thy lustre. Fill thou the spacious earth full with thine ashes.

22 Harm not the Waters, do the Plants no damage. From every place, King Varuṇa, thence save us.
Their saying that we swear our oath by sacred cows, by Varuṇa,
O Varuṇa, save us therefrom.
To us let Waters and let Plants be friendly; to him who hates us, whom we hate, unfriendly.

23 These waters teem with sacred food: rich in that food, one longs for them.
Rich be the holy rite therein. In sacred food be Sûrya rich.

24 I set you down in Agni's seat whose home is indestructible.
Indra-and-Agni's share are ye, Mitra-and-Varuṇa's share are ye.
The share of all the Gods are ye.
May waters gathered near the Sun, and those wherewith the Sun is joined,
Speed on this sacred rite of ours.

25 Thee for the heart, thee for the mind, thee for the heaven, thee for the Sun.
Bear up erect to heaven, to Gods, this rite, these sacrificial calls.

---

22 He addresses the heart-spit, the stick on which the victim's heart has been roasted, and which is now buried where dry ground and moist ground meet. *Waters...plants*: being between both and not touching either. *From every place*: the St. Petersburg Lexicon suggests that *dhâmno-dhâmnaḥ* of the text is a corruption of *dâmno-dâmnaḥ*, 'from every bond or fetter.' *Their saying*: the meaning is not clear. Perhaps, Save us from our enemies' blame when they find fault with us for swearing by cows and by Varuṇa, when an oath on cows alone would be sufficient.

23 *These waters*: the Vasatîvarî waters, to be used in pressing out the Soma juice. *Rich in that food*: the Sacrificer.

24 The text is taken from R. V. I. 23. 17.

25 The Adhvaryu takes Soma down from the cart, lays him on the pressing-stones, and recites the text. *Heart ....mind*: I take thee down in order to fulfil the wish and purpose of the Sacrificer. *Sacrificial calls*: or, according to Mahîdhara, the seven chief priests themselves.

26 Descend, O Soma, King, to all thy people. Down, unto thee, go, one and all, thy people!

May Agni with his fuel hear my calling. Hear it the Waters and the Bowls, Divine Ones! Hear, Stones, as knowing sacrifice, my calling. May the God Savitar hear mine invocation. All-hail!

27 Waters Divine, your wave, the Waters' offspring, fit for oblation, potent, most delightful—

Upon those Gods among the Gods bestow it, who drink the pure, of whom ye are the portion. All-hail!

28 Drawing art thou: I draw thee up that Ocean ne'er may waste or wane.

Let waters with the waters, and the plants commingle with the plants.

29 That man is lord of endless strength whom thou protectest in the fight,

Agni, or urgest to the fray.

30 By impulse of God Savitar I take thee with arms of Asvins, with the hands of Pûshan,

Free with thy gifts art thou. Perform for Indra this deep, most excellently ordered worship.

With the most noble bolt I pay the worship enriched with strengthening food and milk and sweetness.

Ye are Nigrâbhyâ waters, heard by Deities: make me content.

---

26 *Bowls:* there is some doubt as to the exact meaning of *dhishaṇâs* here. From the context sacrificial implements of some kind are clearly implied. See Oldenberg, Vedic Hymns, II. 121. Mahîdhara explains the word as meaning Divine Voices or Words, *i. e.* hymns. *Stones:* for pressing Soma.

27 He pours butter into the water and recites the text. *The pure:* Soma.

28 *Drawing:* or ploughing. He removes the oblation by means of the Maitrâvaruṇa priest's cup, that is, he makes the sediment float away. *I draw:* he takes some water in the Maitrâvaruṇa's cup. *Waters with the waters:* the Vasatîvarî water and that in the cup, which he brings together. *Plants with the plants:* beans, lentils, etc., with rice and other grains.

29 If the ceremony be the liturgical rite called Agnishṭoma (Praise of Agni), an oblation is to be offered with this text taken from R. V. I. 27. 7.

30 Formulas for the Morning Soma-Pressing. *I take thee:* the stone called Upâmsusavana or Low-voiced Presser. *Most noble bolt:* Soma, like a thunderbolt in power. *I pay the worship:* or, I make the Soma; the words are understood. *Nigrâbhyâ:* the technical name of the Vasatîvarî waters when poured into the Hotar's cup. This water is now brought, and the rest of the text, with the verse that follows, is recited over it.

31 Content my mind, content my speech, content my breath, content mine eye, content mine ear, content my soul, content my progeny, content my herds, content the troops of men about me: never may the bands of men about me suffer thirst.

32 For Indra girt by Vasus and accompanied by Rudras, thee. For Indra with Âdityas, thee. For Indra foe-destroyer, thee. Thee for the Soma-bringing Hawk. For plenty-giving Agni, thee.

33 Soma, what light there is of thine in heaven, what on the earth, what in mid-air's wide region,
Therewith give broad space to the Sacrificer for his enrichment: Comfort thou the giver.

34 Auspicious are ye, conquerors of Vṛitra, formed for bestowing wealth, the Immortal's Consorts.
Lead to the Gods this sacrifice, Divine Ones! and at our invitation drink of Soma.

35 Be not afraid; shake not with terror. Take thou strength.
Ye two Bowls, being firm, stay firm, and take ye strength.
Mishap—not Soma—hath been killed.

36 East, west, north, south, from every side to meet thee let the regions run.
Fill him, O Mother, let the noble meet together.

37 Thou, verily, O Mightiest, as God shalt gladden mortal man.
O Bounteous Lord, there is no comforter but thou. Indra, I speak my words to thee.

---

32 He measures out Soma on the Upâṃsu press-stone, five handfuls with a formula for each. *Soma-bringing Hawk:* see V. 1.

33 He touches the measured-out Soma.

34 He pours the Nigrâbhyâ waters on the Soma. *Conquerors of Vṛitra:* as blended with Soma the inspirer and strengthener of Indra. Cf. I. 13. *The Immortal's Consorts:* as closely connected with the imperishable Soma.

35 He addresses the Soma which he beats with the press-stone. *Take thou strength:* give sap or juice, according to Mahîdhara. *Two Bowls:* Heaven and Earth; or the sacrificial implements, bowls or boards, may be meant. See verse 28, note. *Take ye strength:* or, put juice (into the Soma). *Killed:* by the beating.

36 *Thee:* Soma. *Fill him:* or, satisfy him; the formula is obscure. "I take the last part of the formula to mean, 'May he (Soma) win (or, perhaps, join) the longing (waters).'"—Eggeling, Sacred Books of the East, XXVI. 245. *Mother:* each Region.

37 *Thou:* Indra. The text is taken from R. V. I. 84. 19. *Mortal man:* the Sacrificer.

# BOOK THE SEVENTH.

FLOW for Vâchaspati, cleansed by hands from the two off-shoots of the Bull.

Flow pure, a Deity thyself, for Deities whose share thou art.

2 Sweeten the freshening draughts we drink.

Soma, whatever name thou hast, unconquerable, giving life,

To that thy Soma, Soma! Hail!

3 Self-made art thou from all the Powers that are in heaven and on the earth.

May the Mind win thee, thee, All-hail! for Sûrya, O thou nobly-born.

Thee for the Deities who sip light-atoms.

Truly fulfilled, O Plant divine, be that for which I pray to thee.

With ruin falling from above may So-and-So be smitten, crash!

Thee for out-breathing, thee for breath diffused!

4 Taken upon a base art thou. Hold in, Rich Lord! be Soma's guard.

Be thou protector of our wealth: win strengthening food by sacrifice.

---

Formulas for the Grahagrahaṇa or drawing cups or libations of Soma juice. He first presses and draws the Upâṃśu Graha or draught, so named from the Upâṃśusavana or Low-voiced Press-stone used for the purpose. See VI. 30, note.

1 *Flow:* O Soma. *Vâchaspati:* Lord of Speech; Prâṇa, Breath, the Genius of Life which remains in the human body as long as the power of speech. *Hands:* of the priests. *Offshoots of the Bull:* two sprigs of the mighty Soma through which the juice is poured. *Flow pure:* he draws a second cup.

2 He draws a third cup, still addressing the Soma.

3 *Self-made:* the Upâṃśugraha is said to be Prâṇa or Breath. *The Mind:* meaning Prajâpati. *Thee for the Deities:* he wipes off and addresses the Soma that has adhered to the cup. *Sip light-atoms:* or, according to Mahîdhara, guard the motes of light which are distinct from the rays of the Sun. *Truly fulfilled:* this formula is to be used when the Sacrificer wishes to invoke a curse upon an enemy. *Plant:* a sprig of the Soma plant. *So-and-So: asau*; iste: the name of the enemy is to be supplied. *Thee:* I put thee, the cup, down. *Out-breath: prâṇa.* *Breath diffused: vyâna*; another of the five or more vital airs, that which circulates or is diffused through the whole body. He puts down the Upâṃśu press-stone which he addresses.

4 *Taken upon a base:* a frequently recurring expression for an offering that is supported or held up. The base or support being the cup or the earth on which it is deposited. Here the Antaryâma Graha (a cup to be drawn after sunrise with suppression of voice and breath) is addressed. *Hold in: antaryachha*; a play upon the word; retain the juice in the vessel, or, withhold from our enemies certain fiendish powers. *Rich Lord:* Indra is addressed.

5 The heaven and spacious earth I lay within thee, I lay within thee middle air's wide region.
Accordant with the Gods lower and higher, Rich Lord, rejoice thee in the Antaryâma.

6 Self-made art thou . . . . . light-atoms (verse 3 repeated).
Thee for the upward breath.

7 O Vâyu, drinker of the pure, be near us: a thousand teams are thine, All-bounteous Giver.
To thee the rapture-giving juice is offered, whose first draught, God, thou takest as thy portion.

8 These, Indra-Vâyu! have been shed; come for our offered dainties' sake:
The drops are yearning for you both.
Taken upon a base art thou. For Vâyu, Indra-Vâyu, thee.
This is thy home. Thee for the close-knit friends.

9 This Soma hath been shed for you, Law-strengtheners, Mitra-Varuṇa!
Here listen ye to this my call.
Taken upon a base art thou. For Mitra thee, for Varuṇa.

10 May we, possessing much, delight in riches, Gods in oblation, and the kine in pasture;
And that Milch-cow who shrinks not from the milking, O Indra-Varuṇa, give to us daily.
This is thy home. Thee for the righteous Twain.

11 Distilling honey is your whip, Aṣvins, and full of pleasantness:
Sprinkle therewith the sacrifice.
Taken upon a base art thou. Thee for the Aṣvins. This is thy home. Thee for the Honey-lovers.

---

7 Formulas for the Aindra-Vâyava Graha, libation to the dual deity Indra-Vâyu. This verse is taken from R. V. VII. 92. 1. *Of the pure:* Soma. *First draught:* cf. R. V. I. 134. 1; 135. 1; IV. 46. 1; V. 43. 3; VIII. 89. 2.

8 Taken from R. V. I 2. 4. *These:* Soma juices. *Thou:* the Soma. *Thee:* 'I draw' understood. *This:* the earth, on which he deposits the cup. *Thy:* Indra and Vâyu or Indra-Vâyu being regarded as one Deity. *The close-knit friends:* Indra and Vâyu.

9 Formulas for the Maitrâ-Varuṇa Graha, libation to Mitra-Varuṇa. The text is taken from R. V. II. 41. 4.

10 He mixes the Soma with milk symbolizing wealth in cattle. The text is taken from R. V. IV. 42. 10. The added formula is repeated from verse 8. *Milch-cow:* wealth. *The righteous Twain:* Mitra and Varuṇa. *Ṛitâyubhyâm,* dative dual of *ṛitâyu,* observing the Law, devoted to the Right, is explained in the Ṣatapatha Brâhmana (Sacred Books of the East, XXVI. p. 272) as Ṛita, Right or Truth, that is, Mitra, and Âyu, Life, meaning Varuṇa.

11 Formulas for the Âṣvina Graha, the cup or libation offered to the Aṣvins. *Whip:* this Whip is glorified in A. V. IX. 1. It signifies, perhaps,

12 Thou in the first old time, as all were wont, so now drawest from him, light-finder, throned on sacred grass;
Preëminence and strength, from him turned hither, swift, roaring, who winneth those whereby thou waxest strong.
Taken upon a base art thou. Thee for Saṇḍa.
This is thy home. Protect thou manly power.
Saṇḍa hath been removed, may Deities who drink the pure libation lead thee forward. Invincible art thou.

13 Well stored with heroes and begetting heroes, with growth of wealth surround the Sacrificer.
The Bright, conjoined with Heaven and with Earth, with the brightly-shining one.
Expelled is Saṇḍa. Thou art Sukra's dwelling.

14 May we, O radiant Soma, be the keepers of thine uninjured strength and growth of riches.
This is the first all-bounteous Consecration: he the first, Varuṇa, Mitra, and Agni.

15 He is the first Bṛihaspati, the Prudent. Offer ye juice with Svâhâ! to that Indra.
Content be priestly offices, those with good sacrifice of meath, those that are pleased when they have gained fair offerings with the solemn Hail!
The Kindler of the Fire hath sacrificed.

16 See, Vena, born in light hath driven hither on chariot of the air the calves of Pṛisni.

---

the early stimulating and life-giving morning breeze which accompanies the first appearance of the Asvins, the Lords of Light, who precede and herald Dawn, and represents in the Atharva-veda hymn all creative, vivifying, and sustaining power. But see Prof. Max Müller, Vedic Hymns, Part I. p. 187. The Commentators explain *kaśâ*, whip, as a name of Vâk, Voice, or Speech. *Honey-lovers:* or lovers of sweetness, the Asvins. The text is taken from R. V. I. 22. 3.

12 Formulas for the Sukra Graha, or libation to the Bright One, the Sun. The text, taken with a variation from R. V. V. 44. 1, is hopelessly obscure. *Thou:* Indra. *Him:* Soma. *Those:* the sacrificial waters. See the Hymns of the Ṛigveda, where the verse is differently interpreted. *Saṇḍa:* an Asura or demon, for whom the cup is drawn, and then offered to a deity. He is said to be Sukra's son. *Invincible art thou:* the right hip of the high altar, on which the Adhvaryu deposits his cup, is addressed and secured from the attacks of demons.

13 The Sukra cup or libation is addressed by the Adhvaryu.

14 *Keepers:* givers, according to Mahîdhara.

15 *Priestly offices:* meaning, apparently, the priests themselves. According to Mahîdhara the deified sacrificial metres are intended. *Kindler of the Fire:* the Agnîdh, who is the last to sacrifice.

16 He draws the Manthin cup of Soma juice mixt with meal, with the very obscure text from R. V. X. 123. 1. Manthin is said to be the Moon,

Singers with hymns caress him as an infant there where the waters and the sunlight mingle.

Taken upon a base art thou. Thee for Marka.

17 To his oblation, swift as thought ye hurried and welcomed eagerly the prayers he offered.

With arrows in his hand the Very Mighty forced from him all obedience of a servant.

This is thy dwelling-place. Protect the people. Marka hath been removed.

Gods, drinkers of the Manthin, lead thee forward! Invincible art thou.

18 Well stored with people and begetting people, with growth of wealth surround the Sacrificer.

The Manthin joined with Heaven and Earth and with the Manthin-shining one.

Expelled is Marka. Thou art Manthin's dwelling.

19 O ye eleven Gods whose home is heaven, O ye eleven who make earth your dwelling.

Ye who with might, eleven, live in waters, accept this sacrifice, Ye Gods, with pleasure.

20 Taken upon a base art thou. Thou art Âgrayaṇa, good first libation.

Be thou the guard of sacrifice: protect the sacrifice's lord.

Vishṇu with might protect thee. Guard thou Vishṇu. Guard on all sides the Soma sacrifices.

21 Soma flows pure, Soma flows pure for this Priesthood, for the Nobility, pure for the worshipper who presses out the juice, flows pure for food and energy, for waters and for plants; flows pure for general prosperity. Thee for the Universal Gods. This is thy home. Thee for the Universal Gods.

---

as Ṣukra is the Sun. *Vena:* the loving Sun; apparently the Sun rising in the mist of morning. *Priṣni:* the Speckled Cow, the variegated cloud. Her *calves* are the masses of mist which the Sun dispels. *Marka:* son of Ṣukra, and Purohita or tribal priest of the Asuras.

17 The text as it stands, taken from R. V. X. 61. 3, seems unintelligible and is probably corrupt. See The Hymns of the Rigveda, new ed. Vol. II. 465. The following formula is, *mutatis mutandis*, identical with that in verse 12. *Manthin:* Soma juice mixed and stirred up with meal.

18 The Pratiprasthâtar or assistant priest, on the north side of the Sacrificial Stake, addresses a chip of the Stake which he has sprinkled, and throws it on the Âhavanîya fire. Cf. verse 13.

19 The formula for the Âgrayaṇa Graha, a libation offered to the All-Gods, with the text taken from R. V. I. 139. 11. *Waters:* of air.

20 *Vishṇu:* the Sacrifice.

21 *Thee:* he deposits the cup.

22 Taken upon a base art thou. For Indra Lord of the Bṛihat, strong with vital vigour, I take thee lover of the invocation.
Indra, what mighty vigour thou possessest, for that do I take thee, take thee for Vishṇu.
This is thy home. Thee for the recitations.
For the Gods take I thee, the Gods' protector; yea, for the sacrifice's life I take thee.

23 For Mitra-Varuṇa thee, the Gods protector, yea, for the sacrifice's life I take thee.
For Indra, thee, etc. For Indra-Agni, thee, etc. For Indra-Varuṇa, thee, etc. For Indra-Bṛihaspati thee, etc. For Indra-Vishṇu thee, etc.

24 Him, messenger of earth and head of heaven, Agni Vaiśvanara, born in holy Order,
The Sage, the King, the Guest of men, a vessel fit for their mouths, the Gods have generated.

25 Taken upon a base art thou. Firm, firmly resting, the firmest of the firm, the most securely grounded of those who never have been shaken.
This is thy home. Thee for Vaiśvânara.
I pour forth with firm mind, with voice, firm Soma. So now may Indra verily make our people all of one heart and mind and free from foemen.

26 Whatever drop of thine leaps forth, whatever stalk from the bowls' lap, shaken by the press-stone,
From the Adhvaryu's hand or from the filter, that, consecrated in my mind with Vashaṭ I offer unto thee with cry of Svâhâ!
Thou art the way by which the Gods ascended.

---

22 Formula for the Ukthya Graha. *Bṛihat:* the Great (Psalm); one of the most important Sâma hymns, Sâmaveda II. ii. i. 12, taken from R. V. VI. 46. 1, 2 *Recitations:* Ukthas or hymns of praise.

23 *For Mitra-Varuṇa:* he gives a portion of the draught to the Maitrâvaruṇa priest. *For Indra:* to the Brâhmaṇâchhaṃsî. *For Indra-Agni:* to the Achhâvâka.

24 Formula for the Dhruva Graha, or Firm Libation; probably so called because, drawn in the morning, it remains unoffered till the evening. The text is taken from R. V. VI. 7. 1.

25 *Firm: dhruva.*

26 Formula for the Viprud-Homa or Drop-Oblation, to expiate any dropping of Soma during the ceremony of pressing and drawing the juice. *Vashaṭ:* the sacrificial exclamation, May he (Agni) carry (it to the Gods). The text is taken, with two variations, from R. V. X. 17. 12. *Thou:* the Châtvâla or pit, into or towards which the Adhvaryu throws one of two blades of grass taken from the altar. *Ascended:* through sacrifice to heaven.

27 Giver of splendour, grow thou pure for splendour for my outward breath.

Giver of splendour, grow thou pure for splendour for my spreading breath.

Giver, etc. ... ... ... for my upward breath.

Giver, etc. ... ... ... for my power of speech.

Giver, etc. ... ... ... for my sense and will.

Giver, etc. ... ... ... for my hearing power.

Givers of splendour, grow ye pure for splendour for my orbs of sight.

28 Giver of splendour, grow thou pure for splendour for my living self.

Giver, etc. ... ... ... for my energy.

Giver, etc. ... ... ... for my vital power.

Givers of splendour, grow ye pure for splendour for all sprung from me.

29 Who art thou? Which of all art thou? Whose art thou? Who art thou by name?

Even thou on whose name we have meditated, thou whom we have delighted with our Soma.

30 Taken upon a base art thou. For Madhu thee. Taken upon a base art thou. For Mâdhava thee.

Taken, etc. For Ṣukra thee. Taken, etc. For Ṣuchi thee. Taken, etc. For Nabhas thee. Taken, etc. For Nabhasya thee. Taken, etc. For Food thee. Taken, etc. For Energy thee. Taken, etc. For Sahas thee. Taken, etc. For Sahasya thee. Taken, etc. For Tapas thee. Taken, etc. For Tapasya thee. Taken, etc. For Aṃhasaspati thee.

---

27 The Avakâṣa formulas, the Sacrificer being made to look at the libation cups in the order in which the offerings have been made, with a slightly varied formula addressed to each. *Givers:* he looks at and addresses the Ṣukra and the Manthin cups.

28 *Givers:* he looks at the two Soma troughs, Pûtabhṛit and Âdhavanîya.

29 He looks at the Droṇakalaṣa or large wooden Soma reservoir. *Who?:* Ka, Prajâpati, according to Mahîdhara. See I. 6, note. *Which of all?:* or, Eminently Prajâpati. *Whose?:* or Prajâpati's.

30 Formulas for the Ṛitu Grahas or libations to the deified Seasons. The cups are drawn in turn by the Adhvaryu and the Pratiprasthâtar. *Madhu:* Honey, or sweetness; here a name of the first month of the year, Chaitra, Mid-March to Mid-April. *Thee:* 'I take' understood. *Mâdhava:* Honey-like, vernal; the month Vaisâkha, April-May. *Ṣukra:* Bright; the month Jyaishṭha, May-June. *Ṣuchi:* Pure; Âshâḍha, June-July. *Nabhas:* Mist; Ṣrâvaṇa, July-August. *Nabhasya:* Misty; Bhâdra, August-September. *Food:* Ish; Âṣvina, September-October. *Energy:* Ûrj; Kârtika, October-November. *Sahas:* Strength; Mârgasîrsha, November-December. *Sahasya:* Strong; Pushya, December-January. *Tapas:* Pain; Mâgha, January-February. *Tapasya:* Painful; Phâlguna, February-March. *Aṃhasaspati:* Lord of Trouble; the Genius of the thirteenth or intercalary month.

31 Moved, Indra-Agni, by our hymns, come to the juice, the precious dew.
Drink ye thereof, impelled by song.
Taken upon a base art thou. For Indra-Agni thee. This is thy dwelling. Thee for Indra-Agni.

32 Hitherward! they who light the flame and straightway strew the sacred grass,
Whose Friend is Indra ever young.
Taken upon a base art thou. For Indra-Agni thee. This is thy dwelling. Thee for Indra-Agni.

33 Ye Viṣvedevas who protect, reward, and cherish men, approach
Your worshipper's drink-offering.
Taken upon a base art thou. Thee for the Universal Gods.
This is thy home. Thee for the Viṣvedevas.

34 O ye All-Gods, come hitherward: hear this my invocation: seat
Yourselves upon this sacred grass.
Taken upon a base art thou. Thee for the Universal Gods.
This is thy home. Thee for the Viṣvedevas.

35 Here drink the Soma, Indra girt by Maruts! as thou didst drink the juice beside Ṣâryâta.
Under thy guidance, in thy keeping, Hero! the singers serve, skilled in fair sacrifices.
Taken upon a base art thou. For Indra girt by Maruts thee.
This is thy home. For Indra girt by Maruts thee.

36 The Bull whose strength hath waxed, whom Maruts follow, free-giving Indra, the Celestial Ruler,
Mighty, all-conquering, the victory-giver, him we invoke to give us new protection.
Taken upon a base art thou. For Indra girt by Maruts thee.
This is thy home. For Indra girt by Maruts thee.
Taken upon a base art thou. Thee for the Maruts' energy.

---

31 The Adhvaryu draws the Aindrâgna Cup, or libation to Indra and Agni, with the text from R. V. III. 12. 1. *This:* the mound on which he deposits the cup.

32 This text, from R. V. VIII. 45. 1, is also recited.

33 He draws the cup for the Viṣvedevas, the All-Gods or Universal Gods, with the text taken from R. V. I. 3. 7.

34 He recites another text, from R. V. II. 41. 13.

35 The Morning-Pressing having been finished, the formulas for the Mâdhyamdina-savana or Midday-Pressing begin. First the Marutvatîya Cups are drawn for Indra Marutvân or Marut-girt. The text for the first cup is taken from R. V. III. 51. 7. *Beside Ṣâryâta:* that is, at the sacrifice offered by Ṣâryâta, said to have been a king, son of Ṣaryâta who may be identified with Ṣaryâti son of Manu Vaivasvata. See R. V. I. 51. 12; 112. 17.

36 He draws the second cup for Indra Marutvân with the text taken from R. V. III. 47. 5.

37 Indra, accordant with the banded Maruts, drink Soma, Hero! as wise Vṛitra-slayer.
Slay thou our foemen, drive away assailants, and make us safe on every side from danger.
Taken, etc. For Indra girt by Maruts thee. This is thy home. For Indra girt by Maruts thee.

38 Drink, Indra Marut-girt, as Bull, the Soma: for joy, for rapture even as thou pleasest.
Pour down the wave of meath within thy belly: thou art the King of juices shed fortnightly.
Taken, etc..........Maruts thee (as above).

39 Great, hero-like, controlling men is Indra, unwasting in his powers, doubled in vastness.
He, turned to us, hath grown to hero vigour: broad, wide, he hath been decked by those who serve him.
Taken upon a base art thou. Thee for Mahendra.
This is thy dwelling-place. Thee for Mahendra.

40 Indra, great in his power and might, and like Parjanya rich in rain,
Is magnified by Vatsa's lauds.
Taken, etc. ( as in 39 ).

41 His bright rays bear him up aloft, the God who knoweth all that lives,
Sûrya, that all may look on him. All-hail!

42 The brilliant presence of the Gods hath risen, the eye of Mitra, Varuṇa, and Agni.
Soul of all moving, soul of all that moves not, the Sun hath filled the air and earth and heaven.

43 By goodly paths lead us to riches, Agni, thou God who knowest every sacred duty.
Remove the sin that makes us stray and wander: most ample adoration will we bring thee.

44 Wide room and comfort may this Agni give us, and go before us cleaving down our foemen.

---

37 An offering-prayer taken from R V. III. 47. 2.

39 He draws the Mâhendra Graha; the Cup for Mahendra, Great Indra, with the text taken from R. V. VI. 19. 1.

40 The text is from R. V. VIII. 6. 1. *Parjanya:* God of the rain-cloud. *Vatsa:* the seer of the hymn.

41 The text, taken from R. V. I. 50. 1, accompanies an offering (Dâkshiṇa-homa or oblation in the Southern fire) to Sûrya.

42 A second oblation is offered to Sûrya with the text from R. V. I. 115. 1.

43 The text, from R. V. I. 189. 1, accompanies an oblation in the Âgnîdhra fire to Agni.

44 He offers again with the text. Verses 43, 44 occur also in V. 36. 37.

May he win booty in the fight for booty: may he quell foes in his triumphant onset.

45 I through your beauty have attained to beauty. The Tutha, the omniscient, allot you!

Go forth, bright-gifted! on the path of Order. Look thou upon the heaven and air's mid-region. Unite thee with the priests who keep the Sadas.

46 This day may it be mine to find a Brâhman sprung from a lauded father and grandfather,

Offspring of Ṛishis and himself a Ṛishi, the fit recipient of priestly guerdon.

Go to the Gods, bestowed by me, and enter into him who gives.

47 To Agni, yea, to me let Varuṇa give thee. May I gain life that shall endure for ever.

Be thou strong vital power to him who gives thee, and comfort unto me the gift's receiver.

To Rudra, yea, to me let Varuṇa............for ever.

Be thou the breath of life to him who gives thee, and vigour unto me the gift's receiver.

To me Bṛihaspati let Varuṇa..............for ever.

Be thou a covering skin to him who gives thee, and comfort unto me the gift's receiver.

To Yama, yea, to me let Varuṇa...... .....for ever.

Be thou a steed to him who gives the guerdon, and vital power to me the gift's receiver.

48 Who hath bestowed it? Upon whom bestowed it?

Desire bestowed it, for Desire he gave it. Desire is giver and Desire receiver. This, O Desire, to thee is dedicated.

---

45 The Sacrificer, having some gold with him, addresses the cows that are to be given to the priests. *The Tutha:* the Brahman priest, or, according to Mahîdhara, Prajâpati in his form. Cf. V. 31. *Allot you:* distribute you among the officiating priests. *Order:* the sacrificial ceremony. *Look thou:* he addresses the representative cow, meaning, I, through you cows, behold the heavenly world. *Unite thee with:* or, exert thyself to enrich. *Sadas:* the priests' shed. See V. 28.

46 The Sacrificer goes to the Agnîdh or Fire-Kindler and recites the text. *Go to the Gods:* he sits down beside the Agnîdh and gives him the gold and other gifts which are thus addressed. *Enter into:* return to me, the Sacrificer, in the shape of earthly and heavenly blessings.

47 The Adhvaryu recites the first formula as he receives the guerdon of gold. *Thee:* the gold. *To Rudra:* spoken as he receives the cow. *To me, Bṛihaspati:* spoken as he receives a cloth. *To Yama:* God of the Dead; spoken as he receives the horse.

48 Spoken on the receipt of any additional gift such as gruel, sesamum, etc. *Desire bestowed it:* the reward has been given in hope of receiving blessings in return. The text is taken, with variations, from A. V. III. 29. 7.

## BOOK THE EIGHTH.

TAKEN upon a base art thou. Thee for the Âdityas.

Here, O Far-striding Vishṇu, is thy Soma. Guard it from injury. Let them not harm thee.

2 Ne'er art thou fruitless, Indra; ne'er dost thou desert thy worshipper.

But now, O Liberal Lord, thy bounty as a God is poured forth ever more and more. Thee for the Âdityas.

3 Never art thou neglectful: thou guardest both races with thy care.

The Soma feast, O Fourth Âditya, is thy strength. Amrit is stablished in the heavens. Thee for the Âdityas.

4 The sacrifice obtains the Gods' acceptance. Be graciously inclined to us, Âdityas.

Hitherward let your favour be directed and be our best deliverer from trouble. Thee for the Âdityas.

5 This is thy Soma draught, O bright Âditya: take delight therein.

To this mine utterance, O ye men, give credence, what good the man and wife obtain by praying:

A manly son is born and gathers riches, and thrives for ever sinless in the dwelling.

6 Fair wealth, O Savitar, to-day, to-morrow, fair wealth produce for us each day that passes.

May we, through this our song, be happy gainers, God! of a fair and spacious habitation.

---

This Book contains the formulas required for the Third or Evening Soma-Pressing, and first, as a preliminary ceremony, for the Âditya Graha or Libation to the Âdityas.

1 The Pratiprasthâtar draws the Soma from the trough into the Âditya vessel. *Thee:* 'I pour out' understood. *Here*: in the Sthâlî, bowl, or pot into which he pours the juice from the Âditya vessel which is then placed on it as a cover. *Them:* the evil spirits.

2 He draws the Âditya cup with the text from R. V., Vâlakhilya III. 7.

3 He withdraws the cup, and again takes the juice with the text taken with a variation from R. V. Vâlakhilya IV. 7. *Both races:* Gods and men. *Fourth Âditya:* next to Varuṇa, Mitra, Aryaman. *Amrit:* or Ambrosia; celestial Soma.

4 He mixes the Âditya libation with sour milk with the text from R. V. I. 107. 1.

5 *Bright Âditya:* Sûrya the Sun is addressed. *To this:* the Sacrificer's wife recites the text which is taken partly, and with variations, from A. V. XIV. 2. 9.

6 He draws the Sâvitra Graha or Cup for Savitar, with the text from R. V. VI. 71. 6.

7 Taken upon a base art thou.
Savitar's giver of delight art thou. Giver of joy art thou: vouchsafe me joy.
Speed thou the sacrifice, speed thou the sacrifice's lord to win his share. Thee for the God, for Savitar.

8 Taken upon a base art thou.
Thou art a good protector, firmly stablished. To the Great Bull be reverential homage. Thee for the Viṣvedevas.
This is thy home: Thee for the Viṣvedevas.

9 Taken upon a base art thou.
May it be mine to prosper the libations of thee Bṛihaspati's son, O radiant Soma, of thee, strong Indu, mated with thy Consorts.
I am in heaven above, on earth beneath it. The intermediate region was my father.
I saw the Sun both from above and under. I am what Gods in secret hold the highest.

10 Agni, associate with the Dames, accordant with the God Tvashṭar, drink. All-hail!
Thou art Prajâpati, strong male, impregner: may I obtain from thee, strong male, impregner, a son who shall himself become a father.

11 Taken upon a base art thou.
Thou art bay-coloured, Yoker of Bay Coursers. Thee for the pair of tawny-coloured horses.
United with the Soma, ye, for Indra, are corn for his two tawny steeds to feed on.

12 That draught of thine which winneth cows or horses, offered with sacrificial text and lauded

---

7 He addresses the Soma in the cup.

8 He draws from the Pûtabhrit, a vessel containing strained Soma juice, the Mahâvaisvadeva Cup or Libation to the Great All-Gods. *The Great Bull:* Prajâpati, the Lord of Creatures.

9 He drawn the Pâtnîvata Cup or Libation to Him with Consorts, here meaning Soma. *Bṛihaspati's son:* poured forth by priests whose representative is Bṛihaspati. *Indu:* drop, juice; a common name of Soma. *Consorts;* the waters with which Soma is mixed. *I am in heaven, etc.:* the Adhvaryu recites, identifying himself in his sacerdotal character with the Supreme Self.

10 He offers the Pâtnîvata Cup to Agni. *The Dames:* the Consorts of the Gods; with a reference also in this place to the wife of the Sacrificer. *Thou art Prajâpati;* spoken by the Matron who is led up by the Neshṭar (see V. 31) and directed to look at and address the Udgâtar or Sâma-Chanter. *From thee:* through thy favour.

11 He draws the Hâriyojana Cup, or Libation to Indra Harnesser of the Haris or Bay Steeds. *Ye:* grains of parched corn which he throws into the cup.

12 The priests smell the grains taken from the cup, and throw them on the high altar.

With chanted hymns and songs of adoration—of that permitted do I take permitted.

13 Of sin against the Gods thou art atonement. Of sin against mankind thou art atonement.

For sin against the Fathers thou atonest. Of sin against oneself thou art atonement.

Of every sort of sin thou art atonement. The sin that I have knowingly committed, the sin that unawares I have committed, of all that wickedness thou art the atonement.

14 We with our bodies have again united, with lustre, vital sap, and happy spirit.

Giver of boons, may Tvashṭar grant us riches and smooth whate'er was injured in our body.

15 Lead us with thought to wealth in kine, O Indra, to princes, Lord of Bounty! and to welfare.

Lead thou us on to God-inspired devotion, to favour of the Gods who merit worship. All-hail!

16 Verse 14 repeated.

17 May this please Savitar and liberal Dhâtar, Prajâpati the Treasure-Guard, bright Agni,

Tvashṭar, and Vishṇu: blessing him with children, grant store of riches to the Sacrificer.

18 Gods, we have made your seats easy of access, who, pleased with us, have come to this libation.

Bearing and bringing hitherward your treasures, grant to this man, good Lords, abundant riches. All-hail!

19 The willing Gods whom, God, thou hast brought hither, send them to their own dwelling-place, O Agni.

As all of you have eaten and have drunken, approach the air, the heat, the light of heaven.

---

13 *Thou:* a splinter of the Sacrificial Stake. Six of these splinters are thrown on the fire and severally addressed with a formula.

14 The priests touch the Chamasas, cups or bowls, filled with water, and recite the text taken from A. V. VI. 53. 3.

15 He makes nine offerings called Samishṭayajuses or final sacrificial texts and oblations, and with the first he recites the text taken from R. V. V. 42. 4. *Princes:* wealthy sacrificers who will liberally reward our services.

16 The second offering is made with repetition of verse 14.

17 The third offering, with the text from A. V. VII. 17. 4. *This:* our oblation. *Liberal:* or *râti* may mean the Oblation personified. *Dhâtar:* the Creator, or Ordainer. *Grant:* ye, the Deities mentioned.

18 The fourth, with the text whose first three Padas are taken from A. V. VII. 97. 4. *Easy of access:* sacrifice leading the worshipper to heaven.

19 The fifth, with the text from A. V. VII. 97. 3. *Eaten:* the sacrificial rice-cakes. *Drunken:* libations of Soma.

20 Here, Agni, as this sacrifice proceedeth, have we elected thee to be our Hotar.
Special have been thine offerings and thy labour. Well knowing sacrifice, as sage, come near us.

21 Do ye, O Gods, discoverers of the Pathway, go forward on the path when ye have found it.
O God, thou Lord and Master of the Spirit, bestow—All-hail!—this sacrifice on Vâta.

22 Go, Sacrifice, to the sacrifice: seek thou the sacrifice's lord, seek thine own home. All-hail!
Lord of the sacrifice, this is thy sacrifice, followed by many heroes, loud with hymns of praise. Accept it thou. All-hail!

23 Become no serpent thou, become no viper.
King Varuṇa hath made a spacious pathway, a pathway for the Sun wherein to travel.
Where no way was he made him set his footstep, and warned afar whate'er afflicts the spirit.
To Varuṇa be reverential homage! Varuṇa's noose beneath our feet is trampled.

24 The waters, face of Agni, have I entered, O Waters' Child, repelling evil spirits.
Offer the fuel in each home, O Agni. Let thy tongue dart —All-hail!—to meet the butter.

25 Thy heart is in the flood, within the waters. With thee let plants and waters be commingled,
That, Lord of Sacrifice, we may adore thee with singing praise and telling forth our homage. All-hail!

26 This, O celestial Waters, is your offspring. Support him dearly loved and gently nurtured.

---

20 The sixth, with the text whose first line is taken from A. V. VII. 97. 1.

21 The seventh, with the text repeated from II. 21. *Pathway:* the sacrifice. *The path:* your own homeward way. *O God:* Prajâpati.

22 The eighth, with the text. *This is thy sacrifice:* he offers the ninth and last oblation of the series.

23 After this set of oblations, the Adhvaryu throws the black-buck's horn (see IV. 10, note) and the girdle into the Châtvâla or pit. *Thou:* the girdle of rope (see VI. 12). The Sacrificer then recites the text from R. V. I. 24. 8. *To Varuṇa:* spoken by the Sacrificer as he steps into the Avabhṛitha or other water. *Varuṇa's noose;* affliction sent as a punishment for sin by the Moral Governor of the world.

24 The Sacrificer throws a kindling-stick into the water and makes an offering thereon with four ladlefuls of butter.

25 The Adhvaryu floats a jar containing the dregs of the Soma, and recites the text. *Thy heart:* O Soma.

26 *This:* Soma. *Bring .... ward off:* I follow Mahîdhara. Prof. Eggeling refers *vakshva* in both cases to *vaksh* instead of *vaḥ:* 'thrive thou well therein and thrive thou thoroughly.'

This is thy station, O celestial Soma; therein bring happiness and ward off evil.

27 O restless Purifying Bath, thou glidest onward restlessly.
May I with aid of Gods remove the stain of sin against the Gods, and wash away with mortals' help the wrong that hath been done to men. Preserve me, God, from injury, from the loud-roaring demon foe. Thou art the fuel of the Gods.

28 Let, still unborn, the ten-month calf move with the following after-birth.
Even as the wind is moving, as the gathered flood of ocean moves,
So may this ten-month calf come forth together with the after-birth.

29 O thou who hast a womb of gold and offspring meet for sacrifice,
Him with all limbs unbroken have I brought together with his dam. All-hail!

30 Multiform, rich in wondrous operation, the strong juice hath enrobed itself with greatness.
Let the worlds praise her uniped and biped, three-footed and four-footed and eight-footed. All-hail!

31 Verily, best of guardians hath he in whose dwelling-place ye drink,
O Maruts, giants of the sky.

32 May Heaven and Earth, the Mighty Pair, besprinkle this our sacrifice,
And feed us full with nourishments.

---

27 He immerses the jar. *Purifying Bath:* he addresses the Avabhritha. The text is repeated from III. 48. *Thou art the fuel:* he puts a kindling-stick on the Âhavanîya fire.

28 A course of expiation to be followed when a sacrificial cow, supposed to be barren, is found after immolation to be in calf. Cf. R. V. V. 78. 7—9, which Sâyaṇa calls 'the liturgy of child-birth.' *Ten-month:* 'although the embryo be not of ten months' growth', says Mahîdhara, 'the priest makes it such by prayer and sacrificial text.'

29 *O thou:* the Vaṣâ or Sacrificial Cow is addressed. *Him:* the embryo calf.

30 *Multiform:* the fat juice of the embryo, with butter poured over it, is offered as an oblation. *Greatness:* derived from the cow. *Praise:* or celebrate; *prakhyâtâm kurvantu:* Mahîdhara. *Uniped:* as containing one chief element of sacrifice, the omentum. *Biped:* containing omentum and limbs for sacrifice. *Three-footed:* with elements of by-offerings in addition. *Eight-footed:* when in calf. Cf. R. V. II. 7. 5.

31 When the Samishṭayajus oblations are finished, he takes the embryo wrapped in a bandage and offers it on the sacrificial hearth to the Maruts, with the text from R. V. I. 86. 1.

32 The embryo is covered up with coals, and the text from R. V. I. 22. 13 is recited.

33 Slayer of Vṛitra, mount thy car: thy Bay Steeds have been yoked by prayer.
May, with its voice, the pressing-stone draw thine attention hitherward.
Taken upon a base art thou. For Indra thee, for Shoḍaśî. This is a dwelling-place for thee. For Indra thee, for Shoḍaśî.

34 Harness thy pair of strong Bay Steeds, long-maned, whose bodies fill the girths,
And, Indra, Soma-drinker, come to listen to our songs of praise.
Taken upon a base, etc., as in 33.

35 His pair of tawny Coursers bring Indra of unresisted might
Hither to Ṛishis' songs of praise and sacrifice performed by men.
Taken upon a base, etc., as in 33.

36 Than whom there is none other born more mighty, who hath pervaded all existing creatures—
Prajâpati, rejoicing in his offspring, he, Shoḍaśî, maintains the three great lustres.

37 Indra chief Lord and Varuṇa the Sovran have made this draught of thine the first and foremost.
I, after, drink their draught. May she, the Goddess of Speech, rejoicing, sate herself with Soma—All-hail!—with Prâṇa as her feast-companion.

38 Skilled in thy task, O Agni, pour lustre and hero strength on us,
Granting me wealth and affluence.
Taken upon a base art thou. For Agni thee, for splendour.
This is thy home. For Agni thee, for splendour.
Thou, lustrous Agni, mid the Gods art splendid. May I among mankind be bright with lustre.

---

33 Formulas for additional Soma sacrifices, and, first, the Shoḍaśî (sixteen-fold, or sixteen-hymned) libation to Indra who is called Shoḍaśî as connected with this service. The libation is drawn at the Morning-Pressing in a four-cornered cup of Khadira wood, with the text from R. V. I. 84. 3.

34 Or this text from R. V. I. 16. 3 may be recited.

35 Or a third text from R. V. I. 84. 2.

36 He approaches the cup and recites the text. *Three great lustres:* Agni, Vâyu, Sûrya, or Fire, Wind, and Sun.

37 He drinks the cup. *The Goddess of Speech:* Sarasvatî. *Prâṇa:* the Genius of Vital Breath.

38 Formulas for the Dvâdaśâha or Twelve-Day Ceremonial, of which the Prishṭhyashaḍaha, a period of six sacrificial days, forms part. On the first three days of this period the three Atigrâhyas (Additional or Superiority Cups) are drawn with appropriate texts for Indra, Agni, and Sûrya. The first cup is for Agni, with the text in Gâyatrî from R. V. IX. 66. 21.

39 Arising in thy might thy jaws thou shookest, Indra, having drunk
The Soma which the mortar pressed.
Taken upon a base art thou. For Indra thee, for mighty strength.
This is thy home. For Indra thee, for might.
Among the Gods thou art the mightiest, Indra. Among mankind I fain would be most mighty.

40 His herald rays are seen afar refulgent o'er the world of men,
Like flames of fire that burn and blaze.
Taken upon a base art thou. For Sûrya, for the Bright One, thee.
This is thy home. For Sûrya, for the Bright One, thee.
Thou among Gods art brightest, brightest Sûrya. Among mankind I fain would be the brightest.

41 His herald rays bear him aloft, the God who knoweth all that lives, Sûrya, that all may look at him.
Taken upon a base, etc., as in 40.

42 Smell thou the vat. Let Soma drops pass into thee, O Mighty One.
Return again with store of sap. Pour for us wealth in thousands thou with full broad streams and floods of milk. Let riches come again to me.

43 Idâ, delightful, worshipful, loveable, splendid, shining One,
Inviolable, full of sap, the Mighty One, most glorious,
These are thy names, O Cow: tell thou the Gods that I act righteously.

---

39 The second Atigrâhya is drawn for Indra with the text in Gâyatrî from R.V. VIII. 65. 10. *Shookest:* in delight.

40 The third cup is drawn for Sûrya with a Gâyatrî text from R. V. I. 50. 3.

41 A Gâyatrî text from R. V. 50. 1. to accompany the drawing of an Atigrâhya Cup for Sûrya on the middle day of the great twelve-months sacrificial Sattra or Session called Gavâmayana or Procession of the Cows. The rest of the formula is repeated from verse 40.

42 Formulas for the Gargatrirâtra, a festival of three days, in which a thousand cows are given to the officiating priests, three hundred and thirty-three each day. The full number of a thousand is to be completed with a red cow who is led up to the sacrificial enclosure and stationed between the Havirdhâna shed and the Agnîdhra hearth where she is made to smell the Droṇakalaśa or large wooden Soma vat or reservoir. *O Mighty One:* the red cow is addressed.

43 *Idâ:* one of the cow's sacrificial names: see III. 27; IV. 22. *Inviolable:* more literally, 'unrestrained, or Aditi,' another name of the cow: see III. 27. *Full of sap:* or Sarasvatî, also a name of the cow.

44 O Indra, beat our foes away, humble the men who challenge us:
Send down to nether darkness him who seeks to do us injury.
Taken upon a base art thou. For Indra, foe-dispeller, thee.
This is thy home. For Indra, foe-dispeller, thee.

45 Let us invoke to-day, to aid our labour, the Lord of Speech, the thought-swift Viṣvakarman.
May he hear kindly all our invocations, who gives all bliss for aid, whose works are righteous.
Taken upon a base art thou. For Indra Viṣvakarman thee.
This is thy home. For Indra Viṣvakarman thee.

46 With strengthening libation, Viṣvakarman, thou madest Indra an undying guardian.
The people of old time bowed down before him because the Mighty One was meet for worship.
Taken upon a base, etc., as in 45.

47 Taken upon a base art thou.
I take thee lord of Gâyatrî for Agni. For Indra take I thee the lord of Trishṭup.
I take thee lord of Jagatî for All-Gods. Anushṭup is the song that sings thy praises.

48 I stir thee for the fall of cloud-borne waters. I stir thee for the fall of streams that gurgle. I stir thee for the fall of those that gladden. I stir thee for their fall who are most lovely. I stir thee for their fall that are the sweetest. I stir thee for the waters' fall, I stir thee, pure one, in the pure, in the day's form, in Sûrya's beams.

49 The Bull's majestic form is shining brightly, the pure the pure's preceder, Soma Soma's.
Whatever name invincible, stimulating, is thine, O Soma, for that name I take thee.
All-hail to Soma, unto thee, O Soma.

---

44 Formulas for the drawing of the Mahâvratîya Graha, or Great Vow Libation, on the penultimate day of the Gavâmayana. He draws the cup for Indra with the text from R. V. X. 152. 4. *Foe-dispeller:* Vimṛidh; 'Averter of Scorn': Eggeling.

45 A second text for Viṣvakarman, the Omnific Indra, called also Vâchaspati, Lord of Speech.

46 A third alternative text. *Undying: avadhyam;* not slayable.

47 Formulas for drawing the Adâbhya Graha, the Undeceivable or Invincible Libation. *Lord of:* accompanied by. *Agni:* to whom the Gâyatrî metre is specially devoted. Three sprigs of the Soma plant are thrown into the vessel containing the Nigrâbhyâ (VI. 30) waters.

48 He approaches the Âhavanîya fire-house, and stirs the Nigrâbhyâ waters with the Soma sprigs. *I stir thee:* Soma. *In the pure:* water.

49 *The Bull's majestic form:* the Sun, identified with Soma.

50 O radiant Soma, eagerly draw nigh to Agni's well-loved food.
O radiant Soma, willingly go to the food that Indra loves.
Go, radiant Soma, as our friend, to the All-Gods' belovèd food.

51 Here is delight: enjoy yourselves; here surety, surety of your own. All-hail!
Loosing the suckling to his dam, the suckling as he milks his dam—
May he maintain the growth of wealth among us. All-hail!

52 Thou art the Session's happy termination.
We have attained the light and grown immortal.
We have gone up from earth to sky, have found the Gods and heaven and light.

53 Indra and Parvata, our champions in the fight, drive ye away the man who fain would war with us, drive him far from us with the bolt.
Welcome to him concealed afar shall be the lair that he hath found.
So may the Render rend our foes on every side, rend them, O Hero, everywhere.
Earth! Ether! Sky! May we be rich in offspring, rich in brave sons and rich in food to feed us.

54 Parameshṭhin when contemplated. Prajâpati in uttered speech.
Food when approached. Savitar in the partition. Visvakarman in Consecration. Pûshan in the Soma-purchasing cow.

---

51 Formulas for the Sattrotthâna or Rising up from the Sacrificial Session. Two oblations are offered in the Ṣâlâdvârya, or Sacrificial Hall Door fire, and two texts are recited. *Here is delight:* the cows are addressed. *Loosing the suckling:* he offers the second oblation. *The suckling* is Agni, and *his dam* is the Earth whose moisture he drains, or whose produce in the shape of sacrificial food he consumes. *He:* Agni.

52 *Thou:* the Soma in the cup. *We have attained, etc.:* cf. R. V. VIII. 48. 3.

53 The Sacrificers creep eastward under the axle of the southern Havirdhâna or Soma cart with the text from R. V. I. 132. 6. *Parvata:* mountain; the presiding Genius of mountains and clouds, frequently associated with Indra, or, according to Sâyaṇa, another form of that God.

54 This and the four following verses contain thirty-four formulas for rectifying and expiating any neglect, error or mischance in the sacrificial performance. If the cow who should supply milk for the Gharma or Warm Libation fails to give any, another is to be milked and thirty-four oblations of butter are to be offered on her right tail-bone. See Sacred Books of the East, XXVI. 411, 412. The sacrifice, Soma, is identified with each of the Deities and sacred objects whose names are mentioned. *Parameshṭhin:* Supreme Lord; an epithet applied to various Deities. *Soma-purchasing cow:* see IV. 19, 26.

55 As Indra and the Maruts he is stationed ready for the sale: Asura, being bought and sold. Mitra when purchased; Vishṇu Sipivishṭa when on the Sacrificer's thigh he resteth; Vishṇu Narandhisha brought on the barrow;

56 Soma when come: when seated on the platform, Varuṇa; Agni in the sacred fire-place;
Indra upon the sacrificial barrow; Atharvan when deposited for pounding;

57 All-Gods when offered in the scattered fragments; Vishṇu, the guard of those who soothe his anger, when he is filled and swelling in the waters; Yama in pressing; Vishṇu in collection;
Vâyu what time they cleanse and purify him; the Bright when cleansed; the Bright with milk about him; Manthin commingled with the meal of barley;

58 All-Gods when he is drawn away in beakers; Life when uplifted for the fire-oblation; Rudra when offered; Vâta when reverted; Man-viewer when beheld; drink when they drink him; deposited, the Nârâṣaṃsa Fathers;

59 Sindhu when ready for the bath that cleanses; the sea when he is carried to the waters; Water is he when he is plunged beneath it.
To those most mighty hath it gone, most manly in vigour, by whose strength the worlds were stablished,
Who rule as Lords resistless in their grandeur, Vishṇu and Varuṇa, at the prayer of morning.

---

55 *Asura:* Lord; Divine Being. *Ṣipivishṭa:* a title of Vishṇu of uncertain etymology and meaning. 'Invested with rays of light,' according to Sâyaṇa. See The Hymns of the Rigveda, VII. 100. 6, note. *Sacrificer's thigh:* see IV. 27, note. *Narandhisha:* variously explained by Mahîdhara as 'world-destroying,' 'not injuring men,' and, in XXII. 20, as 'man-praising.' According to the St. Petersburg Lexicon the meaning is probably 'man-observing.'

56 *Atharvan:* an ancient priest, the first who obtained fire and instituted the worship of Agni.

57 *Fragments:* the severed stalks or filaments of the plant. *Filled and swelling:* see V. 7, note. *In collection:* when he is being procured and prepared for sacrifice. *The Bright:* Ṣukra. See VII. 13. *Manthin:* said to mean the Moon. See VII. 16.

58 *Vâta:* =Vâyu, the Wind-God. *Reverted:* carried away, for partition, to the Sadas or Priests' shed. *Nârâṣaṃsa:* so called as referred to in certain Soma libations at which the name of Agni Narâṣaṃsa, or Praise of Men, is mentioned.

59 *Sindhu:* the Indus, or, River. Water is now to be poured on any Soma that has been spilt during the performance, with recitation of the text taken, with variation, from A. V. VII. 25. 1. *Hath it gone:* the spilt portion of Soma.

60 To Gods, to sky the sacrifice hath gone: come riches thence to me!
To men, to air the sacrifice hath gone: come riches thence to me!
To Fathers, earth, the sacrifice hath gone: come riches thence to me!
Whatever sphere the sacrifice hath reached, may wealth come thence to me.

61 The threads that have been spun, the four-and-thirty, which stablish this our sacrifice with Svadhâ,
Of these I join together what is broken. All-hail! to Gods go the warm milk oblation!

62 Spread far and wide is sacrifice's milking: eightfold along the heaven hath it extended.
Pour, Sacrifice! in plenty on mine offspring: may I obtain prosperity for ever. All-hail!

63 Soma, send wealth in gold and steeds and heroes. All-hail! bring hitherward booty in cattle.

---

61 *The threads:* the sacrificial formulas which have now come to an end. See verse 54. *With Svadhâ:* with the appropriate oblation.

62 The Sacrificer recites the text. *Eightfold:* directed to the quarters of the sky and the intermediate points.

63 He touches the spilt Soma as he recites the text.

# BOOK THE NINTH.

OUR sacrifice, God Savitar, speed onward: speed to his share the sacrifice's patron.

May the celestial Gandharva, cleanser of thought and will, make clean our thought and purpose: the Lord of Speech sweeten the food we offer.

2 Thee, firmly set, settled in man, in spirit.

Taken upon a base art thou. I take thee, draught acceptable to Indra. This is thy home. Thee, welcomest to Indra.

Thee set in waters, butter, realm of ether. Taken upon ......Indra.

Thee seated in the sky, earth, air's mid-region, among the Gods and in the vault of heaven. Taken, etc. as above.

3 The strength-arousing essence of the waters, gathered in the Sun, Essence of waters' essence, that, most excellent, I take for you.

Taken, etc., as above.

4 Cups of strength-giving sacrifice, inspirers of the sage's hymn—

Of you, the handleless, have I collected all the sap and strength.

Taken, etc., as above.

United are ye twain: with bliss unite me. Parted are ye: keep me apart from evil.

---

Books IX. and X. contain the formulas required for the performance of two important modifications of the Soma sacrifice, the Vâjapeya, Draught of Strength or Cup of Victory, and the Râjasûya, Inauguration or Consecration of a King. For the Vâjapeya, see Sacred Books of the East, XLI. pp. 1—40; Hillebrandt, Ritual-Litteratur, pp. 141—143; Weber, Über den Vâjapeya (Sitzungsberichte der K. Preussischen Akademie der Wissenschaften, pp. 765—813).

1 The Sacrificer offers an oblation of butter and recites the text. *Celestial Gandharva:* the God in the form of the Sun's disc, according to Mahîdhara. *Lord of Speech:* Prajâpati. *The food: vâjam.*

2 *Thee:* the first of the five Vâjapeya Cups which he draws for Indra. *Thee set in waters:* he draws the second cup. The rest of the formula is repeated from lines 2 and 3. *In the sky, etc.:* he draws the third cup. The rest as in lines 2 and 3. Soma is considered as pervading the three worlds, Earth, Air, and Sky.

3 He draws the fourth cup. *Gathered in the Sun:* meaning the purifying Vâyu or Wind. *That most excellent:* meaning Prajâpati. *For you:* O Gods. The rest of the formula is repeated as above.

4 He draws the fifth cup. *Handleless:* or noseless, or jawless; without spouts or side-handles. *Ye twain:* a cup of Soma and another of Surâ, a kind of wine or beer made from rice or barley with a kind of leaven to make it ferment. See Zimmer, Altindisches Leben, p. 280.

5 Thou art the thunderbolt of Indra, winner of wealth: with thee may this man win him riches.
In gain of wealth we celebrate with praises her, Aditi by name, the Mighty Mother,
On whom this Universe of life hath settled. Thereon God Savitar promote our dwelling!

6 Amrit is in the Waters, in the Waters healing medicine. Yea, Horses! at our praises of the Waters grow ye fleet and strong.
Whatever wave, O ye celestial Waters, wealth-giving, towering high, and swiftly rushing, is yours, therewith may this man win him riches.

7 It was the wind, or it was thought, or the Gandharvas twenty-seven—
These at the first harnessed the horse: they set the power of speed in him.

8 Steed, being yoked grow wind-swift: be beauteous as Indra's right-hand steed.
Omniscient Maruts harness thee! Tvashṭar put swiftness in thy feet!

9 What speed, O Horse, was laid in thee in secret, what passed in wind, bestowed upon the falcon,
With that same strength be strong for us, O Courser, wealth-winning and victorious in battle.
Starting to run your course, winners of riches, smell ye Bṛihaspati's portion, O ye Horses.

10 By impulse of God Savitar, true Impeller, may I ascend Bṛihaspati's highest heaven.

---

5 Here begin the formulas for the chariot-racing which is a characteristic and important part of the Vâjapeya. The Sacrificer addresses the Chariot which he takes down from its stand, draws to the south of the Châtvâla or pit, and places by the altar. *On whom:* as Earth.

6 He takes water and sprinkles the chariot horses, reciting the text from A. V. I. 4. 4., the first line of which is taken from R. V. I. 23. 19. *Amrit:* nectar or ambrosia.

7 He harnesses the off horse with the text. *Wind . . . thought:* as emblems of rapidity. *Gandharvas*: see II. 3. note; here representing the Nakshatras, Lunar Mansions or stages through which the Moon passes, and signifying the flight of time.

8 He yokes the near horse. *Omniscient*: or, All-possessing.

9 He yokes a third horse as off side-horse. *In secret:* in the region of thy heart. *In battle*: or, at the gathering (of the Gods at sacrifice), according to the Ṣatapatha-Brâhmaṇa. *Bṛihaspati's portion:* a mess of boiled wild-rice, dedicated to Bṛihaspati the representative of the priesthood. The horses are made to smell it in order to assure their victory.

10 The Brahman mounts a chariot-wheel placed on a post, with the following line of text if the Sacrificer is a Brâhman. *Indra:* as the represen-

By impulse of God Savitar, true Impeller, may I ascend the highest heaven of Indra.

By impulse of God Savitar, true Impeller, Bṛihaspati's highest heaven have I ascended.

By impulse of God Savitar, true Impeller, I have ascended Indra's loftiest heaven.

11 Bṛihaspati, win the prize. Lift up your voices to Bṛihaspati. Make ye Bṛihaspati win the prize.

Do thou, O Indra, win the prize. To Indra lift your voices up. Make Indra winner of the prize.

12 True hath been this your league whereby ye made Bṛihaspati win the prize.

Bṛihaspati have ye caused to win the prize. Be freed, ye Forest-lords.

Faithful was this your league whereby ye have made Indra win the prize.

Ye have made Indra win the prize. Be ye set free, ye Forest-lords.

13 Through impulse of God Savitar, true Impeller, mine be Bṛihaspati's prize who winneth prizes.

On to the goal, ye Steeds, winners of prizes, blocking the ways and meting out the courses!

14 Bound by the neck and at the flanks and in the mouth, that vigorous Courser lends new swiftness to his speed.

---

tative of the Kshatra or nobility; this part of the text being used when the Sacrificer is a Râjanya, a man of the princely, noble, or military class. The third line also is to be used when the Brahman descends from the wheel, if the Sacrificer be a Brâhman, and the fourth when he is a Râjanya.

Seventeen being the number sacred to Prajâpati, whose favour is to be won in the ceremony, seventeen four-horse chariots have been prepared and assembled, the goal round which they have to turn being the branch of an Udumbara tree (Ficus Glomerata) planted in the ground at a distance of seventeen bowshots from the starting-place.

11 The Brahman beats one of the seventeen drums ranged along the edge of the altar ground, and recites the text, the rest of the drums being considered to be simultaneously beaten. *Bṛihaspati:* this, if the Sacrificer is a Brâhman. *Lift up:* O Drums. *O Indra:* this, if the Sacrificer is a Râjanya.

12 After the racing he takes down, with the text, the drum that has been beaten, and the others in silence. *Your league:* the union of your voices. *Bṛihaspati . . . Indra:* as in verse 11. *Forest-lords:* trees, the drums made chiefly of wood.

13 This refers to an earlier stage of the proceedings when the Sacrificer mounts the chariot.

14 The Adhvaryu makes an offering of butter, or addresses the running horses with two verses taken respectively from R. V. IV. 40. 4, 3. *Dadhikrâs,* or in the crude form, Dadhikrâ: a kind of divine horse, probably a personification of the morning Sun. The word appears to be an apocopated form of Dadhikrâvan in the following verse, with which it is interchangeable.

Drawing himself together as his strength allows, Dadhikrâs speeds along the windings of the paths. All-hail!

15 His pinion, rapid runner, fans him on his way, as of a bird that hastens onward to its aim,

And, as it were a falcon's gliding through the air, strikes Dadhikrâvan's side as he speeds on with might. All-hail!

16 Bless us the Coursers when we call, while slowly they move, strong singers, to the Gods' assembly.

Crushing the wolf, the serpent, and the demons, may they completely banish all affliction. All-hail!

17 May all those vigorous Coursers listen to our cry, hearers of invocation, speeders on their way;

Winners of thousands, fain to win where meed is won, who gather of themselves great wealth in every race.

18 Deep-skilled in Law Eternal, wise, immortal, O Coursers, help us in each fray for booty.

Drink of this meath, be satisfied, be joyful: then go on paths which Gods are wont to travel.

19 To me come plenteous growth of wealth! Approach me these, Heaven and Earth, who wear each form and figure!

Hither may Father come to me, and Mother. Soma with immortality approach me!

20 To the Friend, Hail! To the Good Friend, Hail! To the Later-born, Hail! To Resolution, Hail! To the Vasu, Hail! To the Lord of Days, Hail! To the Failing Day, Hail! To the Failing sprung from the Transitory, Hail! To the Transitory sprung from the Final, Hail! To the Final Mundane, Hail! To the Lord of the World, Hail! To the Sovran Lord, Hail!

---

16 He addresses the horses with the text from R. V. VII. 38. 7. *Strong singers:* or, perhaps, high-mettled.

17 He addresses them again with the text from R. V. X. 64. 6. *Meed:* the priestly fee.

18 He addresses them a third time with the text from R. V. VII. 38 8. *This meath:* a mess made of wild-rice which the horses are made to smell before the race and to drink after it. See verse 9.

19 The Sacrificer having dismounted from the chariot touches the mess of wild-rice and recites the text. *Father:* Heaven. *Mother:* Earth; or perhaps the Sacrificer's parents are intended.

20 The Adhvaryu makes twelve oblations with the dipping-spoon, or makes the Sacrificer recite the following twelve formulas, one for each month, addressed to Prajâpati as the Presiding Genius of the Year. *The Friend:* perhaps the first month after the winter solstice when the weather becomes milder. *The Lord of Days:* the month containing the longest day. The meaning of some of these fanciful expressions is obscure, and their applicability to the respective months is not apparent. Cf. XVIII. 28; XXII. 32.

21 May life succeed through sacrifice. May life-breath thrive by sacrifice. May the eye thrive by sacrifice. May the ear thrive by sacrifice. May the back thrive by sacrifice. May sacrifice thrive by sacrifice.

We have become the children of Prajâpati. Gods, we have gone to heaven. We have become immortal.

22 In us be your great might and manly vigour, in us be your intelligence and splendour.

Obeisance to our Mother Earth! Obeisance to our Mother Earth!

This is thy Sovranty. Thou art the ruler, thou art controller, thou art firm and stedfast.

Thee for land-culture, thee for peace and quiet, thee for wealth, thee for increase of our substance.

23 Of old the furtherance of strength urged onward this Sovran Soma in the plants and waters.

For us may they be stored with honey: stationed in front may we be watchful in the kingdom. All-hail!

24 The furtherance of strength extended over this heaven and all the worlds as sovran ruler.

He, knowing, makes the churl a bounteous giver: wealth may he grant us with full store of heroes. All-hail!

25 Surely the furtherance of strength pervaded all these existing worlds in all directions.

From olden time the King moves round, well knowing, strengthening all the people and our welfare.

26 As suppliants, for aid we grasp Soma the King, and Agni, the Âdityas, Vishṇu, Sûrya, and the Brahman-priest Bṛihaspati.

---

21 He offers six oblations, or makes the Sacrificer recites the following six formulas, one for each season, belonging to Prajâpati as Lord of the Year. *Sacrifice:* meaning the Vâjapeya now in course of performance. *The back:* or, possibly, a special arrangement of Sâmans called Pṛishṭha. *We have gone to heaven:* or, to light; here the Sacrificer, mounting by a ladder, touches the dough cap or head-piece of the sacrificial stake. *Become immortal:* he mounts higher till his head is above the top of the stake.

22 He looks towards the four quarters of the sky and the intermediate points, and addresses the text to them or to their presiding deities. *Obeisance:* here he looks on the ground. *Thy Sovranty:* he points to a seat of Udumbara wood, on which he spreads a goat-skin. *Thou:* addressed to the Sacrificer whom he seats on the Âsandi or throne. *Thee:* 'I seat' understood.

23 He offers oblations of milk, rice and other grain collected in a vessel of Udumbara wood, and recites seven texts. These offerings are called Vâjaprasavanîya, Strength-Furthering, the first three texts beginning with *Vâjasya . . . prasavaḥ*, the furtherance of strength. *Of old:* in the beginning of creation. *The churl:* literally, 'him who is unwilling to give.'

26 Taken with a variation from R. V. X. 141. 3.

27 Urge Aryaman to send us gifts, and Indra, and Bṛihaspati, Vâk, Vishṇu, and Sarasvatî, and the strong Courser Savitar.

28 Agni, speak kindly to us here, be graciously inclined to us. Winner of thousands, grant us boons, for thou art he who giveth wealth.

29 Let Aryaman vouchsafe us wealth, and Pûshan, and Bṛihaspati.
May Vâk the Goddess give to us. All-hail!

30 Thee by the radiant Savitar's impulsion, with arms of Aṣvins, with the hands of Pûshan.
To Vak Sarasvatî's controlling guidance, here the controlling leader, I consign thee.
I with Bṛihaspati's supreme dominion endow thee by the balm of consecration.

31 With the monosyllable Agni won vital breath: may I win that. With the dissyllable the Aṣvins won bipeds: may I win those. With the trisyllable
Vishṇu won the three worlds: may I win those. With quadrisyllabic metre
Soma won four-footed cattle: may I win those.

32 With five-syllable metre Pûshan won the five regions: may I win them.
With six-syllable metre Savitar won the six seasons: may I win them.
With seven-syllable metre the Maruts won the seven domestic animals:
May I win them. With octosyllabic metre Bṛihaspati won the Gâyatrî: may I win that.

33 With nine-syllable metre Mitra won the Trivṛit Stoma: may I win that. With decasyllabic metre Varuṇa won Virâj: may I win that.

---

27 Taken from R. V. X. 141. 5, Vâk, the Goddess of Speech, being substituted for Vâta the Wind-God.

28 Taken with a slight variation from R. V. X. 141. 1.

29 The first line is taken from R. V. X. 141. 2, Pûshan being substituted for Bhaga the Distributor of food or wealth.

30 *Thee:* 'I besprinkle' understood. The priest sprinkles the Sacrificer with the remainder of the sacrificial elements. *I endow thee:* addressing him by his name.

31 He offers oblations, or makes the Sacrificer recite the Ujjitis or Victory. Formulas. *Monosyllable:* metre of one syllable. *Six Seasons:* Spring, Summer, Rains, Autumn, Winter, Dews. See II. 32.

32 *Seven domestic animals:* ox, horse, sheep, goat, mule, ass, man. See The Hymns of the Atharva-veda, II. 34. 1, note; III. 10. 6 and note.

33 *Trivṛit Stoma:* Triple Praise-Song; a recitation in which first the first three verses of each triplet of R. V. IX. 11 are sung together, then the second verses, and lastly the third.

With hendecasyllabic metre Indra won Trishṭup: may I win that.

With dodecasyllabic metre the All-Gods won Jagatî: may I win that.

34 The Vasus by thirteen-syllable metre won the Thirteenfold Stoma: may I win that. The Rudras by fourteen-syllable metre won the fourteenfold Stoma: may I win that. The Âdityas with fifteen-syllable metre won the Fifteenfold Stoma: may I win that. Aditi with sixteen-syllable metre won the Sixteenfold Stoma: may I win that. Prajâpati with seventeenfold metre won the Seventeenfold Stoma: may I win that.

35 This is thy portion, Nirṛiti! Accept it graciously. All-hail!

To Gods whose guide is Agni, to the eastward-seated Gods, All-hail!

To Gods whose guide is Yama, to the southward-seated Gods, All-hail!

To Gods whose guides are the All-Gods, those who are seated westward, Hail!

Hail to the northward-seated Gods, to those whose guides are Mitra and Varuṇa or the Marut host!

To Gods whose guide is Soma, who, worshipful, sit on high, All-hail!

36 Gods who have Agni as their guide, whose seat is eastward, Hail to them!

Gods who have Yama as their guide, whose seat is southward, Hail to them!

Gods who have All-Gods as their guides, whose seat is westward, Hail to them!

Gods who have Mitra-Varuṇa for guides, north-seated, Hail to them!

Gods who have Soma as their guide, high-seated, worshipful, Hail to them!

37 Agni, subdue opposing bands and drive our enemies away.
Invincible, slay godless foes: give splendour to the worshipper.

---

35 Here begin the formulas for the Râjasûya or King's Inauguration, the Ceremony in verse 30 being merely an *entr'acte*. A rice-cake is prepared for Anumati or Divine Favour; then the Sacrificer takes a firebrand, goes towards the south, and having made up a fire in a natural cleft in the ground, or on barren land, offers to Nirṛiti, or Earth in her lowest depths. *This:* mess of meal. He offers in five fires, or in five parts of the fire, to the five classes of Gods mentioned, with an address to each class.

37 He then offers the Apâmârga oblation, an exorcising ceremony performed with seeds of the Apâmârga plant (Achyranthus Aspera: see The Hymns of the A. V. IV. 17. 6), having taken a firebrand from the southern fire, and reciting the text from Ṛ. V. III. 24. 1.

38 Thee at the radiant Savitar's impulsion, with Aṣvins' arms and with the hands of Pûshan,
I offer with the strength of the Upâṃṣu. Slain is the demon brood. All-hail!
Thee for the slaughter of the brood of demons. The demons have we slain, have slain. So-and-So, So-and-So is slain.

39 Savitar quicken thee for sway of rulers, Agni of householders, of the trees Soma,
Bṛihaspati of Speech, for lordship Indra, Rudra for cattle, Mitra for true-speaking, Varuṇa for the sway of Law's protectors.

40 Gods, quicken him that none may be his rival, for mighty domination, mighty lordship,
Him, son of Such-a-man and Such-a-woman, of Such-a-tribe. This is your King, ye Tribesmen. Soma is Lord and King of us the Brâhmans.

---

38 He puts the fire together and offers an oblation of Apâmârga seeds. *Upâṃṣu:* the Soma libation so named. See VI. 30. *Thee for the slaughter:* with these words he throws the dipping-spoon towards the place where he offers oblation. *So-and-So:* in the performance of the ceremony the name of the enemy whom the Sacrificer wishes to destroy is to be substituted for the *asau* (iste) of the text. Cf. VII. 3.

39 Oblations are prepared for the eight Devasûs, Quickening or Furthering Gods, and the Adhvaryu recites the formulas holding the Sacrificer by the right arm, and proclaiming his name and parentage. *Rulers:* or 'orders,' according to Mahîdhara; *savânâm,* from *su* 'to impel,' the root of Savitar, Impeller. *Householders:* Gṛihapati, Lord of the Household, being a little of Agni. *Trees:* Soma being called Vanaspati, Tree or Plant *par excellence.* *Speech:* Bṛihaspati being Lord of Speech, i. e. Prayer. *Lordship:* or preëminence, Indra representing royalty and being King of Gods. *Cattle:* Rudra being Paṣupati, Lord of Beasts or Cattle. *True-speaking:* Mitra, as the Sun, being called the Truthful (Solem quis dicere falsum Audeat?). *Law's:* Varuṇa being the Moral Governor of the world.

40 *Him:* he pronounces the name of the Sacrificer. *Such-a-man, etc.:* he declares the names of the Sacrificer's parents. *Tribe:* or people. *Tribesmen:* or, people: here the name of the tribe or people, e. g. Ye Kurus, or Pañchâlas, or Bharatas, as the case may be, is to be substituted in the performance of the ceremony.

## BOOK THE TENTH.

THE Gods drew waters with their store of sweetness, succulent and observant, king-creating,
Wherewith they sprinkled Varuṇa and Mitra, wherewith they guided Indra past his foemen.

2 Wave of the male art thou, giver of kingship. Do thou—All-hail!—bestow on me the kingdom.
Wave of the male art thou, giver of kingship. Do thou on So-and-So bestow the kingdom.
Thou hast a host of males, giver of kingship. Do thou—All-hail!—bestow on me the kingdom.
A host of males hast thou, giver of kingship. Do thou on So-and-So bestow the kingdom.

3 Swift at your work are ye, givers of kingship. Do ye—All-hail!—bestow on me the kingdom.
Swift at your work are ye, givers of kingship. Do ye on So-and-So bestow the kingdom.
Endowed with strength are ye, givers of kingship, etc.
O'erflowing floods are ye, etc.
The Waters' Lord art thou, giver of kingship. Do thou, etc.
The Waters' Child art thou, etc.

---

The Râjasûya Ceremony is continued, with formulas for the collection and mixing of waters from different streams and sources for the Abhisheka, Aspersion or Consecration of a King. For fuller details of the Sacrifice, see Sacred Books of the East, XLI. pp. 73 seq.; Weber, Über den Râjasûya; Hillebrandt, Ritual-Litteratur, pp. 143—147.

1 The Adhvaryu first takes water brought from the Sarasvatî, the sacred river of the earlier Hindus, and recites the text. *Varuṇa and Mitra:* predecessors, as Kings, of Indra.

2 *Of the male:* raised by a male animal, beast or man. He steps into the water, and takes the ripple that rises in front of him. *On me:* to be transferred to the Sacrificer. *So-and-So:* the Sacrificer who is to be consecrated King, and whose name he mentions. *Host of males:* the ripples are likened to an opposing band of armed men. With this formula he takes up the wavelet that rises behind him.

3 Stanzas 1 and 2 are formulas for taking water from a tank or pool—that in stanza 1 being mixed with Sarasvatî water; he now takes water from a stream. *So-and-So:* as in verse 2. *Endowed with strength:* which is to be conferred upon the Sacrificer. He takes water that runs in the opposite direction. *O'erflowing:* signifying abundant wealth. He takes water that escapes from its channel. *Waters' Lord:* he takes water that has been brought from the sea. *Waters' child:* he takes water from an eddy.

4 With sun-bright skins are ye, givers, etc.
Brilliant as Suns are ye, etc.
Bringers of joy are ye, etc.
Dwellers in cloud are ye, etc.
Desirable are ye, etc.
Most powerful are ye, etc.
Endowed with might are ye, etc.
Man-nourishing are ye, etc.
All-nourishing are ye, etc.
Self-ruling Waters are ye, giving kingship. On So-and-So do ye bestow the kingdom.
Together with the sweet let sweet ones mingle, obtaining for the Kshatriya mighty power.
Rest in your place inviolate and potent, bestowing on the Kshatriya mighty power.

5 Brilliance of Soma art thou: may my brilliance grow like thine.
To Agni Hail! To Soma Hail! To Savitar Hail! To Sarasvati Hail! To Pûshan Hail! To Bṛihaspati Hail! To Indra Hail! To the Noise Hail! To Fame Hail! To Aṃśa Hail! To Bhaga Hail! To Aryaman Hail!

6 Ye are two strainers, Varuṇa's own possession. I make you pure at Savitar's impulsion, with flawless strainer, with the beams of Sûrya.
Thou, friend of speech, heat-born, art undefeated. Soma's share art thou. Hail, ye king-producers!

---

4 *With sun-bright skins:* he takes water from a pool on which the sun shines. *Brilliant:* rain-water that falls in sunshine. *Bringers of joy:* water from a lake. *Dwellers in cloud:* 'fold-dwellers': Eggeling; waters from a well. *Desirable:* or, perhaps, obedient: the water of dew-drops. *Most powerful:* he takes flowing honey. *Endowed with might:* fluids of an unborn calf. *Man nourishing:* milk. *All-nourishing:* clarified butter. *Self-ruling:* sun-motes which, after taking seventeen kinds of water, he takes and mingles with them. *Together:* he mixes them all in a vessel of Udumbara wood. *The Kshatriya:* the prince who is being consecrated King.

5 He spreads a tiger-skin, one of the emblems of royalty, before the Maitrâvaruṇa's *dhishṇyâ* or fire-hearth, and recites the formulas. *Of Soma:* because Indra became a tiger after he had drunk Soma, says the Commentator. The tiger, in the Atharva-veda, is the king of beasts and the type of heroic strength and courage. See A. V. IV. 8. 4, 7. *The Noise:* of his proclamation as king. *Aṃśa:* the name of one of the Âdityas.

6 He makes two strainers (see I. 3), and interweaves them with gold. *Friend of speech:* the mingled waters are addressed in the singular number. Man, it is said, has the power of speech so long as there is water in his vital airs or breathings. *Heat-born:* from fire smoke, from smoke cloud, from cloud water. *Soma's share:* when the priests moisten the plant with water.

7 Sharers in joy are these majestic Waters, inviolate, industrious, investing.

In these as homes hath Varuṇa made his dwelling, he, Child of Waters, in the best of mothers.

8 Thou art the inner caul of princely power. Thou art the outer caul of princely power. Of princely power thou art the womb, the navel.

Thou art the Vṛitra-slaying arm of Indra. Mitra's art thou, thou Varuṇa's possession. With thee to aid may this man slaughter Vṛitra.

Cleaver art thou; thou Render; thou art Shaker. Protect him ye in front, protect him rearwards; protect him sidewards; from all quarters guard him.

9 Visible, O ye men. Informed is Agni, Master of the Household. Informed is Indra of exalted glory. Informed are Mitra-Varuṇa, Law-Maintainers. Informed is Pûshan, Lord of all Possessions. Informed are Heaven and Earth, the All-propitious. Informed is Aditi who gives wide shelter.

10 Appeased by sacrifice are biting creatures. Ascend the East. May Gâyatrî protect thee, the psalm Rathantara, the triple praise-song, the season Spring, and the rich treasure, Priesthood.

---

7 *Sharers in joy:* 'playmates': Eggeling. He moves them into various consecration vessels of Palâsa and Udumbara wood. *Investing:* forming the raiment of Varuṇa in the ocean of air. *Best of mothers:* or, most maternal, as nourishing all life.

8 The royal Sacrificer puts on various garments, first a *târpya*, perhaps a silk under-garment (See Sacred Books of the East, XLI. 85 note) which is addressed in the first formula of the verse. *Inner caul:* or amnion. *Outer caul:* or chorion; he puts on a woollen garment which is thus addressed. *The womb:* he puts on a mantle. *The navel:* he puts on a turban with the ends hanging down, which is thus addressed. These garments symbolize the development of an embryo till it reaches maturity, and the progressive stages of the King's Consecration. *Vṛitra-slaying arm:* the Adhvaryu strings a bow, an emblem of military and princely rank. *Mitra's:* he addresses the right end of the bow. *Varuṇa's:* the left end. *Thee:* the bow. *Vṛitra:* the typical enemy; all foes. He then gives the King three arrows, and addresses each by name. *Shaker:* Kshumâ; causing the foe to tremble.

9 He recites the formulas announcing and introducing the newly-consecrated King. *Visible:* he stands before you. *Lord of all possessions:* or, all-knowing.

10 He puts a piece of copper in the mouth of a long-haired person, that is, a eunuch, seated in the Sadas. *Biting creatures:* such as serpents, or Râkshasas who disturb sacrifices. *Rathantara:* one of the most important Sâmans, consisting of verses 22, 23 of R. V. VII. 32=Sâmaveda II. i. i. 11. *Triple praise-song:* or Trivṛit Stoma. See IX. 33.

11 Ascend the South. Be thy protectors Trishṭup, the Bṛihat Sâman, the fifteenfold praise-song, the season Summer, and the treasure Kingship.

12 Ascend the West. May Jagatí protect thee, the psalm Vairûpa, the seventeenfold praise-song, the Rain-time, and that store of wealth, the People.

13 Ascend the North. Thy guardians be Anushṭup, Vairâja psalm, the twenty-onefold praise-song, the season Autumn, that rich treasure Fruitage.

14 Ascend the Zenith. Paṅkti be thy keeper, Sâkvara, Raivata the pair of Sâmans,
Praise-songs the thirty-threefold and thrice-ninefold, both seasons, Winter, Dews, that treasure lustre.
The head of Namuchi hath been cast from me.

15 Brilliance of Soma art thou, may my brilliance grow like thine.
Save me from death. Vigour art thou, victory, everlasting life.

16 With golden bodies, at the flush of morning, ye rise on high, two Sovran Lords, and Sûrya.
Ascend your car, O Varuṇa and Mitra: thence view infinity and limitation.
Thou art Mitra, thou art Varuṇa.

17 Thee with the strength of Soma, Agni's lustre, with Sûrya's splendour, Indra's might I sprinkle.
Be lord of princes: safe past arrows guard him.

---

11 The King is now called on to ascend, that is, to master, the four quarters of the sky and the zenith and so to assume universal sovranty. *Bṛihat:* See VII. 22 note.

12 *Vairûpa:* the name of an important Sâman

13 *Anushṭup:* a Vedic metre of four octosyllabic Pâdas or quarter-verses. *Vairâja:* another important Sâman.

14 *Paṅkti:* a metre of five octosyllabic Pâdas. *Ṣâkvara, Raivata:* two important Sâmans. *Dews:* one of the six seasons, comprising the months Mâgha and Phâlguna. *Lustre:* spiritual light. *The head of Namuchi:* he kicks away a piece of lead which has been placed on the hinder part of the tiger-skin (see X. 5). The lead symbolizes the head of the demon Namuchi torn off by Indra. See The Hymns of the Ṛigveda, Index.

15 The first line is repeated from X. 5. The King steps on the tiger-skin. *Save me:* he addresses a piece of gold placed under his foot. *Vigour art thou:* another piece of gold, pierced with nine holes, and placed on the King's head.

16 The Adhvaryu raises the King's arms, with the text taken, with variations, from R. V. V. 62. 8. *Infinity and limitation:* or Aditi and Diti, the former being infinite Nature and the latter a vague abstract conception regarded as a Goddess in contrast to her; the two together meaning the entire aggregate of visible nature.

17 The Purohita (the King's household priest) or the Adhvaryu sprinkles him as he stands looking eastward. He is also sprinkled by his brother,

18 = IX. 40.

19 Forth from the summit of the bull, the mountain, pouring spontaneously, the ships keep moving.

They, lifted up, have turned them back and downward, still flowing onward, after Ahibudhnya.

Thou art the stepping-forth of Vishṇu: thou art Vishṇu's outstep; Vishṇu's step art thou.

20 Prajâpati, thou only comprehendest all these created forms, and none beside thee.

Give us our heart's desire when we invoke thee. So-and-So's father is this man. Sire of this man is So-and-So.

May we—All-hail!—be lords of rich possessions.

What active highest name thou hast, O Rudra, therein thou art an offering, art an offering at home. All-hail!

21 Indra's bolt art thou. I by the direction of Mitra-Varuṇa, Directors, yoke thee.

I, the uninjured Arjuna, mount thee for firmness, thee for food.

By quickening of the Maruts be thou victor. May we obtain by mind: with power united.

22 Let us not, Indra, conqueror of the mighty, unfit through lack of prayer fail to obtain thee.

Ascend the car which thou whose hand bears thunder controllest, and the reins with noble horses.

---

a friendly Râjanya, and a Vaisya, man of the people or third class, from the three other vessels of consecrating water, made respectively of Udumbara, Banyan or Ficus Indica, and Asvattha (Ficus Religiosa) wood. *Guard him:* O Soma, according to Mahîdhara.

19 *The bull, the mountain:* originally meaning a mighty cloud, and here the King, preëminent over all, from whose head the drops of consecrating water flow. *Ships:* streams of water. *Lifted up:* from the earth by the Sun. *Ahibudhnya:* a mysterious atmospheric deity, regent of the depths of the firmament; the Dragon of the Deep. See The Hymns of the Rig-veda, Index. *The stepping-forth:* the Sacrificer is made to take three steps on the tiger-skin in imitation of Vishṇu's three strides, as the Sun, over earth and through firmament and heaven.

20 The Sacrificer, with his son holding on to him behind offers an oblation in the fire at the door of the sacrificial hall (the Gârhapatya fire) and recites the text, taken, with additions, from R. V. X. 121. 10. *So-and-So's......So-and-So:* the names of son and father are to be substituted. *Rudra:* addressed as Lord of Cattle, the chief wealth of the earlier Hindus. *Active:* powerful to injure: Mahîdhara. *Thou:* he addresses the oblation of the residue of the sacrificial material.

21 He takes down the Vâjapeya chariot from its stand (see IX. 5) and yokes the four horses at the right corner of the altar. *Arjuna:* a name of Indra, whom the Sacrificer, as King, represents. *Be thou victor:* he addresses the off yoke horse. *By mind:* he stops the chariot in the midst of the assembled cows. *By power:* he touches a cow with the end of the bow.

22 He gives the owner of the cows, his brother, as many as, or more than, he has taken by the symbolical act of touching one in verse 21, and

23 All hail to Agni, Master of the Household! All-hail to Soma, Sovran of the Forest!
All-hail to the great vigour of the Maruts! All-hail to the effectual might of Indra!
Injure me not, O Mother Earth, and may I never injure thee.

24 The Haṃsa throned in light, the Vasu in mid-air, the Priest beside the altar, Guest within the house,
Dwelling in noblest place, mid men, in truth, in sky, born of flood, kine, truth, mountain, he is mighty Law.

25 So great art thou: life art thou; give me life.
Mate art thou: thou art splendour; give me splendour.
Strength art thou: give me strength. I draw you downward, two arms of Indra mighty in achievement.

26 Fair art thou, good to sit on, womb of kingship.
Sit on the fair one, sit on that which offers a pleasant seat: sit in the womb of kingship.

27 Varuṇa, Law's maintainer, hath sat down among his people, he Most wise, for universal sway.

28 Supreme Lord art thou. May these five regions of thine be prosperous. Brahman! Thou art Brahman. Savitar art thou, faithful in impulsion. Varuṇa art thou, he whose power is real. Indra art thou, whose strength is of the people. Rudra art thou, the very kind and gracious.

---

then passes on in front of the Sacrificial Stake and stops the chariot before the hall where he recites the text which is partly taken, with variations, from R. V. V. 33. 3.

23 He offers the four Rathavimochanīya or Car-unharnessing oblations with their respective formulas.

24 He dismounts from the chariot reciting the text taken from R. V. IV. 40. 5. *Haṃsa:* or Swan; the Sun who floats through the sky.
*In truth:* or in the sacrifice. *Kine:* or rays of light. *Mountain:* cloud behind which he rises. *Mighty Law:* 'the great truth': Eggeling.

25 The Sacrificer touches one of two gold discs or beads fastened on the right wheel of the car-stand, and addresses it with the text. *Life:* cf. X.15. *Strength art thou:* he touches and addresses a branch of an Udumbara tree which has been hidden in the wheel-track. *I draw:* the Adhvaryu draws the Sacrificer's arms down to the mess of curds placed on the tiger-skin.

26 *Fair art thou:* the Adhvaryu addresses a throne of Khadira wood (Acacia Catechu) which has been placed on the tiger-skin. *Good to sit on:* he spreads a mantle on the seat. *Womb of kingship:* investing the embryo King. *Sit:* he addresses the Sacrificer.

27 The Adhvaryu touches the Sacrificer's breast with the text from R. V. I. 25. 10. *Varuṇa:* the moral Governor of the world, typifying the new King.

28 He puts five dice into the Sacrificer's hand, in the shape of golden shells, representing the four quarters of the sky and the zenith. See S. B. E. XLI. 10. 6, note. *Brahman!:* the Sacrificer addresses the Brahman priest.

Doer of much, Improver, Wealth-increaser!
Indra's bolt art thou. Be therewith my vassal.

29 May spacious Agni, Lord of Duty, gladly, vast Agni, Duty's Lord, accept the butter. All-hail!
Hallowed by Svâhâ, with the beams of Sûrya, strive for his central place among the kinsmen.

30 I creep forth urged onward by Savitar the Impeller; by Sarasvatî, Speech; by Tvashṭar, created forms; by Pûshan, cattle; by this Indra; by Bṛihaspati, Devotion; by Varuṇa, Power; by Agni, Brilliance; by Soma, the King; by Vishṇu the tenth Deity.

31 Get dressed for the Asvins. Get dressed for Sarasvatî. Get dressed for Indra the Good Deliverer.
Soma the Wind, purified by the strainer, Indra's meet friend, hath gone o'erflowing backward.

32 What then? As men whose fields are full of barley reap the ripe corn, removing it in order,
So bring the food of these men, bring it hither, who pay the Sacred Grass their spoken homage.
Taken upon a base art thou. Thee for the Asvins.
Thee for Sarasvatî, and thee for Indra, for the Excellent Protector.

---

*Thou art Brahman:* the priest's reply. *Varuṇa, etc.:* the priest's second reply to the Sacrificer's second address. *Indra art thou:* the third reply to the address repeated for the third time. *Rudra:* as above, the fourth time. *Doer of much:* the priest addresses the Sacrificer for the fifth time. *Indra's bolt:* the wooden sacrificial sword is addressed, which the Purohita or the Adhvaryu hands to the Sacrificer. It is to be used for marking out the gaming-ground; on which the dice are thrown, and the winning numbers presented to the King as tokens of victory and supremacy.

30 Formulas for the Dasapeya (To be Drunk by Ten) Libations or Sacrifices. The priests, officiating and others, a hundred in number, meet together at the ceremony on a Soma-pressing day, and having each counted ten ancestors who have offered Soma sacrifices, perform the Saṃsṛip or Creeping oblation, so called because the priests creep along to their respective fire-hearths. The formula is recited by each of the priests.

31 Formulas follow for the performance of the Sautrâmaṇî, a ceremony originally instituted to obviate or atone for excess in Soma drinking, subsequently a supplement to other sacrificial rites. *Get dressed:* he addresses the Surâ (see IX. 4) prepared for the ceremony. *Good Deliverer:* Sutrâman, whence the name of the sacrifice is formed. *Soma:* he purifies the Surâ in a vessel with blades of Darbha grass. *The Wind:* meaning, according to Mahîdhara, (purified) by the wind. According to the St. Petersburg Lexicon, *vâyu* here means 'inviting,' a rendering adopted by Prof. Eggeling. The word may, perhaps, mean 'purifying.' Cf. the plural *vâyavaḥ*, 'breezes,' I. 1.

32 He throws meal of Badarî or Jujube fruit into the purified Surâ and draws a draught of the liquor in a vessel of Vaikaṅkata (Flacourtia Sapida) wood, with the text, taken, with an important variation in the last Pâda, from R. V. X. 131. 2.

33 Ye Asvins, Lords of Splendour, drank full draughts of grateful Soma juice,
And aided Indra in his deeds with Namuchi of Asura birth.

34 As parents aid a son, both Asvins aided thee, Indra, with their wondrous powers and wisdom.
When thou with might hadst drunk the draught that gladdens, Sarasvatî, O Bounteous Lord, refreshed thee.

---

33 The Sacrificer recites two Inviting Texts taken from R. V. X. 131. 4, 5. *Namuchi:* see X. 14. This Asura, the friend of Indra, is said to have drunk up, with Surâ and Soma, the manly strength of Indra who, on his complaining to the Asvins and Sarasvatî, received from them a thunderbolt in the shape of the waters' foam with which he cut or tore off Namuchi's head.

# BOOK THE ELEVENTH.

HARNESSING, first of all, the mind, Savitar having stretched the thought
With reverent look upon the light of Agni bore them up from earth.

2 By impulse of God Savitar we with our spirit harnessed strive
With might to win the heavenly.

3 Savitar, having harnessed Gods who go to light and heavenly thought,
Who will create the lofty light—Savitar urge them on their way!

4 The priests of him the lofty priest well skilled in hymns, harness their spirit, yea, harness their holy thoughts.
He only, skilled in rules, assigns their priestly tasks. Yea, lofty is the praise of Savitar the God.

5 I yoke with prayer your ancient inspiration: may the laud rise as on the prince's pathway.
All Sons of the Immortal One shall hear it, who have resorted to celestial dwellings.

---

Books XI.—XVIII. contain formulas for the construction of altars or hearths for the various sacrificial fires, and first and chiefly for building up with about 10,800 bricks, all laid with special consecrating texts, the Uttaravedi or High Altar which represents the Universe and is identified with Agni himself. This ceremony, called the Agnichayana requires a year for its complete performance and is of corresponding importance (see Sacred Books of the East, XLIII., Introduction). The High Altar is constructed in the shape of an outspread bird, probably an eagle or a falcon.

1 *Harnessing:* applying to the holy work. *Savitar:* the Impeller, here meaning Prajâpati, the Lord of creatures, who is identified with Agni, that is the Fire Altar which is now to be built. *Them:* oblations; or bricks, according to Mahîdhara. With this and the seven following formulas the Adhvaryu offers an eightfold oblation, that is, a single oblation of eight dipping-spoonfuls of clarified butter poured into the offering-ladle.

2 *To win the heavenly:* to merit heaven by the due performance of our task.

3 *Having harnessed:* engaged them in Agni's service. *By thought:* or devotion, or skill. *Lofty light:* the Sun, Agni. *On their way:* to perform their task.

4 Taken from R. V. V. 81. 1. *The lofty Priest:* Savitar; or Agni-Prajâpati. *Well skilled in hymns:* or 'inspirer of devotion': Eggeling. *Rules:* that regulate sacrifice.

5 Taken from R. V. X. 13. 1. *Your:* referring to the Sacrificer and his wife, according to Mahîdhara. *Inspiration: brahma;* according to Mahîdhara, the vital airs, the Seven Rishis, and Brâhmans who are engaged in the holy work. *The prince's pathway:* the prince or noble is the Sacrificer, whose praise is to pervade earth and heaven. *Sons of the Immortal One:* the Gods whose father is Prajâpati.

6 Even he, the God whose going forth and majesty the other Deities have followed with their might,
He who hath measured the celestial regions out by his great power, he is the Courser Savitar.

7 Our sacrifice, God Savitar! speed forward: speed to his share the sacrifice's patron.
May the celestial Gandharva, cleanser of thought and will, make clean our thoughts and wishes.
The Lord of Speech sweeten the words we utter!

8 God Savitar, speed this God-loved sacrifice of ours, friend-finding, ever-conquering, winning wealth and heaven.
Speed praise-song with the sacred verse, Rathantara with Gâyatra, Bṛihat that runs in Gâyatra. All-hail!

9 By impulse of God Savitar I take thee, with arms of Asvins, with the hands of Pûshan, in Angiras' manner, with Gâyatrî metre.
From the earth's seat bring thou Purîshya Agni, as Angiras was wont, with Trishṭup metre.

10 Spade art thou; woman art thou. Ours be power with thee to dig out Agni in his dwelling, as Angiras was wont, with Jagatî metre.

11 Savitar, bearing in his hand the gold spade which he took therewith,
Looking with reverence on the light of Agni, raised it from the earth,
With the Anushṭup metre and as Angiras was wont to do.

12 Run hither, urged to speed, O Horse, along the most extended space.

---

6 Taken from R. V. V. 81. 3.

7 Repeated from IX. 1. *Celestial Gandharva:* Savitar, the Sun-God

8 *Praise-song: stoma. Sacred verse: rich;* recited verse of praise. *Rathantara:* see X. 10. *Bṛihat:* see VII. 22; X. 11.

9 *Thee:* the spade (see V. 22; VI. 1.) that is to be used for digging up earth and clay for the construction of the Altar. *In Angiras' manner:* as Angiras, one of the institutors of Agni's worship, and the priestly members of his family did aforetime. *Purîshya:* an epithet of Agni identified with the Altar, abiding in the loose earth or rubble used as mortar to fill the spaces between the bricks and to bind them together. Mahîdhara gives another meaning also: good to *purîshas*, that is, cattle. See III. 40.

10 *Woman: nârî;* the word for spade, *abhri*, being feminine. According to Mahîdhara, *nârî = na + ariḥ*, may mean, not having an enemy. See V. 22, note.

11 A formula to be used on taking up the spade.

12 Holding the spade, he addresses the animals, a horse, an ass, and a he-goat, that have been posted looking eastward. First the horse is addressed as representing the Sun in heaven, Vâyu in mid-air, and Agni on earth.

Thy loftiest birthplace is in heaven, thy navel is in air's mid-realm, the womb that bare thee is on earth.

13 Upon this course, O lords of wealth, harness, ye twain, the Ass who bears
Agni, and kindly favours us.

14 In every need, in every race we call, as friends, to succour us,
Indra, the mightiest of all.

15 Come, speeding on and trampling imprecations, come gladdening to the chieftainship of Rudra.
Speed through the wide air thou whose paths are pleasant, with Pûshan for thy mate, providing safety.

16 From the Earth's seat, like Angiras, bring thou Purîshya Agni forth.
After the wont of Angiras we to Purîshya Agni go.
Agni Purîshya we will bear after the wont of Angiras.

17 Agni hath looked along the van of Mornings, looked on the days, the earliest Jâtavedas,
And many a time along the beams of Sûrya: along the heaven and earth hast thou extended.

18 The Courser, started on his way, shakes from him all hostilities.
He longs to look with reverent eye on Agni in the mighty seat.

---

13 *Lords of wealth:* the Sacrificer and the Adhvaryu.

14 He addresses the goat with the text taken from R. V. I. 30. 7.

15 Without touching the animals he makes them go eastward. He addresses the horse. *Imprecations:* ill-wishes, or slanderous words of the Sacrificer's enemies. *Rudra:* as Paṣupati, Lord of Beasts. *Speed:* here he addresses the ass, the steed of the Aṣvins. *Pûshan:* here said to mean Earth.

16 He addresses the goat, sacred to Agni. *Thou:* the spade. *We:* the three fires having been lighted, the Sacrificer, the Brahman, and the Adhvaryu go to the lump of clay, representing Agni Purîshya, which has been prepared for making the Ukhâ or Fire-pan and placed in a square hole in the ground. *Will we bear:* with this formula the Adhvaryu looks at the puppet or mock-man, the *anaddhâpurusha* (one of no use to Gods, men, or Manes), to which a passive part in the ceremony is assigned. Prof. A. Hillebrandt, (Ritual-Litteratur, p. 165) suggests that this doll or effigy may be a figure representing some enemy of the Sacrificer; and Prof. A. Weber that it is a sort of *corpus vile*, intended to bear the blame of any accidental hitches and oversights in the performance of the ceremony.

17 A hollow ant-hill is placed between the lump of clay and the Âhavanîya fire, and through the cavity the Adhvaryu looks at the clay, reciting the text taken, with variations, from A. V. VII. 82. 5.

18 He addresses the horse. *Hostilities:* attacks, toils and troubles, and evils of all kinds. *Agni:* represented by the lump of clay. *On the mighty seat:* manifested on the sacrificial ground.

19 O Courser, having come to earth, seek Agni with a longing wish.
Tell us by trampling on the ground where we may dig him from the earth.

20 Heaven is thy back, the earth thy seat, the air thy soul, the sea thy womb.
Looking around thee with thine eye trample the adversaries down.

21 Wealth-giver, Courser, from this place step forth to great felicity.
May we enjoy Earth's favour while we dig forth Agni from her lap.

22 Down hath he stepped, wealth-giver, racer, courser. Good and auspicious room on earth thou madest.
Thence let us dig forth Agni, fair to look on, while to the loftiest vault we mount, to heaven.

23 I thoughtfully besprinkle thee with butter, thee dwelling near to all existing creatures.
Broad, vast through vital power that moves transversely, conspicuous, strong with all the food that feeds thee.

24 I sprinkle him who moves in all directions: may he accept it with a friendly spirit.
Agni with bridegroom's face and lovely colour may not be touched when all his form is fury.

25 Round the oblation hath he paced, Agni the wise, the Lord of Strength,
Giving the offerer precious boons.

26 We set thee round us as a fort, victorious Agni, thee a Sage,
Of hero lineage, day by day destroyer of our treacherous foes.

27 Thou, Agni, with the days, fain to shine hitherward, art brought to life from out the waters, from the stone,

---

19 He puts the horse's near forefoot on the lump of clay. *With a longing wish: ruchâ;* or, perhaps, with thy light, or eye.

20 He holds his hand over the horse's back. *The sea:* the ocean of air in which the Sun, represented by the horse, springs to birth.

21 He removes the horse's foot from the clay lump.

23 He sits down and offers two oblations on the lump of clay and the horse's hoof-print, and recites two texts taken (the first with variations) from R. V. II. 10. 4, 5. *Thee:* Agni, represented by the clay. Line 1 of verse 23 is first recited, then line 2 of 24; then line 2 of 23 and line 1 of 24.

24 *With bridegroom's grace:* or, 'revered by men.'

25 He draws a line with the spade three times round the lump of clay, and recites the texts taken respectively from R. V. IV. 15. 3; X. 87. 22; II. 1. 1.

27 *The waters:* of the firmament, as lightning. *Forest trees:* in the conflagrations caused by the friction of dry branches.

From out the forest trees and herbs that grow on ground, thou, Sovran Lord of men, art generated pure.

28 At Savitar's, the Shining One's, impulsion, with arms of Asvins and with hands of Púshan,

As Ángiras was wont to do, I dig thee forth from the seat of Earth, Agni Purîshya.

Thee, Agni, luminous and fair of aspect, resplendent with imperishable lustre, gracious to living creatures, never harming,

As Angiras was wont to do, we dig thee forth from the seat of Earth, Agni Purishya.

29 Thou art the Waters' back, the womb of Agni, around the ocean as it swells and surges.

Waxing to greatness, resting on the lotus, spread thou in amplitude with heaven's own measure.

30 Yea are a shelter and a shield, uninjured both, and widely spread.

Do ye, expansive, cover him : bear ye Purishya Agni up.

31 Cover him, finders of the light, united both with breast and self,

Bearing between you Agni, the refulgent, everlasting One.

32 Thou art Purîshya, thou support of all. Atharvan was the first, Agni, who rubbed thee into life.

Agni, Atharvan brought thee forth by rubbing from the lotus, from

The head of Viṣva, of the Priest.

33 Thee too as Vṛitra-slayer, thee breaker of forts, the Sage Dadhyach,

Son of Átharvan, lighted up.

---

28 He digs round the lump of clay and recites the text.

29 Northward of the hole from which he has dug the hidden lump of clay (see verse 16. note) he spreads a black-antelope's skin with the neck turned to the east; on this he puts a lotus-leaf, and on this the lump of clay. *Thou:* he address the lotus-leaf representing the sky. *Waxing:* Agni, represented by the lump of clay. *Spread forth:* as the Sun, fill the whole heaven with thy grandeur

30 *Ye:* the antelope skin and the lotus-leaf, both of which he touches as he recites the two texts.

32 He touches the lump of clay reciting the first line of the text taken, in part, from R. V VI. 16. 13. *Purîshya:* according to Mahîdhara = *paṣavya*, favourable to cattle. See XI. 9, note. *Atharvan:* see VIII. 56. Here he takes hold of the lump of clay with both hands. *The lotus:* the sky, or the waters of the air. *Viṣva:* perhaps Heaven personified; or the Universe. The last line of the text is obscure, and has been variously explained. See Sacred Books of the East, XII. 217, 218, note.

33 Taken from R. V. VI. 16. 14. *Dadhyach:* see The Hymns of the Rigveda, I. 84. 13.

34 Pâthya the Bull, too, kindled thee the Dasyus' most destructive foe,
Winner of spoil in every fight.

35 Sit, Hotar, in the Hotar's place, observant: lay down the sacrifice in the place of worship.
Thou, dear to Gods, shalt serve them with oblation. Agni, give long life to the Sacrificer.

36 Accustomed to the Hotar's place, the Hotar hath seated him, bright, splendid, passing mighty,
Whose foresight keeps the Law from violation, excellent, pure-tongued, bringing thousands, Agni.

37 Seat thee, for thou art mighty: shine, best entertainer of the Gods.
Worthy of sacred food, praised Agni! loose the smoke, ruddy and beautiful to see.

38 Pour heavenly Waters honey-sweet here for our health, for progeny.
Forth from the place whereon they fall let plants with goodly berries spring.

39 May Vâyu Mâtariṣvan heal and comfort thy broken heart as there supine thou liest.
Thou unto whom the breath of Gods gives motion, to Ka, yea, unto thee, O God, be Vashaṭ!

40 He, nobly born with lustre, shield and refuge, hath sat down in light.
O Agni, Rich in Splendour, robe thyself in many-hued attire.

41 Lord of fair sacrifice, arise! With Godlike thought protect us well.

---

34 From R. V. VI. 16. 15. *Pâthya the Bull:* or, the hero Pâthya, probably some celebrated Sacrificer. Prof. Max Müller (Vedic Hymns, Part I. p. 153) takes *vrishâ* here as a Proper Name, Vrishan Pâthya. *Dasyus:* hostile aborigines.

35 *Hotar:* Agni, the Sacrificing Priest, or Invoker, of the Gods. The text is taken from R. V. III. 29. 8.

36 The text is taken from R. V. II. 9. 1.

37 Taken from R V. I. 36. 9. *Seat thee:* on the lotus-leaf.

38 He pours water into the hole from which the lump of clay was taken. *Pour:* O Spade, or O Heaven, or O Adhvaryu: Mahîdhara.

39 He fans air into the hole, and with the first line of the text addresses the wounded earth. *Mâtariṣvan:* in the R. V. generally a name or form of Agni, here a designation of Wind as breathing, moving, or growing in his mother the Air. See I. 2, note. *Ka:* Prajâpati (see I. 6, note), that is, Vâyu in his form. *Vashaṭ:* a sacrificial exclamation; benediction.

40 He takes up the edges or corners of the antelope-skin and the lotus-leaf, ties them together, and wraps them round the lump of clay, reciting the text.

41 He takes the wrapped up lump of clay and stands up reciting the text. Cf. R. V. VIII. 23. 5.

With great light splendid to behold come, Agni, through sweet hymns of praise.

42 Rise up erect to give us aid, stand up like Savitar the God;
Erect as strength-bestower when we call aloud, with unguents and with priests on thee.

43 Thou, being born, art Child of Earth and Heaven, parted, fair Babe, among the plants, O Agni.
The glooms of night thou, brilliant child, subduest, and art come forth, loud roaring, from the Mothers.

44 Steady be thou, and firm of limb. Steed, be a racer fleet of foot.
Broad be thou, pleasant as a seat, bearing the store which Agni needs.

45 Be thou propitious, Angiras, to creatures of the human race.
Set not on fire the heaven and earth, nor air's mid-region, nor the trees.

46 Forth with loud neighing go the Steed, the Ass that shouteth as he runs.
Bearing Purîshya Agni on, let him not perish ere his time,
Male bearer of male Agni, Child of Waters, Offspring of the Sea. Agni, come hither to the feast.

47 The Law the Truth, the Law the Truth. As Angiras was wont to do, we bear Purîshya Agni on.
Ye Plants, with joyous welcome greet this Agni, auspicious One who cometh on to meet you.
Removing all distresses and afflictions, here settle down and banish evil purpose.

---

42 With uplifted arms he holds it up towards the east, and recites the text taken from R. V. I. 36. 13. *Unguents...priests:* or, shining ministrants; priests who bear oblations.

43 *Among the plants:* the shrubs that serve as fuel; or phosphorescent plants in which he dwells; or, according to Mahîdhara, rice and other plants from which sacrificial cakes are made. *The Mothers:* the trees whose dry wood feeds him. The text is taken from R. V. X. 1. 2.

44 He addresses the ass (see verse 12). *The store:* the equipment of Agni, all that is required to make the Altar complete. See V. 13, note.

45 He addresses the goat, here called Angiras, a name of Agni (see III. 3), as sacred to that God.

46 He holds the lump of clay over the animals without touching them, first over the horse, reciting the text. *The Ass:* here ironically coupled with the horse. *Bearing:* the horse. *Male:* the ass, over which he now holds the lump of clay. *Offspring of the Sea:* born as lightning in the aërial ocean. *Agni, come hither:* he takes the lump down.

47 He holds the clay-lump over the goat, and recites the first Pâda or quarter-division of the text. *The Law, etc.:* meaning Agni as the Sun, being himself both Law and Truth.

48 Welcome him joyfully, ye Plants, laden with bloom and goodly fruit.
This seasonable Child of yours hath settled in his ancient seat.

49 Resplendent with thy wide-extending lustre dispel the terrors of the fiends who hate us.
May lofty Agni be my guide and shelter, ready to hear our call, the good Protector.

50 Ye, Waters, are beneficent, so help ye us to energy
That we may look on great delight.

51 Give us a portion of the sap, the most propitious that ye have.
Like mothers in their longing love.

52 To you we gladly come for him to whose abode ye lead us on:
And, Waters, give us procreant strength.

53 Mitra, having commingled earth and ground together with the light—
For health to creatures mix I thee Omniscient and nobly born.

54 The Rudras, having mixed the earth, set all aglow the lofty light.
Bright and perpetual their light verily shines among the Gods.

55 The lump of clay that hath been mixed by Vasus, Rudras, by the wise,
May Sinîvâlî with her hands soften and fit it for the work.

56 May Sinîvâlî with fair braids, with beauteous crest, with lovely locks,
May she, O mighty Aditi, bestow the Fire-pan in thy hands.

---

49 The lump of clay has been deposited on a mound sprinkled and covered with gravel. It is now freed from its wrapper (see verse 40), with the text taken from R. V. III. 15. 1. Some of the goat's hair is then cut off, and the three animals are driven towards the north-east.

50 He pours on the lump of clay water that has been heated with the gum of the Parṇa or Palâśa tree, and recites the triplet from R. V. X. 9. 1—3.

53 He mixes the clay with the goat's hair and recites the text. *Mitra:* the Sun. *Earth:* meaning sky, according to Mahîdhara. *Light:* symbolized by the hair of the goat sacred to Agni. *Thee:* Agni, identified with the clay.

54 He mixes with gravel, iron-filings or rust, and small stones, and recites the text. *Rudras:* the Maruts, sons of Rudra the Storm-God.

55 He mixes the mass more thoroughly, and recites three texts. *Sinîvâlî:* the presiding Goddess of the day of New Moon, associated with child-birth.

56 *Fire-pan: ukhâ;* a sort of saucepan; a pot or cooking-vessel.

57 Aditi shape the Fire-pan with her power, her arms, her intellect,
And in her womb bear Agni as a mother, in her lap, her son.

58 With Gâyatrî, like Angiras the Vasus form and fashion thee!
Stedfast art thou, thou art the Earth. Establish in me progeny, command of cattle, growth of wealth, kinsmen for me the worshipper.
With Trishṭup may the Rudras, like Angiras, form and fashion thee.
Stedfast art thou, thou art the Air. Establish in me, etc., as above.
With Jagatî, like Angiras, Âdityas form and fashion thee!
Stedfast art thou, thou art the Sky. Establish in me, etc.
Friends of all men, the All-Gods with Anushṭup form thee Angiras-like.
Stedfast art thou, thou art the Quarters. Establish in me, etc.

59 The zone of Aditi art thou. Aditi seize thy hollow space.
She, having made the great Fire-pan, a womb for Agni, formed of clay,
Aditi, gave it to her Sons and, Let them bake it, were her words.

60 The Vasus make thee fragrant, as Angiras did, with Gâyatrî!
The Rudras make thee fragrant with the Trishṭup, as did Angiras!
With Gâyatrî, like Angiras, may the Âdityas perfume thee.
Dear to all men, may the All-Gods with the Anushṭup sweeten thee, as Angiras was wont to do.
May Indra make thee odorous. May Varuṇa make thee odorous. May Vishṇu make thee odorous.

---

57 *Aditi:* as Mother of the Gods. *Thou:* the lump of clay out of which the Fire-pan is to be made, representing the hearth of the Âhavanîya fire. *Of sacrifice:* or of Makha, a certain mythical being. Cf. XXXVII. 3—10; R. V. IX. 101. 13; X. 171. 2.

58 He spreads the clay which is to form the bottom of the Fire-pan. *The Rudras:* here he lays down the first lower side of the pan. *Âdityas:* here he adds the upper side. With the rest of the formulas he continues the work.

59 He puts on the rim and addresses it. *Aditi seize:* he takes hold of the pan by the mouth. *She:* he places the completed pan on the ground. *Her Sons:* the Gods.

60 He fumigates the pan with the smoke of seven lumps of horse-dung, reciting seven formulas, one for each Deity or class of Deities mentioned.

61 Pit! Angiras-like may Aditi the Goddess, beloved by all Gods, dig thee in Earth's bosom.

Pan! Angiras-like may the Gods' heavenly Consorts, dear to all Gods, in the Earth's bosom place thee.

Pan! Angiras-like may Dhishaṇâs, Divine Ones, dear to all Gods, in the Earth's bosom light thee.

Pan! Angiras-like may the divine Varûtrîs, dear to all Gods, in the earth's bosom heat thee,

Pan! Angiras-like may the celestial Ladies, dear to all Gods, in the earth's bosom bake thee.

Angiras-like may the celestial Matrons, beloved by all the Gods, with unclipped pinions, within the lap of Earth, O Fire-pan, bake thee.

62 The gainful grace of Mitra, God, supporter of the race of man,

Is glorious, of most wondrous fame.

63 With lovely arms, with lovely hands, with lovely fingers may the God Savitar make thee clean, yea, by the power he hath.

Not trembling on the earth fill thou the regions, fill the Quarters full.

64 Having arisen wax thou great, yea, stand thou up immovable.

To thee, O Mitra, I entrust this Fire-pan for security. May it remain without a break.

65 Thee may the Vasus, Angiras-like, fill with the metre Gâyatrî.

Thee may the Rudras, Angiras-like, fill with the Trishṭup metre full.

---

61 He digs a square hole and addresses it with the first line of the text. *Pan!:* he deposits it, with the mouth downwards, in the hole, on the north-side of the Invincible brick, the first-laid brick of the Altar. *Consorts:* the wives of the Gods are here said to be the life-supporting Plants. *Dhishaṇâs:* apparently regarded as Goddesses of Wealth and Abundance. See Prof. H. Oldenberg, Vedic Hymns, Part II. pp. 120—122. Here he deposits silently in the hole the bricks called All-lights, and heats the Fire-pan with fire from the Dakshiṇa or southward hearth, reciting the three following formulas. *Varutrîs:* Protecting Goddesses, said to be the Nychthemera or Days-and-Nights. *Celestial Ladies:* the Gnâs, or Divine Dames, said to be the deities of the sacred Metres. *Celestial Matrons:* the presiding deities of the stars. *With unclipped pinions:* moving freely and without interruption.

62 He trims the fire, reciting the text from R. V. III. 59. 6.

63 He removes the ashes, and recites the text. *Not trembling:* he turns the pan, and sets it down with the mouth upwards.

64 He takes up the Fire-pan with both hands, reciting the first line. *To thee:* he deposits it on another vessel that has been placed for the purpose.

65 He pours goat's milk into it, and recites the formulas.

Thee may Âdityas, Angiras-like, fill with the metre Jagatî.
With the Anushṭup metre may the All-Gods, dear to all men, fill thee full, as Angiras was wont.

66 Intention, Agni, Motive, Hail! Mind, Wisdom, Agni, Motive, Hail!
Thought, Knowledge, Agni, Motive, Hail! Rule of Speech, Agni, Motive, Hail!
To Manu Lord of creatures, Hail! To Agni dear to all men, Hail!

67 May every mortal man elect the friendship of the guiding God.
Each one solicits him for wealth: let him seek fame to prosper him. All-hail!

68 Break not, nor suffer any harm. Endure, O Mother, and be brave;
This work will thou and Agni do.

69 Be firm for weal, O Goddess Earth. Made in the wonted manner thou
Art a celestial design.
Acceptable to Gods be this oblation. Arise thou in this sacrifice uninjured.

70 Wood-fed, bedewed with sacred oil, ancient, Invoker, excellent,
The Son of Strength, the Wonderful.

71 Abandoning the foeman's host, pass hither to this company:
Assist the men with whom I stand.

72 From the remotest distance come, Lord of the Red Steeds, hitherward.
Do thou Purîshya, Agni, loved of many, overcome our foes.

---

66 Having offered the five Audgrabhaṇa oblations customary at Soma sacrifices (see IV. 7), he now offers seven connected with the building of the Fire-altar, and recites the appropriate formulas. *Intention:* our determination to build the altar. *Manu:* the representative Man, identified with Prajâpati.

67 He offers to Savitar with the text from R. V. V. 50. 1, repeated from Book IV. 8.

68 The Sacrificer or the Adhvaryu, standing towards the north-east, places the Fire-pan embedded in Muñja grass and hemp, on the Âhavanîya fire, and addresses it with the two texts.

69 *Earth:* the Fire-pan being made of clay.

70 When the fire has burnt up, he places on it a kindling-stick of Kṛimuka wood (a tree unknown to European botanists) with the text taken from R. V. II. 7. 6. *Son of Strength:* Agni, as sprung from the violent agitation of the fire-drill.

71 He puts on a stick of Vaikaṅkata (Flacourtia Sapida) with the text from R. V. VIII. 64. 15.

72 He puts on a third stick, of Udumbara (Ficus Glomerata) with the text. *Our foes: mṛidhaḥ;* 'the scorners': Eggeling.

73 O Agni, whatsoever be the fuel that we lay on thee,
May that be butter unto thee. Be pleased therewith, Most Youthful God.

74 That which the termite eats away, that over which the emmet crawls—
Butter be all of this to thee. Be pleased therewith, Most Youthful God.

75 Bringing to him, with care unceasing, fodder day after day as to a stabled courser,
Joying in food and in the growth of riches, may we thy neighbours, Agni, ne'er be injured.

76 While on earth's navel Agni is enkindled, we call, for ample increase of our riches,
On Agni joying in the draught, much-lauded, worshipful, victor conquering in battle.

77 Whatever hosts there are, fiercely assailant, charging in lengthened lines, drawn up in order,
Whatever thieves there are, whatever robbers, all these I cast into thy mouth, O Agni.

78 Devour the burglars with both tusks, destroy the robbers with thy teeth.
With both thy jaws, thou Holy One, eat up those thieves well champed and chewed.

79 The burglars living among men, the thieves and robbers in the wood,
Criminals lurking in their lairs, these do I lay between thy jaws.

80 Him who would seek to injure us, the man who looks on us with hate
Turn thou to ashes, and the man who slanders and would injure us.

---

73 He puts on a stick of some sacrificial tree, that has not been cut off but has fallen or been blown off by the wind, and recites the text from R. V. VIII. 91. 20.

74 He adds a fifth stick, that has been found lying on the ground, with the text from R. V. VIII. 91. 21. *Termite:* commonly called white ant, a great devourer of wood and a most destructive pest in houses.

75 He puts on, with eight texts, eight kindling-sticks of Palâsa wood. The first text is taken from A. V. XIX. 55. 1, 'day after day' being substituted for 'night after night.'

76 *Earth's navel:* the central and most important spot where Agni is now kindled.

81 Quickened is this my priestly rank, quickened is manly strength and force,
Quickened is his victorious power of whom I am the Household priest.

82 The arms of these men have I raised, have raised their lustre and their strength.
With priestly power I ruin foes and lift my friends to high estate.

83 A share of food, O Lord of Food, vouchsafe us, invigorating food that brings no sickness.
Onward, still onward lead the giver. Grant us maintenance both for quadruped and biped.

---

81 He puts on eleven sticks in ordinary cases, but twelve for a Kshatriya or a Purohita. In the latter case he recites the text taken, with variations, from A. V. III. 19. 1. *Quickened:* or, sharpened, intensified.

82 In the case of a prince or noble (Râjanya, Kshatriya) being the Sacrificer, he recites this text, the second line of which is taken from A. V. III. 19. 3.

83 He dips a kindling-stick in the vow-milk (see IV. 11, note) presented by the Adhvaryu, lays it on the fire, and recites the text.

## BOOK THE TWELFTH.

FAR hath he shone abroad like gold to look on, beaming imperishable life for glory.
Agni by vital powers became immortal when his prolific Father Dyaus begat him.

2 Night and Dawn, different in hue, accordant, meeting together, suckle one same infant.
Golden between the heaven and earth he shineth. The wealth-possessing Gods supported Agni.

3 The Sapient One arrays himself in every form: for quadruped and biped he hath brought forth good.
Excellent Savitar hath looked on heaven's high vault: he shineth after the outgoings of the Dawn.

4 Thou art the goodly-pinioned Bird: thou hast the Trivṛit for thy head.
Gâyatra is thine eye, thy wings are Bṛihat and Rathantara.
The hymn is self, the metres are his limbs, the formulas his name.
The Vâmadevya Sâman is thy form, the Yajñâyajñiya thy tail, the fire-hearths are thy hooves.
Thou art the goodly-pinioned Bird: go skyward, soar to heavenly light.

---

This Book contains formulas relating chiefly to the treatment of Ukhya Agni or Agni of the Fire-pan, and the preparation of the Âhavanîya Fire-Altar.

1 The Sacrificer binds on his neck a circular piece of gold with twenty-one knobs sewed up in the black-antelope's skin and strung above his navel on a hempen string of three strands. The gold plate symbolises the Sun, that is, Agni, and the knobs represent the months, five seasons, the three worlds, and the Sun. He then recites the text taken from R. V. X. 45. 8.

2 With two small round mats of Muñja grass he takes hold of the Fire-pan and recites the text taken, with variations, from R. V. I. 96. 5, setting it down on a seat or stool of Udumbara wood as he recites the last sentence. The two mats symbolize Heaven and Earth, the Fire-pan is Agni or the Sun, and the seat is the ground. *One same infant:* Agni as the Sun.

3 He ties round his neck the main cord of the suspensory sling in which the Fire-pan is to be carried about, and recites the text from R. V. V. 81. 2. *The Sapient One:* the Sun, Agni. *Every form:* every object that he discloses after the darkness of night.

4 He raises up the sling, and addresses Ukhya Agni with the text. *Trivṛit:* the hymn of three triplets (see IX. 32). *The hymn:* meaning the Pañchadaśa Stoma or form of recitation in fifteen verses. *Formulas:* sacrificial prayers and texts. *Vâmadevya:* belonging to Vâmadeva, the Ṛishi or inspired seer of Book IV. of the R. V., the name given to various Sâmans. *Yajñâyajñiya:* a Sâman named after the beginning (Yajñâ-yajñâ, at every sacrifice) of R. V. I. 168. 1. The text expresses the form (that of an eagle) in which the Fire-altar is to be built.

5 Thou art the rival-slaying stride of Vishṇu. Mount the Gâyatra metre: stride along the earth.
Thou art the foe-destroying stride of Vishṇu. Mount the Trishṭup metre: stride along mid-air.
Thou art the traitor-slaying stride of Vishṇu. Mount the Jagatî metre: stride along the sky.
Thou art the foeman-slaying stride of Vishṇu. Mount Anushṭup metre: stride along the Quarters.

6 Agni roared out like Dyaus what time he thunders: licking full oft the earth round plants he flickered.
At once, when born, he looked about, enkindled: he shineth forth between the earth and heaven.

7 Return to me, thou still-returning Agni, with life, with lustre, progeny, and treasure,
With profit, wisdom, riches, and abundance.

8 A hundred, Agni Angiras! be thy ways, a thousand thy returns.
With increment of increase bring thou back to us what we have lost. Again bring hitherward our wealth.

9 Return again with nourishment; Agni, again with food and life. Again preserve us from distress.

10 Agni, return with store of wealth. Swell with thine overflowing stream that feedeth all on every side.

11 I brought thee: thou hast entered in. Stand stedfast and immovable.
Let all the people long for thee. Let not thy kingship fall away.

12 Varuṇa, from the upmost bond release us, let down the lowest and remove the midmost.
So in thy holy law may we made sinless belong to Aditi, O thou Âditya.

---

5 He makes four strides representing the course of Vishṇu as the Sun, with an address to each stride.

6 He holds up Ukhya Agni towards the east, reciting the text taken from R. V. X. 45. 4. *Round plants he flickered:* 'stroking the plants,' 'literally anointing (? either furbishing, or impregnating': Eggeling.

7 He brings the Fire-pan lower and lower four times, reciting a text each time.

11 Holding the Fire-pan above his navel he addresses Agni with the text taken, with the exception of the first Pâda, from R. V. X. 173. 1.

12 He unties the cord of the suspensory sling and the string of the gold disc, reciting the text taken from R. V. I. 24. 15. *Varuṇa:* addressed in the original hymn as the Moral Governor of the world, armed with a noose or cord with which he binds the wicked.

13 High hath the Mighty risen before the Mornings, and come to us with light from out the darkness.
Fair-shapen Agni with white-shining splendour hath filled at birth all human habitations.

14 The Haṃsa homed in light, the Vasû in mid-air, the Priest beside the altar, Guest within the house,
Dweller in noblest place, mid men, in truth, in sky, born of flood, kine, truth, mountain, he is holy Law. The Great.

15 Knowing all holy ordinances, Agni, be seated in the lap of this thy mother.
Do not with heat or glowing flame consume her: shine thou within her with refulgent lustre.

16 Within this Fire-pan with thy light, O Agni, in thy proper seat,
Glowing with warmth, be gracious thou, O Jâtavedas, unto her.

17 Being propitious unto me, O Agni, sit propitiously.
Having made all the regions blest, in thine own dwelling seat thyself.

18 First Agni sprang to life from out of heaven, the second time from us came Jâtavedas.
Thirdly the Manly-souled was in the waters. The pious lauds and kindles him Eternal.

19 Agni, we know thy three powers in three stations, we know thy forms in many a place divided.
We know what name supreme thou hast in secret: we know the source from which thou hast proceeded.

20 The Manly-souled lit thee in sea and waters, Man's Viewer lit thee in the breast of heaven.
There as thou stoodest in the third high region the Bulls increased thee in the waters' bosom.

---

13 He holds Agni up to the south-east with the text taken from R. V. X. 1. 1.

14 He lowers him with the text (repeated from X. 24) taken from R. V. IV. 40. 5, and a sacrificial formula of one word. *The Great; brihat;* Truth, understood; that is, Agni. As he pronounces this formula he lays Agni on the seat.

15 He stands by Ukhya Agni, reverencing him with three texts.

18 He worships with the Vâtsapra rite, the recitation of Hymn 45 of Book X. of the Rigveda, ascribed to the Rishi Vatsaprî son of Bhalanda. *From out of Heaven;* or, from Dyaus or Heaven his father, in the shape of the Sun. *From us:* produced by men in the shape of sacrificial and domestic fire. *In the waters:* of the firmament, in the shape of lightning, the third form of Agni. *Manly-souled:* or, Friend of men.

19 *In secret:* unknown to those who know not the Veda: Sâyaṇa.

20 *Manly-souled:* or, Friend of men; Varuṇa, according to Sâyaṇa, and Prajâpati, according to Mahîdhara. Prof. Ludwig thinks that Dyaus (cp. verse 8) may be meant, and Prof. Grassmann that Indra, the kindler of the lightning, is intended. *The Bulls;* or, the Mighty Ones; the Maruts.

21 Agni roared out, etc. (verse 6 repeated).

22 The spring of glories and support of riches, rouser of thoughts and guardian of the Soma,
Good Son of Strength, a King amid the waters, in forefront of the Dawns he shines enkindled.

23 Germ of the world, ensign of all creation, he sprang to life and filled the earth and heaven.
Even the firm rock he cleft when passing over, when the Five Tribes brought sacrifice to Agni.

24 So among mortals was immortal Agni stablished as cleansing, wise, and eager envoy.
He waves the red smoke that he lifts above him, striving to reach the heaven with radiant lustre.

25 Far hath he shone, etc. (verse 1 repeated).

26 Whoso this day, O God whose flames are lovely, makes thee a cake, O Agni, mixed with butter,
Lead thou and further him to higher fortune, to bliss bestowed by Gods, O thou Most Youthful.

27 Endow him, Agni, with a share of glory, at every song of praise sung forth enrich him.
Dear let him be to Sûrya, dear to Agni, preëminent with son and children's children.

28 While, Agni, day by day men pay thee worship they win themselves all treasures worth the wishing.
Allied with thee, eager and craving riches, they have disclosed the stable filled with cattle.

29 Agni, man's gracious Friend, the Soma's keeper, Vaiṣvânara, hath been lauded by the Ṛishis.
We will invoke benignant Earth and Heaven: ye Deities, give us wealth with hero children.

30 Pay service unto Agni with your fuel, rouse your Guest with oil:
In him present your offerings.

---

23 *The firm rock:* the massive cloud, according to Sâyaṇa and Mahîdhara. Some extraordinary forest conflagration may, perhaps, be referred to. *The Five Tribes:* literally, the five men; according to Sâyaṇa, men in general, and according to Mahîdhara, the institutor of the sacrifice and the four chief priests. But some special and remarkable occasion seems to be referred to, such as the associated sacrifice offered by representatives of the Five Confederate Âryan races or tribes. See The Hymns of the Ṛigveda, Index.

28 *Stable filled with cattle:* a common expression for great possessions.

29 *Soma's keeper:* as connected with the Moon, the great receptacle of the celestial Soma, the nectar or ambrosia of the Gods. See A. Hillebrandt, Vedische Mythologie, I. 330—336.

30 Formulas for the Vanîvâhanam or Driving Hither and Thither of Agni. The Sacrificer stations a car northward of Ukhya Agni, turned towards the east, and lays a kindling-stick on the fire, reciting the text.

31 May all the Gods, O Agni, bear thee upward with their earnest thoughts:
Not to be looked on, rich in light, be thou propitious unto us.

32 Agni, go forth resplendent, thou with thine auspicious flames of fire.
Shining with mighty beams of light harm not my people with thy form.

33 Agni roared out, etc. (verse 21 repeated.)

34 Far famed is this the Bharata's own Agni: he shineth like the Sun with lofty splendour.
He who hath vanquished Púru in the battle, the heavenly Guest hath shone for us benignly.

35 Receive these ashes, ye celestial Waters, and lay them in a fair place full of fragrance.
To him bow down the nobly-wedded Matrons! Bear this on waters as her son a mother.

36 Agni, thy home is in the floods: into the plants thou forcest way,
And as their child art born anew.

37 Thou art the offspring of the plants, thou art the offspring of the trees:
The offspring thou of all that is, thou, Agni, art the Waters' Child.

38 With ashes having reached the womb, the waters, Agni! and the earth,
United with the mothers, thou blazing hast seated thee again.

39 Seated again upon thy seat, the waters, Agni! and the earth,
In her, thou, most auspicious One, liest as in a mother's lap.

---

31 He lifts up Ukhya Agni together with the seat (see verse 3), and standing on the south side puts him on the car.

32 He yokes in silence two oxen, and goes eastward reciting the text.

33 When the axle creaks he mutters the text repeated from XII. 6 and 21.

34 At his dwelling he takes down Ukhya Agni on a spot that has been raised and sprinkled, lays a kindling-stick on the fire, and recites the text taken from R. V. VII. 8. 4. *Bharata's:* God of Vasishtha, the Purohita or Tribal Priest of the Bharatas, a warlike tribe. *Púru:* the Púrus (one of the Five Âryan Tribes) who opposed the Bharatas. According to Mahîdhara, Puru was a Râkshasa or demon.

35 He takes the ashes from the Fire-pan in a basket or tray made of the leaves of a Palâśa, Ficus Indica (banyan), or other sacred tree, and throws them into water, reciting the text. *To him:* Agni in the ashes. *Nobly wedded:* Consorts of Varuṇa who rules over the waters.

36 He takes ashes in the basket again, and throws them into the water as before, with two texts, the first of which is taken from R. V. VIII. 43. 9.

38 With his little finger he takes some ashes from the water, and throws part of them back, reciting the four texts.

40, 41 Return again, etc. Agni, return, etc. (verses 9 and 10 repeated).

42 Mark this my speech, Divine One, thou Most Youthful, offered to thee by him who gives most freely:
One hates thee, and another sings thy praises. I thine adorer laud thy form, O Agni.

43 Be thou for us a liberal Prince, Giver and Lord of precious things.
Drive those who hate us far away.
To the Omnific One All-hail!

44 Again let the Âdityas, Rudras, Vasus, and Brâhmans with their rites light thee, Wealth-bringer!
Increase thy body with presented butter: effectual be the Sacrificer's wishes.

45 Go hence, depart, creep off in all directions, both ancient visitors and recent comers.
Yama hath given a place on earth to rest in. This place for him the Fathers have provided.

46 Knowledge art thou: accomplishment of wishes. In me be the fulfilment of thy wishes.
Thou art the ashes, thou the mould of Agni. Rankers are ye, rankers around. Rankers right upward, be ye fixed.

---

42 Having returned from the pool he throws into the Fire-pan some of the ashes taken from the water, and stands by the fire worshipping with two texts taken respectively from R. V. I. 147. 2 and II. 6. 4, the last line of the verse being an original Yajus or sacrificial formula.

43 *Prince:* or Patron.

44 He stands up after a burnt offering of butter and replaces the same fire-stick on the Ukhya Agni reciting the text.

45 Formulas for the construction of the Gârhapatya hearth, representing the domestic fire-place of the householder who institutes sacrifice. The Adhvaryu sweeps the ground where the hearth is to be built with a Palâsa branch, and throws away the grass and rubbish, reciting a Pâda of the text (see R. V. X. 14. 9) as he sweeps each side beginning with the east. *Go hence:* in the original funeral hymn this is, according to Sâyaṇa, addressed to the Pisâchas and other evil spirits that haunt the place of cremation. Here, says Mahîdhara, the ministers of Yama, Lord Paramount of the ground, are meant. *For him:* for the Sacrificer.

46 Over the site of the future altar he scatters saline earth, when he has thrown out the Palâsa branch towards the north, and addresses it with the text. *Knowledge:* of the cattle, inasmuch as they smell out and lick the soil on which a saline efflorescence appears. *Completion of thy wishes: mayi te paśavo bhûyâsuḥ;* on me may there be cattle for thee: Mahîdhara. *Thou art the ashes:* here he spreads sand over the saline earth. *Rankers:* he surrounds the altar site with twenty-one small enclosing stones, forming a range or rank, *Round:* set in a circle. *Upward:* set upright in the ground.

47 This is that Agni where the longing Indra took the pressed Soma deep within his body.
Winner of spoils in thousands like a courser, with prayer art thou exalted, Jâtavedas.

48 The splendour which is thine in heaven, O Agni, in earth, O Holy One, in plants, in waters,
Wherewith thou hast o'erspread mid-air's broad region, that light is brilliant, billowy, man-surveying.

49 O Agni, to the flood of heaven thou mountest, thou callest hither Gods, the thought-inspirers.
The waters, those beyond the light of Sûrya, and those that are beneath it here, approach thee.

50 May the Purîshya Agnis in accord with those that spring from floods,
May they, benevolent, accept the sacrifice, full, wholesome draughts.

51 As holy food, Agni, to thine invoker give wealth in cattle, lasting, rich in marvels.
To us be born a son and spreading offspring. Agni, be this thy gracious will to us-ward.

52 This is thine ordered place of birth whence, sprung to life, thou shonest forth.
Knowing this, Agni, mount on high and cause our riches to increase.

53 Ranker art thou: Angiras-like sit steady with that Deity.
Ranker-round art thou: Angiras-like sit steady with that Deity.

---

47 Sitting on the south of the circle and looking northward the Adhvaryu lays down four bricks in the middle of the circle, the first with the text from R. V. III. 22. 1.

48 He lays the second brick with the text from R. V. III. 22. 2.

49 He lays the third brick with the text from R. V. III. 22. 3.

50 He lays the fourth with the text from R. V. III. 22. 4. *Purîshya:* according to Mahîdhara, friendly to cattle; 'Fires that dwell in mist': The Hymns of the R. V. *Born from floods:* the meaning of *prâvaṇebhiḥ* is uncertain.

51 He sits on the north side facing the south, and lays down the southward one of the two hinder bricks with the text from R. V. III. 22. 5.

52 He lays down the northern one with the text, repeated from III. 14, taken from R. V. III. 29. 10.

53 Sitting on the south side, facing the north, he lays the northern one of the two front bricks, reciting the text. *Angiras-like:* as thou wast wont to do with the ancient Fire-priest Angiras. *Ranker-round:* he lays down the second southward brick. *That Deity:* according to Mahîdhara, that famous deity Vâyu.

54 Fill up the room, supply the void, then settle steady in thy place.
Indr-Âgni and Brihaspati have set thee down in this abode.

55 The dappled kine who stream with milk prepare his draught of Soma juice—
Clans in the birthplace of the Gods, in the three luminous realms of heaven.

56 All sacred songs have magnified Indra expansive as the sea,
The best of warriors borne on cars, the Lord, the very Lord of Strength.

57 Combine ye two and harmonize together, dear to each other, brilliant, friendly-minded,
Abiding in one place for food and vigour.

58 Together have I brought your minds, your ordinances, and your thoughts.
Be thou our Sovran Lord, Agni Puríshya; give food and vigour to the Sacrificer.

59 Thou art Puríshya Agni, thou art wealthy, thou art prosperous.
Having made all the regions blest, here seat thee in thine own abode.

60 Be ye one-minded unto us, both of one thought, free from deceit.
Harm not the sacrifice, harm not the Patron of the sacrifice.
Be gracious unto us to-day, ye knowers of all things that be.

61 Even as a mother bears her son, Earth, Ukhâ hath borne within her womb Puríshya Agni.
Maker of all, accordant with the All-Gods and Seasons, may Prajâpati release her.

62 Seek him who pours not, offers not oblation; follow the going of the thief and robber.

---

54 He lays down three *lokamprinás* or Space-filling bricks—those that have no special prayer appropriated to them—, and addresses each. *Indr-Âgni*: the two Gods combined as a dual Deity.

55 As he settles the two bricks (verse 53) he recites the text called the Sûdadohas from the word *sûdadohasaḥ*, streaming with milk, taken from R. V. VIII. 58. 3.

56 He brings mould from the place of the pit and throws it on the Gârhapatya hearth that is building, with the text taken from R. V. I. 11. 1.

57 He throws the Ukhya Agni, that is the fire in the pan, on the Gârhapatya hearth, with the four following texts.

61 He fills the Fire-pan with sand, looses it from the suspensory sling, and sets it down at the distance of a cubit north of the fire, reciting the text.

62 Formulas for averting Nirriti, the Goddess of Destruction. He lays down the black bricks dedicated to Nirriti, that have been baked with rice-husks, Nirriti's perquisites, in some natural hollow in the ground or a barren place, with the following texts.

This is thy way; leave us and seek some other. To thee, O Goddess Nirṛiti, be homage.

63 To thee, sharp-pointed Nirṛiti, full homage! Loose and detach this iron bond that binds him.
Unanimous with Yama and with Yamî to the sublimest vault of heaven uplift him.

64 Thou, Awful One, thou in whose mouth I offer for the unloosing of these binding fetters,
Whom people hail as Earth with their glad voices, as Nirṛiti in every place I know thee.

65 The binding noose which Nirṛiti the Goddess hath fastened on thy neck that none may loose it,
I loose for thee as from the midst of Âyus. Sped forward now, eat thou the food we offer.
To Fortune, her who hath done this, be homage.

66 Establisher, the gatherer of treasures, he looks with might on every form and figure.
Like Savitar the God whose laws are constant, like Indra he hath stood where meet the pathways.

67 Wise, through desire of bliss with Gods, the skilful bind the traces fast, and lay the yokes on either side.

68 Lay on the yokes and fasten well the traces: formed is the furrow, sow the seed within it.
Through song may we find hearing fraught with plenty: near to the ripened grain approach the sickle.

---

63 *Yama:* here meaning Agni. *Yamî:* Yama's sister. See The Hymns of the Rigveda, X. 10. *Him:* the Sacrificer. *Iron bond:* of sin.

65 He throws down on the farther side of the bricks the suspensory sling, the cord of the gold plate (see 1) the two reed mats (2) and the wooden seat (2), and addresses the Sacrificer with the text. *From the midst of Âyus:* from the Gârhapatya hearth which is the middle of Agni: Mahîdhara. 'Âyus may rather have to be taken in the sense of 'life' or 'vital power': Eggeling. *Sped forward:* by being freed from the bonds of Nirṛiti. *To Fortune:* he pours out a jarful of water.

66 The Brahman-priest, the Sacrificer, and the Adhvaryu return to the sacrificial enclosure from the place where the Nirṛiti bricks were laid down, and the Adhvaryu stands worshipping Agni, in the form of the Gârhapatya hearth, with the texts, taken with variations, from R. V. X. 139. 3. *Pathways:* the R. V. has *dhanânâm*, that is in the meeting or conflict for booty; and Mahîdhara explains *pathînâm*, of the pathways, by 'with robbers or infesters of the way.'

67 Standing behind the right or southern hip of Agni or the Fire-altar, the Adhvaryu addresses the plough to which oxen are being yoked for the purpose, with two texts from R. V. X. 101, 4, 3. *Through desire of bliss with Gods:* or, through desire of pleasing the Gods; 'with mind devoted to the Gods': Eggeling.

69 Happily let the shares turn up the ploughland, happily go the ploughers with the oxen!
Suna and Sîra, pleased with our oblation, cause ye our plants to bear abundant fruitage.

70 Approved by Visvedevas and by Maruts, balmed be the furrow with sweet-flavoured fatness.
Succulent, teeming with thy milky treasure, turn hitherward to us with milk, O Furrow.

71 The keen-shared plough that bringeth bliss, good for the Soma-drinker's need,
Shear out for me a cow, a sheep, a rapid drawer of the car, a blooming woman, plump and strong!

72 Milk out their wish, O Wishing-Cow, to Mitra and to Varuṇa,
To Indra, to the Asvins, to Pûshan, to people and to plants.

73 Be loosed, inviolable, Godward-farers! We have attained the limit of this darkness: we have won the light.

74 The year together with the darksome fortnights; Dawn with the ruddy-coloured cows about her; the Asvins with their wonderful achievements; the Sun together with his dappled Courser; Vaisvânara with Idâ and with butter. Svâhâ!

75 Herbs that sprang up in time of old, three ages earlier than the Gods,—
Of these, whose hue is brown, will I declare the hundred powers and seven.

---

69 On the site of the Altar, near the enclosing stones, he ploughs four furrows, south, west, north, and east, with four texts, one for each furrow. The first text is from A. V. III. 17. 5, the first half being taken from R. V. IV. 57. 8. *Suna and Sîra:* two deities or deified objects which bless or are closely connected with agriculture. See A. V. III. 17, 5, note.

70 Taken from A. V. III. 17. 9.

71 Taken from A. V. III. 17. 3. with a variation. See S. B. E. XLI. 328.

72 *O Wishing-Cow:* O Furrow, productive as the Cow of Plenty.

73 He looses and addresses the oxen. *Inviolable: aghnyâ,* not to be slain or injured. The word is usually applied to cows. *Godward-farers:* as assistants at sacrifice. *Limit of this darkness:* R. V. I. 92. 6. Darkness here meaning distress arising from hunger and thirst, according to Mahîdhara.

74 He places a bunch of Kusa grass in the middle of the Altar site and offers an oblation with five takings of sacrificial butter, reciting the formula of thirteen utterances (Svâ-hâ, divided, counting as two) each of which represents a layer of the Fire-altar. See S. B. E. XLI. 334.

75 Having poured fifteen jars of water on the Altar site he sows the seed of various plants and herbs reciting five triplets. Verses 75—96 are taken from R. V. X. 97 which is a physician's charm addressed to the medicinal herbs, some of which he is about to apply to a patient. *Pâkâru:* perhaps dyspepsia; or some disease of the mouth, abscess or gumboil.

76 Ye, Mothers, have a hundred homes, yea, and a thousand are your growths.
Do ye who have a thousand powers free this my patient from disease.

77 Be glad and joyful in the Plants, both blossoming and bearing fruit,
Plants that will lead us to success like mares who conquer in the race.

78 Plants, by this name I speak to you, Mothers, to you the Goddesses:
Steed, cow, and garment may I win, win back thy very self, O man.

79 The Holy Fig tree is your home, your mansion is the Parṇa tree:
Winners of cattle shall ye be if ye regain for me this man.

80 He who hath store of Herbs at hand like Kings amid a crowd of men,—
Physician is that sage's name, fiend-slayer, chaser of disease.

81 Herbs rich in Soma, rich in steeds, in nourishment, in strengthening power,—
All these have I provided here, that this man may be whole again.

82 The healing virtues of the Plants stream forth like cattle from the stall,—
Plants that shall win me store of wealth, and save thy vital breath, O man.

83 Reliever is your mother's name, and hence Restorers are ye called.
Rivers are ye with wings that fly: keep far whatever brings disease.

84 Over all fences have they passed, as steals a thief into the fold.
The Plants have driven from the frame whatever malady was there.

85 When, bringing back the vanished strength, I hold these herbs within my hand,
The spirit of disease departs ere he can seize upon the life.

86 He through whose frame, O Plants, ye creep member by member, joint by joint,—
From him ye drive away disease like some strong arbiter of strife.

87 Fly, Spirit of Disease, begone, with the blue jay and kingfisher.
Fly, with the wind's impetuous speed, vanish together with the storm.

88 Help every one the other, lend assistance each of you to each,
All of you be accordant, give furtherance to this speech of mine.

89 Let fruitful Plants, and fruitless, those that blossom, and the blossomless,
Urged onward by Bṛihaspati, release us from our pain and grief;

90 Realese me from the curse's plague and woe that comes from Varuṇa;
Free me from Yama's fetter, from sin and offence against the Gods.

91 What time, descending from the sky, the Plants flew earthward, thus they spake:
No evil shall befall the man whom while he liveth we pervade.

92 Of all the many Plants whose King is Soma, Plants of hundred forms,
Thou art the Plant most excellent, prompt to the wish, sweet to the heart.

93 O all ye various Herbs whose King is Soma, that o'erspread the earth,
Urged onward by Brihaspati, combine your virtue in this Plant.

94 All Plants that hear this speech, and those that have departed far away,
Come all assembled and confer your healing power upon this Herb.

95 Unharmed be he who digs you up, unharmed the man for whom I dig:
And let no malady attack biped or quadruped of ours.

96 With Soma as their Sovran Lord the Plants hold colloquy and say:
O King, we save from death the man whose cure a Brâhman undertakes.

97 Most excellent of all art thou, O Plant: thy vassals are the trees.
Let him be subject to our power, the man who seeks to injure us.

98 Banisher of catarrh art thou, of tumours and of hemorrhoids;
Thou banishest Pâkâru and Consumption in a hundred forms.

99 Thee did Gandharvas dig from earth, thee Indra and Bṛihaspati.
King Soma, knowing thee, O Plant, from his Consumption was made free.
100 Conquer mine enemies, the men who challenge me do thou subdue,
Conquer thou all unhappiness: victorious art thou, O Plant.
101 Long-lived be he who digs thee, Plant, and he for whom I dig thee up.
So mayst thou also, grown long-lived, rise upward with a hundred shoots.
102 Most excellent of all art thou, O Plant; thy vassals are the trees.
Let him be subject to our power, the man who seeks to injure us.
103 May he not harm me who is earth's begetter, nor he whose laws are faithful, sky's pervader;
Nor he who first begot the lucid waters. To Ka the God let us present oblation.
104 Turn thyself hitherward, O Earth, to us with sacrifice and milk.
Thy covering skin Agni, urged forth, hath mounted.
105 All, Agni, that in thee is bright, pure, cleansed, and meet for sacrifice,
That do we bring unto the Gods.
106 I from this place have fed on strength and vigour, the womb of holy Law, stream of the mighty.
In cows let it possess me and in bodies. I quit decline and lack of food, and sickness.
107 Agni, life-power and fame are thine: thy fires blaze mightily, thou rich in wealth of beams!
Sage, passing bright, thou givest to the worshipper, with strength, the food that merits laud.
108 With brilliant, purifying sheen, with perfect sheen thou liftest up thyself in light.
Thou, visiting both thy Mothers, aidest them as Son: thou joinest close the earth and heaven.

---

103 With the wooden sword he takes from outside the fire altar four bricks, each made of a lump of clay, and lays them on the body of the altar site, reciting a text as he deposits each. The first is from the front. *Earth's begetter:* Prajâpati.

104 He lays down a brick from the south. *Covering skin:* the surface of the earth.

105 He lays down a clay brick from behind.

106 He lays down a clay brick from the north.

107 He throws sand on the High Altar with six verses from R. V. X. 140.

109 O Jâtavedas, Son of Strength, rejoice thyself, gracious, in our fair hymns and songs.
In thee are treasured various forms of strengthening food, born nobly and of wondrous help.

110 Agni, spread forth, as Ruler, over living things: give wealth to us, Immortal God.
Thou shinest out from beauty fair to look upon: thou leadest us to conquering power.

111 To him, the wise, who orders sacrifice, who hath great riches under his control,
Thou givest blest award of good, and plenteous food, givest him wealth that conquers all.

112 The men have set before them for their welfare Agni, strong, visible to all, the Holy.
Thee, Godlike One, with ears to hear, most famous, men's generations magnify with praise-songs.

113 Soma, wax great. From every side may vigorous powers unite in thee.
Be in the gathering-place of strength.

114 In thee be juicy nutriments united, and power and mighty foe-subduing vigour.
Waxing to immortality, O Soma, win highest glory for thyself in heaven.

115 Wax, O most gladdening Soma, great through all thy filaments, and be
A friend of most illustrious fame to prosper us.

116 May Vatsa draw thy mind away, even from thy loftiest dwelling-place,
Agni, with song that yearns for thee.

117 Agni, best Angiras, to thee all people who have pleasant homes
Apart have turned to gain their wish.

118 In dear homes, Agni, the desire of all that is and is to be,
Shines forth the One Imperial Lord.

---

113 He touches the sand that has been spread on the body of the altar, reciting the texts taken from R. V. I. 91. 16, 18, 17.

116 The following verses are addressed to the Fires as they are led forward, preceded by a horse, a white one by preference, representing Agni as the Sun; or, if no horse is available, by a bullock (see Sacred Books of the East, XII. 297). The first verse is taken from R. V. VIII. 11. 7.

117 Taken from R. V. VIII. 43. 18.

# BOOK THE THIRTEENTH.

I TAKE within me Agni first, for increase of my wealth, good offspring, manly strength:
So may the Deities wait on me.

2 Thou art the waters' back, the womb of Agni, around the ocean as it swells and surges.
Waxing to greatness, resting on the lotus, spread forth in amplitude with heaven's own measure.

3 Eastward at first was Brahma generated. Vena o'erspread the bright Ones from the summit,
Disclosed his deepest nearest revelations, womb of existent and of non-existent.

4 In the beginning rose Hiraṇyagarbha, born Only Lord of all created being.
He fixed and holdeth up this earth and heaven. Worship we Ka the God with our oblation.

5 The Drop leaped onward through the earth and heaven, along this place and that which was before it.

---

This Book contains formulas for the laying down of the Lotus-leaf, the solemn setting of various bricks, the burial of the Tortoise, the disposal of the Victims' Heads, and other ceremonies connected with the construction of the Âhavanîya Fire-altar.

1 The Sacrificer standing on the farther side of the High Altar offers an oblation and recites the text. *I take Agni:* in order that Ágni, that is, the Fire-Altar, may be made out of Agni himself.

2 He lays down a lotus-leaf, representing the sky, on a tuft of Kusa grass, with the text which is repeated from XI. 29.

3 Upon the lotus-leaf he lays the piece of gold hung round his neck (see XII. 1), with the text from A. V. IV. 1. 1. *Brahma:* or the Prayer. Prayer originated in the eastern heaven: when Vena, the Loving One, the early Sun, first rose in his glory he poured forth the type of human prayer, his morning song of joy and praise. See III. 8, note. According to Mahîdhara, Brahma here is the Sun. *O'erspread the Bright Ones:* or, disclosed bright flashes. According to Mahîdhara, *the Bright Ones* are the worlds. *Non-existent:* but possessing the potentiality of future existence.

4 On the piece of gold he lays a golden figure of a man, on his back, with his face eastward, a symbol of Prajâpati, Agni, and the Sacrificer, and recites the two texts taken respectively from R. V. X. 121. 1, and, with variations, from R. V. X. 17. 11. *Hiraṇyagarbha:* 'the Gold Germ,' 'Source of Golden Light,' the Sun-God identified with Prajâpati. *Ka:* Prajâpati. Or, What God (other than Prajâpati) shall we adore with our oblation? See I. 6, note.

5, 6, 7 *The Drop:* meaning, say the Commentators, Âditya, the Sun. *Oblations: hotrâs,* meaning, it is said, the regions of the sky. The Sacrificer thus establishes the Sun in heaven. See Sacred Books of the East, XLI. p. 368. The Sacrificer stands by the golden figure worshipping with the three following formulas. *Serpents:* see two hymns addressed to Serpents as powerful superhuman beings, A. V. III. 26. 27. *Demons' darts:* sent by Râkshasas and other evil beings to bite and kill men.

I offer up, throughout the seven oblations, the Drop still moving to the common dwelling.

6 Homage be paid to Serpents unto all of them that are on earth,

To those that dwell in air, to those that dwell in sky be homage paid.

7 To those that are the demons' darts, to those that live upon the trees,

To all the Serpents that lie low in holes be adoration paid.

8 Or those that are in heaven's bright sphere, or those that dwell in the Sun's beams:

Serpents, whose home has been prepared in waters, homage unto them!

9 Put forth like a wide-spreading net thy vigour: go like a mighty King with his attendants.

Thou, following thy swift net, shootest arrows: transfix the fiends with darts that burn most fiercely.

10 Forth go in rapid flight thy whirling weapons: follow them closely glowing in thy fury.

Spread with thy tongue the wingèd flames, O Agni: unfettered cast thy firebrands all around thee.

11 Send thy spies forward, fleetest in thy motion: be, ne'er deceived, the guardian of this people

From him who, near or far, is bent on evil, and let no trouble sent from thee o'ercome us.

12 Rise up, O Agni, spread thee out before us, burn down our foes, thou who hast sharpened arrows.

Him, blazing Agni! who hath worked us mischief, consume thou utterly like dried-up stubble.

13 Rise, Agni, drive off those who fight against us: make manifest thine own celestial vigour.

Slacken the strong bows of the demon-driven: destroy our foemen whether kin or stranger.

I settle thee with Agni's fiery ardour.

---

9 He sits down and offers an oblation on the gold figure with butter taken in five ladlefuls, reciting five texts, demon-slaying charms, taken from R. V. IV. 4. 1—5.

11 *Spies:* the first flames, sent forward as if to reconnoitre.

13 *Demon-driven:* those whom evil spirits incite to attack us. *I settle thee:* with this formula he lays down on the south side a ladle made of the wood of the Kârshmarya tree (Gmelina Arborea filled with clarified butter,

14 Agni is head and height of heaven, the Master of the earth is he:
He quickeneth the waters' seed.
I settle thee with the great strength of Indra.

15 Thou art the leader of the rite and region to which with thine auspicious teams thou tendest.
Thy light-bestowing head to heaven thou liftest, making thy tongue the oblation-bearer, Agni!

16 Steady art thou, sustainer, laid by Viṣvakarman in thy place.
Let not the ocean nor the bird harm thee: unshaking, steady earth.

17 Thee let Prajâpati settle on the waters' back, in Ocean's course,
Thee the capacious, widely spread. Thou art the Wide One: spread thee wide!

18 Thou art the earth, the ground, thou art the all-sustaining Aditi, she who supporteth all the world.
Control the earth, steady the earth, do thou the earth no injury.

19 For all breath, out-breath, through-breath, upward-breathing, for high position, for prescribed observance,
May Agni keep thee safe with great well-being, with the securest shelter. As aforetime with Angiras, with that Deity lie steady.

20 Upspringing from thine every joint, upspringing from each knot of thine,

---

14 He lays down on the north side a ladle of Udumbara (Ficus Glomerata) wood, filled with inspissated sour milk (*dadhi; dahî* in Hindî), and recites the text, repeated from III. 12, taken from R. V. VIII. 44. 16, and the additional formula, I settle thee, etc.

15 He recites also the text from R. V. X. 8. 6.

16 He lays on the golden man a Svayamâtriṇṇâ, a naturally perforated or porous brick; one with grit and gravel in its composition. *The ocean:* the gold disc. *The bird:* the golden man. *Viṣvakarman:* the Omnific; Prajâpati, the Creator. *Steady earth:* keep the ground on which the altar is to be built firm and unmoved.

17 *The waters' back:* the Earth. *The Wide One: prithivî*, feminine of *prithu*, wide; the common name of the earth, and Earth personified as a Goddess. *Spread thee wide: prathasva.*

19 *High position:* 'for a resting-place': Eggeling. *Prescribed observance:* 'for a moving-place': Eggeling. *As aforetime with Angiras:* that is, as thou layest steady in the case of. or when laid down by, Angiras.

20 On the porous brick he lays a Dûrvâ brick, that is Dûrvâ or Dûb grass, with roots and tops, to form a layer. This creeping grass spreads rapidly, throwing out perpetually new branchlets. He recites two texts. Do thou stretch us out: or, Lengthen out our line (of descendants).

Thus with a thousand, Dûrvâ! with a hundred do thou stretch us out.

21 Thou spreading with a hundred, thou that branchest with a thousand shoots,—
Thee, such, with our oblation will we worship, O celestial Brick.

22 Thy lights, O Agni, in the Sun that with their beams o'erspread the sky,—
With all of those assist thou us to-day to light and progeny.

23 Lights of yours in the Sun, O Gods, or lights that are in kine and steeds,
O Indra-Agni, with all those vouchsafe us light, Bṛihaspati!

24 The Far-Refulgent held the light. The Self-Refulgent held the light.
Thee, luminous, may Prajâpati settle upon the back of Earth.
Give, to all breathing, all the light, to out-breath, to diffusive breath.
Thy Sovran Lord is Agni. With that Deity, as with Angiras, lie firmly settled in thy place.

25 Madhu and Mâdhava, the two Spring seasons—thou art the innermost cement of Agni.
May Heaven and Earth, may Waters, Plants and Agnis help, separate, accordant, my precedence.
May all the Fires 'twixt heaven and earth, one-minded, well-fitted, gather round these two Spring seasons,
As the Gods gathering encompass Indra: firm with that Deity, Angiras-like, be seated.

26 Thou art Ashâḍhâ, Conquering One. Conquer our foemen, conquer thou the men who fain would fight with us.
A thousand manly powers hast thou: so do thou aid and quicken me.

---

22 Close to the porous brick, on its eastern side, he lays a Dviyajus brick, so called because it was originally seen and used by the two Gods, Indra and Agni, and recites the two texts.

24 He lays down two Retaḥsich, or Seed-pouring, bricks, close to the Dviyajus, eastward, one on each side of the backbone of the altar, and recites the first line of the text. *Thee, luminous:* he lays down a Viṣvajyotis, or All-light, brick, and recites the rest of the text.

25 He lays down two Ṛitavyâ, or Seasonal, bricks, in front of the All-light brick, one on each side of the backbone of the altar. *Madhu:* honey, a name of Chaitra (Mid-March to Mid-April). *Mâdhava:* honey-like; Vaiṣâkha (Mid-April to Mid-May). *Thou:* the two regarded as one Spring. *Be seated:* the seasonal bricks are addressed. *Of Agni:* that is, of the Fire-altar.

26 He lays down the brick Ashâḍhâ, or Invincible, on the front of the altar, on its backbone.

27 The winds waft sweets, the rivers pour sweets for the man who keeps the Law:

So may the plants be sweet for us.

28 Sweet be the night and sweet the dawns, sweet the terrestrial atmosphere:

Sweet be our Father Heaven to us.

29 May the tall tree be full of sweets for us and, and full of sweets the Sun:

May our milch-kine be sweet for us.

30 Seat thyself in the deepness of the waters, lest Sûrya, lest Vaiśvânara Agni scorch thee.

With wing unclipped, survey created beings: may rain that cometh down from heaven attend thee.

31 He crept across the three heaven-reaching oceans, the Bull of Bricks, the Master of the Waters.

Clad in the world with his, the Well-Made's, vesture, go whither those before thee have departed.

32 May Heaven and Earth, the Mighty Pair, besprinkle this our sacrifice,

And feed us full with nourishments.

33 Look ye on Vishṇu's works whereby the Friend of Indra, close allied,

Hath let his holy ways be seen.

---

27 He anoints a tortoise, said to represent the Sun or Prajâpati, with mixed sour milk, honey, and butter, and recites the three texts taken from R. V. I. 90. 6—8.

30 He lays down the tortoise on a bed of Avakâ plants (Blyxa Octandra, growing in marshy places) on the right side of the brick Invincible, looking towards the golden figure. The custom of building living animals, sometimes human beings, into the foundations of a house to secure its stability, is of very great antiquity, and was formerly very widely spread. See S. Baring-Gould, Strange Survivals, pp. 1—35 The tortoise may have been chosen here with reference to the belief that the world rests upon a tortoise as an incarnation of Vishṇu. See A. Weber, Indische Streifen, p. 58. *Waters:* the heavenly waters in the orb of the Sun.

31 He keeps his hand on the tortoise and shakes it as he recites the text. *The Bull:* the chief. *The Well-made:* Agni whose vesture is said to be cattle whose form the tortoise is supposed to assume. *Those before thee:* former tortoises employed in similar ceremonies.

32 He puts the tortoise on the altar site with the text, repeated from VIII. 32, taken from R. V. I. 22. 13.

33 On the north side of the chief and representative porous brick he places a pestle and mortar of Udumbara wood, reciting the text, repeated from VI. 4, taken from R. V. I. 22. 19.

34 Firm art thou, a sustainer. Hence engendered, forth from these wombs at first came Jâtavedas.

By Gâyatrî, by Trishṭup, by Anushṭup, may he who knows bear to the Gods oblation.

35 Take thou thine ease for food, for store of riches, for might in splendour, and for strength and offspring.

Thou art all-ruling, independent Ruler: both fountains of Sarasvatî protect thee!

36 O radiant Agni, harness thou thy steeds which are most excellent!

They bear thee as thy spirit wills.

37 Yoke, Agni, as a charioteer, thy steeds who best invoke the Gods:

As ancient Hotar take thy seat.

38 Like rivers our libations flow together, cleansing themselves in inmost heart and spirit.

I look upon the flowing streams of butter: the golden reed is in the midst of Agni.

39 Thee for the praise-verse, thee for sheen, thee for bright splendour, thee for light.

This hath become the energetic spirit of all the world and of Vaiśvânara Agni.

40 Agni, all-luminous with light, splendid with splendour, golden One.

Giver of thousands art thou: for a thousand thee.

---

34 Having first silently placed the Fire-pan on the mortar he pounds the prepared clay and throws it on the ground before the Fire-pan which is then set upon it with the two following formulas. *Firm art thou*: see verse 16.

35 *Both fountains*: Mind and Speech; according to Mahîdhara, the Rigveda and the Sâmaveda.

36 He offers two oblations on the Fire-pan with two texts taken respectively from R. V. VI. 16. 43 and VIII. 64. 1.

38 The heads of the victims slaughtered for the ceremony were set aside at an early stage of the proceedings, and he now thrusts a splinter of gold, the symbol of purity and immortality, into the mouth of each, with the text taken, with transposition and a variation, from R. V. IV. 58. 6, 5. *The golden reed*: the golden figure of a man (see verse 4). *Agni*: here meaning the Fire-altar.

39 *Thee for the praise-verse*: *richê*; 'for praise': Eggeling. He thrusts a splinter of gold into each victim's left nostril. *For sheen*: into the right nostril. *For bright splendour*: into the right eye. *For light*: into the left eye. *This hath become*: with this, a splinter of gold is trust into the left ear.

40 With the first line he thrusts a splinter of gold into each victim's right ear. *Giver of thousands*: he addresses the golden figure's head which he takes up and deposits, with the other heads, in the Fire-pan.

41 Balm thou with milk the unborn babe Âditya, wearing all forms, creator of a thousand.
Spare him with heat, nor plot against him: give him a hundred years of life while thou art building.

42 The wind's impetuous rush, Varuṇa's navel! the horse that springs to life amid the waters!
The rivers' tawny child, based on the mountain, harm not, O Agni, in the loftiest region.

43 Unwasting Drop, red, eager, pressing forward, Agni I worship with repeated homage.
Forming thyself with joints in proper order, harm not the Cow, Aditi widely ruling!

44 Her who is Tvashṭar's guardian, Varuṇa's navel, the Ewe brought forth from out the loftiest region,
The Asura's mighty thousandfold contrivance, injure not in the highest sphere, O Agni.

45 The Agni who from Agni had his being, from heat of Earth or also heat of Heaven,
Whereby the Omnific One engendered creatures, him may thy fierce displeasure spare, O Agni.

46 The brilliant presence of the Gods hath risen, the eye of Mitra, Varuṇa, and Agni.
The soul of all that moveth not or moveth, the Sun hath filled the air, and earth and heaven.

47 Injure not, thousand-eyed, while thou art building for sacrifice, this animal, the biped.

---

41 *With milk:* with reference to the milk, representing wealth in cattle, put into the Fire-pan with the sand mentioned in XII. 61, note. *Âditya:* the Sun, that is, Agni of the Fire-altar. *Wearing all forms:* regarded as the Sun. *Him:* the Sacrificer.

42 He puts the horse's head on the north-east side, and recites the text.

43 He puts the ox's head on the south-east side, and recites the text. The *Drop* is Soma represented by the ox.

44 The ram's head is similarly placed on the north-west side. *Tvashtar's guardian:* as providing warm clothing for human beings created by him. *Asura's:* the Divine Being's. But see S. B. E. XLI. 406. *Thousandfold:* infinitely precious, or fit for a thousand services.

45 On the south-western side he puts the head of the he-goat. *The Agni:* in the form of the goat. *From Agni:* that is Prajâpati. *Whereby:* by the goat (or, by the Birthless) representing Vâk, Speech, the Word, by which the Omnific Prajâpati created all things. See Weber, Indische Studien, IX. 473 sq., and Muir, Original Sanskrit Texts, V. 391.

46 He offers an oblation on the human head, or head of the figure, reciting the text, repeated from VII. 42, taken from R. V. I. 115. 1.

47 After worshipping he removes the human head, reciting the text. *Pith:* or marrow, the essential part of sacrificial food. *Man's counterfeit:* *mayu* is explained by *kimpurusha*, perhaps, monkey. Perhaps the head of a puppet or doll, representing a man, is intended. See XI. 16, note.

Accept as pith man's counterfeit the victim, Agni: therewith building thy forms, be settled.

Let thy flame reach man's counterfeit: let thy flame reach the man we hate.

48 Harm not this animal whose hooves are solid, the courser neighing in the midst of coursers.

I dedicate to thee the forest Gaura: building thy bodies up with him be settled.

Let thy flame reach the Gaura, let thy flame reach him whom we detest.

49 Thousandfold, with a hundred streams, this fountain, expanded in the middle of the waters,

Infinite, yielding butter for the people, harm not, O Agni, in the highest region.

This wild bull of the forest I assign thee: building thy bodies up therewith be settled.

Let thy flame reach the wild bull, etc. (as in 48).

50 This creature clothed in wool, Varuṇa's navel, the skin of animals quadruped and biped,

The first that was produced of Tvashṭar's creatures, O Agni, harm not in the highest region.

The forest buffalo do I assign thee: building, etc., as above *mutato mutando.*

51 From Agni's warmth the he-goat had his being: he looked at first upon his generator.

Thereby the Gods at first attained to Godhead: those meet for worship to the height ascended.

The forest Ṣarabha do I assign thee: building, etc.

52 Do thou, Most Youthful God, protect the men who offer, hear their songs,

Protect his offspring and himself.

---

48 He removes the horse's head. *Gaura:* the Gaur or Gour (Bos Gaurus), a species of wild ox.

49 He removes the head of the ox representing the cow. *Wild bull:* Gavaya; the Gayal (Bos Gavaeus).

50 He removes the head of the ram. *Skin:* provider of clothing. *Quadrupeds:* horses, cows, mules, etc.

51 He removes the head of the he-goat. *Agni's warmth:* meaning Prajāpati's. *Thereby:* by the goat (or the Birthless). See v. 45, note. *Ṣarabha:* a mythical eight-legged animal, supposed to live on the Snowy Mountains and to equal or surpass the lion in strength, like our unicorn.

52 He worships the half-finished Fire-altar with the text from R. V. VIII. 73. 3. *The men who offer:* or, the Sacrificer's men. *His:* The present Sacrificer's.

53 I set thee in the passage of the waters. I set thee in the swelling of the waters. I set thee in the ashes of the waters. I set thee in the lustre of the waters. I set thee in the way which waters travel. I set thee in the flood, the place to rest in. I set thee in the sea, the place to rest in. I set thee in the stream, the place to rest in. I set thee in the water's habitation. I set thee in the resting-place of waters. I set thee in the station of the waters. I set thee in the meeting-place of waters. I set thee in the birthplace of the waters. I set thee in the refuse of the waters. I set thee in the residence of waters. I settle thee with the Gâyatrî metre. I settle thee with the Trishṭup metre. I settle thee with the Jagatî metre. I settle thee with the Anushṭup metre. I settle thee with the Paṅkti metre.

54 This, in front, is Bhuva. His offspring, Breath, is Bhauvâyana. Spring is Prâṇâyana. The Gâyatrî is the daughter of Spring. From the Gâyatrî comes the Gâyatra tune. From the Gâyatra the Upâṃśu. From the Upâṃśu the Trivṛit. From the Trivṛit the Rathantara. The Ṛishi Vasishṭha. By thee, taken by Prajâpati, I take vital breath for creatures.

55 This on the right, the Omnific. His, the Omnific's offspring, Mind. Summer sprang from Mind. The Trishṭup is the daughter of Summer. From the Trishṭup came the Svâra song. From the Svâra the Antaryâma. From the Antaryâma the Pañchadaśa. From the Pañchadaśa the Bṛihat. The Ṛishi Bharadvâja. By thee, taken by Prajâpati, I take Mind for creatures.

---

53 He mounts on the altar behind the porous brick and lays down the Apasyâs, or Watery, bricks, five in each quarter, corresponding with the number of the sacrificial victims, and addresses a formula to each. *Passage:* explained as the wind. *Swelling:* the plants. *Ashes:* foam. *Lustre:* lightning. *Way:* the earth. *Flood:* the breath. *Sea:* the mind. *Stream:* speech. *Habitation:* the eye. *Resting-place:* the ear. *Station:* the sky. *Meeting-place:* the air. *Birthplace:* the sea. *Refuse:* sand. *Residence:* food. *I settle:* he then lays down four Chhandasyâs, or Metre, bricks, with a formula for each.

54 He lays down the Prâṇabhṛitas, or Breath-supporting, bricks, two at a time, with a formula for each set. *Bhuva:* a name of Agni; 'the Existent': Eggeling. *Bhauvâyana:* sprung from the Existent; or Mundane. *Prâṇâyana:* sprung from breath. *Upâṃśu:* see VI. 30 sq. *Trivṛit:* the nine-verse hymn. *Vasishṭha:* meaning the vital breath, the word signifying best, most precious. *Taken:* created, or established.

55 He lays down the third set (after the ten of the following verse). *The Omnific:* meaning Vâyu the Wind-God. *Svâra:* a Sâman that has the *svara*, or first rising and then falling pitch of the final vowel, for its finale. *Antaryâma:* a special Soma cup and libation. See VII. 4, note. *Pañchadaśa:* a hymn with fifteen verses. *Bharadvâja:* another famous Vedic Ṛishi, here meaning Mind.

56 This on the western side, the All-Embracer. His, the All-Embracer's offspring, the Eye. The Rains sprang from the Eye. The Jagatî is the daughter of the Rains. From the Jagatî came the Ṛiksama. From the Ṛiksama the Sukra. From the Sukra the Saptadaṣa. From the Saptadaṣa the Vairûpa. The Ṛishi Jamadagni. By thee, taken by Prajâpati, I take the Eye for creatures.

57 This on the north side, heaven. This, heaven's offspring, the Ear. Autumn, the daughter of the Ear. The Anushṭup sprang from Autumn. From the Anushṭup came the Aiḍa. From the Aiḍa the Manthin. From the Manthin the Ekaviṃṣa. From the Ekaviṃṣa the Vairâja. The Ṛishi Viṣvâmitra. By thee, taken by Prajâpati, I take the Ear for creatures.

58 This above, Intellect. Its, Intellect's offspring, Speech. Winter the offspring of Speech. Paṅkti sprang from Winter. From Paṅkti the Nidhanavat. From the Nidhanavat came the Âgrayaṇa. From the Âgrayaṇa the Triṇava and the Trayastriṃṣa. From the Triṇava and the Trayastriṃṣa the Ṣâkvara and the Raivata. The Ṛishi Viṣvakarman. By thee, taken by Viṣvakarman, I take Speech for people.

Fill up the room, etc. The dappled kine, etc. All sacred songs, etc., three texts repeated from XII. 54—56.

---

56 He lays down the second set of ten. *All-Embracer:* the Sun. *Ṛiksama:* similar to a Ṛich; a certain kind of Sâman. *Ṣukra:* a certain Soma cup and libation. See VII. 12. *Saptadaṣa:* a hymn of seventeen verses. *Vairûpa:* an important Sâman. *Jamadagni:* a famous Vedic Ṛishi, here representing the Eye.

57 He lays down the fourth set. *Aiḍa:* the name of Sâmans which have the word *iḍâ* (refreshment; libation) for their finale or chorus. *Manthin:* a Soma libation. See VII. 16. *Ekaviṃṣa:* a hymn of twenty-one verses. *Vairâja:* an important Sâman. *Viṣvâmitra:* the name of a celebrated Vedic Ṛishi, here meaning the Ear, because one hears with it on all (*viṣva*) sides, and because it has a friend (*mitra*) on all sides.

58 He lays down the fifth set. *Intellect:* meaning the Moon. *Nidhanavat:* a Sâman with a special finale or chorus. *Âgrayaṇa:* a certain Soma cup and libation. See VII. 20. *Triṇava:* a hymn consisting of thrice nine verses. *Trayastriṃṣa:* a hymn of thirty-three verses. *Ṣâkvara...Raivata:* two important Pṛishṭha-Sâmans, Ṣâkvara meaning Potent, and Raivata Wealthy. See Haug, Aitareya-Brâhmaṇam, IV. 13. *Viṣvakarman:* meaning, all-effecting Speech.

# BOOK THE FOURTEENTH.

WITH stedfast site and birthplace thou art stedfast: settle thou duly in thy stedfast birthplace, rejoicing in the Ukhya's first appearance.

Here let the Aṣvins, the Adhvaryus, seat thee.

2 Nesting, intelligent, dripping with butter, in the auspicious seat of earth be seated.

Let Rudras, Vasus welcome thee with praises: fill full these prayers for our propitious fortune.

Here let the Aṣvins, the Adhvaryus, seat thee.

3 Here, Guard of Strength, with thine own powers be seated for the Gods' happiness and great enjoyment.

Even as a father to his son, be friendly: with easy entrance enter with thy body. Here let the Aṣvins, the Adhvaryus seat thee:

4 Thou art the filling-stuff of earth called Apsas. May all the Gods celebrate thee with praises.

Enriched with songs of praise, Pṛishṭhas and butter, sit here and give us wealth with store of children.

Here let the Aṣvins, etc.

5 Upon the back of Aditi I lay thee the sky's supporter, pillar of the Quarters,

Queen over creatures. Wave and drop of waters art thou; and Viṣvakarman is thy Ṛishi.

6 Ṣukra and Ṣuchi, seasons, both, of summer—thou art the innermost cement of Agni.

May Heaven and Earth, may Waters, Plants and Agnis help, separate, accordant, my precedence.

---

He now sets the second layer of bricks, the first layer representing this terrestrial world.

1 He lays down the first brick called Âṣvinî, belonging to the Aṣvins, because they as the divine Adhvaryus laid down for the Gods the second layer of the Celestial Altar of the Universe, representing what is between the earth and the middle-air. *Ukhya's:* Agni's.

2 He lays down the second Âṣvinî brick. *Earth:* meaning the first layer.

3 He lays down the third Âṣvinî brick.

4 He lays down the fourth Âṣvinî brick. *Filling-stuff: purîsha;* 'soil-cover': Eggeling. *Apsas:* according to Mahîdhara, the moisture that is the formal cause of water, *ap.*

5 He lays down the fifth Âṣvinî brick. *Aditi:* Earth in the form of the first layer. *Thou:* as constituting one season. *Viṣvakarman:* Prajâpati the Creator.

6 He lays down two Ṛitavyâ, or Seasonal, bricks on the two Seasonal bricks of the first layer. See XIII. 25. *Ṣukra and Ṣuchi:* May-June and June-July. The formula is almost identical with XIII. 25.

Let all the Agnis 'twixt the earth and heaven gather together round these summer seasons, as the Gods gather in their hosts round Indra,

Firm, with that Deity, Angiras-like, be seated.

7 Associate with the Seasons, with the Modes with the Gods, with the health-establishing Gods—may the Aṣvins the Adhvaryus settle thee here for Agni Vaiṣvânara.

Associate...............with the Vasus, etc.

Associate...............with the Rudras, etc.

Associate...............with the Âdityas, etc.

Associate...............with the Viṣvedevas, etc.

8 Guard thou my breath. Guard my out-breathing. Guard my through-breathing. Illume mine eye with far-reaching vision. Give power of hearing to mine ear. Pour forth waters. Quicken plants. Protect bipeds. Protect quadrupeds. Send rain from heaven.

9 The head is vital vigour. Prajâpati became the metre. Royalty is vital vigour, health-giving metre. The Supporter is vital vigour, the Sovran Lord the metre. Viṣvakarman is vital vigour, Parameshṭhin the metre. The he-goat is vital vigour, excellent the metre. The bull is vital vigour, extensive the metre. Man is vital vigour, languid the metre. The tiger is vital vigour, invincible the metre. The lion is vital vigour, covering the metre. The four-year bull is vital vigour, Bṛihatî the metre. The ox is vital vigour, Kakup the metre. The steer is vital vigour, Satobṛihatî the metre.

---

7 He lays down five Vaiṣvadevî bricks, so called as beloning to the Visvedevas or All-Gods. *Associate:* or, in accord; the brick is addressed. *Modes:* meaning the waters by which everything was created and arranged. *Health-establishing Gods:* the vital breathings by which life is supported. The four following formulas differ only in substituting 'Vasus,' 'Rudras,' etc. for 'the Gods.'

8 He lays down the Prâṇabhṛitas or Breath-supporting bricks (see XIII. 54) with five formulas. *Pour forth waters:* here he lays down the Apasyâs or Watery bricks (XIII. 53) with five formulas, one for each brick.

9 He lays down the nineteen Vayasyâs or Vital-vigour bricks, called in the Ṣatapatha-Brâhmaṇa Chhandasyâs or Sacred-metre bricks, with a formula addressed to each. According to the legend, Prajâpati after he had performed the work of creation became disjointed, relaxed, or agitated, and the cattle, having assumed the forms of the sacred metres, went from him. Then Prajâpati in the form of the Gâyatrî, which is connected with cattle, and the other metres followed and overtook them through the vital power of the Gâyatrî. *The head:* Prajâpati.

10 The bullock is vital vigour, Paṅkti the metre. The milch-cow is vital vigour, Jagatî the metre. The eighteen-month calf is vital vigour, Trishṭup the metre. The two year old steer is vital vigour, Virâj the metre. The thirty-month old ewe is vital vigour, Gâyatri the metre. The three year old steer is vital vigour, Ushṇih the metre. The four year old ox is vital vigour, Anushṭup the metre. Fill up the room, etc. The dappled kine, etc. All sacred songs, etc. are three texts repeated from XII. 54—56. See also XIII. 58.

11 Indra and Agni, in its place securely set the unshaking brick.
Thou with thy back sunderest heaven and the broad earth and firmament.

12 On the air's back let Viṣvakarman set thee, thee the capacious, thee the far-extended.
Control the air, fix firm the air, do thou the air no injury.
For all breath, out-breath, through-breath, upward breathing, for high position, for prescribed observance,
May Vâyu keep thee safe with great well-being, with securest shelter. In the manner of Angiras, with that Deity lie steady.

13 Queen art thou, Quarter of the East. Wide-ruler, Quarter of the South. West Quarter, thou art Sovran. Thou Autocrat, Quarter of the North.
Queen Paramount art thou, the Lofty Point.

14 On the air's back may Viṣvakarman set thee luminous.
Control all light for all breath, for out-breath, up-breath, through-breath.
Thy Lord is Vâyu, with that Deity, Angiras-like, lie firm.

15 Two Rainy Seasons, Nabhas and Nabhasya—thou art the innermost cement of Agni, etc. (as in XIII. 25).

---

11 He now sets the third layer of the Altar. *Indra and Agni:* as in the case of the first layer. *Unshaking brick:* the central porous brick which represents the layer. *Thou:* the brick is addressed.

12 See XIII. 18, 19.

13 He lays down five Diṣyâs or Regional bricks on the spines above the Vaiṣvadevî bricks of the second layer, with a formula addressed to each. *Lofty Point:* the zenith.

14 He lays down a Viṣvajyotis or All-light brick just above the Viṣvajyotis brick of the second layer. *Air's back:* the second layer representing mid-air as the first represents the earth.

15 He lays down two Ṛitavyâ or Seasonal bricks, called *Nabhas and Nabhasya:* Mist and Misty; July-August and August-September. The rest of the formula is repeated from XIII. 25.

16 Isha and Ûrja, two Autumnal Seasons—thou art the innermost cement of Agni, etc.

17 Preserve my life. Preserve my breath. Guard mine outbreath. Preserve mine eyes. Preserve mine ears. Strengthen my voice. Quicken my mind. Preserve my self. Vouchsafe me light.

18 Mâ metre. Pramâ metre. Pratimâ metre. Asrivayas metre. Paṅkti metre. Ushṇih metre. Bṛihatî metre. Anushṭup metre. Virâj metre. Gâyatrî metre. Trishṭup metre. Jagatî metre.

19 Earth metre. Sky metre. Heaven metre. Years metre. Nakshatras metre. Vâk metre. Mind metre. Husbandry metre. Gold metre. Cow metre. She-goat metre. Horse metre.

20 The Deity Agni. The Deity Vâta. The Deity Sûrya. The Deity Moon. The Deity Vasus. The Deity Rudras. The Deity Âdityas The Deity Maruts. The Deity Viṣvedevas. The Deity Bṛihaspati. The Deity Indra. The Deity Varuṇa.

21 Chief art thou, bright, supporting, firm, thou art the great sustainer, Earth.

Thee for life, thee for lustre, thee for tillage, thee for peace and rest.

22 Controller, brilliant art thou, managing controller, firm sustainer. For strength, for energy thee, for riches thee, for prosperity thee.

Fill up the room, etc. The dappled kine, etc. All sacred songs, etc. (as in 10).

---

16 He lays two more Seasonal bricks on the first two; called Isha and Ûrja, Sap and Vigour, September-October and October-November. The rest of the formula as in XIII 25.

17 He lays down the Prâṇabhṛitas or Breath-supporting bricks, ten in number with a formula for each.

18 He lays down the Chhandasyâs or Metrebricks, thirty-six in number, in sets of twelve, with a formula for each. The first four names of the bricks are fanciful. *Mâ:* measure; signifying the measured earth. *Pramâ:* forward measure; mid-air. *Pratimâ:* counter-measure; the heavenly world copied in mid-air. *Asrivayas:* said to represent the three worlds of earth, air, and heaven. The following eight are real metres and names of the bricks.

19 The next twelve bricks are laid down and addressed as the metres of the deified objects enumerated.

20 The next twelve are named after the deities enumerated.

21 He lays down the bricks called Vâlakhilyâs, representing the vital breathings, seven in front and seven behind.

22 *Thee:* that is, I lay thee down. *Fill space, etc:* these three formulas are repeated from XII. 54—56.

23 The Swift, the triple praise-song. The Shining, the Pañchadaṣa hymn. Heaven, the Saptadaṣa. The Supporter, the Ekaviṃṣa. Speed, the Ashṭâdasa. Ardour, the Navadasa. Triumphant Onset, Saviṃṣa, Vigour, Dvâviṃṣa. Maintenance, Trayoviṃṣa. Womb, Chaturviṃṣa. Embryos, Pañchaviṃṣa. Energy, the Triṇava. Intention, the Ekatriṃṣa. The Basis, the Trayastriṃṣa. The Bright One's Station, the Chatustriṃṣa. The Vault of Heaven, the Shaṭtriṃṣa. The Revolving One, the Ashṭâchatvâriṃṣa. The Support, the Four-divisioned praise-song.

---

23 He begins the fourth layer, setting eighteen bricks that represent the Stomas or hymns of praise, with a formula addressed to each, 'thou art' being understood in each case. *Triple praise-song:* the Trivṛit, or nine-verse hymn. *The Shining:* or the impatient, the Moon or the thunderbolt according to Mahîdhara. *Pañchadaṣa:* a form of recitation sacred to Indra as wielder of the thunderbolt; or referring to the days of the waxing and waning of the Moon. *Heaven:* or the Year, according to Mahîdhara; in the former case meaning Prajâpati who is Saptadaṣa or Seventeenfold; the Year being also seventeenfold with twelve months and five seasons. Saptadaṣa is also the name of a Stoma or praise-song in seventeen verses. *Supporter:* the Sun; *Ekaviṃṣa:* the Stoma of twenty-one verses; or the Sun, the twenty-onefold, with 12 months, 5 seasons, 3 worlds, and himself. *Speed:* the Year. *Ashṭâdaṣa:* eighteenfold, with 12 months, 5 seasons, and itself; or the hymn of 18 verses. *Ardour:* or Heat, the Year. *Navadaṣa:* Nineteenfold, with 12 months, 6 seasons, and itself; or the hymn of 19 verses. *Triumphant Onset:* the Year. *Saviṃṣa:* Twentyfold, of 12 months, 7 seasons, and itself; or the hymn of 20 verses. *Vigour:* the Year. *Dvâviṃṣa:* twenty-twofold, with 12 months, 7 seasons, day and night, and itself; or the hymn of 22 verses. *Maintenance:* the Year. *Trayoviṃṣa:* Twenty-threefold; consisting of 13 months (one intercalary), 7 seasons, day and night, and itself, or the hymn of 23 verses. *Womb:* the Year. *Chaturviṃṣa:* Twenty-fourfold, of 24 half-months; or the hymn of 24 verses. *Embryos:* the Year. *Pañchaviṃṣa:* Twenty-fivefold, of 24 half-months and itself; also the hymn of 25 verses. *Energy:* the Year. *Triṇava:* Thrice-ninefold, with 24 half-months, day and night, and itself; meaning also the hymn of thrice-nine verses. *Intention:* the Year. *Ekatriṃṣa:* Thirty-onefold, of 24 half-months, 6 seasons, day and night and itself; also the hymn of 31 verses. *The Basis:* the Year. *Trayastriṃṣa:* Thirty-threefold, of 24 half-months, 6 seasons, day and night, and itself; also the hymn of 33 verses. *The Bright One's Station:* the place of the Sun; the Year. *Chatustriṃṣa:* Thirty-fourfold, consisting of 24 half-months, 7 seasons, day and night, and itself; also the hymn of 34 verses. *The Vault of Heaven:* the Year. *Shaṭtriṃṣa:* Thirty-sixfold, consisting of 24 half-months, and 12 months; also the hymn of 36 verses. *The Revolving One:* the intercalary Year. *Ashṭâchatvâriṃṣa:* Forty-eightfold, consisting of 26 half-months, 16 months, 7 seasons, day and night; also the hymn of 48 verses. *The Support:* Vâyu, the Wind. *Four-divisioned:* a hymn made up of four Stomas, Trivṛit, Pañchadaṣa, Saptadaṣa, and Ekaviṃṣa. This completes the setting of eighteen bricks with eighteen formulas.

24 Thou art the portion of Agni, chief control of Consecration. The Priesthood is saved; the Trivṛit Stoma.
Thou art the portion of Indra, the sovranty of Vishṇu. The Nobility is saved; the Pañchadaṣa Stoma.
Thou art the share of the Man-beholders; the supremacy of the Creator; the birthplace is saved; the Saptadaṣa Stoma.
Thou art the share of Mitra, the sovranty of Varuṇa. Rain of heaven and wind are saved; the Ekaviṃṣa Stoma.

25 Thou art the share of the Vasus, the sovranty of the Rudras. Quadrupeds are saved; the Chaturviṃṣa Stoma.
Thou art the share of the Âdityas; the sovranty of the Maruts. The Embryos are saved; the Panchaviṃṣa Stoma.
Thou art the share of Aditi; the sovranty of Pûshan. Strength is saved; the Triṇava Stoma.
Thou art the share of God Savitar; the sovranty of Bṛihaspati. The universal Quarters are saved; the Chatushṭoma Stoma.

26 Thou art the share of the Yavas; the sovranty of the Ayavas. Creatures are saved; the Chatuṣchatvâriṃṣa Stoma.
Thou art the share of the Ṛibhus; the sovranty of the Viṣvedevas. The Being is saved; the Trayastriṃṣa Stoma.

27 Sahas, Sahasya, the two Winter Seasons—thou art the innermost cement of Agni, etc. (as in XIII. 25).

28 With one they praised; creatures were produced. Prajâpati was over-lord.
With three they praised; the Priesthood was created. Bṛihaspati was over-lord.

---

24 He lays down the bricks called Spṛitas or Deliverers, symbolical of Prajâpati's deliverance, with the help of the Gods, of all beings from death and evil. *Thou:* the first brick. *The portion...chief control:* each God and deified entity that aided the work of deliverance received by agreement a portion and chief control or sovereignty. *Consecration:* here meaning Vâk or Speech. *The Trivṛit Stoma:* 'was the means of deliverance,' being understood. According to Mahîdhara the nominative case is used for the instrumental *trivṛitâ stomena,* by means of the T. S. *Man-beholders:* the Gods. *The birthplace: janitram;* the Vaisya caste, 'the peasantry': Eggeling. The word is almost equivalent to our 'proletariate.'

26 *Yavas:* the first halves of the months when the Moon is waxing. *Ayavas:* the last or dark halves.

27 He lays down two Ṛitavyâs or Seasonal bricks (see XIII. 25). *Sahas and Sahasya:* Force and Forceful; mid-November to mid-January. The rest of the formula is repeated from XIII. 25.

28 He lays down the bricks called Sṛishṭis, or Creations, symbolical of Prajâpati's creation of living beings by the sacrifice of himself. *One.* Vâk, Speech. *They:* the deities of the Vital Airs. *Three:* out-breath, upward breath, diffusive breath. *Five:* four vital breaths and mind. *Seven:* vital airs of the head; ears, eyes, nostrils, voice.

With five they praised; beings were created. The Lord of Beings was over-lord.

With seven they praised; the Seven Ṛishis were created. Dhâtar was over-lord.

29 With nine they praised; the Fathers were created. Aditi was Sovran Lady.

With eleven they praised; the Seasons were created. The Season-Lords were over-lords.

With thirteen they praised; the Months were created. The Year was over-lord.

With fifteen they praised; the Nobility was created. Indra was over-lord.

With seventeen they praised; domestic animals were created. Bṛihaspati was over-lord.

30 With nineteen they praised; Ṣûdra and Ârya were created. Day and Night were Sovran Ladies.

With twenty-one they praised; solid-hoofed animals were created. Varuṇa was over-lord.

With twenty-three they praised; small animals were created. Pûshan was over-lord.

With twenty-five they praised; forest animals were created. Vâyu was over-lord.

With twenty-seven they praised; earth and heaven came apart. Vasus, Rudras, Âdityas followed separately, so they were over-lords.

31 With twenty-nine they praised; Trees were created. Soma was over-lord.

With thirty-one they praised; creatures were created. The Yavas and the Ayavas were over-lords.

With thirty-three they praised; living beings were happy. Prajâpati, the Supreme in Place, was over-lord.

Fill up the room, etc. The dappled kine, etc. All sacred songs, etc. Repeated from XII. 14—16.

---

29 *Nine:* seven vital airs of the head and two below. *Eleven:* ten vital airs and the body. *Season-lords:* or Sections of the year. *Thirteen:* ten vital airs, the feet, and the body. *Fifteen:* ten fingers, the fore-arm and upper arms, and the part above the navel. *Seventeen:* ten toes, the thighs and knees and the part below the navel.

30 *Nineteen:* ten fingers and nine vital airs. *Twenty-one:* 20 fingers and toes and the body. *Twenty-three:* the two feet added. *Twenty-five:* fingers, toes, hands, feet, and body. *Twenty-seven:* fingers, toes, arms, thighs, feet, and body.

31 *Twenty-nine:* fingers, toes, and nine vital airs. *Thirty-one:* fingers, toes, ten vital airs, and the body. *Thirty-three:* fingers, toes, ten organs of perception and action, the feet, and the body. *Soma:* as the most excellent of plants, and also as the moon which is believed to influence the growth of trees.

## BOOK THE FIFTEENTH.

DRIVE our born enemies away, O Agni; drive from us foes unborn, O Jâtavedas.
Graciously-minded, free from anger, bless us: may we enjoy thy firm thrice-guarding shelter.

2 Drive off with might our foemen born and living: keep off those yet unborn, O Jâtavedas.
Benevolent in thought and spirit bless us. May we remain alive: drive off our foemen.

3 The Sixteenfold Stoma, strength and wealth. The Forty-fourth Stoma, splendour and wealth.
Apsas art thou, the complement of Agni. As such may all the Gods greet thee with praises.
Enriched with songs of praise, Pṛishṭhas, and butter, sit here and give us wealth with store of children.

4 Course metre. Space metre. Happy metre. Encompassing metre. Covering metre. Mind metre. Expanse metre. River metre. Sea metre. Water metre. Kakup metre. Trikakup metre. Kâvya metre. Aṅkupa metre. Aksharapaṅkti metre. Padapaṅkti metre. Vishṭârapaṅkti metre. Kshurabhrâja metre.

5 Covering metre. Clothing metre. Collecting metre. Parting metre. Bṛihat metre. Rathantara metre. Group metre. Vivadhra metre. Swallower metre. Bright metre. Saṃsṭup metre. Anushṭup metre. Course metre. Space metre. Vigour metre. Vigour-giving metre. Emulating metre. Spacious metre, Inaccessible metre. Slow metre. Aṅkâṅka metre.

---

He begins the fifth layer with the bricks called Asapatnâs, or Free from Enemies; reciting two texts addressed to Agni as he sets one brick in front and one behind.

3 He lays a brick on the right, and addresses it with the formula, 'Thou art' being understood. Then one on the left with *The Forty-fourfold Stoma:* etc. Then one in the middle with 'Thou art the *complement,* etc.' repeated with 'Agni' instead of 'Earth' from XIV. 4.

4 He lays down the Virâj bricks, which are named after that metre, by sets of ten, corresponding to the ten regions of the sky, 'Thou art' being understood before each formula. *Course:* in which all living creatures move, that is, this world. *Space:* the middle air or firmament. *Happy:* the sky. *Encompassing:* the regions. *Covering:* food. *Mind:* Prajâpati. *Expanse:* the Sun. *River:* the breath. *Sea:* mind. *Water:* Speech. *Kakup:* breath. *Trikakup:* upward breathing. *Kâvya:* the three Vedas. *Aṅkupa:* water. *Aksharapaṅkti:* the heavenly world. *Padapaṅkti:* this world. *Vishṭârapaṅkti:* the region or regions. *Ksharabhrâja:* Bright Razor; the Sun.

5 *Covering:* food. *Clothing:* food. *Collecting:* night. *Parting:* day. *Bṛihat:* yonder world. *Rathantara:* this world. *Group:* the wind. *Vivadhra:* (Yoke): the air, *Swallower:* food. *Bright:* fire. *Saṃsṭup* and

6 With the ray for truth quicken thou truth. With advance by duty quicken duty. With following by heaven quicken heaven. With union by middle air quicken middle air. With Pratidhi by Earth quicken Earth. With support by rain quicken rain. With blowing away by day quicken day. With following by night quicken night. With clarified butter by the Vasus quicken the Vasus. With perception by the Âdityas quicken the Âdityas.

7 With the thread by prosperity quicken prosperity. With the creeper by revelation quicken revelation. With refreshment by plants quicken plants. With the best by bodies quicken bodies. With the invigorating by religious study quicken religious study. With the victorious by brilliance quicken brilliance.

8 Thou art Pratipad, for Pratipad thee. Thou art Anupad, for Anupad thee. Thou art Sampad, for Sampad thee. Thou art brilliance, for brilliance thee.

9 Trivṛit (triple) art thou, thee for Trivṛit. Pravṛit art thou, thee for Pravṛit. Vivṛit art thou, thee for Vivṛit. Savṛit art thou, thee for Savṛit. Thou art attack, thee for attack. Thou art concurrence, thee for concurrence. Thou art ascent, thee for ascent. Thou art upstriding, thee for upstriding. With Energy as over-lord quicken food-essence.

10 Thou art the Queen, the Eastern region. The bright Vasus are thine over-lords. Agni is thy warder-off of hostile weapons. May the Trivṛit Stoma assist thee on earth. The Âjya Uktha fix thee firmly against slipping. The Rathantara Sâman establish thee in the sky for secure station. May the first-born Ṛishis extend thee among the

---

*Anushṭup:* food. *Course ..Expanse:* see verse 4. *Vigour:* food. *Vigour-giving:* Agni. *Emulating:* yonder world. *Spacious:* this world. *Cover:* the air. *Inaccessible:* the Sun. *Slow:* the Paṅkti. *Aṅkâṅka:* water.

6 He lays down the bricks called Stoma-bhâgas or Laud-sharers, 29 in number, with a formula addressed to each. *The ray:* the Sun, which as the giver of light is food. *Advance:* meaning food. *By duty:* according to Mahîdhara, in this and the following formulas of this verse the instrumental case is used for the dative; for duty, etc.

7 According to Mahîdhara, *the thread: the creeper: the best:* etc., mean 'food,' and he gives the same meaning to *Pratipad, Anupad,* etc., in the following verse.

9 *Trivṛit:* triple, threefold; food, says Mahîdhara, as produced from ploughing, seed, and rain. He gives similar explanations of the other untranslatable words in the verse.

10 He lays down the Nâkasadas or Sky-seated bricks. *Thou:* the brick laid down in front. *Âjya Uktha:* a litany to Agni. *Ṛishis:* the Vital Airs. *Disposer:* Speech. *Over-lord:* Mind.

Gods by the measure and amplitude of heaven. May this Disposer and the Over-Lord extend thee. May all, concordant, settle thee on the ridge of heaven in the world of Svarga.

11 Thou art Far-ruling, the Southern region. The bright Rudras are thine over-lords. Indra is thy warder-off of arrows. May the Pañchadaṣa Stoma support thee on earth. The Praüga Uktha fix thee firmly against slipping. The Bṛihat Sâman establish thee in the sky, etc. (the rest as in 10).

12 Thou art Universal Ruler, the Western region. The Âdityas are thine over-lords. Varuṇa is thy warder-off of missiles. The Saptadaṣa Stoma support thee on earth. The Marutvatiya Uktha fix thee firmly against slipping. The Vairûpa Sâman establish thee, etc. (as above).

13 Thou art Independent Ruler, the Northern region. (The rest is identical with 12, with the substitution of Maruts ...Soma....Vimṣa Stoma ...Nishkevalya Uktha....Vairâja Sâman for the corresponding names).

14 Thou art Lady-Paramount, the Lofty region. (The rest as above, Viṣvedevas...Bṛihaspati ..Triṇava and Trayastriṃṣa Stomas...Vaiṣvadeva and Mâruta Ukthas...Sâkvara and Raivata Sâmans being substituted for the corresponding names.

15 This one in front, golden-tressed, with sunbeams; the leader of his host and his chieftain are Rathagṛitsa and Rathaujas, and Puñjikasthalâ and Kratusthalâ his Apsarases. Biting animals are his weapon, homicide his missile weapon; to them be homage: may they protect us, may they have mercy upon us. In their jaws we place the man whom we hate and who hates us.

---

11 He lays a brick on the right side. *Far-ruling:* Virâj. *Praüg Uktha:* name of a hymn at the morning libation.

12 He lays a brick behind. *Universal Ruler:* Samrâj. *Marutvatiya Uktha:* a litany to Indra Lord of the Maruts.

13 *Independent Ruler:* Svarâj. *Nishkevalya Uktha:* a litany to Indra exclusively, beginning with Abhi tvâ, Ṣûra, nonuma (R. V. VII. 32. 22).

14 He lays a brick in the middle.

15 He lays the Pañchachûḍâs or Five-crested bricks on the Nâkasadas (10). *This in front:* the brick representing Agni. *Rathagṛitsa and Rathaujas:* Skilled with the Car, and Mighty with the Car; meaning the two Spring months. *Puñjikasthalâ and Kratusthalâ:* allegorical names of Celestial Nymphs representing the region and the sub-region.

16 This one on the right, the Omnific; the leader of his host and his chieftain are Rathasvana and Rathechitra, and Menakâ and Sahajanyâ his Apsarases. Yâtudhânas are his weapon, Râkshasas his missile weapon; to them be homage, etc. (as in 15).

17 This one behind, the All-comprising; the leader of his host and his chieftain are Rathaprota and Asamaratha, and Pramlochantî and Anumochlantî are his Apsarases. Tigers are his weapon, Serpents his missile weapon; to them be homage, etc.

18 This one on the left, Lord of uninterrupted riches; the leader of his host and his chieftain are Târkshya and Arishṭanemi, and Viṣvâchî and Ghṛitâchi his Apsarases. Water is his weapon, wind his missile weapon; to them be homage, etc.

19 This one above, Wealth-giver; the leader of his host and his chieftain are Senajit and Susheṇa, and Urvaṣî and Pûrvachitti his Apsarases. Thundering is his weapon and lightning his missile weapon; to them be homage, etc.

20 Agni is head and height of heaven, the Master of the earth is he. He quickeneth the waters' seed.

21 This Agni is the Master of spoil thousandfold and hundredfold, the sapient one, the head of wealth.

22 Agni, Atharvan brought thee forth by rubbing from the lotus-leaf, the head of Viṣva, of the Priest.

---

16 He sets a brick on the south or right side. *The Omnific:* Viṣvakarman, meaning Vâyu, the Wind. *Rathasvana*: Car-rattling. *Rathechitra:* Glittering on his Car. These two are the two Summer months. *Menakâ and Sahajanyâ:* Celestial Nymphs, representing portions of the sky, or heaven and earth.

17 He sets a brick behind. *All-comprising:* the Sun. *Rathaprota:* Car-seated. *Asamaratha: Peerless-carred:* the two Rain months.

18 He sets a brick on the left side. *Lord of uninterrupted riches:* the sacrifice. *Târkshya* and *Arishṭanemi* (whose fellies are uninjured): both originally personifications of the Sun; meaning here the two Autumn months. *Viṣvâchî and Ghṛitâchî:* representing the quarter and the mid-quarter of the sky.

19 He sets a brick in the middle above. *Wealth-offerer:* Parjanya, God of the Rain-cloud. *Army-conqueror:* or Senajit. *Well-armied:* or Susheṇa. These are the two Winter months. *Urvaṣî and Pûrvachitti:* representing a quarter and a mid-quarter of the sky. For Urvaṣî see R. V. X. 95.

20 He lays down the Chhandasyâs or Metre bricks, and first three bricks representing the Gâyatrî with formulas in that metre. The first formula repeated from III. 12) is taken from R. V. VIII. 44. 16.

21 The formula is taken from R. V. VIII. 64. 4.

22 The formula (repeated from XI. 32 b.) is taken from R. V. VI. 16. 13.

23 Guide of the rite art thou and of the region to which with thine auspicious teams thou tendest.
Thy light-bestowing head to heaven thou liftest, making thy tongue oblation-bearer, Agni.

24 Agni is wakened by the people's fuel to meet the Dawn who cometh like a milch-cow.
Like young trees shooting up on high their branches his flames are rising to the vault of heaven.

25 To him adorable, sage, strong and mighty we have sung forth our song of praise and homage.
Gavishṭhira hath raised with prayer to Agni this laud far-reaching as the gold in heaven.

26 Here by ordainers was this God appointed first Invoker, best at worship, to be praised at rites;
Whom Apnavâna and the Bhṛigus caused to shine bright-coloured in the wood, spreading to every house.

27 The watchful Guardian of the people hath been born, Agni the very strong, for fresh prosperity.
With oil upon his face, with high heaven-touching flame, he shineth splendidly, pure for the Bharatas.

28 Agni, Angirases discovered thee what time thou layest hidden, fleeing back from wood to wood.
Thou by attrition art produced as conquering might, and men, O Angiras, call thee the Son of Strength.

29 Offer to Agni, O my friends, your seemly food, your seemly praise;
To him supremest o'er the folk, the Son of Strength, the Mighty Lord.

30 Thou, mighty Agni, gatherest up all that is precious for thy friend.
Bring us all treasure as thou art enkindled in libation's place.

---

23 He lays down the three Trishṭup bricks with formulas in that metre. The first formula (repeated from XIII. 15) is taken from R. V. X. 8. 6.

24 Taken from R. V. V. 1. 1.

25 Taken from R. V. V. 1. 12. *Gavishṭhira:* the Seer of the original hymn. *The gold:* the Sun.

26 He lays down three Jagatî bricks with formulas in that metre, 48 syllables in a stanza. The first formula is taken from R. V. IV. 7. 1. It has occurred also in III. 15.

27 Taken from R. V. V. 11. 1. *Bharatas:* warriors; or men of a tribe so named; or according to Sâyaṇa and Mahîdhara, the priests.

28 Taken from R. V. V. 11. 6. *Layest hid:* alluding to the flight and capture of Agni. See R. V. I. 65.

29 He lays down three Anushṭup bricks with formulas in that metre. The first formula is taken from R. V. V. 7. 1.

30 The second from R. V. X. 191. 1.

31 O Agni, loved of many, thou of fame most wondrous, in their homes
Men call on thee whose hair is flame to be the bearer of their gifts.

32 With this my reverent hymn I call Agni for you, the Son of Strength,
Dear, wisest envoy, served with noble sacrifice, immortal messenger of all.

33 Immortal messenger of all, immortal messenger of all,
His two red steeds, all-cherishing, he harnesseth: let him, well-worshipped, urge them fast.

34 Let him well-worshipped urge them fast, let him well-worshipped urge them fast.
Then hath the sacrifice good prayer and happy end, and heavenly gift of wealth to men.

35 O Agni, thou who art the Lord of wealth in kine, the Son of Strength,
Vouchsafe to us, O Jâtavedas, high renown.

36 He, Agni, kindled, good and wise, must be exalted in our song:
Shine, thou of many forms, shine radiantly on us.

37 O Agni, shining of thyself by night and when the morning breaks,
Burn, thou whose teeth are sharp, against the Râkshasas.

38 May Agni, worshipped, bring us bliss, may the gift, Blessèd One! and sacrifice bring bliss,
Yea, may our praises bring us bliss.

39 Yea, may our praises bring us bliss. Show forth the mind that brings success in war with fiends, wherewith thou conquerest in fights:

40 Wherewith thou conquerest in fights. Bring down the many firm hopes of our enemies, and let us vanquish with thine aid.

---

31 The third from R. V. I. 45. 6.

32 He lays down three Bṛihatî bricks with formulas in Bṛihatî metre, 8+8+12+8 syllables. The first formula is taken from R. V. VII. 16. 1.

33 The verses of the original hymn (R. V. VII. 16) being alternately Bṛihatî and Satobṛihatî, the second and third verses of this triplet are made up out of verse 2 with the aid of repetitions.

35 He lays down three Ushṇih bricks with a triplet in that metre (8+8+12 syllables) from R. V. I. 79. 4—6.

38 He lays down the three Kakup bricks with a triplet in that metre (8+12+8), verse 1 taken from R. V. VIII. 19. 19, verses 2 and 3 pieced together out of the Satobṛihatî verse 20 of the original hymn, with pâdas repeated as in 33 and 34.

41 I value Agni, that good Lord, the home to which the kine return;
Whom fleet-foot coursers seek as home, and strong enduring steeds as home. Bring food to those who sing thy praise.

42 'Tis Agni whom we laud as good, to whom the milch-kine come in herds,
To whom the coursers swift of foot, to whom our well-born princes come. Bring food to those who sing thy praise.

43 Thou, brilliant God, within thy mouth warmest both ladles of the oil.
So fill us also in our hymns abundantly, O Lord of Strength. Bring food to those who sing thy praise.

44 Agni, with lauds this day may we bring thee that which thou lovest,
Right judgment, like a horse, with our devotions.

45 For thou hast ever been the car-driver, Agni, of noble
Strength, lofty sacrifice, and rightful judgment.

46 Through these our praises come thou to meet us, bright as the sunlight,
O Agni, well-disposed, with all thine aspects.

47 Agni I hold as Herald, the munificent, the gracious Son of Strength who knoweth all that live, as holy singer knowing all;
Lord of fair rites, a God with form erected, turning to the Gods,
He, when the flame hath sprung forth from the sacred oil, the offered fatness, longeth for it with his glow.

48 O Agni, be our nearest Friend, be thou a kind deliverer and a gracious Friend.
Come as good Agni, come as excellent and give us wealth most splendidly renowned.
To thee then, O most bright, O radiant God, we come with prayer for happiness for our friends.

---

41 He lays down the three Paṅkti bricks with formulas in the corresponding metre (8 × 5) taken from R. V. V. 6. 1, 2, 9.

44 He lays down the three Padapaṅkti bricks with formulas in that metre (5 × 5). This 'consists of two lines, the first embracing three or four feet of five syllables each, having the ictus on the first and fourth syllables, and resembling the last line of a Sapphic verse. The second line is simply a Trishṭup.' M. Müller, S. B. E., XXXII. p. xcviii. The triplet of formulas is taken from R. V. IV. 10. 1—3.

47 He lays down an Atichhandas or Hypermeter brick with a formula taken from R. V. I. 127. 1.

48 He lays down three Dvipadâ bricks with a formulary triplet from R. V. V. 24. 1, 2, 4. Cf. III. 25, 26.

49 With what devotion, winning light, the Rishis came, kindling Agni, to the holy session,
Even with that in heaven I stablish Agni whom men call him whose sacred grass is scattered.

50 Gods, let us follow him with wives beside us, with sons, with brothers, with our gold adornments,
Grasping the sky up in the world of virtue, on the third height, the luminous realm of heaven.

51 This Agni mounted up to Speech's Centre, Lord of the Brave, observant, ever-active.
Laid on the back of Earth, may he, resplendent, cast under foot those who would fight against us.

52 May this most manly Agni, strength-bestower, giver of thousands, shine with care that fails not.
Resplendent in the middle of the water, make thine approach to the celestial mansions.

53 Make him go forth from all sides: meet, approach ye. O Agni, make the paths for Godward travel.
Making the Parents young with life's renewal, the out-spun thread in thee have they extended.

54 Wake up, O Agni, thou, and keep him watchful. Wish and fruition, meet, and he, together.
In this and in the loftier habitation be seated, All-Gods! and the Sacrificer.

55 Convey our sacrifice to heaven that it may reach the Gods, with that

---

49 He lays down the Punaschiti (Piling up again), a second layer of eight bricks, on the top of the Gârhapatya or Householder's Hearth. See XII. 45 sqq. The ceremony is performed with eight formulas, six in Trishṭup and two in Anushṭup metre.

51 He lays down the third brick. *Speech's Centre:* the part of the pile in which he is established. *Ever-active: bhuraṇyu;* the world's supporter, according to Mahîdhara.

52 He lays the fourth brick.

53 He lays the fifth brick. *Make him:* he addresses the Rishis. *Make the paths:* according to Mahîdhara the plural verb is used for the singular and refers to Agni. If, as grammar requires, the verb refers to the Rishis, *Agneḥ*, of Agni, must be read instead of *Agne:* 'Make ye Agni's paths to lead to the Gods': Eggeling. *Parents: pitarâ;* meaning Vâk and Manas, Speech and Mind. *Outspun thread:* of sacrifice. *They extended:* the Rishis according to Mahîdhara: but the verb is in the singular: 'in thee hath he spun out this thread': Eggeling.

54 He lays the sixth brick. *Wish and fruition:* the heavenly rewards of pious actions. *He:* the Sacrificer.

55 He lays the seventh brick. The formula is taken from A. V. IX. 5. 17. *With that:* power, understood.

Whereby thou, Agni, bearest wealth in thousands and all precious things.

56 This is thine ordered place of birth whence sprung to life thou shonest forth.

Knowing this, Agni, rise thou up and cause our riches to increase.

57 Tapa, Tapasya, pair of Dewy Seasons: thou art, etc. (as in XIII. 25).

58 On the sky's back may Parameshṭhin lay thee, etc. (as in XIV. 14).

Thy Lord is Sûrya, etc. (as in XIV. 14).

59 Repeated from XII. 54.

60 Repeated from XII. 55.

61 Repeated from XII. 56.

62 Like a horse neighing, eager for the pasture, when he hath stepped forth from the great enclosure:

Then the wind following blows upon his splendour, and, straight, the path is black which thou hast travelled.

63 In Âyu's seat I set thee, in the shadow of the protector in the heart of Ocean,

Thee luminous, bright with eyes, thee who illumest the sky, the earth, and air's broad realm between them.

64 On the sky's back may Parameshṭhin set thee, etc. (as in XIV. 12, substituting sky for air and Sûrya for Vâyu).

65 Thou art the measure of a thousand. Thou art the representative of a thousand. Thou art the equivalent of a thousand. Thou art worth a thousand. Thee for a thousand.

---

56 He lays the eighth brick. The formula, taken from R. V. III. 29. 10, has occurred in III. 14 and XII. 52.

57 He lays two Ritavyâs or Seasonal bricks. See XIII. 25. *Tapa, Tapasya:* January-February, and February-March. *Thou art:* the rest of the formulas as in XIII. 25.

58 He lays down a Visvajyotis or All-light brick. *Parameshṭhin:* the Supreme. The rest is as in XIV. 14, with the substitution of Sûrya for Vâyu.

59 He lays the Lokampriṇâs, Room-filling or Complementary bricks, with the three formulas employed in XII. 54—56.

62 He scatters loose soil over the layer and sets the brick called Vikarnî and the porous or Svayamâtṛiṇṇâ. The Vikarṇî with the formula taken from R. V. VII. 3. 2.

63 The Svayamâtṛiṇṇâ with the following formula. *Ayu's:* of Vital Power, or of the Sun.

65 He stands by the Altar and consecrates it by scattering over it a thousand bits of gold, two hundred at the recitation of each formula. *Measure of a thousand:* bricks. *Thee:* I sprinkle. *For a thousand:* for the attainment of countless benefits.

## BOOK THE SIXTEENTH.

HOMAGE be paid unto thy wrath, O Rudra, homage to thy shaft: to thy two arms be homage paid.

2 With that auspicious form of thine, mild, Rudra! pleasant to behold,
Even with that most blessèd form, look, Mountain-haunter! here on us.

3 The shaft which, Mountain-haunter, thou art holding in thy hand to shoot,
Make that auspicious, Mountain-Lord! Injure not man nor moving thing.

4 O Dweller on the Mountain, we salute thee with auspicious hymn;
That all, yea, all our people may be healthy and well-satisfied.

5 The Advocate, the first divine Physician, hath defended us.
Crushing all serpents, drive away all Yâtudhânis down below.

6 That most auspicious One whose hue is coppery and red and brown,
And those, the Rudras who maintain their station in the regions, who surround him in a thousand bands, of these we deprecate the wrath.

7 May he who glides away, whose neck is azure, and whose hue is red,
He whom the herdsmen, whom the girls who carry water have beheld, may he when seen be kind to us.

8 Homage to him the Azure-necked, the thousand-eyed, the bountiful,
Yea, and his spirit ministers—to them I offer reverence.

---

This Book consists of the Ṣatarudriya, a litany, accompanying 425 oblations, addressed to the hundred Rudras, or the hundred forms and powers of Rudra representing life and nature in their more terrible phases. Agni, that is, the Fire-altar, has on completion become Rudra, and this ceremony is performed to avert his wrath and secure his favour. The Taittirîya recension of the text—which has been regarded as a special Upanishad, or treatise on esoteric religious doctrine—has been translated and annotated by Prof. A. Weber, Indische Studien, II. pp 14 ff., and the White Yajurveda text has been transliterated and translated by J. Muir, Original Sanskrit Texts, IV. pp. 322—331. There is also a complete translation of the formulas in Sacred Books of the East, XLIII. pp. 150—155.

2 *Auspicious form:* the God having two forms, one terrific and the other gentle and auspicious.

5 *Hath defended us:* 'May he plead for us': Eggeling. *Yâtudhânis:* sorceresses, or female goblins.

7 *He who glides away:* in the form of the Sun. *Whose neck is azure:* from drinking up the world-destroying poison produced at the Churning of the Ocean by the Gods.

9 Loosen thy bowstring, loosen it from thy bow's two extremities,
And cast away, O Lord Divine, the arrows that are in thy hand.

10 Now stringless be Kapardin's bow, his quiver hold no pointed shaft.
The shafts he had have perished and the sheath that held his sword is bare.

11 Thy weapon, O Most Bountiful, the bow that resteth in thy hand,—
With that, deprived of power to harm, protect thou us on every side.

12 So may the arrow of thy bow, in all directions, pass us by,
And in a place remote from us lay thou the quiver that thou hast.

13 Having unbent thy bow O thou hundred-eyed, hundred-quivered One!
And dulled thy pointed arrows' heads, be kind and gracious unto us.

14 To thy fierce weapon, now unstrung, be reverent obeisance paid.
Homage be paid to both thine arms, and to thy bow be reverence!

15 Do thou no injury to great or small of us, harm not the growing boy, harm not the full-grown man.
Slay not a sire among us, slay no mother here, and to our own dear bodies, Rudra! do no harm.

16 Harm us not in our seed or in our progeny, harm us not in our life or in our cows or steeds.
Slay not our heroes in the fury of their wrath. We with oblations ever call on only thee.

17 Homage to the golden-armed leader of hosts, lord of the regions, to the trees with their green tresses, to the Lord of beasts be homage; homage to him whose sheen is like green grass, homage to the radiant Lord of paths, homage to the golden-haired wearer of the sacrificial cord, homage to the Lord of the well-endowed.

---

10 *Kapardin:* he whose hair is coiled and braided; an epithet in the Rigveda of Pûshan as well as of Rudra.

15, 16 are taken, with variations, from R. V. I. 114. 7, 8.

17 *Lord of beasts:* either originally regarded as the protector of grazing cattle which are specially exposed to the fury of the Storm-God, or as the lord of sacrificial victims, as Prof. Weber thinks must be the explanation. *Well-endowed* : or, physically, 'full-fed' (Muir); 'strong-bodied': Eggeling.

18 Homage to the brown-hued piercer, to the Lord of food be homage. Homage to Bhava's weapon, homage to the Lord of moving things! homage to Rudra whose bow is bent to slay, to the Lord of fields homage, homage to the charioteer who injures none, to the Lord of forests be homage.

19 Homage to the red architect, to the Lord of trees homage! Homage to him who stretched out the earth, to him who gives relief be homage. Homage to the Lord of Plants, homage to the prudent merchant! Homage to the Lord of bushes, to the shouting Lord of foot-soldiers who makes foes weep be homage.

20 Homage to the runner at full stretch, to the Lord of ministering spirits, homage! Homage to the conquering, piercing Lord of assailing bands, homage to the towering sword-bearer, to the Lord of thieves homage! Homage to the gliding robber, to the roamer, to the Lord of forests homage!

21 Homage to the cheat, to the arch-deceiver, to the Lord of stealers homage! Homage to the wearer of sword and quiver, to the Lord of robbers homage! Homage to the boltarmed homicides, to the Lord of pilferers homage! Homage to the sword-bearers, to those who roam at night, to the Lord of plunderers homage!

22 To the turban-wearing haunter of mountains, Lord of land-grabbers homage! Homage to you who bear arrows and to you who carry bows. Homage to you with bent bows, and to you who adjust your arrows, to you who draw the bow and to you who shoot be homage!

23 Homage to you who let fly and to you who pierce, homage to you who sleep and to you who wake, homage to you who lie and to you who sit, homage to you who stand and to you who run.

24 Homage to assemblies and to you lords of assemblies, homage to horses and to you masters of horses, homage to you hosts that wound and pierce, to you destructive armies with excellent bands be homage.

---

18 *Bhava:* the Existent, or the Eternal; here a name of Rudra.

20 *Thieves...robber:* assuming their forms in sport, says Mahîdhara.

24 *Armies:* or, alternatively, Goddesses, according to Mahîdhara; the feminine participle standing without a noun.

25 Homage to the troops and to you lords of troops be homage.
Homage to the companies and to you lords of companies, homage.
Homage to sharpers and to you lords of sharpers, homage.
Homage to you the deformed, and to you who wear all forms, homage!

26 Homage to armies and to you the leaders of armies, homage.
Homage to you car-borne and to you who are carless, homage.
Homage to the charioteers and to you drivers of horses, homage.
Homage to you the great and to you the small, homage.

27 Homage to you carpenters, and to you chariot-makers homage.
Homage to you potters and to you blacksmiths, homage.
Homage to you Nishâdas and to you Puñjishṭhas, homage.
Homage to you dog-leaders, and to you hunters, homage.

28 Homage to dogs, and to you masters of dogs, homage.
Homage to Bhava, and to Rudra homage, homage to Ṣarva and to Paṣupati, and to Nîlagrîva and Ṣitikaṇṭha, homage.

29 Homage to him with braided hair and to him with shaven hair, homage! homage to the thousand-eyed and to him with a hundred bows, homage!
To the mountain-haunter and to Ṣipivishṭa, homage!
To the most bountiful, armed with arrows, homage!

30 Homage to the short, and to the dwarf, homage, homage to the great and to the adult, homage! Homage to the full-grown and to the growing, to the foremost and to the first be homage.

31 Homage to the swift, and to the active be homage, and to the hasty and to the rapid mover be homage! Homage to him who dwells in waves, and in still waters, to him who dwells in rivers and on islands.

32 Homage to the eldest and to the youngest, to the first-born and to the last-born, homage! Homage to the middle-most and to the immature, to the lowest and to him who is in the depth, be homage!

---

27 *Nishâdas*: men of certain wild aboriginal tribes. *Puñjishṭhas*: fishermen, or fowlers.

28 *Ṣarva*: a name or form of Rudra, of frequent occurrence in the A. V. *Paṣupati*: Lord of Beasts. *Nîlagrîva*: Blue-neck. See verse 7. *Ṣitikaṇṭha*: White-throated.

29 *Ṣipivishṭa*: in the R. V. a name of Vishṇu. See VIII. 55.

33 Homage to Sobhya and to the dweller in the magic amulet, homage! Homage to him who is allied to Yama, to him who prospers be homage! Homage to the famous and to the endmost, to him of the sown corn-land and to him of the threshing-floor be homage.

34 Homage to him in woods and to him in bushes, homage! Homage to him as sound and to him as echo, homage! Homage to him with swift armies and to him with swift chariots, homage! Homage to the hero, and to him who rends asunder be homage.

35 Homage to him who wears a helmet, and to him who wears a cuirass, homage! To him who wears mail and defensive armour, homage! To the renowned one and to him whose army is renowned be homage, to him who is in drums and to him who makes himself known by beating them.

36 Homage to the bold one and to the prudent, homage to him who carries sword and quiver, homage to him who hath keen arrows and is armed with weapons, homage to him who hath good weapons and a good bow.

37 Homage to him who dwells on paths and roads, homage to him who dwells in rugged spots and on the skirts of mountains, homage to him who dwells in water courses and lakes, homage to him who dwells in rivers and meres.

38 Homage to him who dwells in wells and pits, homage to him who dwells in bright sky and sunlight. Homage to him who dwells in cloud and lightning, homage to him who dwells in rain and to him who dwells in fair weather.

39 Homage to him who dwells in wind and to him who dwells in tempest, homage to the dweller in houses and to the house-protector. Homage to Soma and to Rudra, homage to the copper-coloured and to the ruddy One.

40 Homage to the giver of weal, and to Paşupati, homage to the fierce and to the terrific. Homage to him who slays in front and to him who slays at a distance, homage to the slayer and to the frequent slayer, homage to the green-tressed trees, homage to the deliverer.

41 Homage to the source of happiness and to the source of delight, homage to the causer of happiness and to the causer of delight, homage to the auspicious, homage to the most auspicious.

---

33 *Sobhya:* said to mean, dweller in Sobha the City of the Gandharvas. *Magic amulet:* a string bound round the neck or arm with incantations. *Allied to Yama:* in Yama's (death's) power: Eggeling.

42 Homage to him who is beyond and to him who is on this side, homage to him who crosses over and to him who crosses back. Homage to him who is in fords and on river banks, homage to him who is in tender grass and in foam.

43 Homage to him who is in sand and to him who is in running water, homage to him who is on pebbly ground and to him who is where still water stands. Homage to him who wears braided hair and to him whose hair is smooth. Homage to him who is in deserts and to him who is on broad roads.

44 Homage to him who is in herds of cattle and to him who is in cow-pens, homage to him who is on beds and to him who is in houses. Homage to him who is in hearts, and to him who is in whirlpools, homage to him who is in wells and to him who is in abysses.

45 Homage to him who is in dry things and to him who is in green things. Homage to him who is in dust and to him who is in vapour. Homage to him who is in inaccessible places, homage to him who is in creeping plants, homage to him who is in the earth and to him who is in good soil.

46 Homage to him who is in leaves and to him who is in the falling of leaves. Homage to him with the threatening voice and to him who slays, homage to him who troubles and to him who afflicts. Homage to you arrow-makers and to you bow-makers, homage to you sprinklers, to the hearts of the Gods. Homage to the discerners, homage to the destroyers; homage to the indestructible.

47 Pursuer, Lord of Soma juice, thou cleaver, coloured blue and red,
Cleave not, destroy not one of these our children, nor of these our beasts, let nothing that is ours be sick.

48 To the strong Rudra bring we these our songs of praise, to him the Lord of Heroes, with the braided hair,
That it be well with all our cattle and our men, that in this village all be healthy and well-fed.

49 Rudra, with that auspicious form of thine which healeth every day,
Auspicious, healer of disease, be kind to us that we may live.

---

46 *Sprinklers:* senders of rain. *The hearts of the Gods:* meaning, according to Mahîdhara, Agni, Vâyu, and Sûrya; 'the sparkling hearts of the gods': Eggeling.

48 Taken from R. V. I. 114. 1.

50 May Rudra's missile turn aside and spare us, the great wrath of the impetuous One avoid us.
Turn, Bounteous God, thy strong bow from our princes, and be thou gracious to our seed and offspring.

51 Most bounteous, most auspicious, be auspicious, well inclined to us.
On some remotest tree lay down thy weapon, and clad in robe of skin approach, bearing thy bow come hitherward.

52 O Wound averter, purple-hued, to thee be homage, holy Lord!
May all those thousand darts of thine strike dead another one than us.

53 Thousands of thousands are the shafts, the missiles ready in thy hands:
Thou holy Lord, who hast the power, turn thou their points away from us.

54 Innumerable thousands are the Rudras on the face of earth:
Of all these Rudras we unbend the bows a thousand leagues away.

55 Bhavas there are above us in this mighty billowy sea of air,
Of all of these do we unbend, etc.

56 Rudras are dwelling in the sky, whose necks are blue, whose throats are white:
Of these do we unbend the bows a thousand leagues away from us.

57 Ṣarvas haunt realms beneath the earth—their necks are blue, their throats are white:
Of these, etc.

58 Those, green like young grass, in the trees, with azure necks and purple hue,
Of those, etc.

59 Those, ministering spirits' lords, with no hair-tufts, with braided locks,
Of these, etc.

60 Those, the protectors of the paths, bringers of food, who fight for life, Of these, etc.

61 Those who with arrows in their hand, and armed with swords, frequent the fords, Of these, etc.

62 Those who, inhabiting the food, vex men while drinking from their cups, etc.

---

50 Taken from R. V. II. 33. 14.

63 Rudras so many and still more, lodged in the quarters of the sky, etc.

64 Homage to Rudras, those whose home is sky, whose arrows floods of rain.

To them ten eastward, southward ten, ten to the south, ten to the north, ten to the region uppermost!

To them be homage! May they spare and guard us. Within their jaws we lay the man who hates us and whom we abhor.

65 Homage to Rudras, those whose home is air, whose arrows is the rain. To them, etc.

66 Homage to Rudras, those whose home is earth, whose arrows is men's food.

To them be homage, etc.

---

64 *To them:* 'I stretch out' understood. *Ten:* 'fingers' understood. That is, he extends both hands, with the finger tips placed together in sign of adoration to the omnipresent Rudras, towards the four quarters of the sky.

Dr. Muir observes: 'Many of the epithets in this Śatarudriya are not found in other books; and it is difficult, and perhaps of little importance to discover their real sense. Others, as the reader will have observed, are of the most fantastic character.'

## BOOK THE SEVENTEENTH.

THE food and strength contained in stone and mountain, drink gathered from the plants and trees and waters,
That food and strength, Maruts! free-givers, grant us.
In the stone is thy hunger. In me is thy food. Let thy pain reach the man we hate.

2 O Agni, may these bricks be mine own milch kine: one, and ten, and ten tens, a hundred, and ten hundreds, a thousand, and ten thousand a myriad, and a hundred thousand, and a million, and a hundred millions, and an ocean middle and end, and a hundred thousand millions, and a billion.
May these bricks be mine own milch-kine in yonder world and in this world.

3 Ye are the Seasons, strengthening Law, fixed in due season, strengthening Law,
Called Splendid, dropping butter down and honey, yielders of every wish, imperishable.

4 With the lake's mantling need we robe thee, Agni: to us be purifying and auspicious.

5 With cold's investing garb we gird thee, Agni: to us be purifying and auspicious.

---

After the performance of the Ṣatarudriya Oblation, propitiatory and preparatory ceremonies in connexion with Agni and the Fire-altar are continued in this Book.

First he sprinkles the altar with water from a pitcher, beginning from a stone which he has placed at the junction of the right wing of the altar with the body.

1 *In the stone:* he puts the pitcher on the stone which represents Agni. According to Mahīdhara, *aṣman* (rock, stone) here means 'eater,' the devouring Fire. *In me:* he takes up the pitcher. *Thy pain:* the fiery heat and attendant suffering. Here, having put the stone in the pitcher, he throws it southward.

2 He takes possession of the bricks of the altar, stretching over it and touching as much of it as he can. *An ocean:* a fantastic name for a thousand million.

3 *Ye:* the bricks.

4 He draws a frog, an Avakā (Blyxa Octandra, a water-weed), and a shoot of bamboo, all emblems of coolness, eastward along the right part of the body of the altar. See R. V. X. 16. 14.

5 He draws them along from the south to the north hip of the altar.

6 Descend upon the earth, the reed, the rivers : thou art the gall, O Agni, of the waters.
With them come hither, female Frog, and render this sacrifice of ours bright-hued, successful.

7 This is the place where waters meet; here is the gathering of the flood.
Let thy shaft burn others than us : be thou cleanser, propitious unto us.

8 O Agni, purifier, God, with splendour and thy pleasant tongue
Bring hither, and adore, the Gods.

9 So, Agni, purifying, bright, bring hither to our sacrifice,
To our oblation bring the Gods.

10 He who with purifying, eye-attracting form hath shone upon the earth as with the light of Dawn;
Who speeding on, as in the fleet steed's race, in fight, cometh untouched by age, as one athirst in heat.

11 Obeisance to thy wrath and glow! Obeisance to thy fiery flame!
Let thy shot missiles burn others than us : be thou cleanser, propitious unto us.

12 To him who dwells in man, Hail! To him who dwells in waters, Hail!
To him who dwells in sacred grass, Hail! To him who dwells in the wood, Hail! To him who finds the light, Hail!

---

6 He draws them along from the north hip to the south shoulder of the altar. *Gall:* meaning heat, which is regarded as characteristic of the bilious humour.

7 He draws then along from the north to the south shoulder.

8 He draws them over the right wing of the altar. The formula is taken from R. V. V. 26. 1.

9 He draws them over the tail of the bird-shaped altar, with the formula from R V. VI. 15. 5.

10 *Fleet steed's:* or Etaṣa's, one of the horses of the Sun.

11 The Adhvaryu takes chips of gold and a mixture of clarified butter and honey, with a bunch of Kuṣa grass, and mounts the altar reciting the formula addressed to Agni.

12 Mounted on the altar he offers an oblation, on the chief Porous brick, of clarified butter taken in five ladlefuls, pronouncing five formulas. *Who dwells in man:* Agni. seated as vital breath in human beings. *Hail!: vet*, a sacrificial exclamation of unknown derivation, somewhat similar to *vashat*. *In waters:* in the shape of submarine fire, according to Mahidhara. *In sacred grass:* in the shape of the Âhavanlya fire. *In the wood:* in the trees which he penetrates and consumes. *The light:* or heaven, in the form of the Sun.

13 Worshipful Gods of Gods who merit worship, those who sit down beside their yearly portion,
Let them who eat not sacrificial presents drink in this rite of honey and of butter.

14 Those Gods who have attained to Godhead over Gods, they who have led the way in this our holy work,
Without whose aid no body whatsoever moves, not on heaven's heights are they, nor on the face of earth.

15 Giver of breath, of out-breath, breath diffusive, giver of lustre, giving room and freedom,
Let thy shot missiles burn others than us : be thou cleanser, propitious unto us.

16 May Agni with his sharpened blaze cast down each fierce devouring fiend.
May Agni win us wealth by war.

17 He who sate down as Hotar priest, the Ṛishi, our Father offering up all things existent—
He, seeking with his wish a great possession, came among men on earth as archetypal.

18 What was the place whereon he took his station ? What was it that upheld him ? What the manner,
Whence Viṣvakarman, seeing all, producing the earth, with mighty power disclosed the heavens ?

---

13 He sprinkles the altar, the enclosing stones, and outside them, with sour curds, honey, clarified bulter, and Kuṣa grass, reciting two formulas. *Worshipful Gods:* in the shape of the Vital Airs, who are not eaters of oblations.

14 *Holy work: brahman;* according to Mahîdhara, Agni is intended. *No body...moves:* 'no dwelling-place becometh pure': Eggeling. *Not on heaven's height, etc.:* that is, the Vital Airs, although deities, exist in living creatures only.

15 He descends from the altar, and recites the formula addressed to Agni.

16 He goes to the sacrificial hall and offers clarified butter taken in five ladlefuls in the Hall-Door Fire, with the formula taken from R. V. VI. 16. 28:

17 He offers clarified butter in a ladle filled with sixteen spoonfuls, in two oblations, with eight formulas for each. and the formula of verse 16. The verses 17-23 are taken from R. V. X. 81. *He who sate down:* Viṣvakarman, the Omnific, the universal Father and Generator, the Architect of the worlds and Cretor of all things, here identified with Prajâpati, Agni the Fire-altar. *All things existent:* regarded as contained in the offerings presented by Viṣvakarman. *His wish:* his desire to create. *Archetypal:* the meaning of *prathamachhad* is uncertain ; 'first investing ( Agni with the worlds )', according to Sâyaṇa's explanation; 'first appearing' : Ludwig ; 'first worshipper' : Wallis.

19 He who hath eyes on all sides round about him, a mouth on all sides, arms and feet on all sides,
He the sole God, producing earth and heaven, weldeth them with his arms as wings together.

20 What was the tree, what wood in sooth produced it, from which they fashioned out the earth and heaven?
Ye thoughtful men, inquire within your spirit whereon he stood when he established all things.

21 Thine highest, lowest sacrificial natures, and these thy midmost here, O Viṣvakarman,
Teach thou thy friends at sacrifice, O Blessèd, and come thyself, exalted, to our worship.

22 Bring those, thyself exalted with oblation, O Viṣvakarman, Earth and Heaven to worship.
Let enemies around us live in folly: here let us have a rich and liberal patron.

23, 24 = VIII. 45, 46.

25 The Father of the eye, the Wise in spirit, created both these worlds submerged in fatness.
Then when the eastern ends were firmly fastened, the heavens and the earth were far extended.

26 Mighty in mind and power is Viṣvakarman, Maker, Disposer, and most lofty Presence.

---

19 *Weldeth them*: Cf. R. V. IV. 2. 17; X. 72. 2. *With his arms as wings*: fanning the flame in which the material is smelted. Prof. Ludwig thinks that whirlwinds, produced by the action of hands, feet, and wings, are intended.

20 *They*: the makers of the world, directed by Parameṣvara the Supreme God.

21 *Come thyself*: 'exhilarated, thyself offer up thyself': Muir; 'do thou sacrifice to thyself delighting thyself': Wallis. According to Mahidhara, the meaning is that man is incompetent to worship the Creator, that is, in his forms, and that the worship must be performed by the Creator himself.

22 Bring......*Earth and Heaven to worship*: or, sacrifice to them.

23, 24 = VIII. 45, 46.

25 This and the following six verses are taken from R. V. X. 81. *The father of the eye*: Viṣvakarman, who made the light which enables the eye to see. *Submerged in fatness*: Sāyaṇa explains *ghritām* here by 'water':—'engendered the water, (and then) these two (heaven and earth) floating (on the waters).' – Wilson.

26 *Most lofty Presence*: literally, the highest apparition; the highest image or object of spiritual contemplation. *Their offerings*: the offerings, or perhaps the wishes, of the Fathers, semi-personified. *The Seven Rishis*: the great Rishis Marichi, Atri, Angiras, Pulastya, Pulaha, Kratu, and Vasishtha. The meaning is that the spirits of the blest enjoy the fulfilment of all their desires beyond the starry heavens where the One Being, the great Creator, dwells.

Their offerings joy in rich juice where they value One, only One beyond the Seven Ṛishis.

27 Father who made us, he who, as Disposer, knoweth all races and all things existing,
Even he alone, the Deities' name-giver,—him other beings seek for information.

28 To him in sacrifice they offered treasures,—Ṛishis of old, in numerous troops, as singers,
Who, in the distant, near, and lower region, made ready all these things that have existence.

29 That which is earlier than this earth and heaven, before the Asuras and Gods had being,—
What was the germ primeval which the waters received where the first Gods beheld each other?

30 The waters, they received that germ primeval wherein the Gods were gathered all together.
It rested set upon the Unborn's navel, that One wherein abide all things existing.

31 Ye will not find him who produced these creatures: another thing hath risen up among you.
Enwrapt in misty cloud, with lips that stammer, hymn-chanters wander and are discontented.

32 First was the God engendered, Viṣvakarman: then the Gandharva sprang to life as second.
Third in succession was the plants' begetter: he laid the waters' germ in many places.

33 Swift, rapidly striking, like a bull who sharpens his horns, terrific, stirring up the people,
With eyes that close not, bellowing, Sole Hero, Indra subdued at once a hundred armies.

---

27 *For information:* to learn who is the Supreme God; or what their several functions are.

28 *Distant, near, and lower region:* meaning, apparently, the heavenly, the earthly, and the intermediate atmosphere.

30 *The Unborn*, Aja, seems here to be identified with Viṣvakarman. See *Vedic India*, pp. 423, 424.

31 *Another thing:* meaning, according to the Commentator, 'Viṣvakarman is a different entity from you who are sentient beings, who have individual consciousness, and so forth.'—See editor's note in Wilson's translation. *Enwrapt*, etc.: You who are engaged in the enjoyments of this world or the next, being subject to false knowledge or ignorance, have no knowledge of the Truth. See The Hymns of the R. V. and the authorities referred to in the note on the passage.

32 *The Gandharva:* the Sun, that is, Agni. *The plants' begetter:* Parjanya, the God of the Rain-cloud.

33 This verse and the eleven that follow are taken from R. V. X. 103, which is a prayer to Indra for aid and victory in battle.

34 With him loud-roaring, ever watchful, Victor, bold, hard to overthrow, Rouser of battle,
Indra the Strong, whose hand bears arrows, conquer, ye warriors, now, now vanquish in the combat.

35 He rules with those who carry shafts and quivers, Indra who with his band brings hosts together,
Foe-conquering, strong of arm, the Soma-drinker, with mighty bow, shooting with well-laid arrows.

36 Bṛihaspati, fly with thy chariot hither, slayer of demons, driving off our foemen.
Be thou protector of our cars, destroyer, victor in battle, breaker-up of armies.

37 Conspicuous by thy strength, firm, foremost fighter, mighty and fierce, victorious, all-subduing,
The Son of Conquest, passing men and heroes, kine-winner, mount thy conquering car, O Indra.

38 Cleaver of stalls, kine-winner, armed with thunder, who quells an army and with might destroys it,—
Follow him, brothers! quit yourselves like heroes, and like this Indra show your zeal and courage.

39 Piercing the cow-stalls with surpassing vigour, Indra, the pitiless Hero, wild with anger,
Victor in fight, unshaken and resistless,—may he protect our armies in our battles.

40 Indra guide these: Bṛihaspati precede them, the guerdon, and the sacrifice, and Soma;
And let the banded Maruts march in forefront of heavenly hosts that conquer and demolish.

41 Ours be the potent host of mighty Indra, King Varuṇa, and Maruts, and Âdityas.
Uplifted is the shout of Gods who conquer, high-minded Gods who cause the worlds to tremble.

42 Bristle thou up, O Bounteous Lord, our weapons: excite the spirits of my warring heroes.
Urge on the strong steeds' might, O Vṛitra-slayer, and let the din of conquering cars go upward.

43 May Indra aid us when our flags are gathered: victorious be the arrows of our army.
May our brave men of war prevail in battle. Ye Gods protect us in the shout of onset.

---

40 *Guide these:* be the leader of our troops. *The guerdon:* the reward of the priests who perform the sacrifice offered before battle.

43 *When our flags are gathered:* 'apparently comparable with the signis collatis of the Romans': Ludwig.

44 Bewildering the senses of our foemen, seize thou their bodies and depart, O Apvâ.
Attack them, set their hearts on fire and burn them: so let our foes abide in utter darkness.

45 Loosed from the bowstring fly away, O Arrow, sharpened by our prayer.
Go to the foemen, strike them home, and let not one of them escape.

46 Advance, O heroes, win the day. May Indra be your sure defence.
Exceeding mighty be your arms, that none may wound or injure you.

47 That army of our enemies, O Maruts, that comes against us with its might, contending,
Meet ye and wrap it in unwelcome darkness so that not one of them may know another.

48 There where the flights of arrows fall like boys whose locks are yet unshorn,
May Indra, may Bṛihaspati, may Aditi protect us well, protect us well through all our days.

49 Thy vital parts I cover with thine armour: with immortality King Soma clothe thee.
Varuṇa give thee what is more than ample, and in thy triumph may the Gods be joyful.

50 Worshipped with butter, Agni, lead this man to high preëminence.
Vouchsafe him growth of riches and multiply him with progeny.

---

44 *Apvâ:* according to Sâyaṇa, a female deity who presides over sin; according to Mahîdhara, sickness or fear. Apparently Apvâ was a sort of colic, or dysentery, likely to attack soldiers in the field of battle. *And depart:* or, pass us by; do not attack us.

45 Taken from R. V. VI. 75. 16.

46 Taken from R. V. X. 103. 13.

47 Taken from A. V. III. 2. 6.

48 This and the following verse are taken from R. V. VI. 75. 17, 18. *Like boys*, etc.: 'the point of the comparison is not very obvious, but it may mean that the arrows fall where they list, as boys before they are left with the lock of hair, before the religious tonsure, play about wherever they like.': Wilson. Prof. von Roth separates *viśikhâ* from *kumârâ*, and translates: 'where the arrows fly, young and old': that is, feathered and unfeathered.

49 *Thy vital parts:* the *varman*, or coat of mail, protected the shoulders, back, chest, and lower parts of the body. If not made of metal, it was strengthened with metal of some kind.

50 He puts three logs of Udumbara wood on the fire, with a formula for each.

51 Indra, lead him to eminence : controller of his foes be he.
Vouchsafe him lustre : let him give their sacred portions to the Gods.

52 The man within whose house we pay oblation, Indra, prosper him.
May the Gods bless and comfort him, they and this Brahmaṇaspati.

53 May the All-Gods, O Agni, bear and lift thee upward with their thoughts.
Fair to be looked on, rich in light, be thou propitious unto us.

54 May the Five Regions guard, divine, our worship, Goddesses chasing lack of thought and hatred,
Giving the Sacrificer growth of riches. Let sacrifice be based on growth of riches.

55 Inspirited above enkindled Agni, adorable, winged with hymns, was it accepted,
When the Gods offered sacrifice with viands, circling the heated caldron, paying worship.

56 Lord of a hundred draughts, benign, God-serving—to him divine, establisher, protector,
The Gods approached the sacrifice, encircling. Gods for the Gods stood fain for sacred service.

57 When the fourth sacrifice reaches the oblation, accepted offering which hath been made ready, fit for the Immolator's sacrificing,
Thence bless us prayers and holy recitations !

58 Savitar, golden-hued, hath lifted eastward, bright with the sunbeams, his eternal lustre,
He at whose furtherance wise Pûshan marches surveying all existence like a herdsman.

---

52 *This Brahmaṇaspati:* or Bṛihaspati, Lord of Prayer, who is specially present.

53 The Pratiprasthâtar lifts up a kindled log of fuel representing Agni. The text has occurred in XII. 31.

54 He goes forward to the altar.

55 *Inspirited:* 'glorifying' : Eggeling. The meaning of the verse is obscure.

56 *Lord of a hundred draughts:* Agni, worshipped with countless libations.

57 *Fourth sacrifice:* coming after the muttering of formulas, the recitation of sacred praise-verses, and the Apratiratha or Irresistible hymn (verses 33--44. Prof. Eggeling remarks with reason that 'these verses are rather enigmatical.'

58 Taken from R. V. X. 139. 1. Savitar, the Impeller, the Sun as a form of Agni.

59 He sits, the measurer, in the midst of heaven, filling the two world-halves and air's mid-region.
He looks upon the rich far-spreading pastures between the eastern and the western limit.

60 Steer, Sea, Red Bird with strong wings, he hath entered the dwelling-place of the Primeval Father.
A gay-hued Stone set in the midst of heaven, he hath gone forth and guards the air's two limits.

61 All sacred songs have glorified Indra expansive as the sea,
The best of warriors borne on cars, the Lord, the Very Lord of strength.

62 May God-invoking sacrifice bring the Gods hitherward to us.
May bless-invoking sacrifice bring the Gods hitherward to us.
May Agni, God, make offering and hither bring the Gods to us.

63 May the abundant growth of wealth with elevation lift me up,
And with his subjugating power may Indra keep my foemen down.

64 Upraising and depression and devotion may the Gods increase.
May Indra, too, and Agni drive my foes away to every side.

65 Go ye by Agni to the sky bearing the Ukhya in your hands.
Reaching the heights of sky and heaven stay intermingled with the Gods.

66 Agni, go forward to the eastern region, well-skilled, be here the fire in front of Agni.
Illuming all the quarters, shine with splendour : supply with food our quadrupeds and bipeds.

---

59 He sets up a stone of various bright colours, representing the Sun, and recites the text from R. V. X. 139. 2. *The measurer:* reaching both ends of the firmament. The original text has 'man-viewing.' *Pastures:* there is no substantive in the text. Sâyaṇa supplies 'quarters of space'; Mahîdhara 'altars'; Prof. Ludwig 'ladles'; Prof. Grassmann 'pastures.' 'He scans the all-reaching, the butter-reaching,' meaning the offering-ladles and the offering-grounds : Eggeling.

60 Taken from R. V. V. 47. 3. *Steer:* mighty. *Sea:* as the attracter and receptacle of waters. *Primval Father:* Dyaus or Heaven.

61 They all go to the altar, with the text (repeated from XII. 56) taken from R. V. I. 11. 1.

63 *May. . . lift:* so Mahîdhara. 'Hath upheaved' : Eggeling.

64 *Upraising:* of us. *Depression:* of our foes. *Devotion:* expressed in sacrifice.

65 They mount the altar. *Ukhya:* the fire contained in the pan.

67 From earth to air's mid-region have I mounted, and from mid-air ascended up to heaven.
From the high pitch of heaven's cope I came into the world of light.

68 Mounting the sky they look not round: they rise to heaven through both the worlds—
Sages who span the sacrifice that pours its stream on every side.

69 Foremost of those who seek the Gods come forward, thou who art eye of Gods and men, O Agni.
Accordant with the Bhṛigus, fain to worship, to heaven in safety go the Sacrificers.

70 Night and Dawn, different in hue, accordant, etc., as in XII. 2.

71 O Agni, thousand-eyed and hundred-headed, thy breaths are hundred, thy through-breaths a thousand.
Thou art the Lord of thousandfold possessions. To thee, for strength, may we present oblation.

72 Thou art the Bird of goodly wing: be seated on the ridge of earth.
Fill air's mid-region with thy glow, supporting with thy light the sky, confirm the quarters with thy sheen.

73 Receiving offerings, fair of aspect, eastward be duly seated in thy place, O Agni.
In this the more exalted habitation be seated All-Gods and the Sacrificer.

74 That wondrous all-mankind-embracing favour of Savitar, choice-worthy, I solicit,
Even his which Kaṇva wont to milk, the mighty, the teeming Cow who yields a thousand milk-streams.

---

67 The Sacrificer speaks, reciting three verses from A. V. IV. 14. 3—5. *Air's mid-regiver*: the firmament. *Heaven*: above the sky. *Heaven's cope*: a still higher region. *World of light*: the abode of the Sun, the empyrean. See M. Müller, Vedic Hymns, Part I. p. 9; and Zimmer, Altindisches Leben, p. 358.

68 *Look not round*: do not regard their sons, cattle, etc.

69 *Bhṛigus*: see I. 18; III, 15.

70 He offers an oblation of milk drawn from a black cow with a white calf (representing Night and the Sun), with the text taken, with variations, from R. V. I. 96. 5.

71 *Thousand-eyed*: his eyes are the chips of gold; see XVII. 11. *Hundred-headed*: identified with the hundred-headed Rudra. See Śatapatha-Brāhmaṇa, IX. 1. 1. 6.

72 He lays down the fire and recites two formulas addressed to Agni.

73 *Thy place*: the fire-altar. *More exalted habitation*: heaven.

74 He puts on the fire three pieces of fuel, of Śamī, Vaikaṅkata, and Udumbara wood respectively, with a formula for each. *Kaṇva*: a famous Vedic Ṛishi.

75 May we adore thee in thy loftiest birth place, Agni ! with praise-songs in thy lower station.
The place whence those hast issued forth I worship. In thee, well kindled, have they paid oblations

76 Shine thou before us, Agni, well enkindled, with flame, most youthful God, that never fadeth.
Unceasing unto thee come sacred viands.

77 Agni, this day with lauds, etc., as in XV. 44.

78 I dedicate the thought with mind and butter so that the Gods may come who love oblation, strengthing Law,
To Viṣvakarman, Lord of all the earth, I offer up day after day the inviolable sacrifice.

79 Seven fuel logs hast thou, seven tongues, O Agni, seven Ṛishis hast thou, seven belovèd mansions.
Seven-priests in sevenfold manner pay thee worship. Fill full—All-hail to thee !—seven wombs with butter.

80 Purely-Bright, Wonderfully-Bright, Really-Bright, All-Luminous,
Bright, Law's-Protector, Safe-from-Ill ;

81 Such, Other-Looking, Equal, Similar, Measured, Commensurate, Jointly-Bearing-up.

82 Right, Real, Firm, Strong-to-Support, Bearer, Disposer, Manager.

83 Winner-of-Right, Winner-of-Truth, Host-Conquering, Lord-of-Goodly-Host,
Whose-Friends-are-Near-at-Hand, Whose-Banded-Enemies-are-Far-Away :

---

75 The formula is taken from R. V. II 9. 3. *Loftiest birthplace:* heaven, the birthplace of Agni as the Sun. *Lower station:* the firmament, where he is produced as lightning. *The place whence thou hast issued:* the fire-altar.

76 Taken from R. V. VII. 1. 3.

77 He offers with the *sruva* or dipping spoon. The formula is taken from R. V. IV. 10. 1.

78 He offers again to Viṣvakarman, the Omnific Agni. *I dedicate:* or, offer up. *The thought:* of the priests and the sacrificer. The metre is Atijagatī, four divisions of thirteen syllables each.

79 He offers a full oblation with the *sruk* or offering-spoon. *Fuel logs:* said to be the vital breathings. *Seven tongues:* called Kālī Karālī, etc. *Ṛishis:* Marīchi and the rest. See XVII. 26. *Mansions:* Gāyatrī and other sacred metres, or the Āhavanīya, Gārhapatya and other fire-hearths. *Sevenfold fashion:* with the Agnishṭoma (Praise of Agni) and other services. *Wombs:* layers of the altar.

80 After offering the Vaiṣvānara rice-cake to Agni the God of All Men, he offers seven rice cakes to the Maruts (consisting of three or nine troops of seven each) with a formula at each offering containing names or titles of these deities.

84 To day in this our sacrifice be present, Such, Looking-Thus, Same, Similar-in-Appearance,
Measured, Commensurate, Joint-Bearers, Maruts!

85 Self-Powerful, Voracious-One, Kin-to-the-Sun, The House-holder,
Play-Lover, Mighty, Conqueror.
Fierce, Terrible, The Resonant, The Roaring, Victorious, Assailant, and Dispeller, All-Hail!

86 The Maruts, clans divine, became the followers of Indra; as
The Maruts, clans divine, became the followers of Indra, so
May clans divine and human be the Sacrificer's followers.

87 Drink in the middle of the flood, O Agni, this breast stored full of sap, teeming with water.
Welcome this fountain redolent of sweetness. O Courser, enter those thy watery dwelling.

88 Oil hath been mixed: oil is his habitation. In oil he rests: oil is his proper province.
Come as thy wont is. O thou Steer, rejoice thee. Bear off the oblation duly consecrated.

89 Forth from the ocean sprang the wave of sweetness: together with the stalk it turned to Amrit,
That which is holy oil's mysterious title: but the Gods' tongue is truly Amrit's centre.

90 Let us Declare aloud the name of Ghṛita, and at this sacrifice held it up with homage.
So let the Brahman hear the praise we utter. This hath the four-horned Buffalo emitted.

---

86 This is muttered by the Adhvaryu at the end of the offerings to the Maruts.

87 Verses 87—99 in praise of Agni are muttered by the Sacrificer at the dictation of the Adhvaryu, or by the Adhvaryu himself. *Flood:* said to mean the world. *Breast:* the ladle. *Water:* flowing butter.

88 Taken from R. V. II. 3. 11.

89—99 Taken from R. V. IV. 58. a hymn in praise of Ghṛita or Clarified Butter. It would be fruitless, as Prof. Ludwig remarks, to repeat all the various explanations which Sâyaṇa gives of the first line of this stanza: they only show the utter uncertainty of tradition in reference to the passage. For instance, *samudra*, ocean, is said to mean sacrificial fire; or celestial fire; or the firmament; or the udder of the Cow; and *ûrmi*, wave, may accordingly mean reward; or rain; or butter. Prof. Ludwig thinks that the sense of the stanza may be: the life-giving essence which develops itself out of the world-ocean turns into Soma in the Moon; but it is neither of these two, but the tongue of the Gods (Agni?) from which the Amrit proceeds and to which it returns. But see A. Hillebrandt, Vedische Mythologie, I. 321, 322.

90 *The Brahman:* according to Mahîdhara, the *ṛitvij* or priest. Probably Agni is meant. The last half-line of the stanza is translated, after Sâyaṇa,

91 Four are his horns, three are the feet that bear him: his heads are two, his hands are seven in number.
Bound with a triple bond the Bull roars loudly: the mighty God hath entered into mortals.

92 That oil in triple shape the Gods discovered laid down within the Cow, concealed by Paṇis.
Indra produced one shape, Sûrya another: by their own power they formed the third from Vena.

93 From inmost reservoir in countless channels flow down these rivers which the foe beholds not.
I look upon the streams of oil descending, and lo! the Golden Reed is there among them.

94 Like rivers our libations flow together, cleansing themselves in inmost heart and spirit.
The streams of holy oil pour swiftly downward like the wild beasts that fly before the bowman.

95 As rushing down the rapids of a river, flow swifter than the wind the vigorous currents,
The streams of oil in swelling fluctuation like a red courser bursting through the fences.

---

by Professor Wilson: 'the fair-complexioned deity perfects this rite,' the epithet 'four-horned' being transferred to 'Brahman.' The God may be called a *buffalo (gaura)* Bos Gaurus, as a type of extraordinary strength. Mahîdhara explains *gaura* by *yajña*, sacrifice, having four horns, that is, four officiating priests.

91 *Four are his horns:* the four horns of Agni as identified with sacrifice are said by Sâyaṇa to be the four Vedas, and, if identified with Âditya, the four cardinal points. The *three feet* are, in the former case, the three daily sacrifices, in the latter, morning, noon, and evening. The two heads are, in the former case, the *Brahmaudana* and the *Pravargya* ceremonies, in the latter, day and night. Similarly, the *seven hands* are explained, alternatively, as the seven metres of the Veda or the seven rays of the Sun; and the *triple bond* as the *Mantra*, *Kalpa*, and *Brâhmaṇa*, prayer, ceremonial, and rationale of the Veda, or the three regions, heaven, firmament, and earth. *The Steer* is, either as sacrifice or Âditya, the pourer down of rewards, and the loud roaring is the sound of the repetition of the texts of the Veda. Mahîdhara's explanation differs from that of Sâyaṇa. The four horns are priests; or nouns, verbs, prepositions, and particles; the three feet are the Vedas, or the first, second, and third persons, or the past, present, and future tenses; the two heads are two sacrifices, or the agent and object; the seven hands are the metres or the cases of the noun; and the three bonds are the three daily sacrifices, or the singular, dual, and plural numbers.

92 *In triple shape:* as milk, curds, and butter, according to Sâyaṇa. The meaning seems to be that Indra, Surya, and Vena (who is probably Agni), restored the power of the elements of sacrifice respectively in heaven, the firmament, and the earth, after they had been rendered ineffectual for a time by the malignant Paṇis.

93 *The Golden Reed:* Celestial Agni.

96 Like women at a gathering fair to look on and gently smiling, they incline to Agni.
The streams of holy oil attain the fuel, and Jâtavedas joyfully receives them.

97 As maidens deck themselves with gay adornment to join the bridal feast, I now behold them.
Where Soma flows and sacrifice is ready, thither the streams of holy oil are running.

98 Send to our eulogy a herd of cattle: bestow upon us excellent possessions.
Bear to the Gods the sacrifice we offer: the streams of oil flow pure and full of sweetness.

99 The universe depends upon thy power and might within the sea, within the heart, within all life.
May we attain that sweetly-flavoured wave of thine, brought, at this gathering, o'er the surface of the floods.

---

98 *Send to our eulogy a herd of cattle:* this is Sâyaṇa's explanation. The Gods are addressed and prayed to reward the singers.

99 *Thy power:* Agni's. *Within the sea:* in the aerial ocean, the firmament, in which Agni is present as lightning. *Within the heart:* as Vaiṣvânara, belonging to all men. *Within all life:* as the vital principle, or heat. The *wave* is the flowing butter of the oblation.

## BOOK THE EIGHTEENTH.

MAY my strength and my gain, and my inclination and my influence, and my thought and my mental power, and my praise and my fame, and my renown and my light, and my heaven prosper by sacrifice.

2 May my breathing and my out-breathing, and my through-breathing and my vital spirit, and my thought and my reflection, and my voice and my mind, and my eye and my ear, and my ability and my strength prosper by sacrifice.

3 May my energy and my force, and my self and my body, and my shelter and my shield, and my limbs and my bones, and my joints and my members, and my life and my old age prosper by sacrifice.

4 May my preëminence and my overlordship, and my wrath and my angry passion, and my violence and my impetuosity, and my victorious power and my greatness, and my breadth and my width, and my height and my length, and my increase and my improvement prosper by sacrifice.

5 May my truth and my faith, and my cattle and my wealth, and my goods and my pleasure, and my play and my enjoyment, and my children and my future children, and my hymn and my pious act prosper by sacrifice.

6 May my religious rite and my immortality, and my freedom from consumption and my freedom from disease, and my life and my longevity, and my freedom from enemies and my freedom from danger, and my happiness and my lying down, and my fair dawn and my fair day prosper by sacrifice.

7 May my controller and my supporter, and my security and my firmness, and my goods and my pleasure, and my knowledge and my understanding, and my begetting and my propagation, and my plough and my harrow prosper by sacrifice.

---

This Book contains the formulas for the performance of the ceremony called Vasordhârâ, the Stream or Shower of Riches, a sort of Consecration Service for Agni as King on the completion of the Fire-altar which is identified with him. The Sacrificer offers an uninterrupted series of four hundred and one oblations of clarified butter poured from a large ladle of Udumbara wood, while the Adhvaryu recites the formulas which are to gain for the Sacrificer all the temporal and spiritual blessings therein indicated.

8 May my welfare and my comfort, and what I hold dear and what I desire, and my love and my gratification, and my enjoyment and my substance, and my happiness and my felicity, and my higher bliss and my fame prosper by sacrifice.

9 May my vigour and my pleasantness, and my milk and my sap, and my butter and my honey, and my meal in company and my drinking in company, and my ploughing and my husbandry, and my superiority and my preëminence prosper by sacrifice.

10 May my wealth and my property, and my prosperity and my growth, and my pervading power and my lordship, and my abundance and my greater abundance, and my bad harvest and my unwasted crop, and my food and my satiety prosper by sacrifice.

11 May my gain and my future gain, and what I have and what I shall have, and my good road and my good path, and my success and my succeeding, and my achievement and my contrivance, and my thought and my good counsel prosper by sacrifice.

12 May my rice-plants and my barley, and my beans and my sesamum, and my kidney-beans and my vetches, and my millet and my Panicum Milliaceum, and my Panicum Frumentaceum and my wild rice, and my wheat and my lentils prosper by sacrifice.

13 May my stone and my clay, and my hills and my mountains, and my pebbles and my trees, and my gold and my bronze, and my copper and my iron, and my lead and my tin prosper by sacrifice.

14 May my fire and my water, and my creepers and my plants, and my plants with culture-ripened fruit and my plants with fruit ripened without culture, and my domestic animals and my wild animals, and my substance and my future substance, and my belongings and my power be produced by sacrifice.

15 May my treasure and my dwelling, and my religious service and my ability to perform it, and my object and my course, and my way and my going prosper by sacrifice.

16 May my Agni and my Indra, and my Soma and my Indra, and my Savitar and my Indra, and my Sarasvati and my Indra, and my Pûshan and my Indra prosper by sacrifice.

---

12 *Panicum:* there are no English names for the two cereals thus designated. Roxburgh describes sixty-two species of the genus.

16 He offers with this and the two following formulas the Ardhendra or Half-Indra oblations to twelve deities, each of whom is coupled with Indra.

17 May my Mitra and my Indra, and my Varuṇa and my Indra, and my Dhâtar and my Indra, and my Maruts and my Indra, and my All-Gods and my Indra prosper by sacrifice.

18 May my earth and my Indra, and my Air and my Indra, and my Sky and my Indra, and my Half-months and my Indra, and my Lunar Mansions and my Indra, and my Sky-regions and my Indra prosper by sacrifice.

19 May my Aṃṣu and my Raṣmi, and my Adhipati and my Upâṃṣu, and my Antaryâma and my Aindra-Vâyava, and my Maitrâ-Varuṇa, and my Âsvina and my Pratiprasthâna, and my Ṣukra and my Manthin proper by sacrifice.

20 May my Âgrayaṇa and my Vaiṣvadeva, and my Dhruva and my Vaiṣvânara, and my Aindrâgna and my Mahâvaiṣvadeva, and my Marutvatiya and my Nishkevalya, and my Sâvitra and my Sârasvata, and my Pâtnivata and my Hâriyojana prosper by sacrifice.

21 May my ladles and my cups, and my Vâyu vessels and my Soma reservoirs, and my pressing-stones and my two press-boards, and my Pûtabhrit and my Âdhavanîya, and my altar and altar-grass, and my Avabhritha and my cries of Good-speed prosper by sacrifice.

22 May my Agni and my Gharma, and my Arka and my Sûrya, and my Prâṇa and my Aṣvamedha, and my Prithivî and my Aditi, and my Diti and my Sky, and my fingers, powers, and sky-regions prosper by sacrifice.

---

19 Three sets of oblations called Grahas follow with their respective formulas enumerating pairs of Soma cups and sets of sacrificial implements. Most of the Soma cups or libations have been mentioned in VII. 1—39, notes. The names of the sacrificial implements also have occurred in preceding Books.

21 *Cries of Good-speed:* exclamations of Svagâ, a benedictory sacrificial formula.

22 He offers two sets of oblations called Yajñakratus or Sacrificial Rites with formulas enumerating objects connected with certain special ceremonies. *Agni:* the Agnichayana or construction of the Fire-altar, or the Agnishṭoma (Praise of Agni. See VI. 29, note). *Gharma:* the Caldron, representing the Pravargya ceremony. See I. 22. *Arka:* the offering of a cake to Indra with Arka the Sun. *Sûrya:* an oblation to that God. *Prâṇa:* the Gavâmayana or Procession of the Cows (see VIII. 41), a solemn sacrificial session usually of twelve months' duration. *Aṣvamedha:* the Horse-Sacrifice. See XXII—XXV. *Prithivî, Aditi, Diti, Sky:* offerings to these deities; *Diti* being a mere abstraction, the antithesis to Aditi, representing limitation as Aditi represents infinity. See X. 16, note. *Fingers:* explained by Mahîdhara as *virâṭpurushâvayavâḥ*, members of Purusha, Embodied Spirit, or Co[illegible] Man. See R. V. X. 90. *Powers:* *ṣakvariyaḥ = ṣaktayaḥ*, according to [illegible]ıdhara.

23 May my vow and my seasons, and my austere devotion, and my day and night, thighs and knees, and two Great Rathantaras prosper by sacrifice.

24 May my One and my Three, and my Three and my Five, and my Five and my Seven (and similarly up to thirty-three) prosper by sacrifice.

25 May my Four and my Eight and my Twelve (and similarly up to forty-eight) prosper by sacrifice

26 May my eighteen-months steer and my eighteen-months heifer, and my two-year bull and cow (and similarly up to four-year) prosper by sacrifice.

27 May my six-year bull and my six-year cow, and my bull and my barren cow, and my young bull and my calf-slipping cow, and my ox and my milch-cow prosper by sacrifice.

28 To strength, Hail! To Gain, Hail! To After-born, Hail! To Power, Hail! To Vasu, Hail! To the Lord of Days, Hail! To the Failing Day, Hail! To the Failing Sprung from the Transitory, Hail! To the Transitory sprung from the Final, Hail! To the Final Mundane, Hail! To the Lord of the World, Hail! To the Sovran Lord, Hail! To Prajâpati, Hail! This is thy kingdom. Thou art a guiding controller for the friend. Thee for vigour, thee for rain, thee for the sovran lordship of creatures.

29 May life succeed through sacrifice. May life-breath thrive by sacrifice. May the eye thrive by sacrifice. May the ear thrive by sacrifice. May the voice thrive by sacrifice. May the mind thrive by sacrifice. May the self thrive by sacrifice. May Brahma thrive by sacrifice. May light succeed by sacrifice. May heaven succeed by sacrifice. May the hymn thrive by sacrifice. May sacrifice thrive by sacrifice; And laud and sacrificial text, and verse of praise and Sâma chant, The Brihat and Rathantara.

---

24 This formula enumerates the Stomas, or Hymns of Praise consisting of uneven numbers of verses.

25 Enumerates the even-versed Stomas, each number after the first increasing by four.

26, 27 Formulas for two sets of Age Libations, enumerating cattle in advancing stages of their lives.

28 Formulas for the Name Libation ceremony, fanciful names of the months, etc. being applied to Agni of whom the months are manifestations. Cf. IX. 20. *Strength:* meaning March-April. *Gain:* April-May. *After-born:* May-June, and so on. Cp. IX. 20. *Prajâpati:* as Genius of the Year. *The friend:* the Sacrificer. *Thee:* I besprinkle and consecrate.

29 He offers the Kalpa or Success Libation with formulas, containing the verb *klṛip*, to succeed, prosper, thrive, repeated from IX. 21.

Gods, we have gone to light. We have become the children of Prajâpati. We have become immortal.

30 In gain of wealth we celebrate, etc. = IX. 5.

31 This day come all the Maruts, all to aid us! Let all the fires be thoroughly enkindled.
May the All-Gods come hither with protection. May we possess all property and riches.

32 May our strength fill the regions seven, fill the four distant places full.
Here may our riches guard us with the All-Gods in the gain of wealth.

33 May strength to-day procure for us donation: strength range the Gods together with the Seasons.
Yea, strength hath made me rich in store of heroes. As lord of strength may I gain all the regions.

34 Strength be before us, in the midst among us. May strength exalt the Gods with our oblation.
Yea, strength hath made me rich in store of heroes. As lord of strength may I gain all the regions.

35 With milk of Pṛithivî do I unite me, unite myself with waters and with plants.
As such may I gain strength, O Agni.

36 Store milk in earth and milk in plants, milk in the sky and milk in air.
Teeming with milk for me be all the regions.

37 Thee by the radiant Savitar's impulsion, with arms of Aṣvins, with the hands of Pûshan,
Controlled by Vâk Sarasvati's Controller, with Agni's sole dominion I besprinkle.

38 Maintainer of Law, true by nature, Agni is the Gandharva. The plants are his Apsarases, namely Delights. May he protect this our Priesthood and Nobility. To him All-hail! Ave! To those All-hail!

---

30 He offers the fourteen Vâjaprasavîya or Strength-quickening Libations, the first seven of the formulas being repeated from IX. 23-29. Of the second set of seven, one is repeated from IX. 5.

35 *Milk of Pṛithivî*: waters and plants used in sacrifice.

37 He anoints the Sacrificer with the remains of the sacrificial material. *Vâk Sarasvatî's Controller*: meaning Prajâpati, according to Mahîdhara; 'by the support of Sarasvatî Vâk, the Supporter': Eggeling.

38 He offers the twelve Râshṭrabhṛitas or Kingdom-supporting Libations with sacrificial butter taken in twelve ladlings. The offerings are made in pairs, first to a male deity and then to females.

39 The Conjoined, Viṣvasâman, Sûrya is the Gandharva. His motes are his Apsarases, Swift-moving. May he protect, etc., as in 38.

40 The Highly-Blessed, the Moon whose rays are like the Sun's, is the Gandharva. The Asterisms are his Apsarases, Luminous. May he protect, etc.

41 The Quick, All-reaching, Wind is the Gandharva. The Waters are his Apsarases, named Energies. May he protect, etc.

42 The Protecting, Strong-winged, Sacrifice is the Gandharva. Guerdons are his Apsarasea, called Praisers. May he protect, etc.

43 The Lord of Creatures, Omnific, Mind is the Gandharva. Richas and Sâmans are his Apsarases, called Wishings. May he protect, etc.

44 Lord of the World, Prajâpati, whose are the homes above and here,
Give great protection unto these, the Priesthood and Nobility.

45 Thou art the vapoury sea that giveth moisture. Blow on me, thou, healthful and blessing-laden.
Thou art the Maruts' own, the band of Maruts. Blow on me, etc.
Seeker of aid art thou, receiving worship. Blow on me, etc.

46 Thy lights, O Agni, in the Sun, etc., as in XIII. 22.

47 Lights of yours in the Sun, O Gods, etc., as in XIII. 23.

---

39 *Conjoined: saṃhitaḥ;* as joiner of night and day. *Viṣvasâman:* wearing the form of all Sâmans.

40 *Luminous:* or Light-givers; this is Mahîdhara's explanation of the doubtful word *bhekuriyaḥ: bhâm hi nakshatrâṇi kurvanti;* for the constellations make light.

41 *Energies:* or, Viands: Eggeling.

42 *Strong-winged:* as soaring to heaven. *Guerdons:* sacrificial fees; priestly honoraria.

43 *Mind:* Prajâpati is so called as Lord of Speech and Thought.

44 He offers oblation with butter taken in five ladlings on the Head, or fore-part, of the War-chariot as it is held over the Âhavanîya fire. *Prajâpati:* identified with Agni.

45 He offers three Wind Libations, having caught the wind in his hollowed hands from outside the altar. *Sea:* meaning the sky. *The Maruts' own:* the stormy region of mid-air. *Seeker of aid:* 'affording protection': Eggeling; this terrestrial world.

46 He offers nine Lustrous oblations with formulas containing the word signifying light or lustre. Verses 46, 47 are repeated from XIII. 22, 23.

48 Give lustre to our holy priests, set lustre in our ruling chiefs: Lustre to Vaiṣyas, Ṣûdras: give, through lustre; lustre unto me.

49 I ask this of thee with my prayer, adoring: thy worshipper asks this with his oblations.
Varuṇa, stay thou here and be not angry: steal not our life from us, O thou Wide-Ruler.

50 Heaven-like is Warmth, Hail! Heaven-like is Arka, Hail! Heaven-like is the Bright One, Hail! Heaven-like is Light, Hail! Heaven-like is Sûrya, Hail!

51 I yoke with power and flowing butter Agni, divine, strong-pinioned, great with vital vigour.
Through him may we approach the Bright One's station, ascending to the loftiest sky, to heaven.

52 With these thy two ne'er-wasting feathered pinions wherewith thou drivest fiends away, O Agni,
Let us fly to the regions of the pious whither have gone the first-born ancient Rishis.

53 The Drop, the powerful, the falcon, righteous, impetuous bird borne on his golden pinions,
Great, stedfast, settled in the habitation—to thee be reverence! Forbear to harm me!

54 Centre of earth, heaven's head art thou, essence of waters and of plants.
Eternal, far-spread refuge. Homage to the Path!

55 Attached thou standest at the head of all the world. Thy heart is in the sea, thy life is in the floods. Give water: cleave the reservoir.

---

48 *Through lustre:* of thine own.

49 He offers again with a formula addressed to Varuṇa, with whom Agni is now identified, taken from R. V. I. 24. 11.

50 He offers the five Arkâsvamedha-santati oblations, combining the worship of Arka (Agni) and the Sun the deity of the Horse-sacrifice.

51 The three following formulas are for the Agniyojana ceremony, the Yoking or Equipment of Agni, causing the sacrificial fire to blaze up. Before the recitation of the Prâtaranuvâka or Morning-Prayer, (see S. B. E. XXVI. p. 229) he begins the ceremony by handling the midmost of the three enclosing-sticks and reciting the first formula. *Bright One's: bradhnasya;* the Sun's: 'the region of the bay': Eggeling.

52 He touches the right-hand stick.

53 He touches the left-hand stick. *The Drop:* or Indu, here meaning Agni.

54 He now unyokes or frees the altar at the points where the sides of the triangle of enclosing-sticks touch the base, and recites two formulas. *The Path:* the Way that leads to heaven, that is, Agni.

55 *The reservoir:* the receptacle of the waters of heaven. *Parjanya:* the God of the Rain-cloud; here the water-laden cloud.

Help us with rain sent from the sky, Parjanya, firmament, or earth.

56 By Bhrigus and by Vasus hath prayer-granting sacrifice been paid.

Come, Wealth, into the house of him our dear, our well-belovèd one.

57 May Agni, served with sacrifice and gifts, protect our offered food:

This homage be Good-speed to Gods!

58 That which hath flowed from purpose or from judgment, or gathered from the wind or from the vision,

Follow ye to the region of the pious whither have gone the first-born ancient Ṛishis.

59 To thee I trust this man, Celestial Dwelling! treasure which Jâtavedas shall bring hither.

After you will the Sacrificer follow. Here recognize him in the highest heaven.

60 Acknowledge him, ye Gods, in highest heaven. Ye who are present, know the shape he weareth.

When he approacheth by the God-ward pathways, reveal to him the meed of pious actions.

61 Wake up, O Agni, etc., as in XV. 54.

62 Convey our sacrifice to heaven, etc., as in XV. 55.

63 With Darbha-bunch, with fencing-wood, with spoon, with altar, holy grass,

With laud, lead this our sacrifice to go to heaven among the Gods.

64 Our gifts, our charitable grants, our pious works, our fees to priests,

May the Omnific's Agni set all this among the Gods in heaven.

---

56 He makes two offerings called Samishṭayajuses or Final Sacrificial Oblations and formulas. See VIII. 15, note.

57 *Good-speed*: *Svagâ*; see note on verse 21.

58 He offers eight oblations with the dipping-spoon, with a formula for each. *Ancient Rishis*: identified with the Vital Airs. The priests are addressed and told to follow sacrifice, from whatever source it may have originated. to the heaven, where the first-born Ṛishis, the earliest existences, are dwelling.

59, 60 Taken with variations form A. V. VI. 123. 1, 2.

60 *Meed of pious actions*: or full fruition of his wishes; the recompense of sacrifices and good works on earth.

61, 62 Repeated from XV. 54, 55.

63 *Darbha-bunch*: the Prastara (see II. 2) which is placed on the Darbha grass covering the High Altar.

64 *The Omnific's*: that is Agni, or the Fire-altar, that belongs to Viṣvakarman or Prajâpati.

65 There where all never-failing streams of honey and of butter flow,
May Agni, Viṣvakarman's own, place us in heaven among the Gods.

66 Agni am I who know by birth all creatures. Mine eye is butter, in my mouth is nectar.
I am the triple light, the region's meter: exhaustless heat am I, named burnt oblation.

67 Praise-verses, sacrificial texts, and chanted hymns am I in name.
Thou art the best of all the Fires among the fivefold race of man
That burn upon this earth of ours. Speed thou us on to lengthened life.

68 O Indra, for the strength that slays Vṛitra and conquers in the fight
We turn thee hitherward to us.

69 Thou, Indra, much-invoked, didst crush to pieces, Kuṇâru, handless fiend who dwelt with Dânus.
Thou with might, Indra, smotest dead the scorner, the footless Vṛitra as he waxed in vigour.

70 O Indra, beat our foes away, etc, as in VIII. 44.

71 Like some dread wild beast roaming on the mountain thou hast approached us from the farthest distance.
Whetting thy bolt and thy sharp blade, O Indra, crush thou the foes and scatter those who hate us.

72 To aid us let Vaiṣvânara come from the distance far away:
Come Agni, to our eulogies!

73 Sought in the sky, sought on the earth, sought after, all plants that grow on ground hath Agni entered.
May Agni, may Vaiṣvânara with vigour, sought for, by day and night from harm preserve us.

---

66 The Sacrificer, identifying himself with Agni, recites the text taken from R. V. III. 26. 7.

67 He regards himself as an incarnation of the three Vedas. *Praise-verses:* of the Ṛigveda. *Sacrificial texts:* formulas of the Yajurveda. *Chanted hymns:* of the Sâmaveda. *Thou:* Agni, the fire of the completed fire-altar.

68 He reverently approaches the completed fire-altar and recites the following formulary texts the first of which is taken from R. V. III. 37. 1.

69 Taken from R. V. II. 30. 8. *Didst crush:* 'crush thou': Eggeling. *Kuṇdru:* the name of a demon of drought. *Dânus:* a class of fiends. *Scorner:* of the Gods, Vṛitra.

70 Repeated from VIII 44, taken from R. V. X. 152,4.

71 Taken from R. V. X. 180. 2.

74 Help us that we may gain this wish, O Agni, gain riches, Wealthy One! with store of heroes.
Desiring strength from thee may we be strengthened, and win, Eternal! thine eternal glory.

75 Approaching with raised hands and adoration, we have this day fulfilled for thee thy longing.
Worship the Gods with most devoted spirit as Priest with no unfriendly thought, O Agni.

76 Home-hider Agni, Indra, and Brahmâ, and bright Bṛihaspati—
May the All-Gods, one-minded, guard our sacrifice in happy place.

77 Guard thou the Sacrificer's men, O Youthfullest, etc., as in XIII. 52.

---

74 Taken from R. V. VI. 5. 7. *Help us:* literally, With thy help may we gain, etc.

75 Taken from R. V. III. 14. 5.

76 *Home-hider:* that is, who frequently changes his dwelling-place.

For the symbolical meaning of the Agnichayana or Construction of the Fire-Altar representing the restoration of the dismembered Agni-Prajâpati (who takes the place of Purusha, the Cosmic Man, R. V. X. 90), the author, by his great self-Sacrifice, of all creation, so as to enable him to repeat continually the sacrifice of himself and thus maintain or re-create the universe, see Eggeling, S. B. E. XLIII. pp xiii.—xx.

## BOOK THE NINETEENTH.

SWEET with the sweet, I sprinkle thee with Soma, strong with the strong, the nectar with the nectar,
The honey-sweet with what is sweet as honey.
Soma art thou. Get dressed for the Aṣvins. Get dressed for Sarasvati. Get dressed for Indra the Good Deliverer.

2 Hence pour ye forth the flowing juice, Soma, best Sacrificial food.
He who, man's friend, hath run within the waters hath with the pressing-stones poured out the Soma.

3 Purified by Vâyu's strainer, Soma that has passed away forward is Indra's proper friend.
Purified by Vâyu's strainer, Soma that has passed away backward is Indra's proper friend.

4 By means of this eternal sieve may Sûrya's Daughter purify
The Soma that flows forth from thee.

5 Soma with Wine, pressed, filtered for the banquet, cleanses priest, noble, brilliancy and vigour.
God, with the Bright give Deities enjoyment; give food with flavour to the Sacrificer.

---

Books XIX—XXI Contain the formulas of the Sautrâmaṇî, a sacrifice originally instituted to expiate and counteract the evil effects of excessive indulgence in Soma-drinking. See X. 31. The ceremony is prescribed as a means of obtaining general eminence; for a dethroned king to procure his restoration, for a Kshatriya to assure victory, for a Vaiṣya to acquire cattle and wealth. It consists mainly in the offering, to the Aṣvins, Sarasvati and Indra, of Surâ a spirituous liquor concocted of *ṣashpa* (husked rice or young grass), *tokman* (green barley), and *lâja* (parched grain) ground up with some roots to serve as yeast, and the liquor of two Odanas or messes of rice, and Ṣyâmâka or millet boiled in water, the mixture being called Mâsara. The prototype of the sacrifice is the cure of Indra, by Sarasvatî and the Aṣvins, when he was suffering from over-indulgence in his favourite beverage. The name is derived from Sutrâman, the Good Deliverer or Protector, Indra. See Hillebrandt, Ritual-Litteratur, pp. 159—161.

1 *Thee:* O Surâ. *Soma art thou:* he addresses the Surâ which by commixture and transubstantiation has sacrificially become Soma.

2 *He:* Soma. *Waters:* with which the stalks are washed and made to swell. Mahîdhara supplies *adhvaryuḥ* (the Adhvaryu) as the understood nominative of 'poured out'.

3 Cf. X. 31. *Vâyu's strainer:* or cleansing power. *Forward:* rejected through the mouth from the over-loaded stomach.

4 Taken from R. V. IX. *Sûrya's Daughter:* Ṣraddhâ or Faith.

5 *Wine:* Surâ. *The Bright:* Soma juice; 'pure vigour', according to Mahîdhara. *Flavour:* clarified butter, etc.

6 What then? As men whose fields are full of barley, etc., as in X. 32.
Taken upon a base art thou. I take thee for the Asvin Pair, Thee for Sarasvatî. Thee for Indra the Good Deliverer.
This is thy home. For splendour thee. Thee for man's vigour. Thee for strength.

7 For each of you is made a God-appointed place; so grant to me a portion in the highest sphere.
Surâ the strong art thou. This here is Soma. Entering thine own place do me no mischief.

8 Taken upon a base art thou. Splendour of Asvins, Sarasvatî's manly vigour, might of Indra.
This is thy home. I take thee for enjoyment, I take thee for delight, take thee for greatness.

9 Thou art lustre: give me lustre. Thou art manly vigour: give me manly vigour.
Thou art strength: give me strength. Thou art energy; give me energy.
Thou art passion; Give me passion. Thou art conquering might: give me conquering might.

10 May she, Vishûchikâ, who guards these two, the tiger and the wolf,
The lion and the wingèd hawk, may she guard this man from distress.

11 When, a delighted boy, I bruised my mother as I sucked her breast,

---

6 He takes three cups of milk for the Asvins, Sarasvatî, and Indra. The first formula is taken from R. V. X. 131. 2, and repeated from X. 32 of this Veda. *For splendour thee:* the Asvins' cup, 'I take' being understood, *Thee for man's vigour:* Sarasvatî's cup. *Thee for strength;* Indra's cup.

7 *For each of you:* Soma and Surâ. *God-appointed place:* an altar where the libations are prepared, approved by the Deities to whom the offerings are made.

8 He deposits the cups, one by one, with a formula for each.

9 After the libation to the Asvins he throws wheat and pounded fruit of the Jujube tree (Ziziphus Jujuba) into the milk and lays two blades of Darbha grass on the vessel that contains it. *Thou:* the milk libation. *Strength . . . energy . . . passion:* represented respectively by wolf's, tiger's, and lion's hair mixed with the Surâ.

10 He purifies the Sacrificer by stroking him with the tail-feathers of an eagle or hawk once above and once below the waist. *Vishûchikâ:* the deity of cholera or diarrhœa. *Guards:* that is, does not attack. *This man:* the Sacrificer.

11 He makes the Sacrificer look at the fire and recite the text. *Bruised:* with my feet. *Thereby:* by looking at the fire which represents Agni. *United:* this part of the formula is repeated from IX. 4, the plural being substituted for the dual as three cups instead of two are addressed.

Free from my debt, O Agni, I become thereby. My parents are by me unharmed.
United are ye all: with bliss unite me. Parted are ye, keep me apart from evil.

12 The Asvins, the Physicians, Gods, stretched out the healing sacrifice,
Sarasvatî with speech was a Physician, all with heroic powers investing Indra.

13 Symbols of Dîkshâ are grass-buds, of Prâyaṇiya sprouts of corn,
Of Soma-purchasing fried grains are symbols, Soma-shoots and meath.

14 Âtithya's sign is Mâsara, the Gharma's symbol Nagnahu.
Three nights with Surâ poured, this is the symbol of the Upasads.

15 Emblem of purchased Soma is Parisrut, foaming drink effused:
Indra's balm milked for Indra by the Asvins and Sarasvatî.

16 The Sacrificer's seat is the throne's symbol, the jar containing Surâ of the Altar.
The mid-space is the northern Altar's symbol: the cloth for filtering is the physician.

17 Altar by Altar is produced, power, holy grass by holy grass.
The stake is by the stake obtained, by Agni Agni carried forth.

18 The Asvins are the Soma store, Sarasvatî the sacred hearth.
For Indra formed is Indra's seat, the Matrons' Hall, the house-lord's fire.

---

12 See X. 33, 34; XIX. first note; R. V. X. 131. 4; Muir's Original Sanskrit Texts, V. 94. *Healing sacrifice:* the prototype of the Sautrâmaṇî. Many miracles of healing are attributed to the Asvins, the divine Physicians, the heralds of light, who recreate the world of life after the darkness of night. See The Hymns of the Rigveda, Index.

13 The purport of this and the eighteen following stanzas is to show the close interconnexion of the Sautrâmaṇî with Soma sacrifice, the sacrificial elements, vessels, implements, lauds and hymns that are used in the former being regarded as forms, types, symbols or reproductions of those employed in the latter. *Dîkshâ:* Consecration. *Grass-buds:* or young grass. See introductory note. *Prâyaṇîya:* the name of an introductory libation at a Soma sacrifice. *Meath:* or honey.

14 *Âtithya:* the ceremonial reception of Soma when brought to the place of sacrifice. See V. 1—4 *Mâsara:* see introductory note. *Gharma:* the caldron for hot libations. *Nagnahu:* a root used as yeast. *Upasads:* see V. 8. *Parisrut:* a kind of beer, prepared from concocted herbs and fermented.

16 *The mid-space:* between the two altars, one for Soma and one for Surâ, used at the Sautrâmaṇî sacrifice. *The physician:* who is to cure Indra.

18 *Sacred hearth:* Âgnîdhra, where the sacrificial fire is kindled. *Matrons' Hall:* see IV. 34. *House-lord's fire:* the Gârhapatya.

19 Orders he gains by orders, by Âpris Âpris of sacrifice,
Post-offerings by fore-offerings, and by calls of Vashaṭ Âhutis.
20 By victims he gains victims, by ground rice-cakes sacrificial food,
By metres kindling-verses, and Vashaṭ-calls by Inviting-prayers.
21 Grain roasted, gruel, barley-meal, grains of rice roasted, milk and curd
Are types of Soma: mingled milk, sweet whey, of sacrificial food.
22 Type of parched corn is jujube-fruit; wheat of the roasted grains of rice; Jujube the type of barley-meal, and Indra-grains of gruel-groats.
23 Symbol of milk are barley-grains, symbol of curd are jujube-fruits.
Whey is the type of Soma, and milk-mixture type of Soma's pap.
24 The Strophe is the cry, Bid hear! the answer is the antistrophe.
Sacrifice! is the Dhâyyâ's form, Pragâthas' the Yajâmahas.
25 By verse-halves comes the Ukthas' type, Nivids by Padas he obtains.
The type of Ṣastras is obtained by Praṇavas, Soma by milk.

---

19 *Orders: praishas;* liturgical directions given by a superior priest to his assistant. *Âpris:* a class of propitiatory hymns addressed to Agni under various forms and titles. See Rigveda, Index. *Post-offerings: Anuyâjas;* oblations of clarified butter offered after the chief sacrifice. *Fore-offerings: prayâjas;* similar offerings preceding the chief sacrifice. *Âhutis:* oblations with fire.

20 *Kindling-verses: samidhenîs;* recited on lighting, or adding fuel to the sacrificial fire. *Inviting-prayers: yâjyâs;* pronounced by the Hotar when oblations are poured into the fire.

21 *Mingled milk:* a mixture of boiled and coagulated milk.

22 *Indra-grains: upavâkas,* or *Indra-yavas;* seeds of the Wrightia Antidysenterica.

23 *Pap: charu;* an oblation of rice, barley, and pulse boiled with butter and milk.

24 *Strophe: stotriyâ;* a verse of eighty syllables used in certain ceremonies. *Bid hear:* the Adhvaryu's call Âṣrâvaya! to the Agnîdhra or Fire-kindler. *The answer:* of the Âgnîdhra, Astu ṣraushaṭ, Yea, let him hear. *Sacrifice! yaja,* the imperative of the verb, addressed to Agni. *Dhâyyâ:* the name of an additional verse inserted in a litany. *Pragâthas:* certain combinations of two verses in different metres. *Yajâmahas:* recitations of R. V. X. 23. 1, beginning with Yajâmaha indram, We worship Indra.

25 *Ukthas:* recitations; songs of praise. *Nivids:* short detached formulas of invocation. *Padas:* verse divisions; quarters of a stanza. *Ṣastras:* recitations; hymns of praise. *Praṇavas:* exclamations of the sacred mystic syllable OM.

26 Gained by the Asvins is the morn's libation, Indra's libation of mid-day by Indra.
Sarasvatî obtains the third outpouring, the offering sacred to the Visve Devas.
27 By Vâyu cups he gains the cups of Vâyu, and by the basket gains the vat for Soma.
By the two jars he gains two cleansing-vessels, and by the cooking-pot the pot for cooking.
28 By sacrificial texts are gained the Grahas, and by the Grahas lauds and laud-arrangements.
By metres are obtained Ukthas and praise-songs, and by the Sâma-chant the Avabhritha.
29 Draughts he obtains by pouring out libations, and wishes by the utterance of praises,
By Samyu he obtains Patnîsamyâjas, and Consummation by Samishtayajus.
30 He gains by vow of fasting Consecration, by Consecration gains the priestly guerdon.
He gains by priestly guerdon faith; by faith comes knowledge of the truth.
31 So far the type of sacrifice was formed by Brahmâ and the Gods.
All this he gains, when juice is shed, in the Santrâmanî sacrifice.
32 The rite with sacred grass, wine, store of heroes, the mighty ones speed on with adorations.
May we, sweet-singing sacrificers, setting Soma mid Gods in heaven, give joy to Indra.

---

27 *Vâyu cups:* wooden Soma cups sacred to Vâyu the Wind-God. *Basket: satu;* a sacrificial vessel made of reeds or cane. *Trough for Soma: dronakalasa*, a large wooden vessel serving as a reservoir. *Two jars:* of Surâ. *Two cleansing vessels:* the Pûtabhrit and the Âdhavanîya; in the latter the Soma is shaken and cleaned, and the former receives the purified juice.

28 *Avabhritha:* the expiatory bath of purification after sacrifice, to atone for any defects in its performance. See III. 48.

29 *Draughts: grahas;* see VII, first note. *Samyu;* an oblation so called, meaning Fortunate. *Patnîsamyâjas:* oblations of clarified butter offered to the Patnîs (Consorts of the Gods), and to Soma, Tvashtar, and Agni. *Consummation; samsthâ;* concluding form of the Soma sacrifice. See S. B E. XXVI. p. 393, note. *Samishtayajus;* see XVIII. 56, note. Mahîdhara explains the second line differently by amplification of the text: By Samyu he obtains Samyu, by Patnîsamyâjas he obtains Patnîsamyâjas, by Consummation he obtains Consummation, by Samishtayajus he obtains Samishtayajus.

30 *Vow of fasting:* see I. 5,

31 *Brahmâ:* or Prajâpati, Lord of Creatures. *He:* the Sacrificer. *Juice:* Surâ representing Soma. That is, the Sautrâmanî becomes a Soma-sacrifice.

32 Here the Adhvaryu offers three milk libations. *Mighty ones:* priests.

33 All essence of thine own in plants collected, all strength of Soma when poured out with Surâ—
Therewith impel with joy the sacrifice, Sarasvatî, the Asvins, Indra, Agni.

34 That which Sarasvatî poured out for Indra, by Asvins brought from Namuchi the demon,
This flowing drop, brilliant and full of sweetness, I drink and feed on here, the King, the Soma.

35 Whatever portion of the savoury fluid is clinging here, what Indra drank with powers,
That drop thereof with pure and holy spirit I drink and feed upon, the King, the Soma.

36 To Fathers who claim Svadhâ be Svadhâ and homage!
To Grandfathers who claim Svadhâ be Svadhá and homage!
To Great-grandfathers who claim Svadhâ be Svadhâ and homage!
The Fathers have eaten. The Fathers have rejoiced. The Fathers have been satisfied. Fathers, be ye purified.

37 Cleanse me the Fathers who enjoy Soma! Grandfathers make me clean!
May Great-grandfathers cleanse me with a sieve that brings a century.
May my Grandfathers cleanse me, may my Great-grandfathers make me clean.
With sieve that brings a century may I obtain full length of life.

38 Agni, thou pourest life: send down upon us food and vigorous strength.
Drive thou misfortune far away.

---

33 With mortars (mortar-shaped cups) of Palâsa wood the Pratiprasthâtar offers libations of Surâ in the Southern fire and recites the formula addressed to the liquor. *Joy:* the exhilaration produced by the spirituous draught.

34 *Namuchi:* who had stolen it from Indra. See X. 33, and Muir, O. S. Texts, V. p. 94, note.

35 *Here:* in the cup whose contents have been offered to Indra.

36 Here follow formulas for oblation and prayer to the Fathers or Manes of departed ancestors. *Svadhâ:* food; oblation; also a sacrificial exclamation. The residue of the three Surâ libations to the Asvins, Sarasvatî, and Indra is now offered outside the enclosing-sticks, on the coals of the Âhavanîya fire, to Ancestral Spirits of three grades.

37 A jar of Surâ pierced with a hundred holes is hung over the Southern fire-place, and a sieve or strainer made of hair of horse, cow, goat, and wool, with gold, is placed beneath. As the liquor drops thereon the Sacrificer recites texts for his purification.

38 Taken from R. V. IX. 66. 19.

39 Cleanse me the companies of Gods! May thoughts with spirit make me clean.
Cleanse me all things that be! Do thou, O Jâtavedas, make me clean.

40 Purify me, O Agni, God, refulgent with thy pure bright sieve,
With powers according to thine own.

41 O Agni, may the cleansing sieve, diffused through all thy fiery glow,
Holy devotion, make me clean.

42 May Pavamâna with his sieve, Guest of all tribes, cleanse us to-day,
He who is Cleanser make us clean.

43 Savitar, God, by both of these, libation, purifying power,
Purify me on every side.

44 Dear to all Gods hath come the cleansing Goddess, she who contains these many smooth-backed figures.
Through her may we in sacrificial banquets taking our pleasure be the lords of riches.

45 The Fathers who in Yama's realm are equal and unanimous—
Their world is Svadhâ, reverence. To Gods let sacrifice be paid.

46 Equals, unanimous, my folk yet living among those who live—
On me be set their glory through a hundred years in this our world.

---

39 Cf. R. V. IX. 67. 27.

40 *Sieve:* the purifying power of fire.

41 Taken, with the exception of the last Pâda, from R. V. IX. 67. 23.

42 Taken from R. V. IX. 67. 22. *Pavamâna:* Soma undergoing purification. *Cleanser:* Potar, Cleaning-Priest.

43 Taken from R. V. IX. 67. 25.

44 A Pravahlikâ or Enigmatical Verse. *Cleansing Goddess:* what Goddess is intended is uncertain. Mahîdhara sugests the Surâ-Jar, or the Sautrâmaṇî, or Vâk, Speech, or the Ukhâ (XI. 16). If the Surâ-Jar is intended, the *smooth-backed figures*, or bodies, may be the drops which fall from its hundred holes. Cf. A. V. VI. 62. 2, from which, with a variation, the second half of the verse is taken.

45 He offers oblation. *Their world:* meaning, according to Mahîdhara, in their world.

46 He offers an oblation of clarified butter.

47 I have heard mention of two several pathways, way of the Fathers, way of Gods and mortals.
On these two roads each moving creature travels, each thing between the Father and the Mother.

48 May this my sacrifice bring store of children, with ten brave sons, full-companied, for welfare—
Life-winning, winning offspring, winning cattle, winning this world of ours and peace and safety.
May Agni make my progeny abundant. Do ye confer food, milk, and manly vigour.

49 May they ascend, the lowest, highest, midmost, the Fathers who deserve a share of Soma.
May Fathers who have gained the world of spirits, gentle and righteous, aid us when we call them.

50 Our Fathers are Angirases, Navagvas, Atharvans, Bhṛigus, who deserve the Soma.
May these the holy look on us with favour: may we enjoy their gracious loving-kindness.

51 Our ancient Fathers who deserve the Soma, who came, most noble, to our Soma banquet—
With these let Yama, yearning with the yearning, rejoicing eat our offerings at his pleasure.

52 Thou, Soma, art preëminent for wisdom: along the straightest path thou art our leader.
Our prudent Fathers by thy wisdom, Soma, dealt out among the Gods their share of treasure.

53 For our sage Fathers, Soma Pavamâna, of old performed by thee their sacred duties.
Fighting unvanquished, open the enclosures: enrich us with large gifts of steeds and heroes.

---

47 He offers an oblation of milk. The formula is taken from R. V. X. 88. 15. *Two several pathways:* the way to the other world and the way back, regarded as distinct. *The Father and the Mother:* heaven and earth.

48 The sacrificer drinks the remains of the milk oblation. *Sacrifice:* sacrificial food. *Do ye:* he addresses the officiating priests.

49 The formula is taken from R. V. X. 15. 1. *Ascend:* rise to higher rank and obtain the best oblation, according to Sâyaṇa. *Lowest, highest, midmost:* dwellers on earth, in heaven, in sky; Barhishads, Somavats, Agnishvâttas. Verses 49-54 are addressed to the highest class.

50 *Angirases, etc:* semi-divine members of half-mythical priestly families of the most ancient times. The formula is taken from R. V. X. 14. 6.

51 Taken from R. V. X. 15. 8.

52. Taken from R. V. I. 91. 1. *Prudent:* "skilled in sacrificing": Mahîdhara.

53 Taken from R. V. IX. 96. 11. *The enclosures:* the obstructions which keep the seasonable rain from falling.

54 Associate with the Fathers thou, O Soma, hast spread thyself abroad through earth and heaven.
So with oblation let us serve thee, Indu, and so let us become the lords of riches.

55 Fathers who sit on sacred grass, come help us: these offerings we have made for you; accept them.
So come to us with most auspicious favour, and give us health and strength without a trouble.

56 I have attained the gracious-minded Fathers, have gained a son and progeny from Vishṇu.
They who enjoy pressed juices with oblation, seated on sacred grass, come oftenest hither.

57 May they, the Fathers, worthy of the Soma, invited to their favourite oblations
Laid on the sacred grass, come nigh and listen: may they be gracious unto us and bless us.

58 May they our Fathers whom the flames have tasted, worthy of Soma, come on God-ward pathways.
Enjoying at this sacrifice their portion, may they be gracious unto us and bless us.

59 Fathers whom Agni's flames have tasted, come ye nigh: ye kindly leaders, take ye each your proper place.
Eat sacrificial food presented on the grass: grant riches with a multitude of hero sons.

---

54 Taken from R. V. VIII. 48. 13, *Indu:* Soma.

55 Three formulas are now addressed to the Barhishads, the Manes who sit on the sacred grass that covers the altar and the floor of the sacrificial hall. The first formula is taken from R. V. X. 15. 4.

56 Taken from R. V. X. 15. 3. *Attained:* won the presence of. *Son and progeny:* the meaning appears to be, as suggested by Prof. Ludwig in his commentary on the original hymn, that the sacrificer has discharged his obligation to the Fathers by begetting a son through the favour of Vishṇu (R. V. X. 184. 1). Still *vikramaṇam:* is an unintelligible expression in this connexion. Another explanation, says Prof. Ludwig, would be to take *napâtam:* as fire, and *vikramaṇam vishṇoḥ:* [Vishṇu's striding forth] as the sun. Prof. Grassmann translates: 'die Kinder und den höchsten Schritt des Vischnu'; the children and the highest stride of Vishṇu. Mahîdhara takes *vishṇoḥ* to mean 'of the sacrifice,' and *napâtam* and *vikramaṇam* as the two paths leading to the Gods and to the Fathers.

57 Taken from R. V. X. 15. 11.

58 Four formulas follow addressed to the Agnishvâttas, those whose bodies have been tasted or consumed by Agni or the fire of the funeral pile.

59 Taken from R. V. X. 15. 11.

60 For those who, burnt with fire or not cremated, joy in their portion in the midst of heaven,
May the Self-Ruler form the world of spirits and this their body as his pleasure wills it.

61 We call the Agnishvâttas, true to seasons, those who drank Soma in the Nârâṣaṃsa.
Prompt to give ear to us be they, the sages, and then let us be lords of wealth and treasure.

62 Bowing the bended knee and seated southward, accept ye, all, this sacrifice with favour.
Injure us not for any sin, O Fathers, which we through human frailty have committed.

63 Lapped in the bosom of the purple Mornings give riches to the man who brings oblation.
Grant to his sons a portion of your treasure, and, present, give us energy, ye Fathers.

64 O Agni Kavyavâhana, cause us to praise before the Gods,
As our associate meet for lauds, wealth which e'en thou reputest wealth.

65 May Agni, Kavya-bearer, who hath worshipped Fathers true to Law,
Announce to Gods and Fathers these our sacrificial offerings.

66 Thou, Agni Kavya-bearer, when entreated, didst bear the offerings which thou madest fragrant,
And gavest to the Fathers who did eat them with Svadhâ. Eat, thou God, the gifts we bring thee.

---

60 Taken, with variations, from R. V. X. 15. 14. *Self-Ruler:* King of the Departed; Yama. *World of spirits: asunîtim;* a difficult word of somewhat uncertain meaning. Sâyaṇa joins it with *tanvam* and explains the two words by 'the body that leads to life', 'that body that is endowed with breath': Wilson. 'Grant thou, O King, that their body may take that life which they wish for', is Prof. Max Müller's translation of the corresponding portion of the original verse in which Yama is addressed. See India, What can it Teach us? p. 227.

61 *True to seasons:* coming at the appointed times for their libations. *Nârâṣaṃsa:* a cup containing Soma juice dedicated to Narâṣaṃsa, Agni the Praise of Men, or Soma, or, as here, the Fathers. Cf. VIII. 58.

62 Taken from R. V. X. 15. 6. This and the following formula from R. V. X. 15. 7 are addressed to all three classes of Manes.

64 Taken, with a variation, from R. V. V. 20. 1. *Kavya-vâhana:* bearer of oblations called Kavya to a class of Manes known also by that title.

65 Taken, with variations, from R. V. X. 16. 11.

66 Taken from R. V. X. 15. 12. *Svadhâ:* the sacrificial exclamation, or, their own allotted portion.

67 Thou, Jâtavedas, knowest well the number of Fathers who are here and who are absent,
Of Fathers whom we know and whom we know not. Accept the sacrifice arranged with portions.

68 Now let us pay this homage to the Fathers, to those who passed of old and those who followed,
Those who have rested in the earthly region and those who dwell among the Mighty Races.

69 As in the days of old our ancient Fathers speeding the work of holy worship, Agni!
Sought pure light and devotion, singing praises, they cleft the ground and made red Dawns apparent.

70 Right gladly do we set thee down, right gladly make thee burn and glow.
Gladly bring yearning Fathers nigh to eat the food of sacrifice.

71 Indra, with waters' foam didst thou wrench off the head of Namuchi,
Subduing all contending hosts.

72 King Soma, pressed, the Drink of Life, left Death behind with Soma-dregs.
By Law came truth and Indra-power, the pure bright drinking-off of juice. The power of Indra was this sweet immortal milk.

73 The Snipe of Angiras by thought from out the waters drank up milk.
By Law came truth, etc., as in 72.

---

67 Taken from R. V X. 15. 13.

68 Taken from R. V. X. 15. 2. *Earthly region:* the part of the firmament nearest to the earth. *Mighty Races:* of the Gods.

69 Taken from R. V. IV. 2. 16. *Cleft the ground:* in constructing an altar, digging a pit, planting a sacrificial stake, and other preparations for sacrifice *Made red Dawns apparent:* the return of the light of day being regarded as the reward of sacrifice and prayer.

70 Addressed to Agni and taken from R. V. X. 16. 12.

71 Taken from R. V. VIII. 14. 13. *With waters' foam:* with a thunderbolt in the shape of foam, according to a later legend. Prof. Lanman (Sanskrit Reader, p. 375) takes Namuchi to be a waterspout in a lake, and 'with foam' to mean 'together with its foam'. The traditional explanation of the name Namuchi, derived from *na* and *much*, 'not loosing', 'Holdfast', makes him a demon who withholds the seasonable rain.

72 The Adhvaryu reverently approaches the libation-cups of milk and Surâ, and recites eight verses illustrative of separation, selection and rejection, with special reference to the Soma drunk by Namuchi (says the Commentator), which though it had mixed with his blood was recovered in a pure state.

73 *The Snipe:* this bird, as well as the swan or flamingo is credited with the power of separating milk from the water with which it has been mixed.

74 The Haṃsa throned in light drank up by metre Soma from the floods.
By Law, etc.

75 Prajâpati by Brahma drank the essence from the foaming food, the princely power, milk, Soma juice. By Law, etc.

76 The generative part enters the *yoni*: it leaves aside the *retas* and the *mûtra*.
The caul-invested embryo leaves by its birth the covering folds. By Law, etc.

77 Viewing both forms Prajâpati gave truth and falsehood different shapes.
Prajâpati assigned the lack of faith to falsehood, faith to truth. By Law, etc.

78 By holy lore Prajâpati drank up both forms, pressed and unpressed.
By Law, etc.

79 Seeing the foaming liquor's sap, Prajâpati with the bright drank out the bright, the milk, the Soma juice. By Law, etc.

80 Wise, with mind, lead, and thread of wool the sages twine an amulet.
Sarasvatî, Savitar, Varuṇa, the Aṣvins span sacrifice and healed his form for Indra.

81 This his immortal shape with mighty powers three Deities bestowing gifts compounded.
His hair they made with sprouts of grass and barley, and roasted grain with skin and flesh supplied him.

82 His inner shape Sarasvatî arranges and, borne on bright paths, the Physician Aṣvins:
With Mâsaras and sieve his bone and marrow, as on the Oxen's hide they lay the liquor.

---

74 *The Haṃsa*: the Swan, the Sun who floats through the sky. Cf. R. V. IV. 40. 1. *By metre*: with his rays in the shape of the metres of the Veda.

75 *Brahma*: sacred lore in the shape of the Gâyatrî.

78 *Pressed and unpressed*: According to Mahîdhara, Soma and milk or the foaming liquor parisrut.

80 With bulls' hoofs—or vessels in their shape—he offers thirty-two oblations of fat or marrow. *The sages*: as skilful men make an amulet as a protective power, so the Deities mentioned span or spread out a remedial sacrifice to cure Indra of his sickness (see introductory note), and recreated his body as described in the verses that follow. *Lead*: employed as a charm against demons and sorcery. See A. V. I. 16. 2; XII. 2. 1, 19, 20, 53.

81 *Three Deities*: the Aṣvins and Sarasvatî.

82 *Mâsaras*: see introductory note. *Liquor*: Surâ.

83 By thought Sarasvatî with both Nâsatyas forms lovely treasure and a beauteous body.
Like shuttle through the loom the steady ferment mixes the red juice with the foaming spirit.

84 By milk they generated bright immortal, productive seed, by Surâ seed from urine,
Chasing afar folly and ill intention, crude food and wind and meat that loads the stomach.

85 Heart with his heart Indra Good Guardian gendered: with rice-cake Savitar gave truth its being.
Varuna, doctoring the lungs and liver, forms, as with Vâyu cups, the gall and kidneys.

86 Cooking-pots pouring honey were the entrails: like a well-milking cow the pans were bowels.
A hawk's wing was the spleen: through mighty powers the stool as mother was navel and belly.

87 The pitcher was the father of the rectum by powers, the womb which first contained the infant.
Plain was the hundred-streaming fount as penis: the jar poured forth libations to the Father.

88 His face the basket, thence his head; the strainer his tongue, his mouth Sarasvatî and Asvins.
The Chapya was his rump, his leech the filter, the bladder was his penis keen with ardour.

89 Asvins with both cups made his eye immortal, the goat and cooked oblation gave it keenness.
With wheat eyelashes and with jujube eyebrows they clothe as 'twere a black and brilliant figure.

90 The sheep, the ram to give his nostril vigour. the immortal path of breath by both libations.
By Indra-grains and sacrificial jujubes Sarasvatî produced through-breath and nose hairs.

---

83 *Nâsatyas:* a title of the Asvins, explained by Indian Commentators as 'not untrue', *na-asatya*. See Macdonell, Vedic Mythology, p. 49. *Ferment:* Nagnahu, the root used as yeast. See verse 14.

85 *Truth:* Indra's quality of truthfulness. *Vâyu cups:* See verse 27.

87 *The pitcher:* or jar, for holding Surâ. *The infant:* in the shape of the Surâ contained in it. *Fount:* the pitcher. See verse 37.

88 *The basket:* see verse 27. *Chapya:* a kind of sacrificial vessel, the use of which is not explained.

89 *Both cups:* libations offered to the Pair. *The goat:* offered in sacrifice. *They:* the Asvins. *Black and brilliant figure:* the eye of Indra.

90 *The ram:* sacred to Sarasvatî, now offered in sacrifice. *By both libations:* 'was made' understood. Cf. XXI. 49.

91 The bull for strength made Indra's form: the immortal hearing for both his ears by two libations.
Barley and sacred grass composed his eyebrows: from his mouth came the jujube and sweet honey.

92 Hair of the wolf was on his waist and body: the beard upon his face was hair of tigers.
Lion's hair were his locks, for fame and beauty, worn on his head, his crest and sheen and vigour.

93 The Aṣvins, Leeches, joined his limbs and body, Sarasvatî put limbs and frame together,
Giving the form and vital power of Indra, hundredfold, deathless and delightful lustre.

94 Sarasvatî, as Consort of the Aṣvins, bears in her womb the nobly-fashioned Infant.
King Varuṇa with waters' wealthy essence begetting Indra in the floods for glory.

95 Splendour of victims, powerful oblation, honey and meath with milk and foaming liquor,
Healing Sarasvatî effused, and Aṣvins; from pressed and unpressed Soma, deathless Indu.

---

91 *Jujube and sweet honey:* his saliva and rheum: Mahîdhara.

94 *Infant:* Indra whom she has helped to recreate.

95 *Pressed and unpressed*: parisrut and milk. *Soma:* 'was produced' understood.

## BOOK THE TWENTIETH.

Birth place of princely power art thou: centre art thou of princely power.

Harm not thyself: do me no harm.

2 Varuṇa, Law's maintainer, hath sat down, etc., as in X. 27. Save me from death. Save me from lightning.

3 Thee, by the radiant Savitar's impulsion, with arms of Asvins, with the hands of Pûshan,

With leech-craft of the Asvins, I besprinkle for splendour, for the lustre of a Brâhman;

With leech-craft of Sarasvatî, besprinkle for manly vigour and for food to feed thee;

Besprinkle thee, by special power of Indra, for strength of body and for fame and glory.

4 Thou art Ka. Noblest Ka art thou. Thee for the state and rank of Ka.

Sumaṅgala! Susloka! Satyarâjan!

5 My head be grace, my mouth be fame, my hair and beard be brilliant sheen!

My breath be King and deathlessness, mine eye Sole Lord, mine ear the Prince!

6 My tongue be bliss, my voice be might, my mind be wrath, my rage self-lord!

Joys be my fingers, and delight my members, conquering strength my friend!

---

The Sautrâmaṇî is continued. An Âsandî or Sacrificer's seat or stool (see XIX. 16, 86) representing a throne, is placed between the two altars, two of its legs being on the southern and two on the northern ground. A black-antelope's skin is spread over it on which the Sacrificer sits and recites the formulas. *Thou:* O Âsandî.

2 *Varuṇa:* the moral Governor of the world, typifying a King. The formula, taken from R. V. I. 26 10, is repeated from X. 27. *Preserve me:* he puts a silver disc under his left foot as a charm against death, and a golden one under the right to protect him from lightning.

3 The Adhvaryu besprinkles the Sacrificer with the remains of the libations of fat which are made to run down to his mouth.

4 *Ka:* or Who? ; Prajâpati. See VII. 29. *Sumaṅgala, etc.:* meaning, Auspicious, Fairfamed, Having-a-real-King; ritual names of the attendants whom the Sacrificer is made to summon.

5 The Sacrificer touches all his members and bodily parts one after another, and recites the benedictory formulas.

7 Let my two arms be Indra's power, my hands be deed of manly might, my soul and breast be princely rule!

8 My ribs be royal government, my belly, shoulders, neck, and hips,
Thighs, elbows, knees, the people, yea, my members universally!

9 My navel intellect, etc., etc. ... ... ... ... ...
Duty am I in legs and feet, established King among the folk.

10 I take my stand on princely power and Kingship, on cows am I dependent, and on horses.
On members I depend, and on the body, on vital breath dependent and on welfare, on heaven and earth and sacrifice dependent.

11 May Deities, eleven threes, the three and thirty bounteous Ones
Whose House-Priest is Bṛihaspati, by impulse of bright Savitar, the Gods protect me with the Gods.

12 May the first Gods with the second, the second with the third, the third with Truth, Truth with Sacrifice, Sacrifice with sacrificial texts, sacrificial texts with Sâmans, Sâmans with praise-verses, praise-verses with fore and after-sentences, fore-sentences with inviting-texts, inviting-texts with Vashaṭ-calls, Vashaṭ-calls with oblations, and oblations, fulfil my desires, Earth! All-hail!

13 My hair is effort and attempt, my skin is reverence and approach.
My flesh is inclination, wealth my bone, my marrow reverence.

14 Gods. Deities, whatever fault of ours have stirred the wrath of Gods,
May Agni set me free from that iniquity and all distress.

15 If in the day-time or at night we have committed acts of sin,
May Vâyu set me free from that iniquity and all distress.

---

10 He steps down on a black-antelope's skin.

12 *Earth!*: Bhûḥ; a mystical exclamation used in sacrifice. Cf. III. 5.

13 The Sacrificer drinks the remainder of the Graha or libation, and recites the formula attributing all-controlling powers and influences to the constituent elements of his body. *Reverence and approach*: that is, approached with reverential intentions. *Reverence*: paid to me by others.

14 The Avabhṛitha or Purificatory Ceremony is begun by floating a jar of Masara (see XIX., introductory note) in water, and reciting the prescribed formulas.

16 If when awake or in our sleep we have committed acts of sin,
May Sûrya set me free from that iniquity and all distress.

17 Each fault in village or in wild, company or corporeal sense,
Each sinful act that we have done to Śûdra or Arya, or to either's disadvantage, e'en of that sin thou art the expiation.

18 Waters, Inviolable ones, etc. Said to be repeated from VI. 22.
O ever-moving Cleansing Bath, etc. Repeated from III. 48.

19 Thy heart is in the flood, etc. Repeated from VIII. 25.
To us let Waters, etc. Repeated from VI. 22.

20 As one unfastened from a stake, or cleansed by bathing after toil,
As butter which the sieve hath purged, let water clean me from my sin.

21 Looking upon the loftier light above the darkness we have come
To Sûrya, God among the Gods, the light that is most excellent.

22 The waters I this day have sought, and to their essence have we come.
Agni, come hither rich in milk, splendour and brilliancy bestow on me, and progeny and wealth.

23 A brand art thou: fain would we thrive. Fuel art thou and splendour: give me splendour.
Earth comes again, the Dawn, the Sun. This Universe all comes again.
May I possess Vaiśvânara's light, may I attain my vast desires. Earth! All-hail!

---

17 *In village or in wild, etc.:* cf. III. 45. *Arya:* one of the third caste; a Vaisya. *To either's disadvantage:* against the interest or wishes of the Sacrificer or his wife, according to Mahîdhara. *Thou:* the jar of Mâsara.

18 This beginning of a verse is the reading of the Taittirîya recension, the Black Yajurveda, differing slightly from the passage referred to. See S. B. E. XXVI. p. 206, note.

20 Taken, with a variation ('water' for 'all') from A. V. VI. 115. 3.

21 Taken from R. V. I. 50. 10.

22 Varied from R. V. I. 23. 24.

23 He takes up a piece of wood and lays it on the Âhavanîya fire. *Earth:* here the Sacrificer offers an oblation of clarified butter. *Comes again:* *sam vartti:* according to Mahîdhara = *naśyati*, is lost, perishes. *Earth!:* see verse 12.

24 O Agni, Master of the Vow, on thee I lay the kindling-stick.
To the fast-vow and faith I come. I, consecrated, kindle thee.

25 Fain would I know that holy world where Deities with Agni dwell,
Where priestly rank and princely power together in accordance move.

26 Fain would I know that holy world where want and languor are unknown,
Where in complete accordance move Indra and Vâyu side by side.

27 Let thy shoot be united with his tendril, joint combine with joint.
Imperishable sap for joy, thine odour be the Soma's guard!

28 They pour it out, they sprinkle it, they scatter it, they make it pure.
In the brown Surâ's ecstasy he says What art thou? What art thou?

29 Indra, at morn accept our cake accompanied with grain and groats, with wheaten bread and hymns of praise.

30 To Indra sing the lofty hymn, Maruts! that slayeth Vṛitra best,
Whereby the Holy Ones created for the God the radiant light that never dies.

31 Adhvaryu, on the straining-cloth pour thou the Soma pressed with stones:
Purify it for Indra's drink.

32 The Sovran Lord of living things, he upon whom the worlds depend,
Mighty, the mighty's King—by him I take thee, take thee on myself.

---

24 He lays three kindling-sticks on the Âhavanîya fire, and recites three formulas. *Master of the Vow:* see I. 5.

27 The Surâ is addressed and mingled with the Soma. *Thy shoot:* the part thou hast in the mixture. *His:* the Soma's part.

28 *He:* Indra, when he tastes Surâ instead of his accustomed Soma.

29 A rice-cake is offered to Indra with a formula taken from R. V. VIII. 78. 1.

30 *Maruts:* chanters of their thunder-psalm; here meaning the loud-voiced singers of the hymn. *The light divine:* the Sun, which the Visve Devas or All-Gods generated or created for Indra.

32 *Thee:* the thirty-third fat or marrow libation, completing the prescribed offerings to the thirty-three Gods, which he takes up in a bull's hoof vessel.

33 Taken upon a base art thou. Thee for the Asvins. This is thy home, etc.

34 Guard of my breath and outward breath, the guardian of mine eye and ear,
All-healer of my voice, thou art the mollifier of my mind.

35 Invited I feed upon thee invited,
Whom Asvins, whom Sarasvatî, whom Indra, Good Protector, made.

36 Kindled in forefront of the Mornings, Indra with forward light, long-active, waxing mighty,
With three and thirty Gods, the Thunder-wielder, smote Vritra dead and threw the portals open.

37 Son of Himself, the Praise of Men, the Hero, measuring out the sacrificial stations,
Rich in bulls' fat, anointing with sweet butter, wise, bright with gauds of gold, he sacrificeth.

38 Lauded by Gods, Lord of Bay Steeds, the Helper, showing his greatness, worshipped with oblations,
Fort-render, Cowpen-cleaver, Thunder-wielder, may he approach our sacrifice rejoicing.

39 May Indra, Lord of Bays, sit by direction eastward on earth accepting our oblation,
And sacred grass, fair, far-spread, widely-stretching, anointed by Âdityas and by Vasus.

40 To the strong Indra go the sounding Portals, dames with a goodly husband, swiftly moving!
Well-manned, divine, wide be the Doors thrown open, expanding in their greatness for the Hero!

---

33 Repeated from X. 32.

34 The officiating priests inhale the odour of the remains of the oblation.

36 The Adhvaryu's part of the ceremony is finished, and the Hotar now begins to officiate. *The portals:* of the rain-cloud, which the demon of drought had obstructed.

37 This and the seven following verses form an Âprî or propitiatory hymn constituting the Inviting-prayers at the *prayâjas:* or fore-offerings of an animal sacrifice. They are addressed to a series of Deities or deified objects, all of which are regarded by Sâyana as manifestations of Agni. See The Hymns of the Rigveda, Index. *Son of Himself:* or, Tanûnapât, Fire, lighted from Fire, a title of Agni. *The Praise of Men:* or Desire of Men, Narâsamsa; Agni. Some families must invoke Tanûnapât and others Narâsamsa as their tutelary Deity.

38 Indra is invited to the sacrifice. *Fort-render:* splitting the cloud-castles of the demons of drought. *Cowpen-cleaver:* opener of the stores of fertilizing rain.

39 *On earth:* on the sacrificial ground.

40 *Portals:* of the sacrificial hall. See R. V. II. 3. 5.

41 Dawn and Night, lofty, sapful, richly-yielding, fair-showing, as they weave with varied colour
The long-extended thread in concert, worship the God of Gods, the lofty Hero Indra.

42 The two first pleasant-voiced celestial Hotars, arranging rites for man in sundry places,
At head of sacrifice stablishing Indra, increase the eastern light with sweet oblation.

43 Thriving by sacrifice may the three Bright Ones, taking delight like wedded dames in Indra,
Sarasvatî, Idâ, Bhâratî all-surpassing, with milk preserve our sacred thread unbroken.

44 May Tvashṭar coming from afar, the active, give strength and plenty to strong glorious Indra,
And strong, prolific, worshipping, the Mighty at sacrifice's head give the Gods honour.

45 Let the divine Stake, like an Immolator, bind, as one ordered, to himself the victim,
And, filling Indra's belly with oblations, season the sacrifice with sweets and butter.

46 Indra the Bull, swift conqueror, wildly rushing bull-like to meet the Indu of the droppings—
Delighting in a mind that scatters fatness, let the immortal Gods rejoice in Svâhâ.

47 May Indra come to us for our protection, here, lauded Hero, be our feast-companion.
May he whose powers are many, waxen mighty, cherish, like Dyaus, the sovran sway of princes.

48 From near or far away may mighty Indra, giver of succour, come for our protection,
Lord of men, armed with thunder, with the Strongest, slaying his foes in conflict, in the battles.

---

41 Cf. R. V. II. 3. 6. *Long-extended thread:* their perpetual course of succession to each other.

42 *Two . . . . Hotars:* Agnî and Vâyu, according to Mahîdhara. According to Sâyaṇa, two Agnis, terrestrial and firmamental.

43 *Three Bright Ones:* or, Goddesses, connected with sacrifice. See R. V. II. 3. 8.

45 *Stake:* Vanaspati, the Tree; the Sacrificial Stake regarded as a form of Agni.

*Immolator:* the priest who slaughters the victim.

46 *Indu of the droppings:* Soma connected with the dripping fat or marrow.

47 Taken from R. V. IV. 21. 1.

48 Taken from R. V. IV. 20. 1. *The Strongest:* the Maruts.

49 May Indra come to us with Tawny Coursers, inclined to us, to favour and enrich us.
May Maghavan, loud-voiced and wielding thunder, stand by us at this sacrifice, in combat.

50 Indra the Rescuer, Indra the Helper, Hero who listens at each invocation,
Ṣakra I call, Indra invoked of many. May Indra, Bounteous Lord, prosper and bless us.

51 May helpful Indra as our Good Protector, Lord of all treasures, favour us with succour,
Baffle our foes and give us rest and safety, and may we be the lords of hero vigour.

52 May we enjoy the grace of him the Holy, yea, may we dwell in his auspicious favour.
May helpful Indra as our Good Preserver drive from us even from afar, our foemen.

53 Come hither, Indra, with Bay Steeds, joyous, with tails like peacock plumes.
Let no men check thy course as fowlers stay the bird: pass o'er them as o'er desert lands.

54 Verily the Vasishṭhas hymn with praises Indra the mighty One whose arm wields thunder.
Praised, may he guard our wealth in men and cattle. Ye Gods, preserve us evermore with blessings.

55 Fire hath been kindled, Aṣvins Twain! the Gharma warmed, the Radiant pressed,
Here the Milch-Cow Sarasvatî hath poured bright Soma, Indra's own.

56 When Soma flows Sarasvatî and both the Aṣvins, Leeches and
Body-guards, bear to Indra strength by passage through the realms of air.

---

49 Taken from R. V. IV. 20. 2. *Maghavan:* the Bounteous Lord, Indra.

50—52 Taken from R. V. VI. 47. 11—13.

53 R. V. III. 45 1.

54 R. V. VII. 23. 6.

55 *The Radiant:* or the Ruler, the Prince; Soma. Twelve propitiatory verses follow in praise of the Aṣvins and Sarasvatî. The Aṣvins, as the divine Physicians, attend Indra as a matter of course, but Sarasvatî's part in his cure is not so easily accounted for. According to the Ṣatapatha-Brâhmana, V. 5. 4. 16, Sarasvatî here is Vâk, Speech, the healing Word. Prof. Weber suggests the rationalistic explanation that Sarasvatî the river, that is, cold water (Amrit is in the waters, in the waters healing medicine. R. V. I. 23. is referred to.

57 When Soma flowed the Asvins Twain, the Leeches, brought sweet medicine,
With Men's Desire Sarasvatî for Indra, Soma, Nagnahu.

58 Worshipped, Sarasvatî bestowed on Indra, senses, manly power.
The Asvins, through oblations paid, combined food, energy, and wealth.

59 The Asvins brought from Namuchi pressed Soma bright with foaming juice.
Sarasvatî with sacred grass brought that to Indra for his drink.

60 Sarasvatî and Indra with the Asvins Twain milked out desires
From heaven and earth, the regions, the resounding and expansive doors.

61 Ye Asvins, Dawn and Night, by day and in the evening, fair of hue,
Accordant, with Sarasvatî, deck Indra with surpassing powers.

62 Guard us, O Asvins, through the day, guards us by night, Sarasvatî.
Celestial Hotars, Leeches! both guard Indra when the juice is pressed.

63 The Asvins, and the Three, apart, Sarasvatî, Idâ, Bhâratî,
As drink to gladden Indra, poured strong Soma with the foaming juice.

64 The Asvins, our Sarasvatî, and Tvashṭar, when the juice was shed,
Gave Indra balm, yea, mead as balm, glory and fame and many a shape.

65 Praising with foaming liquor at due times, Indra, Vanaspati,
Sarasvatî as cow gave forth sweet beverage with the Asvins Twain.

66 Asvins, to Indra ye with cows, with Mâsara and foaming drink
Gave, with Sarasvatî—All hail!—the pressed-out Soma juice and mead.

---

57 *Men's Desire:* or the Praise of Men, Narâsamsa, Agni. Sacrifice, according to Mahîdhara. *Nagnahu:* the drug used for fermenting the Surâ. See XIX. 14, 83.

59 *Namuchi:* see X. 33.

63 *Foaming juice:* Surâ.

65 *Sweet beverage: kilâla.* See II. 34; III. 43.

67 The Asvins and Sarasvatî by wit from fiendish Namuchi
Brought unto Indra sacred food, strength, brilliant treasure, ample wealth.

68 That Indra, strong through sacrifice by Asvins and Sarasvatî,
Cleft Vala through to win him wealth, with Namuchi of Asura birth.

69 Supporting him in sacrifice with sacred food and mighty powers,
Sarasvatî, both Asvins and the cattle hymned that Indra's praise.

70 Indra whom Bhaga, Savitar, and Varuṇa supplied with power,
Lord of the sacrifice, may he, Good Guardian, love the worshipper.

71 Savitar, Varuṇa bestow gifts on the liberal offerer,
Strength, power and treasure which the Good Protector took from Namuchi!

72 Varuṇa giving sway and power, Savitar grace with happiness,
The Good Protector giving strength with fame, obtained the sacrifice.

73 With cows the Asvins, mighty power, with horses manly vigour, strength,
With sacred food Sarasvatî, made Indra, Sacrificer, strong.

74 May those Nâsatyas, fair of form, the Men who ride on paths of gold,
Oblation-rich Sarasvatî, thou, Indra! help us in our rites.

75 Those Leeches righteous in their deeds, She, rich in milk, Sarasvatî,
That Vṛitra-slayer hundred-powered, invested Indra with his might.

76 Ye Asvins and Sarasvatî, joint drinkers of the Surâ draught,
In Namuchi of Asura birth, give aid to Indra in his deeds.

77 As parents aid a son, etc., as in X. 34.

78 He in whom horses, bulls, oxen, and barren cows, and rams, when duly set apart, are offered up,—
To Agni, Soma-sprinkled, drinker of sweet juice, Disposer, with thy heart bring forth a pleasant hymn.

---

68 *Vala:* the rain-with-holding cloud, personified as a demon of drought who stole, like Cacus, the cows of the Gods and concealed them in a cave. See R. V. X. 68. 5—10.

74 *Nâsatyas:* the Asvins.

78 Taken, with variations, from R. V. X. 91. 14. *Disposer:* Arranger of the sacrifice; priest. The Adhvaryu is addressed. *Bring forth:* or, beget.

79 Within thy mouth is poured the offering, Agni, as Soma into cup, oil into ladle.
Vouchsafe us wealth, strength-winning, blest with heroes, wealth lofty, praised by men, and full of splendour.

80 The Asvins gave, with lustre, sight, Sarasvati manly strength with breath.
Indra with voice and might gave Indra vigorous power.

81 With kine, Nâsatyas! and with steeds, come, Asvins, Rudras! to the house, the sure protector of its men;

82 Such, wealthy Gods! as none afar or standing near to us may harm, yea, no malicious mortal foe.

83 Do ye, O longed-for Asvins, lead us on to wealth of varied form, wealth that shall bring us room and rest.

84 Wealthy in spoil, enriched with hymns, may pure Sarasvatî desire with eager love our sacrifice.

85 She who awakens sounds of joy, inspires our hymns, Sarasvatî, she hath allowed our sacrifice.

86 Sarasvatî, the mighty flood, she with her light illuminates, she brightens every pious thought.

87 O Indra, marvellously bright, come, these libations long for thee, thus by fine fingers purified.

88 Urged by the holy singer, sped by song, come, Indra, to the prayers of the libation-pouring priest.

89 Approach, O Indra, hasting thee, Lord of Bay Horses, to the prayer: in our libations take delight.

90 Accordant with Sarasvatî let the two Asvins drink the meath.
May Indra, Vṛitra-slayer, Good Guardian, accept the Soma meath.

---

79 Taken from R. V. X 91. 15.

81—83 Taken from R. V. II. 41. 7—9.

*Rudras:* here a title of the Asvins, the Bright Pair.

84—89 Taken from R. V. I. 3. 10—12, 4—6.

90 *Soma meath:* the sweet libation of Soma juice.

## BOOK THE TWENTY-FIRST.

VARUṆA, hear this call of mine: be gracious unto us this day.
Longing for help I yearn for thee.

2 I ask this of thee with my prayer, etc., as in XVIII. 49.

3 Do thou who knowest Varuṇa, O Agni, put far away from us the God's displeasure.
Best Sacrificer, brightest One, refulgent, remove thou far from us all those who hate us.

4 Be thou the nearest unto us, O Agni, our closest Friend while now this Morn is breaking.
Reconcile Varuṇa to us, be bounteous: show thy compassion and be swift to hear us.

5 We call to succour us the mighty Mother of those whose sway is just, the Queen of Order,
Strong-ruler, far-expanding, ne'er decaying, Aditi gracious guide and good protectress.

6 Sinless may we ascend, for weal, this vessel rowed with good oars, divine, that never leaketh,
Earth our strong guard, incomparable Heaven. Aditi gracious guide and good protectress.

7 May I ascend the goodly ship, free from defect, that leaketh not,
Moved by a hundred oars, for weal.

8 O Mitra-Varuṇa, gracious Pair, with fatness dew our pasturage,
With mead the regions of the air.

---

The formulas of the Sautrâmaṇî are continued.

1, 2 A rice-cake is offered to Varuṇa with an Inviting Prayer (1) taken from R. V. I. 25. 19, and an Offering Prayer (2) from R. V. I. 24. 11, repeated from XVIII. 49.

3, 4 Similar prayers, taken from R. V. IV. 1. 4, 5, addressed to Agni as the Mediator or Intercessor.

5 An Inviting Prayer, taken with a slight variation from A. V. VII. 6. 2, addressed to Aditi to whom a *charu*, or oblation of rice, barley, and pulse boiled with butter and milk, is to be offered.

6 Taken from A. V. VII. 6. 3, varied from R. V. X. 63. 10.

7 *The goodly ship:* sacrifice, which bears us beyond this world to heaven. *Hundred oars:* verses of praise and chanted hymns.

8 Oblations of milk and curds are offered to Mitra and Varuṇa regarded as Rain-Gods (II. 16). The verse is taken from R. V. III. 62. 16. *Fatness:* fertilizing rain.

9 Stretch forth your arms and let our lives be lengthened: with fatness dew the pastures of our cattle.
Ye Youthful, make us famed among the people: hear, Mitra-Varuṇa, these mine invocations.

10 Bless us the Coursers when we call, etc., as in IX. 16.

11 Deep-skilled in Law, etc., as in IX. 18.

12 Kindled is Agni with the brand, yea, kindled well, the excellent.
The metre Gâyatrî, the steer of eighteen months, give power and life!

13 Tanûnapât whose acts are pure. our bodies' guard Sarasvatî,
Ushṇihâ metre and the steer of two years' age give power and life!

14 Agni with offerings, meet for praise, and Soma the immortal God,
Anushṭup metre and the steer of thirty months give power and life!

15 Agni with goodly grass spread out, deathless with Pûshan at his side,
Bṛihatî metre and a steer of three years' age give power and life!

16 The Doors divine, the mighty Regions, Brahmâ, God Bṛihaspati,
The metre Paṅkti, here a bull in his fourth year, give power and life!

17 The two young Dawns of lovely form, the deathless Universal Gods,
The Trishṭup metre, here, a bull in his sixth year, give power and life!

18 The two celestial Hotars, both Physicians, Indra's close-knit friends,
The metre Jagatî, an ox who draws the wain, give power and life!

19 The Three, Iḍâ, Sarasvatî, and Bhâratî, the Marut folk,
Virâj the metre, here, a cow in milk, a bull, give power and life!

---

9 Taken from R. V. VII. 62. 5.

12 This and the ten following verses form an Âprî or Propitiatory Hymn in honour of Indra. *The steer:* to be sacrificed. *Give:* to Indra.

13 *Tanûnapât:* Son of Himself. Agni. See V. 5. *Ushṇihâ:* = Ushṇih.

17 *Two young Dawns:* Morning and Night, inseparably connected and ever born anew. *Here:* in this and other verses meaning 'to Indra.'

18 *Hotars:* Agni and Vâyu, or terrestrial and firmamental Agni.

19 *Folk:* or clans.

20 Tvashṭar the wondrous, full of seed, Indrâgnî furtherers of weal,
Dvipadâ metre, and a cow and vigorous bull give power and life!

21 Our slaughterer Vanaspati, Savitar who promoteth wealth,
The metre Kakup, here, a cow who casts her calf, give power and life!

22 With Svâhâ mighty Varuṇa give healing power to Sacrifice!
The Atichhandas, Bṛihat, and a steer and bull give power and life!

23 With the Spring Season may the Gods the Vasus praised with triple hymn
And with Rathantara, give life to Indra, splendour, sacrifice.

24 With Summer may the Rudras, Gods, praised in the Pañchadaṣa hymn
With Bṛihat, give to Indra strength; with fame, and sacrifice and life.

25 May the Âdityas with the Rains, lauded in Saptadaṣa hymn
And with Vairûpa, with folk, strength, give Indra sacrifice and life.

26 With Autumn may the Ṛibhus, Gods, praised in the Ekaviṃṣa hymn
And with Virâja, give with grace to Indra grace, life, sacrifice.

27 With Winter may the Maruts, Gods, praised in the laud of thrice nine parts,
The Ṣakvarîs, with strength give might to Indra, sacrifice and life.

---

20 *Indrâgnî:* Indra and Agni as a dual Deity. *Dvipadâ:* two-footed; comprising two Pâdas or verse-divisions.

21 *Slaughterer:* Immolator of the victims tied to the Stake. *Kakup:* a metre of 8+12+8 syllables.

22 *Atichhandas:* hypermeter; redundant metre, containing more than forty-eight syllables.

23 *Triple hymn:* the Trivṛit. See IX. 33; X. 10.

24 *Pañchadaṣa:* Fifteenfold; see XII. 4; XIV. 22.

25 *Saptadaṣa:* Seventeenfold. See XIII. 56. *Vairûpa:* a Sâman. See X. 12.

26 *Ṛibhus:* three artificers of ancient time whose wondrous skill and workmanship obtained for them immortality and a place among the Gods. They are usually invoked with Indra. *Ekaviṃṣa:* having twenty-one verses or parts. See XIII. 57; XIV. 23. *Virâja:* See XIII. 57.

27 *Ṣakvarîs:* metres consisting of seven feet.

28 With Dew-time may the deathless Gods praised in the Thirty-three-part laud,
The Revatîs, with truth give sway to Indra, sacrifice and life.

29 Let the Hotar sacrifice with fuel to Agni in the place of libation, to the Asvins, Indra, Sarasvatî. A grey-coloured he-goat with wheat, jujube-fruit and sprouts of rice becomes a sweet salutary remedy, splendour, might, milk, Soma. Let them enjoy sweet butter with foaming liquor. Hotar, present offerings of butter.

30 Let the Hotar, Tanûnapât, worship Sarasvatî. A sheep, a ram, a salutary remedy on the honey-sweet path, bearing to the Asvins and Indra heroic strength, with jujube-fruit, Indra-grains, sprouts of rice, becomes a salutary remedy, milk, Soma. Let them enjoy, etc., as in verse 29.

31 Let the Hotar worship Narâsamsa and the Lord Nagnahu. A ram with Surâ a salutary remedy, Sarasvatî the Physician, the golden car of the Asvins, the victim's omentum, with jujube-fruit, Indra-grains, and rice-sprouts, become a salutary remedy, the manly strength of Indra, milk, Soma. Let them, etc.

32 Let the Hotar, magnified with oblations, offering sacrifice, worship Sarasvatî and Indra, increasing them with strength, with a bull and a cow. Strength and medicine to the Asvins and Indra are meath with jujube-fruit, Mâsara with parched grain, milk, Soma. Let them, etc.

33 Let the Hotar worship the wool-soft Altar-grass, the Physicians Nâsatyas, the Physicians Asvins. A mare with a foal, a milch-cow is a physician. Sarasvatî the Physician yields medicine to Indra, milk, Soma. Let them enjoy, etc.

---

28 *Dew-time* : see II. 32 ; X. 14. *Revatîs :* the name of a verse (R. V. I. 30. 13) beginning with this word, which is called the womb or origin of the Raivata Sâman.

29 *Let the Hotar :* the divine Hotar, the exemplar to be followed by his counterpart on earth *Hotar, present offerings :* the human priest is addressed.

30 *Tanûnapât :* According to Mahîdhara, the nominative case is used in the sense of the accusative : worship, or sacrifice or say the offering-prayer to, Tanûnapât. *Milk, Soma :* Mahîdhara takes these nominatives as accusatives, supplying 'let them drink,' or 'let them enjoy.'

31 *Nagnahu :* the drug used to ferment the Surâ. Mahîdhara turns. *Sarasvatî* and *rathah*, *car*, both nominatives, into accusatives.

33 *A mare, etc. :* with reference to the horses given as fees to the priests.

34 Let the Hotar worship the Doors, the Regions, the resounding, expansive Doors, the Regions, with the Asvins. Indra milks the two milky worlds. The Milch-cow Sarasvatî yields medicine for the Asvins and Indra, pure light and strength. Milk, Soma. Let them, etc.

35 Let the Hotar worship the two fair-formed Dawns. At night and by day the Asvins with Sarasvati compose impetuous power, like healing balm, in Indra, like a falcon, Mâsara with light, thought, and grace. Milk, Soma. Let them enjoy, etc.

36 Let the Hotar worship the two divine Hotars, the Physician Asvins, and Indra. Watchfully by day and night Sarasvatî as Physician, with balms, with lead, yields strength and power. Milk, Soma. Let them enjoy, etc.

37 Let the Hotar worship the three Goddesses. The three active ones, with three sacrificial elements, lay balm and golden hue on Indra. The Asvins, Idâ, Bhâratî—Sarasvatî with Speech yields might and power to Indra. Milk, Soma. Let them enjoy, etc.

38 Let the Hotar worship Tvashtar full of good seed, the Bull active for men, Indra, the Asvins, Sarasvatî the Physician. Vigour, speed, power, a fierce wolf as physician, fame with Surâ is a medicine, Mâsara with grace. Milk, Soma. Let them enjoy, etc.

39 Let the Hotar worship Vanaspati the Immolator, the Lord of Hundred Powers, and awful Passion, the King, the Tiger, and the Asvins, with reverence. Sarasvatî the Physician yields wrath and power to Indra. Milk, Soma. Let them enjoy, etc.

---

34 *The Regions*: that is, the Doors of the sacrificial hall which are as expansive as the Quarters of the sky.

35 *Dawns*: Morning and Night.

36 *With lead*: supernatural virtues are ascribed to this metal. See A. V. I. 16. 2, 4; XII. 2. 1, 19, 20, 53.

37 *Three Goddesses*: of sacrifice and prayer, Sarasvatî, Idâ, Bhâratî. *Three active ones*: the goat, the ram, and the bull which are offered respectively to the Asvins, Sarasvatî, and Indra. *Three sacrificial elements*: constituting chief offerings, secondary offerings, and by-offerings with different parts of their bodies.

38 *Full of good seed*: as the prolific creator of all forms of living beings. *Wolf*: with reference to the wolf's hair mixed with the Surâ. See XIX. 9, note.

39 *Lord of Hundred Powers*: Indra. *Tiger*: the exemplar of royalty, Indra.

40 Let the Hotar worship Agni. Of the drops of clarified butter, Svâhâ! Of the fat, omentum, etc., severally, Svâhâ! Svâhâ! the goat for the Asvins. Svâhâ! the ram for Sarasvatî. Svâhâ! the bull for Indra. To the Lion, to his might, power. Svâhâ! Agni the salutary remedy. Svâhâ! Soma, the power. Svâhâ! Indra the Good Deliverer. Savitar, Varuṇa Lord of Physicians. Svâhâ! Vanaspatî, beloved, food and medicine. Svâhâ! Gods who drink clarified butter. Agni accepting the medicine. Milk, Soma. Let them enjoy, etc.

41 Let the Hotar worship the Asvins with the omentum of a he-goat. Let them enjoy the fat. Hotar, offer the sacrificial oblation.

Let the Hotar worship Sarasvatî with the omentum of a ram. Let her enjoy the fat. Hotar offer the sacrificial oblation.

Let the Hotar worship Indra with the omentum of a bull. Let him, etc.

42 Let the Hotar worship the Asvins, Sarasvatî, Indra the Good Deliverer. These your Somas, pressed, rejoicing with goats, rams, bulls, giving pleasure with rice-shoots, young blades of corn, parched grain, joy-givers adorned with Mâsara, bright, milky, immortal, presented, dropping honey. these let the Asvins, Sarasvatî, Indra the Good Deliverer, Vṛitra-slayer, accept. Let them drink, rejoice in, enjoy the Soma meath. Hotar, sacrifice.

43 Let the Hotar worship the Asvins. Let them eat of the he-goat, the sacrifice. Let them to-day eat the fat, taken from the middle, before those who hate us, before human handling. Yea, let them eat amid the fodder of fields fresh with moisture, with their expanse of barley, limbs of those tasted by Agni, belonging to the Hundred Rudras, portions covered with fat, from the sides, from the thighs, from the fore-feet from the chine. From every member of the divided victims these two make their repast. Thus let the Asvins accept. Hotar, offer the sacrificial oblation.

---

40 *The Lion:* Indra.

43 *Before those who hate us:* before the Asuras and malicious Râkshasas carry off the sacrificial offerings. *Fields:* metaphorically, for the well-nourished limbs of the victims. *Tasted by Agni:* when roasting for sacrifice. *Belonging to the Hundred Rudras:* that is, to Rudra, Lord of Cattle, in his manifold manifestations (XVI., introductory note); according to Mahîdhara, 'lauded with many texts; rudra meaning 'praiser' according to Yâska, Nighaṇṭus, 3. 16.

44 Let the Hotar worship Sarasvatî. Let her approach the ram, the sacrifice.
To-day let her eat, etc., the rest of verse 43 repeated *mutatis mutandis.*

45 Let the Hotar worship Indra, etc., as in 44 *mutatis mutandis.*

46 Let the Hotar worship Vanaspati. He has held with a very well formed and very strong rope. There where the favourite stations of the Asvins are, of the he-goat the sacrifice; of Sarasvatî, of the ram the sacrifice; of Indra, of the bull the sacrifice; there where the favourite stations of Agni are, of Soma, of Indra the Good Deliverer, of Savitar, of Varuṇa, the favourite places of Vanaspati, the favourite stations of Gods who drink clarified butter, and of Agni the Hotar, there let him arrange these victims when he has praised and lauded them, and perform when he has made them very strong. Let divine Vanaspati accept. Hotar, offer oblation.

47 Let the Hotar worship Agni Svishṭakṛit. Let Agni worship the favourite stations of the Asvins, of the he-goat the sacrifice; of Sarasvatî, of the ram the sacrifice; of Indra, of the bull the sacrifice; there, etc., to 'butter' as in 46. Let him worship the favourite stations of Agni the Hotar. Let him worship his own majesty. Let him win for himself by sacrifice food worthy of sacrifice. Let him, Knower of Beings, perform the sacred rites. Let him accept the sacrificial food. Hotar, offer oblation.

48 The Grass divine, for the right Gods, Sarasvatî, the Asvins Twain,
Give Indra splendour, with the Grass, sight of his eyes and mighty strength! For gain of wealth let them enjoy. Thou, Hotar, offer sacrifice.

49 The Doors, the Doors divine, the Two Asvins, Leeches, Sarasvatî—
May they give breath to Indra in his nostrils, and heroic strength.
For gain of wealth, etc., as in verse 48.

---

46 *He has held:* the victims. This is Mahîdhara's explanation of *adhita.* *Stations:* dainties: Eggeling.

47 *Svishṭakṛit:* Maker of Good Sacrifice. *Worship his own majesty:* that is, bring it to the sacrifice. In several of the preceding Âprî verses (30—46) there are difficulties and obscurities, and Mahîdhara's attempted explanations by turning nominatives into accusatives, etc. are futile.

50 May Dawn and Night, the Goddesses, both Aṣvins, and Sarasvatî
Lay, with both Dawns, strength, voice within Indra the Good Deliverer's mouth.
For gain of wealth, etc.

1 Both nursing Goddesses, the Pair of Aṣvins, and Sarasvati
Have with both nurses given strength to Indra, fame, and power to hear.
For gain of wealth, etc.

2 Bringers of strengthening sacrifice, both Goddesses, well-yielding cows,
Sarasvatî, both Aṣvins, the Physicians, these are Indra's guards.
Forth from their breasts by sacrifice they give him brilliant light and power.
For gain of wealth, etc.

3 Both Gods, the Hotars of the Gods, the Aṣvins the Physicians and
Sarasvatî with Vashaṭ-calls, with the two Hotars have bestowed on Indra brilliant light and power, and planted wisdom in his heart.
For gain of wealth, etc.

4 Goddesses three, three Goddesses—Aṣvins, Idâ, Sarasvatî
In Indra's midmost navel have laid store of energy and power.
For gain of wealth, etc.

5 God Narâṣaṃsa, Indra thrice-protecting, whose car moves by Sarasvati and Aṣvins—
May Tvashṭar lay seed, deathless form in Indra, a fitting place of birth and mighty powers.
For gain of wealth, etc.

6 God with the Gods, Vanaspati of golden leaves and goodly fruit
Ripens till Indra finds it sweet, with Aṣvins and Sarasvatî.

7 Strewn, soft as wool, in sacrifice, with Aṣvins and Sarasvatî,
The sacred robe of water-plants be, Indra, a fair seat for thee!
Together with the sacred grass may they, for sovranty, bestow King Passion and great power on thee.
For gain of wealth, etc.

---

51 *Both nursing Goddesses:* Heaven and Earth, or Day and Night.
54 *Sarasvatî:* and Bhâratî, understood.
57 *Robe of water-plants:* mixed with the *barhis* or altar-covering of grass.
*King Passion:* see verse 39. Mahîdhara explains *rájánam* by *dîpyamánam*, glowing.

58 Let the God Agni Svishṭakṛit worship the Gods as is meet and right for each, the two Hotars, Indra, the Aṣvins, Vâk with speech, Sarasvatî, Agni, Soma. Svishṭakṛit has been well worshipped, Indra Good Deliverer, Savitar, Varuṇa the Physician have been worshipped. The God Vanaspati, the Gods who drink clarified butter have been well worshipped, Agni by Agni. Let the Hotar Svishṭakṛit give the Hotar fame, great power, energy, honour, Ancestral libation.

59 To-day this Sacrificer cooking viands, cooking sacrificial rice-cakes, binding a goat for the Aṣvins, a ram for Sarasvati, a bull for Indra, pressing Surâ and Soma juices for the Aṣvins, Sarasvatî, and Indra the Good Deliverer, has chosen Agni as Hotar.

60 To-day the divine Vanaspati has done good service to the Aṣvins with a goat, to Sarasvati with a ram, to Indra with a bull. They have eaten these from the marrow onwards, they have accepted the cooked viands, they have waxed strong with the rice-cakes. The Agnis, Sarasvati, and Indra have drunk the Surâ and Soma draughts.

61 Thee, to-day, O Ṛishi, Ṛishi's son, descendant of Ṛishis, hath this Sacrificer chosen for many collected, saying: This (Agni) shall win by sacrifice for me choice-worthy treasures among the Gods. O God, what gifts the Gods have given, these do thou desire and approve. And thou art a commissioned Hotar, a human Hotar sent forward for benediction, for good speech. Speak thou good words.

---

61 *O Ṛishi:* the Hotar, representative of Agni the divine Hotar, is addressed. *For many:* assembled Gods. *O God:* Agni.

## BOOK THE TWENTY-SECOND.

SPLENDOUR art thou, bright, deathless, life-protector. Protector of my life be thou.
By impulse of God Savitar I take thee with arms of Asvins, with the hands of Púshan.

2 This girdle, which in their religious meetings sages assumed in earlier time of worship,
Is present with us here at this libation, in the Law's hymn, proclaiming rich abundance.

3 Famous art thou, thou art the world, controller and upholder thou.
Go, consecrate by Svâhâ to Agni Vaisvânara widely-famed.

4 For Gods and for Prajâpati I fit thee. For Gods and for Prajâpati, O Brahman,
Will I tie up the horse. Thence may I prosper! Binding him for Prajâpati and Gods be thou successful.

5 Thee welcome to Prajâpati I sprinkle. I sprinkle thee welcome to Indra-Agni. I sprinkle thee acceptable to Vâyu. Thee welcome to the All-Gods I besprinkle. Thee welcome to all Deities I sprinkle.
With fury Varuna attacks the man who fain would slay the steed.
Avaunt the man! Avaunt the dog!

---

Books XXII—XXV. contain the formulas of the Asvamedha or Horse-sacrifice, a very ancient and most important ceremony which only a King can perform. Its object is the acquisition of power and glory, acknowledged preëminence over neighbouring princes, and the general prosperity of the kingdom by the fulfilment of the wishes expressed in verse 22 of this Book.

1 The Adhvaryu ties an ornament of gold, perhaps a chain, round the neck of the Sacrificer, and makes him recite the formula. *Thou:* he addresses the ornament. *Deathless:* as a symbol of the Sun, and identified with light (IV. 17), or, according to Mahîdhara, because gold confers immortality by being presented to the priests. *By impulse, etc.:* repeated from I. 10. *Thee:* a *rasanâ*, girdle, or girth of Darbha grass, thirteen ells in length, with which the sacrificial horse is to be girded.

2 *In the Law's hymn:* when the Sâman of sacrifice is chanted.

3 He girds and addresses the horse.

4 *I fit:* *svagâ*, an indeclinable sacrificial word, Good-speed! and *karomi*, I make or prepare, understood.

5 He sprinkles the horse in standing water. *With fury etc.:* he threatens any man who kills the horse, and so prevents the sacrifice, with the vengeance of the royal Varuna, and a dog is killed (to indicate the punishment of the sinner) by a low-caste man, the son of a Sûdra by a Vaisyâ woman.

6 To Agni Hail! To Soma Hail! Hail to the Waters' Joy! Hail to Savitar! Hail to Vâyu! Hail to Vishṇu! Hail to Indra! Hail to Bṛihaspati! Hail to Mitra! Hail to Varuṇa!

7 Hail to the sound *hiṅ!* Hail to the uttered *hiṅ!* Hail to the neigh! Hail to the down-neigh! Hail to the snort! Hail to the roar! Hail to his smell! Hail to him smelt at! Hail to him seated! Hail to him seated down! Hail to him weary! Hail to him going! Hail to him sitting! Hail to him lying! Hail to him sleeping! Hail to him waking! Hail to him whinnying! Hail to him wakened! Hail to him yawning! Hail to him outstretched! Hail to him drawn together! Hail to him risen! Hail to his going! Hail to his good going! Hail!

8 Hail to him as he goes! Hail to him running! Hail to him running away! Hail to him when he has run away! Hail to the cry Shoo! Hail to him scared with Shoo! Hail to him seated! Hail to him risen! Hail to his speed! Hail to his strength! Hail to him rolling! Hail to him when he has rolled! Hail to him tossing about! Hail to him when he has tossed about! Hail to him listening! Hail to him hearing. Hail to him looking! Hail to him looked at! Hail to him closely looked at! Hail to his closing his eye! Hail to his food! Hail to his drink! Hail to his stale! Hail to him in action! Hail to what he has done!

9 May we attain that excellent glory of Savitar the God:
So may he stimulate our prayers.

10 For our protection I invoke the golden-handed Savitar:
He knoweth, as a God, the place.

11 We specially invoke the grace of Savitar, observant God,
The great good-will that gives true boons.

12 We seek the eulogy and gift of Savitar who strengthens grace,
Yea, of the God who knows our thoughts.

13 I invocate the heroes' Lord, free-giving Savitar, and call
The Cheerer to the feast of Gods.

---

6 The horse is led back to the sacrificial fire, and ten oblations of clarified butter are offered, with their respective formulas to the deities mentioned. *The Waters' Joy:* Soma who delights the waters with which he is sprinkled.

7 He offers an oblation in the Southern fire. *Hiṅ:* onomatopoetic; the horse's low neigh or whinny: originally, the syllable to be uttered, or the sound to be made in reciting Sâma hymns.

9 Six verses follow constituting the Inviting and Offering Prayers of oblations presented to Savitar. The first verse is the famous Sâvitrî, the Gâyatrî *par excellence*, repeated from III. 35, and taken from R. V. III. 62 10.

10 Taken from R. V. I. 22. 5.

14 The judgment of bright Savitar, that cheers the All-Gods' company,
With prayer we estimate as bliss.
15 Wake Agni with thy laud and set the Immortal One aflame, let him
Bestow our offerings on the Gods.
16 Oblation-bearer, well-inclined, immortal, eager Messenger,
Agni comes near us with the thought.
17 Agni, Envoy, I place in front, the oblation-bearer I address:
Here let him seat the Deities.
18 Yea, Pavamâna, thou didst generate the Sun and spread the moisture out with power,
Hasting to us with plenty vivified with milk.
19 Mighty through thy dam, eminent through thy sire, thou
art a horse, thou art a steed, thou art a courser, thou
art a comfort, thou art a racer, thou art a yoke-horse,
thou art a strong steed, thou art a stallion, thou art
manly-minded. Thou art called Yayu, thou art called
Sisu. Follow thou the flight of the Âdityas.

Gods, Warders of the Regions, protect for the Gods this horse besprinkled for sacrifice.

Here is delight. Here take thy pleasure. Here is content. Here is self-content.

20 Hail to Ka! Hail to Who?! Hail to Which?! Hail to
him who has experienced pain! Hail to Prajâpati who
knows the mind! Hail to him who discerns the thought!

---

15 Three Inviting Verses to Agni follow.

16 Taken from R. V. III. 11. 2. *With the thought:* when we think of, or pray to, him.

17 Taken from R. V. VIII. 44. 3. *Place in front:* for adoration.

18 Taken from R. V. IX. 110. 3. Praise and prayer addressed to Soma.

19 The Adhvaryu and the Sacrificer whisper the formula in the horse's right ear. Then the horse (who must be more than twenty four, and less than a hundred years old) is loosed towards the North-east to wander free for a year (or for half a year or a still shorter time according to some authorities), as a sign that his master's paramount sovereignty is acknowledged by all neighbouring princes. The wandering horse is attended by a hundred young men, sons of princes or high Court officials, armed with all sorts of warlike weapons, who are to watch and guard him from all dangers and inconvenience. During the absence of the horse an uninterrupted series of prescribed ceremonies is performed at the Sacrificer's home.

*Yayu:* meaning Goer or Sacrificial. *Sisu:* or Colt; a euphemism for a horse of somewhat mature age.

20 Oblations are offered and homage is paid to various Deities. *Ka... Who? Which?:* Prajâpati. See I. 6, note. *Of the highways:* Pûshan as a Sun-God is guardian of roads and guide of travellers. *Many forms:* of living beings created by him. *Nibhûyapa:* the origin and meaning of the word are unknown. According to Mahîdhara the title means Preserver by means of his repeated incarnations of the Fish, the Tortoise, etc. *Sipivishta:* another title of uncertain meaning. See XVI. 29, note.

Hail to Aditi! Hail to good Aditi! Hail to gracious Aditi! Hail to Sarasvatî! Hail to purifying Sarasvatî! Hail to great Sarasvatî! Hail to Pûshan! Hail to Pûshan of the highways! Hail to Pûshan observer of men! Hail to Tvashṭar! Hail to swift Tvashṭar! Hail to Tvashṭar of many forms! Hail to Vishṇu! Hail to Vishṇu Nibhûyapa! Hail to Vishṇu Șipivishṭa!

21 Let every mortal man elect, etc., repeated from IV. 8.

22 O Brahman, let there be born in the kingdom the Brâhman illustrious for religious knowledge; let there be born the Râjanya, heroic, skilled archer, piercing with shafts, mighty warrior; the cow giving abundant milk; the ox good at carrying; the swift courser; the industrious woman. May Parjanya send rain according to our desire; may our fruit-bearing plants ripen; may acquisition and preservation of property be secured to us.

23 Hail to vital breath! Hail to out-breathing! Hail to diffusive breath! Hail to the eye! Hail to the ear! Hail to Speech! Hail to Mind!

24 Hail to the Eastern Region! Hail to the hitherward Region! Hail to the Southern Region! Hail to the hitherward Region! Hail to the Western Region! Hail to the hitherward Region! Hail to the Northern Region! Hail to the hitherward Region! Hail to the Upward Region! Hail to the hitherward Region! Hail to the Downward Region! Hail to the hitherward Region!

25 Hail to waters! Hail to floods! Hail to water! Hail to standing waters! Hail to flowing waters! Hail to trickling waters! Hail to well waters! Hail to spring waters! Hail to the foaming sea! Hail to the ocean! Hail to the deep!

26 Hail to wind! Hail to mist! Hail to vapour! Hail to cloud! Hail to cloud lightening! Hail to cloud thundering! Hail to it bursting! Hail to it raining! Hail to it pouring! Hail to it violently raining! Hail to it swiftly raining! Hail to it holding up! Hail to it when it has held up! Hail to it sprinkling! Hail to it drizzling! Hail to its drops! Hail to thunderbolts! Hail to hoar frosts!

27 Hail to Agni! Hail to Soma! Hail to Indra! Hail to Earth! Hail to Firmament! Hail to Sky! Hail to Regions! Hail to Quarters! Hail to the Upward Region! Hail to the Downward Region!

---

22 The Adhvaryu whispers to the Brahman priest the blessings which the King hopes the sacrifice will secure to his kingdom.

23 The remaining verses of this Book contain formulas af homage to various Gods and natural and terrestrial objects, accompanying the presentation of oblations made of various materials.

28 Hail to the lunar asterisms! Hail to those connected with the lunar asterisms! Hail to Day and Night! Hail to the half-months! Hail to the months! Hail to the Seasons! Hail to the Season-groups! Hail to the Year! Hail to Heaven and Earth! Hail to the Moon! Hail to the Sun! Hail to his rays! Hail to the Vasus! Hail to the Rudras! Hail to the Âdityas! Hail to the Maruts! Hail to the All-Gods! Hail to roots! Hail to branches! Hail to forest trees! Hail to flowers! Hail to fruits! Hail to herbs!

29 Hail to Earth! Hail to Firmament! Hail to Sky! Hail to Sun! Hail to Moon! Hail to lunar asterisms! Hail to waters! Hail to herbs! Hail to forest trees! Hail to creatures that swim! Hail to things moving and stationary! Hail to things that creep and crawl!

30 Hail to breath! Hail to the Vasu! Hail to the Mighty! Hail to Vivasvân! Hail to the trooping one! Hail to the Troop's Lord! Hail to the Superior! Hail to the Overlord! Hail to Strength! Hail to Saṃsarpa! Hail to the Moon! Hail to light! Hail to Malimlucha! Hail to him who flies by day!

31 Hail to Madhu! Hail to Mâdhava! Hail to Sukra! Hail to Suchi! Hail to Nabhas! Hail to Nabhasya! Hail to Isha! Hail to Ûrja! Hail to Sahas! Hail to Sahasya! Hail to Tapas! Hail to Tapasya! Hail to Aṃhasaspati!

32 Hail to Strength! Hail to impulse! Hail to After-born! Hail to will! Heaven, Hail! Hail to the head! Hail to Vyaṣnuvin! To the final, Hail! Hail to the mundane final! Hail to the Lord of the world! Hail to the Overlord! Hail to the Lord of Creatures!

33 May life succeed by sacrifice, Hail! May breath succeed by sacrifice, Hail! May downward breath, diffusive breath, upward breath, digestive breath, vision, hearing, speech, mind, self, devotion, light, heaven, hymn-arrangement, sacrifice succeed by sacrifice. All-hail!

34 Hail to One! Hail to Two! Hail to Hundred! Hail to Hundred-and-One! Hail to Daybreak! Hail to Heaven!

---

30 *Vivasvân:* the Bright One; the Sun. *The trooping one:* the company of Maruts. *The Troop's Lord:* Indra. *Saṃsarpa:* an intercalary month. *Malimlucha:* another name of the intercalary month.

31 This verse contains names of the months; all of which have occurred in earlier Books. See VII. 30, note. *Aṃhasaspati:* Lord of Trouble; the Genius of the intercalary month. See VII. 30.

32 *After-born:* the intercalary month. Cp. R. V. I. 25. 8. *Vyaṣnuvin:* a Genius of food, according to Mahîdhara. For the rest of the verse, cp. IX. 20.

33 Cf. IX. 21.

34 He salutes the Genii of Numbers.

# BOOK THE TWENTY-THIRD.

In the beginning rose Hiranyagarbha, etc.

2 Taken upon a base art thou. I take thee welcome to Prajâpati.
This is thy place: Sûrya thy majesty.
The majesty that has accrued to thee in the day, in a year, that majesty which has accrued in the wind, in the firmament, to that majesty of thine, to Prajâpati, to the Gods, All-hail!

3 Who by his grandeur hath become sole Ruler of all the moving world that breathes and slumbers;
He who is Sovran of these men and cattle—what God shall we adore with our oblation?

4 Taken upon a base art thou. I take thee welcome to Prajâpati.
This is thy place: the Moon thy majesty.
Thy majesty that has accrued to thee by night, in a year, thy majesty that has accrued in the earth, in Agni, in the stars and in the Moon, to that majesty of thine, to Prajâpati and to the Gods, All-hail!

5 They who stand round him as he moves harness the bright, the ruddy Steed:
The lights are shining in the sky.

6 On both sides to the car they yoke the two Bay Coursers dear to him,
Bold, tawny, bearers of the Chief.

7 When, swift as wind, the Horse has reached the form that Indra loves, the flood,
Again, O singer, by this path bring thou our Courser hitherward.

---

The ceremonies subsequent to the return of the Horse from his wanderings are continued.

1 The Sacrificer offers two Mahiman or Grandeur libations, so called from the name of the golden vessels in which they are presented, and recites the text, repeated from XIII. 4, taken from R. V. X. 121. 1. *Hiranyagarbha*: the Gold-Germ, or Golden Child; Prajâpati, with whom the Sacrificial Horse is identified.

2 *Thou*: the Cup. *Majesty*: or grandeur; *mahimâ*: thy grandeur is like the Sun's.

3 Taken from R. V. X. 121. 3. *What God?*: other than Prajâpati. Or, according to Mahîdhara: Worship we Ka the God. See I. 6, note.

5 He yokes the Horse to a gilded chariot, reciting the text taken from R. V. I. 6. 1.

6 Three other horses are harnessed to the same chariot, with the text from R. V. I. 6. 2.

7 *The flood*: the water to which the Horse is driven to be bathed.

8 Let the Vasus anoint thee with Gâyatrî metre. Let the Rudras anoint thee with Trishṭup metre. Let the Âdityas anoint thee with Jagatî metre. Earth! Ether! Heaven! O Gods, eat this food, parched grains and groats in the product of barley and in the product of cows: eat this food, Prajâpati.

9 Who moveth single and alone? Who is brought forth to life again?
What is the remedy of cold, or what the great receptacle?

10 The Sun moves single and alone. The Moon is brought to life again.
Fire is the remedy of cold; Earth is the great receptacle.

11 What was the antecedent thought? What was the bird of mighty size?
The slippery matron, who was she? Who was the reddish-coloured one?

12 Heaven was the antecedent thought. The Courser was the mighty bird.
The slippery matron was the earth. Night was the reddish-coloured one.

13 Vâyu help thee with cooked viands! Blackneck with goats; Nyagrodha with cups; Sâlmali with increase; this Stallion here, good for the chariot—let him verily come with his four feet. Brahmâkṛishṇa help us! Obeisance to Agni!

---

8 When the Horse has been brought back from the water, the Chief Queen and two other royal Consorts anoint him with clarified butter, reciting their respective formulas. The Chief Queen anoints the fore-quarters, and the others the barrel and hind-quarters. *Earth! etc.*: with these sacrificial exclamations the three Queens, respectively, entwine the hair of the Horse's head, neck, and tail with chains or other ornaments of gold. *O Gods*: the Sacrificer offers the Horse the remains of the night-oblation of grain, which is thrown into the water if he refuses to eat it. *Product of cows*: the sour curds with which the oblation was mixed. *Prajâpati*: meaning the deified Horse.

9 Here intervenes a Brahmodyam, a discussion in question and answer of cosmogonical and mystic-theological doctrine. The questions are couched in designedly enigmatical language, constituting a sort of 'cosmic charade,' as Prof. M Bloomfield calls it. *Who moveth*, etc.: the Brahman questions the Hotar.

10 The Hotar replies.

11 The Hotar questions the Brahman.

12 The Brahman replies. *Heaven*: meaning rain, according to Mahîdhara. *The Courser*: the Sacrificial Horse. *Mighty bird*: that carries the sacrifice of himself to heaven. *Earth*: Mahîdhara's explanation of *aviḥ* (sheep; woollen cloth; Soma-strainer). *Slippery*: after rain.

13 The Horse, a hornless he-goat, and a Gomṛiga or wild ox (Bos Gavaeus) are bound to sacrificial stakes near the fire, and seventeen other victims, a

14 The car is fitted with the rein, the steed is fitted with the rein.
Fitted in waters, water-born, is Brahmâ following Soma's lead.

15 Steed, from thy body, of thyself, sacrifice and accept thyself.
Thy greatness can be gained by none but thee.

16 No, here thou diest not, thou art not injured: only by fair paths to the Gods thou goest.
May Savitar the God in that world place thee where dwell the pious, whether they have journeyed.

17 Agni was the victim. With him they sacrificed. He won this world in which Agni is. This shall become thy world. This shalt thou win. Drink these waters. Vâyu was the victim. With him they sacrificed. He won this world in which Vâyu is. This shall become, etc., as above. Sûrya was the victim, etc. He won the world in which Sûrya is. This shall become, etc.

18 To vital breath, Hail! To out-breathing, Hail! To diffusive breath, Hail!
Ambâ! Ambikâ! Ambâlikâ! No one is taking me away.
The sorry horse will lie beside another, as Subhadrâ the dweller in Kâmpîla.

---

he-goat and a ram among them, are attached to the Horse. To the other stakes are tied a great number of animals, tame and wild, the total, according to the Commentator, amounting to six hundred and nine. *Vâyu help thee:* the Horse is addressed. *Blackneck:* Agni, the fire with its dark smoke. *Nyagrodha:* the Ficus Indica, of whose wood sacrificial vessels are made. *Salmali:* the Seemul or Silk Cotton tree, also used for sacred purposes. *With his four feet:* with all speed. *Brahmâkrishna:* the Brahman in whom there is no black spot; said to mean the Moon.

14 *Fitted:* or, quickened. *Brahmâ:* the Great One, the Horse. *Water-born:* as identified with the Sun who springs out of the ocean of air. See R. V. I. 163. 1. *Soma's lead:* to heaven.

15 The Horse is slaughtered.

16 The Horse is addressed. The first line is taken from R. V. I. 162. 21, and the second from a funeral hymn R. V. X. 17. 4.

17 *Agni was the victim:* offered by the Gods of creation. *Thy world:* the Horse is addressed. *In which Vâyu is:* the firmament. *In which Sûrya is:* the sky.

18 *To vital breath,* etc.: three fire-oblations are offered with these three formulas. *Ambâ, etc.:* women's names. The Chief Queen calls on her fellow-wives for pity, as, to obtain a son, she has to pass the night in disgusting contiguity to the slaughtered Horse: "No one takes me (by force to the horse); (but if I go not of myself), the (spiteful) horse will lie with (another, as) the (wicked) Subhadrâ who dwells in Kâmpila."—Weber, History of Indian Literature, p. 114. *Subhadrâ:* probably the wife of the King of Kâmpila in the country of the Pañchâlas in the North of India. The Chief Queen must submit to the revolting ceremony, or its benefits will go to another woman. See Râmâyana, Book I. Canto XIII. Schlegel's edition.

19 Thee we invoke, troop-lord of troops. Thee we invoke, the loved ones' lord.

Thee, lord of treasures, we invoke. My precious wealth! .

. . . . . . . . . . . .

. . . . . . . . . . . .

32 Now have I glorified with praise strong Dadhikrâvan, conquering steed.

Sweet may he make our mouths: may he prolong the days we have to live.

33 Gâyatrî, Trishṭup, Jagatî, and Paṅkti with Anushṭup joined,
Bṛihatî, Kakup, Ushṇihâ pacify thee with needle-points!

34 Two-footed, those that have four feet, those with three feet and those with five,

Metreless, with one metre, these pacify thee with needle-points!

35 May Mahânâmnis, Revatîs, all far-spread Regions of the sky,
Voices, and lightnings from the cloud pacify thee with needle-points!

36 May married dames of human birth skilfully separate thy hair:

The Regions, Consorts of the Gods, pacify thee with needle-points!

---

19 The three Queens walk nine times round the Horse, reciting the formulas. The Chief Queen then begins the performance of the revolting ceremony.

20 *Mahishî svayamevâśvaśiśnamâkṛishya svayonau sthâpayati.* This and the following nine stanzas are not reproducible even in the semi-obscurity of a learned European language; and stanzas 30, 31 would be unintelligible without them.

32 On the following morning the officiating priests raise the Chief Queen from the place where she has spent the night, and recite the text, taken from R. V. IV. 39. 6, to purify their mouths after the abominable obscenities which they have uttered. *Dadhikrâvan:* or in the shorter form, Dadhikrâs or Dadhikrâ, described as a kind of divine or deified horse, and probably, like Târkshya (XV. 18), a personification of the morning sun. The verse is called the Dâdhikrî, and is used as a purifier after foul language. Cf. The Hymns of the Atharva-Veda, Vol. II. Appendix, p. 457,

33 The three Queens with a hundred and one needles, gold, silver and copper, mark out the lines, on the body of the horse, which the dissector's knife is to follow. *Pacify:* or, send to rest; a sacrificial euphemism.

34 *Two-footed: dvipadâs;* verses with two *padas* or metrical divisions. *With one metre:* having the same metre throughout.

35 *Mahânâmnîs:* whose name is great; nine verses of the Sâmaveda in Śakvarî metre. *Revatîs:* verses from which the Raivata Sâman is formed, so named from R. V. I. 30. 13 in which the word *revatî*, splendid, or wealthy, occurs.

37 They, made of silver, gold, and lead, are used as helpers in the work.
As lines on the strong Courser's skin may they console and give thee rest.

38 What then? As men whose fields are full of barley, etc., as in X. 32.

39 Who flays thee? Who dissects thee? Who prepares thy limbs for sacrifice?
Who is the Sage that slaughters thee?

40 In due time let the seasons as thy Slaughterers divide thy joints,
And with the splendour of the Year sacrifice thee with holy rites.

41 Let the Half-months and let the Months, while sacrificing, flay thy limbs:
Let Day and Night and Maruts mend each fault in sacrificing thee.

42 Let the divine Adhvaryus flay thy body and dissect thy frame,
And let the sacrificing lines prepare thy members joint by joint.

43 May Sky, Earth, Air, and Wind supply each failing and defect of thine:
May Sûrya with the Stars of heaven duly prepare a world for thee.

44 Well be it with thine upper parts, well be it with the parts below!
Well be it with thy bones and with thy marrow and with all thy frame!

45 Who moveth singly? etc., as in verse 9.

46 The Sun moves singly, etc., as in verse 10.

47 What lustre is like Sûrya's light? What lake is equal to the Sea?

---

37 *Lead:* meaning, probably, copper or iron, as Mahîdhara explains.

39 *Who?* or Ka, that is Prajâpati himself performs these sacrificial operations, and not I the human priest.

42 *The divine Adhvaryus:* the Asvins, the Adhvaryus of the Gods. *Sacrificing lines:* traced on the body of the horse to guide the Immolator's knife. See verse 33.

43 *Stars:* or lunar asterisms.

45 Before the *vapâ* or omentum is offered as a burnt-oblation the following Brahmodyam (see verse 9) intervenes. Verses 45, 46 are repeated from 9 and 10.

What is more spacious than the Earth? What thing is that which naught can mete?

48 Brahma is lustre like the Sun. Heaven is a flood to match the Sea.

Indra is vaster than the Earth. Beyond all measure is the Cow.

49 Friend of the Gods, I ask, for information, if thou in spirit hast obtained the knowledge,

Hath Vishṇu this whole Universe pervaded in the three steps wherein the God is worshipped?

50 I also am in those three steps of Vishṇu wherewith this Universe he permeated.

The earth and heaven I circle in a moment and this heaven's summit with a single organ.

51 What are the things which Purusha hath entered? What things hath Purusha contained within him?

This riddle we propound to thee, O Brahman. Why dost thou give no answer to my question?

52 Within five things hath Purusha found entrance: these Purusha hath within himself connected.

This is the thought which I return in answer. Thou art not my superior in wisdom.

53 What was the antecedent thought? etc., as in verse 11.

54 Heaven was the antecedent thought, etc., as in 12.

55 Who, tell me, is the yellowish she? Who is the darkly-yellowish?

Who moves with rapid spring and bound? Who glides and winds along the path?

---

48 *Brahma*: holy lore in the shape of the three Vedas, according to Mahîdhara. *The Cow*: as supplying the elements of sacrifice.

49 The Brahman questions the Udgâtar, the priest who chants the Sâmans. *Three steps*: or places; earth, air, and sky, over and through which he strode as the Sun; according to Mahîdhara, the Gârhapatya, Âhavanîya, and Dakshiṇa fires are intended.

50 The Udgâtar replies. *Single organ*: my mind.

51 The Udgâtar questions the Brahman. *Purusha*: the Person; Personality; the Cosmic Man, or Embodied Spirit; *âtmâ*, the soul or self, according to Mahîdhara.

52 The Brahman replies. *Five things*: the five vital breathings. *These*: the senses; the substrata of hearing, etc.

53 The Hotar questions the Adhvaryu. The question and the answer are repeated from verses 11 and 12.

55 The Adhvaryu questions the Hotar. *Yellowish . . . darkly-yellowish*: the precise colours intended are uncertain.

56 The she-goat, Sir, is yellowish, dark-yellowish is the porcupine.
The hare moves swift with leap and bound: the snake creeps winding on the path.

57 How many different forms hath this, how many syllables, burnt-oblations, brands for kindling?
Here, of the rites of sacrifice I ask thee. How many Hotars in due season worship?

58 Sixfold its form, its syllables a hundred, eighty burnt-offerings, just three brands for kindling.
To thee I tell the rites of sacrificing. Seven Hotars worship in appointed season.

59 Who knoweth this world's central point? Who knoweth the heaven, the earth, and the wide air between them?
Who knows the birthplace of the mighty Sûrya? Who knows the Moon, whence he was generated?

60 I know the centre of the world about us. I know heaven, earth, and the wide air between them.
I know the birthplace of the mighty Sûrya. I know the Moon, whence he was generated.

61 I ask thee of the earth's extremest limit, where is the centre of the world, I ask thee.
I ask thee of the Stallion's genial humour, I ask of highest heaven where Speech abideth.

62 This altar is the earth's extremest limit; this sacrifice of ours is the world's centre.
This Soma is the Stallion's genial humour, this Brahman highest heaven where Speech abideth.

---

56 The Hotar replies. *The she-goat: ajâ* here is explained by Mahîdhara (who takes the word in the sense of birthless) as Mâyâ, Illusion, phenomenal Nature; or Night.

57 The Brahman questions the Udgâtar. *Forms:* according to Mahîdhara, viands or kinds of food. *This:* sacrifice.

58 *Sixfold:* according to Mahîdhara, referring to the six principal tastes, sweet, bitter, salt, etc. *Syllables:* of the sacred metres, twenty-four of the Gâyatrî, etc. *Burnt oblations:* meaning kinds of victims for such offerings. *Eighty:* four tied to each of twenty stakes. *Seven Hotars:* the Hotar, Maitrâvaruṇa, Achchhâvâka, Grâvastut, Brâhmaṇâchchhaṃsî, Âgnîdhra, Potar.

59 The Udgâtar questions the Brahman, who replies in the following verse.

61 The Sacrificer questions the Adhvaryu. The verse is taken from R. V. I. 164. 34.

62 *This altar:* as the place nearest heaven, the place where the Gods visit men. *The Stallion:* Dyaus or Heaven, whose *genial humour* is the fertilizing rain which impregnates the earth. *This Brahman:* who recites the texts of the Veda represents the abiding-place of Speech or the Word.

63 The Strong, the Self-existent One, the First, within the mighty flood
Laid down the timely embryo from which Prajâpati was born.

64 Let the Hotar sacrifice to Prajâpati from the Mahiman-Soma. Let him accept. Let him drink the Soma. Hotar, sacrifice.

65 Prajâpati, thou only, etc., as in X. 20.

---

63 At the end of the Brahmodyam the Adhvaryu draws the Mahiman libation for Prajâpati in a golden cup. *The First:* Purusha; the Self.

64 *The Hotar:* the Hotar of the Gods. *Mahiman-Soma:* contained in the gold cup called Mahiman, Glory, see verse 1, note.

*Hotar, sacrifice:* the human Hotar is addressed.

## BOOK THE TWENTY-FOURTH.

HORSE, hornless goat, Gomṛiga, these belong to Prajâpati. A black-necked goat, devoted to Agni, (is to be bound) in front to the forehead (of the horse); Sarasvatî's ewe below his jaws; two goats belonging to the Asvins, with marks on the lower parts of the body, to his fore-legs; a dark-coloured goat, Soma's and Pûshan's, to his navel; a white and a black, sacred to Soma and Yama, to his sides; Tvashṭar's two, with bushy tails, to his hind feet; Vâyu's white goat to his tail; for Indra the Good Worker a cow who slips her calf; a dwarf belonging to Vishṇu.

2 The red goat, the smoky-red, the jujube-red, these belong to Soma. The brown, the ruddy-brown, the parrot-brown, these are Varuṇa's. One with white ear holes, one with partly white, one with wholly white, belong to Savitar. One with fore-feet white, partly white, wholly white, belongs to Brihaspati. She-goats speckled, with small spots, with big spots, these belong to Mitra-Varuṇa.

3 The bright-tailed, the wholly bright-tailed, the jewel-tailed, these belong to the Asvins. The white, the white-eyed, the reddish, these are for Rudra Lord of Beasts. Long-eared goats are for Yama; proud ones for Rudra; cloud-coloured ones for Parjanya.

---

This Book contains an exact enumeration of the animals that are to be tied to the sacrificial stakes and in the intermediate spaces, with the names of the deities or deified entities to which they are severally dedicated. The principal stake, the eleventh and midmost of the twenty-one, called the Agnishṭha because it stands nearest to the sacrificial fire, is mentioned first. About fifteen victims are bound to each of these stakes, all domestic animals, the total number being 327. In the spaces between the stakes 282 wild animals, from the elephant and the rhinoceros to the bee and the fly, are temporarily confined, to be freed when the ceremony is concluded, bringing the total number of assembled animals up to 609. There is, perhaps, some exaggeration in the number, and some almost impossible animals are mentioned, but it must be remembered that the Asvamedha was a most important tribal solemnity of rare occurrence and that no effort would be spared to assure its performance with all possible splendour.

Several of the wild animals cannot be identified. Some of the names are conjecturally rendered and some are left in their native forms. The Commentator is not of much assistance in doubtful cases, 'a kind of beast' or 'a kind of bird' being all the information that he has to give.

1 *Gomṛiga:* the Gayal or Bos Gavaeus. *Dwarf:* with reference to Vishṇu's Dwarf Incarnation.

3 *Bright-tailed:* 'goat' is to be understood with this and similar epithets.

4 Goats speckled. transversely speckled, upward speckled are for the Maruts. The reddish she-goat, the red-haired, the white, these belong to Sarasvatî. The goat with diseased ears, the short-eared, the red-eared are Tvashṭar's. The black-necked, the white-flanked, one with bright-coloured thighs belong to Indra and Agni. Those with black marks, small marks, large marks belong to Dawn.

5 Parti-coloured female victims belong to the All-Gods; red-coloured, eighteen months old to Vâk; victims without distinguishing marks to Aditi; those of one same colour to Dhâtar; weaned kids sacred to the Consorts of the Gods.

6 Black-necked victims for Agni; white browed for the Vasus; red for Rudra; bright ones for the Âdityas; cloud-coloured for Parjanya.

7 The tall goat, the sturdy, the dwarf, these are Indra-Vishṇu's; the tall, the white fore-footed, the black-backed, Indra-Bṛihaspati's; parrot-coloured the Vâjins'; speckled Agni-Maruts'; dark-coloured Pûshan's.

8 Variegated, Indra-Agni's; two-coloured, Agni-Soma's; dwarf oxen, Agni-Vishṇu's; barren cows, Mitra-Varuṇa's; partly variegated, Mitra's.

9 Black-necked ones, Agni's; brown, Soma's; white, Vâyu's; undistinguished, Aditi's; self-coloured, Dhâtar's; weanlings, the Gods' Consorts'.

10 Black ones for Earth; smoke-coloured for Firmament; tall ones for Sky; brindled ones for Lightning; blotched ones for Stars.

11 Smoke-coloured ones be sacrifices to Spring; white to Summer; black to the Rains; red ones to Autumn; speckled to Winter; reddish-yellow to the Dewy Season.

12 Calves eighteen months old to Gâyatrî; steers of two and a half years to Trishṭup; two year old steers to Jagatî; three year olds to Anushṭup; four year olds to Ushṇih.

13 Four year old steers to Virâj; full grown bulls to Bṛihatî; strong bulls to Kakup; draught oxen to Paṅkti; milch-cows to Atichhandas.

---

7 *Vâjins:* the deified Coursers of the Gods; a class of divinities, according to Sâyaṇa.

11 *Sacrifices:* literally, takes and ties up; a euphemistic expression.

12, 13 The sacred metres are deified as being 'the embodiment of supreme harmony and the efficacy of prayer.'—Eggeling. S. B. E. XII. 80.

14 Black-necked victims sacred to Agni; brown to Soma; spotted to Savitar; weaned she-kids to Sarasvatî; dark-coloured goats to Pûshan; speckled victims to the Maruts; many-coloured to the All-Gods; barren cows to Heaven and Earth.

15 Called contemporary, the dappled belong to Indra-Agni; black ones to Varuṇa; speckled to the Maruts; hornless he-goats to Ka.

16 To Agni foremost in place he sacrifices firstling goats; to the consuming Maruts those born of one mother; to the Maruts who perform domestic rites those born after a long time; to the sportive Maruts those born together; to the self-strong Maruts those born in succession.

17 Called contemporaneous, the dappled belonging to Indra-Agni; those with projecting horns to Mahendra; the many-coloured to Viṣvakarman.

18 Smoke-coloured, those of brownish hue, to be offered to the Soma-possessing Fathers; the brown and the smoky-looking to the Fathers who sit on sacred grass; the black and the brownish-looking to the Fathers who have been tasted by Agni; the black and the spotted belong to Tryambaka.

19 Called contemporaneous, the dappled belong to Ṣuna and Sîra; white ones to Vâyu; white ones to Sûrya.

20 To Spring he offers Kapiñjalas; to Summer sparrows; to the Rains partridges; to Autumn quails; to Winter Kakaras; to the Dewy Season Vikakaras.

21 To the Sea he sacrifices porpoises; to Parjanya frogs; to the Waters fishes; to Mitra Kulîpayas; to Varuṇa crocodiles.

---

15 *Ka:* Prajâpati. See I. 6, note.

16 *Consuming:* or Fiery; *sântapanebhyaḥ*. *Who perform domestic rites: grihamedhibhyaḥ*. *Sportive: krîḍibhyaḥ*. *Self-strong: svatavdbhyaḥ*; see XVII. 85, and S. B. E. XII. pp. 408, 409.

18 Three classes of Fathers are here mentioned; the Somavantaḥ, the Barhishadaḥ, and the Agnishvâttâḥ. *Tryambaka:* a name of Rudra. See III. 58, note.

19 *Ṣuna and Sîra:* two deities or deified objects which bless or are closely connected with agriculture. The words probably mean, as suggested in the St. Petersburg Lexicon, plougshare and plough. See The Hymns of the Atharva-Veda, III. 17. 5, note.

20 *Kapiñjalas:* heathcocks or francolins. *Kakaras... Vikakaras:* unidentified.

21 *Kulîpayas:* unidentified. *Crocodiles:* the exact meaning of *nâkra*, some kind of aquatic animal, is uncertain.

22 To Soma he sacrifices wild geese; to Vâyu female cranes; to Indra-Agni curlews; to Mitra divers; to Varuṇa Chakravâkas.

23 To Agni he sacrifices cocks; to Vanaspatis owls; to Agni-Soma blue jays; to the Aṣvins peacocks, to Mitra-Varuṇa pigeons.

24 To Soma he sacrifices quails; to Tvashṭar Kaulîkas; Mainas to the Gods' Consorts; Kulîkas to the Gods' Sisters; Pârushṇas to Agni Lord of the Homestead.

25 To Day he sacrifices doves; to Night Sîchâpûs; to the Joints of Day and Night bats; to the Months gallinules; to the Year great eagles.

26 To Ground he sacrifices rats; to Firmament field-rats; to Day voles; to the Quarters mungooses; to the Intermediate Spaces brownish ichneumons.

27 To the Vasus he sacrifices black-bucks; to the Rudras stags; to the Âdityas Nyaṅku deer; to the All-Gods spotted deer; to the Sâdhyas Kuliṅga antelopes.

28 To Îṣâna he sacrifices wild asses; to Mitra Gauras; to Varuṇa buffaloes; to Bṛihaspati Gayals; to Tvashṭar camels.

29 To Prajâpati he sacrifices men elephants; to Vâk white ants; to Sight flies; to Hearing black bees.

30 To Prajâpati and to Vâyu a Gayal is to be offered; to Varuṇa a wild ram; to Yama a black ram; to a human king a monkey; to the Tiger a red doe; to the Bull a female Gayal, to the Kshiprasyena a quail; to the Nîlaṅgu a worm; to the Sea a porpoise; to the Snowy Mountain an elephant.

---

22 *Chakravâkas:* ruddy geese, or Brahmany ducks; regarded by Indian poets as types of conjugal love and fidelity. So 'join thou this couple, Indra! like the Chakravâka and his mate':—Nuptial Hymn, A. V. XIV. 2. 64.

24 *Kaulîkas* ... *Kulîkas*...... *Pârushṇas:* unidentified birds. *Mainas: goshâdîs;* 'settling on cows'; Indian starlings (Coracias Indica).

25 *Sîchâpûs:* unidentified. *Joints:* evening and morning twilight, deified.

27 *Sâdhyas:* meaning, probably, 'those who are to be propitiated.' According to Yâska 'the Gods whose dwelling-place is the sky.' In the Amarakosha they are named among the minor deities, but they seem rather to be the most ancient of the Gods. *Nyaṅku...Kuliṅga:* the species have not been identified.

28 *Îṣâna:* Lord, Ruler; one of the names or titles of Rudra. *Wild asses:* or, perhaps, wild buffaloes, the exact animal intended being uncertain.

30 *Kshiprasyena:* perhaps Swift Falcon. *Nîlaṅgu:* said to be a species of worm; perhaps a tape-worm.

31 The Kinnara belongs to Prajâpati; the Ula, the Halikshṇa, the cat belong to Dhâtar; the heron belongs to the Quarters; the Dhuṅkshâ to Agni; sparrow, red snake, Sâras, these are Tvashṭar's; the curlew belongs to Vâk.

32 To Soma an antelope is to be offered; wild goat, mungoose, Ṣakâ, these are Pûshan's; the jackal is the Mâyu's; the Gaura Indra's; Pidva, antelope, cock, these are Anumati's; the Chakravâka is for Echo.

33 The female crane is Sûrya's; Ṣârga, Sṛijaya, Ṣayâṇḍaka, these are Mitra's; to Sarasvatî belongs the human-voiced Maina; to Ground the porcupine; tiger, wolf, viper belong to Passion; to Sarasvân the human-voiced parrot.

34 The eagle is Parjanya's; the Âṭi, the Vâhasa, the woodpecker, these are for Vâyu; for Bṛihaspati Lord of Speech is the Paiṅgarâja; the Alaja belongs to Firmament; pelican, cormorant, fish, these belong to the Lord of Rivers; the tortoise belongs to Heaven and Earth.

35 The buck belongs to the Moon; iguana, Kâlakâ, woodpecker, these belong to the Vanaspatis; the cock belongs to Savitar; the swan is Vâta's: crocodile, dolphin, Kulîpaya, these belong to the Sea; the porcupine to Modesty.

36 The Black-doe belongs to Day; frog, female rat, partridge, these belong to the Serpents; the jackal belongs to the Asvins; the Black-buck to Night; bear, bat, Sushilîkâ, these belong to the Other Folk; the polecat belongs to Vishṇu.

---

31 *Kinnara*: 'What sort of man?', or Mayu; probably a monkey. *Ula*..*Halikshṇa*: unidentified; according to Mahîdhara, the latter is a kind of lion. *Cat*: *vrishdaṃṣa*, "the strong biter,' is thus explained by the Commentator. *Dhuṅkshâ*: a kind of bird, says Mahîdhara. *Sâras*: the Indian or Siberian Crane (Ardea Sibirica); a splendid bird, easily domesticated.

32 *Ṣakâ*: variously explained as bird, fly, long-eared beast. *Mâyu*: probably a Kimpurusha, or manlike monkey. *Pidva*: unidentified. *Anumati*: Divine Favour personified. *Echo*: because the male and female bird are condemned to pass the night on opposite banks of a river, incessantly calling to each other.

33 *Ṣârga, Sṛijaya, Ṣayâṇḍaka*: unidentified. *Sarasvân*: Sarasvatî's Consort.

34 The birds and beasts whose names are left untranslated in this and following verses are unidentified. *Lord of Rivers*: Ocean.

35 *Vanaspatis*: Sacrificial Stakes.

36 *Other Folk*: a euphemistic expression for certain beings who appear to be regarded as spirits of darkness. So, in England, fairies are called Folk, People, Neighbours; in Germany, Little Folk; in Switzerland, Hill People and Earth People.

37 The cuckoo belongs to the Half Months; antelope, peacock, eagle, these are the Gandharvas'; the otter belongs to the Months; tortoise, doe-antelope, iguana, Golathikâ belong to the Apsarases; the black snake belongs to Death.

38 The frog belongs to the Seasons; the vole, the rat, the mouse, these are the Fathers'; the Python, the Balâya belong to the Vasus; Kapiñjala, pigeon, owl, hare belong to Nirṛiti; the wild ram to Varuṇa.

39 The white animal belongs to the Âdityas; the camel, the Ghṛiṇîvân, the rhinoceros to Mati; the Sṛimara belong to the Forest-God; the Ruru buck is Rudra's; Kvayi, cock, gallinule, these are the Vâjins'; the cuckoo belongs to Kâma.

40 The Khaṅga is the All-Gods'; the black dog, the long-eared, the ass, the hyena, these are the Râkshasas'; the boar is for Indra; the lion is for the Maruts; the chameleon, the Pippaka, the vulture, these belong to Śaravyâ; the spotted antelope belongs to the All-Gods.

---

38 *Kapiñjala*: see verse 20. *Nirṛiti*: the Goddess of Death and Destruction. See XII. 62.

39 *Ghṛiṇîvân*: explained by Mahîdhara as the splendid or strong victim. *Mati*: Thought or Devotion. *Vâjins*: see verse 7. *Cuckoo*: *pika*; whose voice (supposed to say *Pî kahâñ*, Where is my darling?) is chiefly heard in Spring, is the favourite bird of Kâma the God of Love.

40 *Śaravyâ*: the arrow personified as a deity.

# BOOK THE TWENTY-FIFTH.

1 I GRATIFY Fresh Grass with his teeth, Avakâ with his gums, Clay with his tooth-sockets, Tegas with his fangs. The tongue-tip for Sarasvati; I gratify the root of the tongue and the palate with his neigh, Vâja with his jaws, the Waters with his mouth, the Stallion with his testicles, the Âdityas with the beard, Path with his eyebrows, Heaven and Earth with his eyelashes, Lightning with the pupils of his eyes. Hail to the white! Hail to the black! Effectual are his eyelashes, irresistible are his lower eyelashes; irresistible are his eyelashes, effectual are his lower eyelashes.

2 With his breath I gratify Vâta; with his outbreath the two Nostrils; with his lower lip the Upayâma; with his upper lip Existence. With his bright look I please Antara, with his reflection Bâhya; the Whirlpool with his head; Thunder with his frontal bone; the Lightning-flash with his brain; Lightning with the pupils of his eyes; Hearing with his external ears; Ears with his internal ears; Blood with his lower neck; Waters with the fleshless part of his neck; Thought with the back neck-tendons; Aditi with his head; Nirṛiti with his ragged head; Vital Breathings with his roars; Tempest with his crest.

3 I gratify Flies with his hair; Indra with his active shoulder; Bṛihaspati with his quick spring; Tortoises with his hoofs; Approach with his fetlocks; Kapiñjalas with his heel-ropes; Speed with his two thighs; the Way with his two fore-legs; the Forest-God with a kneepan; Agni with his two knees; Pûshan with his two fore-feet; the Aṣvins with his shoulders; Rudra with his shoulder-joints.

---

The Horse-sacrifice is continued. In the first nine verses (which constitute a Brâhmana or Exegetical Treatise as distinct from the Texts and Formulas) oblation is made of the roasted flesh, the various parts of the victim being assigned, with the cry of Svâhâ! All-hail! to a host of deities and other objects which are regarded as deified for the occasion.

1 *Avakâ:* a water-plant. See XIII. 30. *Tegas:* the Commentator gives no explanation, and the meaning is unknown. *Vâja:* Strength; or Sacrificial Food. *The Path:* cf. the Way in verse 3. *The white:* the light-coloured part of the body.

2 *Upayâma:* the formula accompanying certain Soma libations: Taken upon a base *(upayâma)* art thou. See VII. 4. *Bright look:* according to Mahîdhara, the gloss on the upper part of his body. *Antara:* interior. *Reflection:* gloss on the lower part of his body, according to the Commentator. *Bâhya:* exterior. *Ragged: nirjarjalpa;* the word (apparently meaningless here) is probably used as a sort of play upon the word *jarjara*, brain.

3 *Hair:* which has so often brushed them away. *Active:* the same word is an epithet of Indra. *Hoofs:* to renovate their shells with the horny material. Cf. A. V. IX. 4. 16: They gave the hooves to tortoises.

4 The first rib is Agni's; the second Vâyu's; the third Indra's; the fourth Soma's; the fifth Aditi's; the sixth Indrâṇî's; the seventh the Maruts'; the eighth Bṛihaspati's; the ninth Aryaman's; the tenth Dhâtar's; the eleventh Indra's the twelfth Varuṇa's; the thirteenth Yama's.

5 (On the left side) the first rib belongs to Indra-Agni; the second to Sarasvatî; the third to Mitra; the fourth to the Waters; the fifth to Nirṛiti; the sixth to Agni-Soma; the seventh to the Serpents; the eighth to Vishṇu; the ninth to Pûshan; the tenth to Tvashṭar; the eleventh to Indra; the twelfth to Varuṇa; the thirteenth to Yama. The right flank belongs to Heaven and Earth, the left to the All-Gods.

6 The shoulders belong to the Maruts; the first rib-cartilages to the All-Gods; the second to the Rudras; the third to the Âdityas; the tail belongs to Vâyu; the hind-quarters to Agni-Soma. I gratify the two Curlews with the hips; Indra-Bṛihaspati with the thighs; Mitra-Varuṇa with the groins; Approach with the buttocks; Strength with the two cavities of the loins.

7 I gratify Pûshan with the rectum; Blind-worms with the large intestines; Serpents with the entrails; Worms with the guts; the Waters with the bladder; Scrotum with the testicles; the Vâjins with his penis; Offspring with his seed; Blue jays with his bile; Fissures with his arms; Kûshmas with his lumps of dung.

8 His chest belongs to Indra; his belly to Aditi; his clavicles to the Quarters; his nether hind-part to Aditi. I gratify Clouds with his aorta; Firmament with his pericardium; Mist with his belly; the two Chakravâkas with his cardiac bones; Sky with his kidneys; Mountains with his ducts; Rocks with his spleen; Ant-hills with his lungs; Shrubs with his heart-vessels; Streams with his veins; Lakes with his flanks; Sea with his belly; Vaiṣvânara with his ashes.

---

4 *Indrâṇî:* Indra's Consort.

6 *The tail belongs to Vâyu:* so at the offering of the typical Sacrificial Bull: Vâta the God receives the tail: he stirs the plants and herbs therewith.—A. V. IX. 4. 13. *Curlews:* regarded, like the Chakravâkas, as semi-sacred birds. See Râmâyaṇa, I. 2. 12ff. for Vâlmîki's curse on the slayer of one of a pair. *Kûshmas:* unexplained and unknown.

8 *Cardiac bones:* two bones, says Mahîdhara, one on each side of the heart. The word *matasne* more probably means kidneys, as I have translated it in XIX. 85.

9 I gratify Separation with his navel; Butter with his flavour; the Waters with his broth; Sunbeams with his drops of fat; Hoar-frost with his heat; Ice with his marrow; Hail-stones with his tears; Thunderbolts with the rheum of his eyes; Râkshasas with his blood; Bright things with his limbs; Stars with his beauty; Earth with his skin. All-hail to Jumbaka!

10 In the beginning rose Hiraṇyagarbha, etc., as in XIII. 4; XXIII. 1.

11 Who by his grandeur, etc., as in XXIII. 3.

12 Whose, by his might, are these snow-covered mountains, and men call sea and Rasá his possession:
Whose are these arms, whose are these heavenly regions. What God shall we adore with our oblation?

13 Giver of vital breath, of power and vigour, he whose commandment all the Gods acknowledge:
The Lord of death, whose shade is life immortal. What God shall we adore with our oblation?

14 May powers auspicious come to us from every side, never deceived, unhindered and victorious,
That the Gods ever may be with us for our gain, our guardians day by day, unceasing in their care.

15 May the auspicious favour of the Gods be ours, on us descend the bounty of the righteous Gods.
The friendship of the Gods have we devoutly sought: so may the Gods extend our life that we may live.

---

9 *Separation: vidhṛiti;* the ritual name of two blades of grass laid crosswise on the altar. See VII. 4; S. B. G. XII. p. 93; XXVI. 89. *Jumbaka:* a name of Varuṇa.

10 Four texts follow constituting the Inviting and Offering Verses of the Sacrifice of the Horse and other victims to Prajâpati. Verse 10 is repeated from XIII. 4 and XXIII. 1.

12 Taken from the same hymn as verses 10 and 11. R. V. X. 121. 4. *Rasá:* the ancient name of a river in the north of India; sometimes regarded as a stream that flows round the earth and the firmament. See Prof. A. Weber, Vedische Beiträge, VII. pp. 10—12. *What God:* other than Prajâpati. Or, God Ka let us, etc.

13 Taken from R. V. X. 121. 2. The first division of the second line is difficult. Prof. M. Müller renders it: 'Whose shadow is immortality, whose shadow is death.' The meaning may be that his cold shadow (his displeasure, or ignorance of him, is death, while the shadow, reflection, or knowledge of his bright glory makes his worshipper immortal.

14 Ten stanzas follow constituting the Inviting and Offering Verses of the oblations of marrow or omentum and rice-cakes to the All-Gods. They are taken from R. V. I. 89. 1—10.

16 We call them hither with a hymn of olden time, Bhaga, the friendly Daksha, Mitra, Aditi,
Aryaman, Varuṇa, Soma, the Asvins. May Sarasvati, auspicious, grant felicity.

17 May the Wind waft to us that pleasant medicine, may Earth our Mother give it, and our Father Heaven,
And the joy-giving stones that press the Soma's juice. Asvins, may ye, for whom our spirits long, hear this.

18 Him we invoke for aid who reigns supreme, the Lord of all that stands or moves, inspirer of the soul,
That Pûshan may promote the increase of our wealth, our keeper and our guard infallible for our good.

19 Illustrious far and wide, may Indra prosper us: may Pûshan prosper us, the Master of all wealth.
May Târkshya with uninjured fellies prosper us: Bṛihaspati vouchsafe to us prosperity.

20 The Maruts, Sons of Pṛisni, borne by spotted steeds, moving in glory, oft visiting holy rites,
Sages whose tongue is Agni and their eyes the Sun,—hither let all the Gods for our protection come.

21 Gods, may we with our ears listen to what is good, and with our eyes see what is good, ye Holy Ones.
With limbs and bodies firm may we extolling you attain the term of life appointed by the Gods.

22 A hundred autumns stand before us, O ye Gods, within whose space ye bring our bodies to decay;
Within whose space our sons become fathers in turn. Break ye not in the midst our course of fleeting life.

23 Aditi is the heaven, Aditi is mid-air, Aditi is the Mother and the Sire and Son.

---

16 *Daksha:* Strength; a creative Power associated with Aditi, and therefore sometimes identified with Prajâpati.

19 *Târkshya:* see XV. 18.

20 *Pṛisni:* see VII. 16.

22 *Hundred autumns:* a hundred years, counted in earlier times by winters, then by autumns, then, as now, by Rains (*varsha* having become the Hindi *baras*, a year), being regarded as the natural duration of human life. Cf. Isaiah. LXV. 20. 'There shall be no more thence an infant of days, nor an old man that hath not filled his days: for the child shall die an hundred years old.'

23 *Aditi:* as the Infinite; Infinite Nature. *Five-classed:* the four castes and Nishâdas or wild aboriginal tribes, according to Sâyaṇa; or 'Fivefold life or being,' that is, Gods, men, Gandharvas and Apsarases, Serpents, and Fathers, according to the same authority.

Aditi is all Gods, Aditi five-classed men, Aditi all that hath been born and shall be born.

24 Slight us not Varuṇa, Aryaman, or Mitra, Ṛibhukshan, Indra, Âyu, or the Maruts,
When we declare amid the congregation the virtues of the Strong Steed, God-descended.

25 What time they bear before the Courser, covered with trappings and with wealth, the grasped oblation,
The dappled goat goeth straightforward, bleating, to the place dear to Indra and to Pûshan.

26 Dear to all Gods, this goat, the share of Pûshan, is first led forward with the vigorous Courser,
While Tvashṭar sends him forward with the Charger, acceptable for sacrifice, to glory.

27 When thrice the men lead round the Steed, in order, who goeth to the Gods as meet oblation,
The goat precedeth him, the share of Pûshan, and to the Gods the sacrifice announceth.

28 Invoker, ministering priest, atoner, fire-kindler, Soma-presser, sage, reciter,
With this well ordered sacrifice, well finished, do ye fill full the channels of the rivers.

29 The hewers of the post and those who carry it, and those who carve the knob to deck the Horse's stake;
Those who prepare the cooking-vessels for the Steed,—may the approving help of these promote our work.

30 Forth, for the regions of the Gods, the Charger with his smooth back is come; my prayer attends him.
In him rejoice the singer and the sages. A good friend have we won for the Gods' banquet.

---

24 The Asvastuti or Eulogy of the Horse follows, comprised in twenty-two verses which form Hymn 162 of Book I. of the Rigveda. *Ribhukshan:* a name of Indra as lord of the Ribhus, the three season-making deities who perhaps represent the past, the present, and the future. *Âyu:* said by Sâyaṇa and Mahidhara to be used in this place for Vâyu. It is apparently a name of Agni, the Living, Lively One, as in V. 9. *God-descended:* sprung from the Gods, or, according to Sâyaṇa, born as the type of various deities. See R. V. I. 163. 2—4.

25 *Grasped oblation:* the offering of clarified butter taken from the remains of a previous burnt-offering. *Goat:* that is to be tied to the Horse at the sacrificial stake. See XXIV. 13. *Pûshan:* said by Sâyaṇa to stand for Agni in this and the two following verses.

28 *Invoker, etc.:* these are the designations of eight of the sixteen priests employed. *Sage:* the Brahman, a priest of profound knowledge (see V. 31; VII. 45) who superintends the ceremony. *Fill full the channels:* obtain blessings in abundance.

31 May the fleet Courser's halter and his heel-ropes, the head-stall and the girths and cords about him,
And the grass put within his mouth to bait him,—among the Gods, too, let all these be with thee.

32 What part of the Steed's flesh the fly hath eaten, or is left sticking to the post or hatchet,
Or to the slayer's hands and nails adhereth,—among the Gods, too, may all this be with thee.

33 Food undigested steaming from his belly, and any odour of raw flesh remaining,
This let the immolators set in order and dress the sacrifice with perfect cooking.

34 What from thy body which with fire is roasted, when thou art set upon the spit, distilleth,—
Let not that lie on earth or grass neglected, but to the longing Gods let all be offered.

35 They who, observing that the Horse is ready, call out and say, The smell is good; remove it;
And, craving meat, await the distribution,—may their approving help promote our labour.

36 The trial-fork of the flesh-cooking caldron, the vessels out of which the broth is sprinkled,
The warming-pots, the covers of the dishes, hooks, carving-boards,—all these attend the Charger.

37 Let not the fire, smoke-scented, make thee crackle, nor glowing caldron smell and break to pieces.
Offered, beloved, approved, and consecrated,—such Charger do the Gods accept with favour.

38 The starting-place, his place of rest and rolling, the ropes wherewith the Charger's feet were fastened,
The water that he drank, the food he tasted,—among the Gods, too, may all these attend thee.

39 The robe they spread upon the Horse to clothe him, the upper covering and the golden trappings,
The halters which restrain the Steed, the heel-ropes,—all these, as grateful to the Gods, they offer.

40 If one, when seated, with excessive urging hath with his heel or with his whip distressed thee,
All these thy woes, as with oblation's ladle at sacrifices, with my prayer I banish.

41 The four-and-thirty ribs of the swift Courser, kin to the Gods, the slayer's hatchet pierces.

---

41 *Four-and-thirty:* so many out of the thirty-six. As the Sacrificial Horse represents the heavens, the thirty-four ribs symbolize the Sun, the

Cut ye with skill so that the parts be flawless, and piece by piece declaring them dissect them.

42 Of Tvashṭar's Courser there is one dissector: this is the custom: two there are who guide him.

Such of his limbs as I divide in order, all these, amid the lumps, in fire I offer.

43 Let not thy dear soul burn thee as thou comest, let not the hatchet linger in thy body.

Let not a greedy clumsy immolator, missing the joints, mangle thy limbs unduly.

44 No, here thou diest not, thou art not injured: only by easy paths to Gods thou goest.

Both Bays, both Spotted Mares are now thy fellows, and to the Ass's pole is yoked the Courser.

45 May this Steed bring us all-sustaining riches, wealth in good kine, good horses, manly offspring.

Freedom from sin may Aditi vouchsafe us; the Steed with our oblations gain us lordship!

46 We will, with Indra and all Gods to help us, bring these existing worlds into subjection.

With the Âdityas, with the band of Maruts, may Indra give us medicine to heal us.

Our sacrifice, our bodies, and our offspring may Indra regulate with the Âdityas.

47 O Agni, be our nearest Friend, etc., as in III. 25.

To thee then, O Most Bright, etc., as in III. 26.

---

Moon, the five planets, and the twenty-seven *nakshatras* or lunar asterisms. See Ludwig, Der Rigveda, III. p. 186. *Piece by piece:* the dissectors are to name the several parts as they divide them, each part being assigned to a separate deity.

42 *One dissector:* in chief. *The lumps:* the portions of meat made up into balls.

43 *Burn thee:* make thee sad.

44 *Both Bays, etc.:* thou art now associated in heaven with the two bay horses of Indra, the two spotted mares of the Maruts, and the ass (representing the grey or dun colour of early morning) that draws the chariot of the Asvins.

46 Taken, with variations, from R. V. X. 157. 1, 3, 2.

For a description of an Asvamedha in later times, see Râmâyaṇa, Book I. 10—15.

The Dakshiṇâs or honoraria bestowed upon the officiating priests are not mentioned in the text. They consisted chiefly of a large proportion of the booty taken from the ruler and the people of the conquered country. According to a Commentator, the spoil of the east was given to the Hotar, and that of the south to the Brahman. The Adhvaryu received a maiden (the daughter of the Sacrificer, says a Commentator), and the Sacrificer's fourth wife. See Hillebrandt, Ritual-Litteratur, p. 152.

# BOOK THE TWENTY-SIXTH.

AGNI and Pṛithivî, closely connected, may they bring low for me the boon I mention.
Vâyu and Firmament, closely connected, may they, etc.
Closely connected Dyaus and the Âditya, may they, etc.
Closely connected Varuṇa and Waters, may they, etc.
Lord of the seven communities and her who forms all beings, eighth,
Make our ways full of pleasantness: may So-and-So and I agree.

2 That I to all the people may address this salutary speech,
To priest and nobleman, Sûdra and Arya, to one of our own kin and to the stranger.
Dear may I be to Gods and guerdon-giver. Fulfilled be this my hope: be that my portion!

3 Give us, Bṛihaspati, that wondrous treasure, that which exceeds the merit of the foeman,
Which shines among the folk effectual, splendid, that, Son of Law, which is with might refulgent.
Taken upon a base art thou. Thee for Bṛihaspati. This is thy home. Thee for Bṛihaspati,

4 Come hither, Indra, rich in kine! Drink Soma, Lord of Hundred Powers,
Effused by braying pressing-stones.
Taken upon a base art thou. Thee for Indra, rich in kine. This is thy home. Thee for Indra, rich in kine.

---

Books XXVI—XXIX contain sacrificial texts and formulas connected with the Lunar Sacrifices, Oblation to the Manes, the Agnihotra, the Seasonal Sacrifices, the Vâjapeya, the Râjasûya, the Sautrâmaṇî, the Asvamedha, etc., which have formed the subjects of earlier Books. To these sacrifices these supplementary formulas are to be applied as occasion requires.

1 *Bring low:* under my control; into my possession. *The boon I mention:* a blank prayer, the special blessing that is desired must be stated when the formula is used. *Seven communities:* probably meaning, all the people. See R. V. VIII. 81. 20. According to Mahîdhara, the seven organs of perception are intended, and Paramâtmâ the Supreme Self, is their Lord. *Eighth:* Earth, or Vâk. These words are in the nominative case, and the verb, *make*, is in the second person singular of the imperative. Mahidhara therefore supplies *He Svâmin, yasya tava*, O Lord, whose are. *So-and-So:* some man with whom the speaker is at variance, and whose name is to be applied as occasion requires. Cp. VII. 3; IX. 38, 40.

2 *Arya:* the Vaisya, the man of the people, the agriculturist and trader, of the third class *Be that:* the special boon prayed for, wealth, kine, sons, or whatever it may be, is to be declared when the formula is used.

3 Taken from R. V. II. 23. 15. *The foeman:* the ungodly man of alien creed. *Son of Law:* who hast thy being in accordance with *ṛita*, Right, Truth, or eternal Law and Order. *Taken upon a base:* see VII. 4. He addresses the cup of Soma juice which he takes or draws for Bṛihaspati.

5 O Indra, Vritra-slayer, come. Drink Soma, Lord of Hundred Powers,
Expressed with stones whose wealth is kine.
Taken upon a base art thou, etc., as in verse 4.

6 Vaiṣvânara the righteous One, the Lord of sacrifice and light,
The heat that wasteth not, we seek.
Taken upon a base art thou. Thee for Vaiṣvânara.
This is thy home: thee for Vaiṣvânara.

7 Still in Vaiṣvânara's grace may we continue: yea, he is King Supreme o'er all things living.
Sprung hence to life upon this All he looketh. Vaiṣvânara hath rivalry with Súrya.
Taken upon a base art thou, etc., as in verse 6.

8 Hitherward come Vaiṣvânara to succour us from far away,
Agni through laud that brings him near!
Taken upon a base, etc, as in verse 6.

9 Agni is Pavamâna, Sage, the Tribe-Priest of the Races Five:
To him of mighty wealth we pray.
Taken upon a base art thou. Thee for lustre. This is thy home. Thee for lustre.

10 May mighty Indra, thunder-armed, may Shoḍaṣî protect us well, and slay the wicked man who hateth us.
Taken upon a base art thou. Thee for Mahendra. This is thy home. Thee for Mahendra.

11 As cows low to their calves in stalls so with our songs we glorify
This Indra, e'en your wondrous God who checks assault, who joys in the delicious juice.

12 Agni's is the most fetching song. Shine mightily, thou rich in light!
Like the Chief Consort of a King, riches and strength proceed from thee.

---

5 *Whose wealth is kine:* libations of Soma juice being thus rewarded.

6 *The heat that wasteth not:* 'Exhaustless heat am I (Agni)':—R. V. III. 26. 7.

7 *Sprung hence:* produced from these two *araṇis*, the fire-drill. The text is taken from R. V. I. 98. 1.

9 Taken from R. V. IX. 66. 20. *Pavamâna:* Self-purifying; an epithet applied both to Soma and to Agni. *Tribe-Priest:* or Purohita. *Races Five:* the four castes and Nishâdas or aboriginal tribes, according to the commentators.

10 *Shoḍaṣî:* a title of Indra. See VIII. 33, note. *Mahendra:* Great Indra.

11 Taken from R. V. VIII. 77. 1. *Cows:* milked for sacrificial purposes and temporarily separated from their calves. See I., introductory note.

12 Taken from R. V. V. 25. 7. *Most fetching:* most effectually attracting and bringing to the sacrifice. *Like the Chief Consort:* like a chief queen proceeding from her home in royal state.

13 Come, here, O Agni, will I sing verily other songs to thee,
And with these drops shalt thou grow strong.

14 The Seasons spread thy sacrifice! the Months protect thine offering!
May the Year guard our sacrifice for thee and keep our children safe.

15 There where the mountains downward slope, there by the meeting of the streams
The sage was manifest with song.

16 High is thy juice's birth: though set in heaven, on earth it hath obtained
Strong sheltering power and great renown.

17 Finder of room and freedom, flow for Indra, meet for worship, flow
For Varuṇa and the Marut host.

18 Striving to win, with him we gain all wealth of the ungodly one,
Yea, all the glories of mankind.

19 May we be prosperous with brave sons, cattle, horses, each wish of ours, and varied blessings,
With quadrupeds, and with the men about us. May the Gods guide our sacrifice in season.

20 O Agni, bring thou hitherward the yearning Consorts of the Gods,
Bring Tvashṭar to the Soma-draught.

21 O Neshṭar girt by Dames, accept our sacrifice: with Ṛitu drink,
For thou art he who giveth wealth.

---

13 Taken from R. V. VI. 16. 16.

15 Taken from R. V. VIII. 6. 28. *The Sage:* Indra. 'Sâyaṇa's conclusion of the purport of the verse is that men ought to worship where *Indra* is said to be manifested.'—Wilson. According to Mahîdhara, the translation should be 'The Sage was gendered with the thought'; that is, he says, the Soma plant sprang to life with the knowledge that men would use it in their sacrifices.

16 Taken from R. V. IX. 61. 10. The verse is addressed to Soma.

17 Taken from R. V. IX. 61. 12. Addressed to Soma. *Meet for worship: yajyave;* according to Prof. M. Müller, the pursuer.

18 Taken from R. V. IX. 61. 11. *Him:* Soma.

20 Taken from R. V. I. 22. 9. *Tvashṭar:* 'probably on account of his creative agency in the womb, Tvaṣṭṛ is closely allied with celestial females *(gnâḥ, janayaḥ)* or the wives of the gods who are his most frequent attendants'—Macdonell, Vedic Mythology. p. 117.

21 Taken from R. V. I. 15. 3. *Neshṭar:* the priest who leads forward the wife of the Sacrificer and prepares the Surâ (see VIII. 10, note). In this place Neshṭar is said to be a title of Tvashṭar from his having on some occasion assumed the function of a Neshṭar priest. *Ṛitu:* with the God Ṛitu, the Season deified; or, in the proper season.

22 He with the Ṛitus fain would drink, Wealth-giver, from the Neshṭar's bowl.
Begin, pay offerings: hasten ye.

23 Thine is this Soma: come thou near, approach it. Drink thou thereof, benevolent, and cease not.
Sit on the sacred grass at this our worship, and take these drops into thy belly, Indra.

24 Come unto us, ye swift to listen! as at home, upon the sacred grass sit and enjoy yourselves.
And, Tvashṭar, well content be joyful in the juice with Gods and Goddesses in gladsome company.

25 In sweetest and most gladdening stream flow pure, O Soma, on thy way,
Pressed out for Indra, for his drink.

26 Fiend-queller, Friend of all men, he hath in the vat attained unto
His place, his iron-fashioned home.

---

22 Taken from R V. I. 15. 9. *With the Ṛitus:* with the deified Seasons; or in due season, as above. *Wealth-giver:* Agni.

23 Taken from R. V. III. 35. 6.

24 *Come unto us:* according to Mahīdhara, the Gods' Consorts are addressed.

25 Taken from R. V. IX. 1. 1.

26 Taken from R V. IX. 1. 2, with a slight variation. *Iron-fashioned home:* receptacle that has been hammered or formed with a tool of *ayas*, iron or perhaps bronze.

# BOOK THE TWENTY-SEVENTH.

HALF-YEARS and Seasons strengthen thee, O Agni, the Years and all the Verities and Rishis!
Flash forth with thy celestial effulgence: illumine all four regions of the heaven.

2 Kindle thee, Agni, wake this man to knowledge: rise up erect for great and happy fortune.
Agni, be those uninjured who adore thee, thy priests be glorious and none beside them!

3 The Brâhmans present here elect thee, Agni: be thou propitious in our sanctuary.
Slayer of rivals, Agni, quell our foemen: watch in thy house with care that never ceases.

4 Even here do thou, O Agni, stablish wealth: let not oppressors injure thee by thinking of thee first.
Light be thy task of ruling, Agni, with thy power: may he who worships thee wax strong, invincible.

5 Kind to the people, grasp thy power, O Agni: contend thou with the Friend by way of friendship.
Placed, Agni, in the centre of our kinsmen, flash forth to be invoked by Kings around thee.

6 Past those who slay, past enemies, past thoughtless men, past those who hate,—
Yea, Agni, drive away all woe and trouble: vouchsafe us opulence with men about us.

7 Holder of sway, shine here refulgent, Agni! invincible, unconquered Jâtavedas.
Light all the regions, chasing human terrors: with happy helps guard us to-day for increase.

---

1 Verses 1—9 are to be used at an animal sacrifice between the 9th and 10th of the normal Gâyatrî kindling-verses recited while the sacrificial fire is being lighted or when additional fuel is applied to it. See Sacred Books of the East, XLI. pp. 167 (note), 168. *Half-years: samâḥ;* the warm halves of the years as distinguished from, and equal (*sama* ὁμος) to the *himâḥ* or winters. See Prof. A. Weber, Vedische Beiträge, VII. pp. 1, 2, and Zimmer, Altindisches Leben, p. 371. Verses 1—3 are taken, with variations, from A. V. II. 6. 1—3.

4 Varied from A. V. VII. 82. 3. *Let not oppressors:* let not the wicked, anticipating our worship, secure thy attention before us, and, as unworthy adorers, insult and degrade thy majesty.

5 A. V. II. 6. 4. *The Friend:* the God Mitra. *By way of friendship: mitradhâ.*

6 A. V. II. 6. 5, slightly varied.

7 Varied, from A. V. VII. 84. 1.

8 Bṛihaspati, Savitar, give this man knowledge: sharpen him thoroughly though already sharpened.
To great and high felicity exalt him: in him let all the Gods rejoice and triumph.

9 As thou, Bṛihaspati, from curse hast freed us, from dwelling yonder in the realm of Yama,
The Aśvins, Leeches of the Gods, O Agni, have chased Death far from us with mighty powers.

10 Looking upon the loftier light, etc., as in XX. 21.

11 Uplifted are the brands that are his fuel: lofty and brilliant are the flames of Agni,
Splendidly bright of the Son fair of aspect.

12 Tanûnapât the Asura, all-possessing, God among Gods, the God with mead and butter shall bedew the paths.

13 With mead to sacrifice thou comest, Agni, comest as friendly-minded Narâśaṃsa, and Savitar righteous God who brings all blessings.

14 He cometh hitherward with power and fatness, the luminous, implored with adoration.
While rites proceed the ladles move to Agni.

15 Let him pay worship to this Agni's greatness, daintily fed: he verily gives enjoyments:
The wisest Vasu he, and best wealth-giver.

16 Widely expansive, ruling by foundation, the Doors divine—and, after, all—
Preserve this Agni's holy works.

17 May Dawn and Night protect—his heavenly Consorts—in his home this our sacrificial worship.

18 Ye two celestial Hotars, greet with praises this lofty rite of ours, the tongue of Agni.
Cause that our sacrifice be well conducted.

---

8 Varied, from A. V. VII. 16. *Bṛihaspati, Savitar:* meaning Agni who is identified with these Gods.

11 Varied, from A. V. V. 27. 1. This and the eleven following verses form an Âprî or Propitiatory Hymn. the whole of which is found, with variations in the same Atharva-veda hymn. *The Son:* Agni is called the Son of the Sacrificer as being produced and supported by him.

12 *Asura:* Lord Divine. *The paths:* the ways or courses of the Sacrifice.

14 *The luminous: vahniḥ;* or, the priest; or, the furtherer (of oblations). See M. Müller, Vedic Hymns, I. pp. 37 sqq.

16 *Doors:* of the sacrificial hall deified. *And all:* there is no substantive; *devâḥ*, Gods, is probably understood.

17 *Dawn and Night:* personified as Goddesses.

18 *Celestial Hotars:* Agni with Âditya or Varuṇa, or Agni terrestrial and firmamental.

19 Upon this grass three Goddesses be seated, Idâ, Sarasvati, Bhârati the Mighty glorified with song.

20 This our productive wondrous flow may Tvashṭar pour down on this man's kin, and wealth and heroes.

21 Vanaspati, presenting of thyself, send God-ward ! Let Agni, Immolator, season our oblation.

22 Pay sacrifice to Indra, Jâtavedas Agni ! with Hail ! All Gods accept the gift we offer !

23 Wise, bright, arranger of his teams, he seeketh men with rich food whose treasures are abundant.
They have stood firm of one accord with Vâyu : yea, the men wrought all noble operations.

24 The God whom both these worlds brought forth for riches, whom heavenly Dhishaṇâ for our wealth appointeth—
His team of harnessed horses waits on Vâyu and, foremost, on the radiant treasure-holder.

25 What time the mighty waters came containing the universal germ, producing Agni,
Thence sprang the Gods' one spirit into being. What God shall we adore with our oblation ?

26 Who in his might surveyed the floods enclosing productive force and generating Worship,
He who is God mid Gods, and none beside him—What God shall we adore with our oblation ?

27 The teams wherewith thou seekest him who offers, within his house, O Vâyu, to direct him,
Therewith send wealth to us with full enjoyment, a hero son and gifts of kine and horses.

28 With thy yoked teams in hundreds and in thousands come to our sacrifice and solemn worship.
O Vâyu, make thee glad at this libation. Preserve us evermore, ye Gods, with blessings.

---

19 *Three Goddesses :* of Prayer and Devotion.

21 *Vanaspati :* the sacrificial stake, regarded as a form of Agni. *Send :* our offerings to the Gods in heaven.

23 This and the following verse, taken respectively from R. V. VII. 91. 3 and 90. 3, are used at the sacrifice of a white hornless he-goat to Vâyu.

24 *Dhishaṇâ :* a Goddess of abundance and prosperity.

25 This and the following verse, in honour of Prajâpati, are taken from R. V. X. 121. 7, 8. *What God shall we adore :* or, Worship we Ka the God.

27 This and the following verse are taken, in continuation of verse 23, from R. V. VII. 91. 3, 5.

29 Drawn by thy team, O Vâyu, come: to thee is offered this, the pure.
Thou visitest the presser's house.

30 Vâyu, the bright is offered thee, best of the meath at holy rites.
Come thou to drink the Soma juice, God longed-for, on thy team-drawn car.

31 Lover of worship, leader, come Vâyu with thought, to sacrifice,
Propitious with propitious teams!

32 With all the thousand chariots that are thine, O Vâyu, come to us,
Team-drawn, to drink the Soma juice.

33 Come thou with one, and ten, O Self-Existent! with two unto the sacrifice, and twenty.
Three are the teams and thirty which convey thee. O Vâyu, in this place unyoke thy coursers.

34 Wonderful Vâyu, Lord of Truth, thou who art Tvashṭar's Son-in-law,
Thy saving succour we elect.

35 Like kine unmilked we call aloud, Hero, to thee and sing thy praise,
Looker on heavenly light, Lord of this moving world, Lord, Indra! of what moveth not.

36 None other like to thee, of earth or of the heavens, hath been or ever will be born.
Desiring horses, Indra, Bounteous Lord! and kine, as men of might we call on thee.

37 That we may win us wealth and power, we poets call on only thee.
In war men call on thee, Indra! the hero's Lord, in the steed's race-course call on thee.

38 As such, O Wonderful, whose hand holds thunder, praised as mighty, Caster of the Stone!

---

29 Taken from R. V. II. 41. 2. *The pure:* Soma juice.
30 Taken from R. V. IV. 47. 1.
32 R. V. II. 41. 1.

34 R. V. VIII. 26. 21. *Tvashṭar's Son-in-law:* the commentators give no satisfactory explanation. Saraṇyu (who is perhaps Ushas, Dawn), Tvashṭar's daughter, was wedded to Vivasvân who cannot be identified with Vâyu. See Hillebrandt, Vedische Mythologie, I. p. 521.

35 R. V. VII. 32. 22. *Moving world:* all animated beings.
36 R. V. VII. 32. 23.
37 R. V. VI. 46. 1. *In war:* literally, in, or among, foes.
38 R. V. VI. 46. 2. *The Stone:* the thunderbolt.

Pour on us boldly, Indra, kine and chariot-steeds ever to be the conqueror's strength.

39 What succour will he bring to us, wonderful, ever-prospering Friend?
With what most mighty company?

40 What genuine and most liberal draught will spirit thee with juice to burst
Open e'en strongly-guarded wealth?

41 Do thou who art protector of us thy friends who praise thee
With hundred aids approach us.

42 Sing to your Agni with each song, at every sacrifice, for strength.
Come, let us praise the Wise and Everlasting God even as a well-belovèd Friend.

43 Protect us, Agni, through the first, protect us through the second hymn.
Protect us through three hymns, O Lord of Power and Might; through four hymns, Vasu! guard thou us.

44 The Son of Strength; for is he not our Friend? Let us serve him for offering our gifts.
In battles may he be our help and strengthener, yea, be the saviour of our lives.

45 Thou art Saṃvatsara; thou art Parivatsara; thou art Idâvatsara; thou art Idvatsara; thou art Vatsara.
Prosper thy Dawns! Prosper thy Day-and-Nights! Prosper thy Half-months, Months, Seasons, and Years!
Combine them for their going and their coming, and send them forward on their ordered courses.
In eagle's shape thou art piled up and layered. With that divinity, Angiras-like, lie steady.

---

39 This and the two following verses are taken from R. V. IV. 31. 1—3.

42 R. V. VI. 48. 1.

43 R. V. VIII. 49. 9. *First, etc.:* the numbers probably have reference to the four quarters of the sky.—Ludwig. According to Mahîdhara, *first* refers to the Ṛig; *second* to the Yajur; *three* to Ṛig, Yajur, Sâma; *four* to these three and Nigada or loud recitation.

44 R. V. VI. 48. 2. A continuation of verse 42. *Son of Strength:* in the accusative case governed by 'let us praise' in the preceding verse.

45 The formulas contained in this verse are to be employed in the Agnichayana ceremony at the time when the Sacrificer touches as much as he can of the surface of the newly-constructed Fire-altar. See XVII. 2. Agni is addressed, as identified with Prajâpati the Presiding Deity of the Year and with the Altar. *Saṃvatsara* and the rest are the names given to the years of the five-year cycle intended, with the aid of an intercalary month, to adjust the difference between the lunar and the solar year. See Zimmer, Altindisches Leben, p. 370. *In eagle's shape:* see XI., first note. *Thou:* the Fire-altar. *Angiras-like:* as thou didst when constructed by Angiras. See XII. 53; XI. 9.

# BOOK THE TWENTY-EIGHTH.

ON the earth's centre, at libation's place let the Priest worship Indra with the kindling-stick.
The mightiest of the lords of men is kindled on the height of heaven.
Let him enjoy the butter. Hotar, worship.

2 Him let the Hotar worship, him Tanûnapât with ready aids; the conqueror never overcome,
Indra, the God who finds heaven's light on paths most rich in pleasant sweets, with Narâṣaṃsa all aglow. Let him enjoy, etc., as in verse 1.

3 With viands let the Hotar worship Indra immortal, praised, receiver of oblations.
The God, the equal of the Gods in vigour, the thunder-wielder, breaker-down of castles. Let him enjoy, etc.

4 Let the Priest worship Indra, Bull who sitteth on sacred grass, doer of manly actions.
Let him be seated on the grass with Vasus and Rudras and Âdityas for companions. Let him enjoy, etc.

5 Let the Priest sacrifice. The Doors have strengthened Indra, his force and conquering might and vigour.
At this our worship let the Doors be opened, easy to pass, the strengtheners of Order: wide let them open out for bounteous Indra. Let them enjoy, etc.

6 Let the Priest sacrifice to Night and Morning, the teeming Cows of Indra, Mighty Mothers.
Indra their calf with lustre have they strengthened, even as two mothers of a calf in common. Let them enjoy, etc.

7 Let the Priest worship both the heavenly Hotars, Friends, Leeches, healing Indra with oblation.
The sages, Gods preëminent for wisdom bestow on Indra his surpassing power. Let them enjoy, etc.

---

This Book is closely connected with, and supplementary to, Books XIX.—XXI. which treat of the Sautrâmaṇî ceremony.

1 Verses 1—11 form an Âprî or Propitiatory Hymn. See XX. 37, note. *The Priest:* the divine Hotar in heaven, whose example the human Hotar is to follow. *Earth's centre:* the altar. *Hotar:* the human Hotar is addressed.

2 *Tanûnapât:* Son of Himself; Agni as continually reproduced from other fire. *Narâṣaṃsa:* Praise or Desire of men; Agni.

3 *Castles:* the cloud-castles of the demons who withhold the rain.

5 *Doors:* of the sacrificial hall.

7 *Hotars:* Firmamental and Terrestrial Agni.

8 Let the Priest offer sacrifice to the three Goddesses and balm.
Let the three triple active Ones, let Iḍâ and Sarasvatî and Bhâratî the mighty Dames, Consorts of Indra, who receive our sacrificial offerings, enjoy the butter, etc.

9 Let the Priest worship Tvashṭar radiant Indra, Physician good at sacrifice, graced with butter,
Multiform and prolific, rich and bounteous. Let Tvashṭar, giving wondrous powers to Indra, enjoy, etc.

10 Let the Priest worship him, the Forest-Sovran, the Immolator, Lord of Hundred Powers, the lover of the prayer, the friend of Indra.
Balming with mead, may he on easy pathways sweeten our sacrifice with savoury butter. Let him enjoy, etc.

11 Let the Priest offer sacrifice to Indra: with Hail! to Gods of butter; with Hail! to Gods of marrow; with Hail! to Gods of drops; with Hail! to Gods of offerings paid with Svâhâ; with Hail! to Gods of sacrificial hymns.
All-hail! May butter-drinking Gods and Indra rejoicing taste the butter. Hotar, worship.

12 Vigorous, strewn by Gods upon the altar the right Gods' sacred Grass hath strengthened Indra.
Cut in the day, cherished by night it hath surpassed those who have sacrificial Grass with wealth. For gain of riches let him taste. Pay sacrifice.

13 Firm, closely joined, the Doors divine have strengthened Indra in the rite.
Pressed by a calf or tender boy may they drive off the courser as he tosses up the sand. For gain of wealth let them enjoy. Pay sacrifice.

14 Morning and Night, the Goddesses, have called on Indra as the rite advanced.
May they well-pleased and ordered well make the Celestial Tribes come forth. For gain of wealth let them enjoy. Pay sacrifice.

---

8 *Three Goddesses:* see XX. 43. *Active Ones:* said to mean Agni, Vâyu, Sûrya.

9 *Radiant Indra:* identified with, or mighty as, Indra. *Multiform:* as creator of all living beings.

10 *Forest-Sovran:* Vanaspati, the Sacrificial Stake. See XX. 45, note.

11 *Of drops:* who enjoy the dripping fat or marrow. Cf. XX. 46.

13 *Pressed by a calf, etc.:* that is, easily closed for protection from raiders. Cf. R. V. VI. 28. 4.

14 *Celestial Tribes:* Vasus, Rudras, Âdityas, All-Gods, Maruts, etc.

15 Two Goddesses, wealth-givers, kind, have heightened radiant Indra's strength.
One drives away hatreds and sins; the other shall bring the Sacrificer boons and treasure.
Instructed, let them both enjoy, for gain of wealth. Pay sacrifice.

16 Bringers of strengthening sacrifice, the Goddesses, the teeming Cows, have prospered Indra with their milk.
Let one bring food and energy, the other feast and banqueting.
Bringers of strengthening sacrifice, allotting the several portions they have put together old energy with new and new with olden, strengthening boons and treasures for the Sacrificer. Instructed, let them, etc., as in verse 15.

17 The two Celestial Hotars, Gods, have heightened radiant Indra's might.
Freed from slain sinners these have brought the Sacrificer wealth and boons. Instructed, let them, etc.

18 Goddesses three, three Goddesses have heightened their Lord Indra's strength.
One, Bhâratî, hath touched the sky, Sarasvatî the sacrifice with Rudras, and, enriched with wealth, Iḍâ the homesteads of the folk. For gain of wealth let them enjoy. Pay sacrifice.

19 The radiant Indra, Praise of Men, thrice-shielding, borne on three car-seats, hath heightened radiant Indra's strength.
Set on a hundred white-backed cows, yea, on a thousand forth he goes. Mitra and Varuṇa alone deserve to be his Hotar-Priests, Bṛihaspati his Chanter, and the Aṣvins his Adhvaryavas. For gain of wealth let him enjoy. Pay sacrifice.

20 Vanaspati, a God with Gods, with golden leaves, sweet boughs, fair fruit, hath heightened radiant Indra's strength.
Sky with his summit hath he touched, and firmament, and stablished earth. For gain of wealth let him enjoy. Pay sacrifice.

---

15 *Two Goddesses:* Heaven and Earth, or Day and Night.

16 *Instructed:* knowing reality or the true nature of things.

19 *Indra:* equal to Indra; endowed with sovereign power. *Praise of Men:* Narâṣaṃsa Agni. *Three car-seats:* the Sadas or Priests' shed, the Havirdhâna or store of sacrificial elements, and the Âgnîdhra or hearth where sacred fire is kindled; or, according to Mahîdhara, the three Vedas. *Cows:* as the sources of the milk and butter required for oblations. *Chanter:* singer of hymns of praise. *Adhvaryavas:* or Adhvaryus; the Aṣvins being invested with the functions of these priests among the Gods.

20 *Firmament:* with his waist. *Earth:* with his foot.

21 The grassy robe of water-plants, divine, hath heightened Indra's strength.
This, the fair seat where Indra sits, hath topped all other sacred grass. For gain of wealth let it enjoy. Pay sacrifice.

22 Agni, Fair-offering-maker, bright, hath heightened radiant Indra's strength.
To-day may Svishṭakṛit, Fair-offering-maker, paying good sacrifice, for us perform it. For gain of wealth let him enjoy. Pay sacrifice.

23 To-day the Sacrificer hath elected—dressing messes of cooked food and a rice-cake, binding a goat for Indra—Agni as his Hotar.
To-day divine Vanaspati hath with a goat served Indra well.
He hath eaten from the fat, he hath accepted the cooked food, he hath waxed strong with the rice-cake.
Thee, to-day, O Ṛishi, etc., as in XXI. 61.

24 Let the Priest worship Agni, Indra, kindled, splendidly kindled, excellent strength-giver,
Lending him mighty power, Gâyatrî metre, a cow aged eighteen months, and vital vigour. Let him enjoy the butter. Hotar, worship.

25 Let the Priest serve with sacrifice him who breaks forth, Tanûnapât, the germ which Aditi conceived, pure Indra who bestoweth strength,
Bringing him mighty power, the Ushṇih metre, an ox of two years old, and vital vigour. Let him enjoy, etc.

26 Let the Priest sacrifice to Soma, Indra, adorable, adored, best Vṛitra-slayer, strength-giver, might, to be adored with viands,
Bringing him mighty power, Anushṭup metre, a cow of thirty months, and vital vigour. Let him enjoy, etc.

27 Let the Priest worship Indra, strength-bestower, immortal, with fair grass, allied with Pûshan, seated on sacred grass, dear, everlasting,
Bringing him mighty power, Bṛihatî metre, a steer of three years' age and vital vigour. Let him enjoy, etc.

28 Let the Priest worship the wide-opening Portals, easy to pass, divine, Law-strengthening, golden, Indra, the Brahman Priest, the strength-bestower,

---

21 *Water-plants:* see XXI. 57.

22 *Fair-offering-maker:* Svishṭakṛit. See XXI. 47.

23 Cf. XXI. 59.

24 Cf. XXI. 60.

Bringing him mighty power, the Paṅkti metre, a bullock four years old, and vital vigour. Let them enjoy the butter. Hotar, worship.

29 Let the Priest worship lofty Night and Morning, well-decked, of varied hue, lovely to look on, Indra the Universal, strength-bestower,

Bringing him mighty power, the Trishṭup metre, a bullock four years old, and vital vigour. Let them enjoy the butter. Hotar, worship.

30 Let the Priest worship both celestial Hotars, the Gods' best glory, sages famed for wisdom, the two companions, Indra strength-bestower,

Bringing him mighty power, Jagatî metre, an ox that draws the wain, and vital vigour. Let them enjoy the butter. Hotar, worship.

31 Let the Priest sacrifice to three well-decorated Goddesses, gold-decked, great, lofty, Bhâratîs, Indra their Lord who giveth strength,

Bringing him mighty power, Virâj the metre, and a cow in milk. Let him enjoy the butter. Hotar, worship.

32 Let the Priest worship Tvashṭar the prolific, strengthener of growth, maintaining varied growth and form, Indra who giveth vital force,

Bringing him Dvipad metre, mighty power, and an ox full-grown. Let him enjoy the butter. Hotar, sacrifice.

33 Let the Priest serve with sacrifice the Forest Lord Vanaspati, the Immolator, hundred-powered, praise-worthy, golden-leafed, who wears the girdle, loved, the gracious Lord, Indra who gives the strength of life,

Giving him Kakup metre, mighty power, a barren, a calf-slipping cow, and vital vigour. Let him enjoy the butter. Hotar, sacrifice.

34 Let the Priest offer worship to the Svâhâkṛiti Goddesses, to Agni Household Lord apart, to Varuṇa the Leech and Sage, might, Indra who bestoweth strength,

Bringing him Atichhandas metre, great and mighty power, a strong bull, in his prime, and vital vigour. Let them enjoy the butter. Hotar, sacrifice.

---

31 *Bhâratîs:* that is, Bhâratî and her two constant companions, Sarasvatî and Iḍâ.

33 *The girdle:* the cord with which the victim is attached.

34 *Svâhâkṛiti Goddesses:* the deities of the Prayâjas or Fore-offerings; Introductory Oblations deified.

35 The Grass divine hath added might to radiant Indra strength-giver,
Laying in Indra wondrous power and sight and strength by Gâyatrî. For gain of wealth let him enjoy the butter. Offer sacrifice.

36 The Doors divine have magnified bright Indra, who bestoweth strength,
With Ushṇih laying mighty power in Indra, vital breath and force. For gain of wealth let them enjoy the butter. Offer sacrifice.

37 Morning and Night, divine Ones, have strengthened bright Indra, strength-giver, the Goddesses advanced the God,
With the Anushṭup laying power in Indra, strength and vital force. For gain of wealth let them enjoy. Pay sacrifice.

38 Kind, bounteous, and divine, they have strengthened bright Indra, force-giver, the Goddesses advanced the God,
Laying in Indra power and force and hearing with the Bṛihatî. For gain of wealth let them enjoy. Pay sacrifice.

39 Bringers of strengthening sacrifice, the Goddesses, two teeming cows, have heightened Indra's power with milk,
Laying bright power in Indra with Pankti, and vital energy. For gain of wealth let them enjoy. Pay sacrifice.

40 The Gods, two heavenly Hotars, have strengthened bright Indra, force-giver, those Gods have magnified the God,
With Trishṭup giving Indra power, impetuous might, and vital strength. For gain of wealth let them enjoy. Pay sacrifice.

41 Goddesses three, three Goddesses have heightened their Lord Indra's strength, his who bestoweth vital force,
Laying in Indra power and might and vital strength with Jagatî. For gain of wealth let them enjoy. Pay sacrifice.

42 The God, the Praise of all men, hath strengthened bright Indra force-giver, the God hath magnified the God,
Laying in Indra with Virâj beauty and power and vital force. For gain of wealth let him enjoy. Pay sacrifice.

43 The God the Forest Sovran hath strengthened bright Indra, force-giver, the God hath magnified the God,
With Dvipad storing Indra with fortune and power and vital strength. For gain of wealth let him enjoy. Pay sacrifice.

---

38 *They:* the deities of the Anuyâjas or Post-offerings.

42 *Virâj:* the metre of that name, four Pâdas of ten syllables each.

44 The Grass divine of water-plants hath helped bright Indra force-giver, the God hath magnified the God,
Laying in Indra mighty power with Kakup, fame and vital strength. For gain of wealth let it enjoy. Pay sacrifice.

45 Agni, the God who makes fair rites, hath strengthened Indra force-giver, the God hath magnified the God,
Laying with Atichhandas power in Indra, sway, and vital strength. For gain of wealth let him enjoy. Pay sacrifice.

46 To-day the Sacrificer hath elected, etc., as in verse 23.
To-day divine Vanaspati, etc. . . . . . . .
Thee, to-day, O Ṛishi, etc. . . . . . . .

---

44 *Kakup:* a metre of three Pâdas, 8 + 12 + 8 syllables.

45 *Atichhandas:* hypermeter; any metre of more than forty-eight syllables.

## BOOK THE TWENTY-NINTH.

DECKING the treasure-house of prayers, O Agni, enkindled, pouring forth sweet-tasted butter,
Swift-moving, bearing curd, O Jâtavedas, bear what they love to the Gods' habitation.

2 Balming the paths that lead to heaven with fatness, let the Steed go unto the Gods well-knowing.
Courser, the Quarters of the sky attend thee! Bestow thou food upon this Sacrificer.

3 Thou, Steed, art meet for laud and veneration; swift, fit for sacrifice art thou, O Courser.
In concert with the Gods and Vasus Agni Omniscient waft thee a contented bearer!

4 Pleased with much Sacred Grass which we have scattered wide spread upon the earth, a pleasant carpet,
Joined with the Gods may Aditi, accordant, bestowing bliss award it happy fortune.

5 May these your Doors divine that wear all colours, auspicious, with uplifted leaves unfolding,
Lofty and closely fitted and sonorous, rich in adornment, offer easy passage.

6 Your two Dawns rich in gold and varied colour, travelling on 'twixt Varuṇa and Mitra,
Acquainted with the face of sacrifices, I settle here within the home of Order.

7 Your two chief Hotars have I pleased, bright-coloured, borne on one car, Gods who behold all creatures,
Those who prepare your rules and ordinances and make you see the light by their direction.

8 Bhâratî with Âdityas love our worship! Sarasvatî with Rudras be our helper,
And Iḍâ in accord, invoked with Vasus! Goddesses, place our rite among the Immortals.

---

This Book is supplementary to Book XXII.—XXV. which treat of the Asvamedha or Horse-Sacrifice.

1 This and the ten following verses form an Âprî or Propitiatory Hymn. See XX. 37, note.

5 *Leaves:* sides of the double door of the sacrificial hall.

6 *Two Dawns:* Morning and closely connected Night. *Varuṇa and Mitra:* representing, respectively, sky and earth.

7 *The light:* according to Mahîdhara, the Âhavanîya fire. *Direction:* commanding them to offer sacrifice.

9 The God-devoted son Tvashṭar produces: from Tvashṭar springs to life your fleet-foot Courser.
Tvashṭar gave being to this All about us. Priest, worship here the mighty work's achiever.

10 Let the Steed seek his home, and balmed with butter go of himself unto the Gods in season.
To the Gods' world Vanaspati, well-knowing, bear our oblations which the fire has tasted!

11 Thou, waxing by Prajâpati's strong fervour, born quickly, guardest sacrifice, O Agni.
With consecrated offering go, preceding, and let the Sâdhyas, Gods, eat our oblation.

12 What time, first springing into life, thou neighedst, proceeding from the sea or cloudy vapour,
Limbs of the deer hadst thou, and eagle pinions. O Steed, thy birth is high and must be lauded.

13 This Steed, bestowed by Yama, Trita harnessed, and Indra was the first to mount and ride him.
His bridle the Gandharva grasped. O Vasus, from out the Sun ye fashioned forth the Courser.

14 Yama art thou, O Horse; thou art Âditya; Trita art thou by secret operation.
From Soma thou art thoroughly divided. They say there are three bonds in heaven that hold thee.

15 Three bonds, they say, thou hast in heaven to bind thee, three in the waters, three within the ocean.

---

11 *Sâdhyas:* see XXIV. 27, and R. V. I. 164. 50; X. 90. 7, 16.

12 This and the twelve following verses are taken from R. V. I. 163. *From the sea:* the Sacrificial Horse identified with the Sun who rises in the ocean of air.

13 *Yama:* according to Sâyaṇa, meaning the Controller, Agni. *Trita:* as a Solar deity, God of the distant birthplace of the Sun. *The Gandharva:* Viśvâvasu, a celestial being connected with the Sun and regarded as the chief of that class of semi-deities.

14 *Yama:* Agni, according to Sâyaṇa. *Âditya:* the Sun. *Secret operation:* the mysterious effect of sacrifice. *From Soma, etc.:* the meaning is obscure. According to Sâyaṇa and Mahîdhara, the translation should be 'With Soma thou art thoroughly united', that is, identified with the Moon. This would certainly be preferable if *vipṛiktaḥ*, excluded separated, could possibly mean 'united.' *Three bonds:* According to Sâyaṇa, his 'media of origin,' the Vasus, Âditya, and Heaven.

15 *The waters:* meaning here, says Sâyaṇa, the habitable world, the *bonds* being seed, rain, and tillage. *Ocean:* of air, in which the *bonds* are cloud, lightning, and thunder. *Varuṇa:* on account of the three bonds with which Varuṇa binds the sinner. See R. V. I. 24. 15.

To me thou seemest Varuṇa, O Courser, there where they say is thy sublimest birthplace.

16 Here, Courser, are the places where they groomed thee; here are the traces of thy hooves as winner.
Here have I seen the auspicious reins that guide thee, which those who guard the holy Law keep safely.

17 Thyself from far I recognized in spirit, a Bird that from below flew through the heaven.
I saw thy head still soaring, striving upward by paths unsoiled by dust, pleasant to travel.

18 Here I beheld thy form matchless in beauty, eager to win thee food at the Cow's station.
Whene'er a man brings thee to thine enjoyment, thou swallowest the herbs, most greedy eater.

19 After thee, Courser, come the car, the bridegroom, the kine come after, and the charm of maidens.
Full companies have followed for thy friendship: the pattern of thy vigour Gods have followed.

20 His horns are golden and his feet are iron. Less fleet than he, though swift as thought, was Indra.
The Gods came only to the oblation-banquet of him who mounted first of all the Courser.

21 Symmetrical in flank, with rounded haunches, mettled like heroes, the celestial Coursers
Put forth their strength like swans in lengthened order when they, the Steeds, have reached the heavenly causeway.

22 A body formed for flight hast thou, O Charger; swift as the wind in motion is thy spirit.
Thy horns are spread abroad in all directions; they move with restless beat in wildernesses.

---

16 *Who guard the holy Law:* the Gods who maintain the order of the universe. Here the reference is to the course of the Sun, with whom the Horse is identified.

17 *A Bird:* the swiftly-moving Sun.

18 *Food:* in the shape of oblations. *The Cow's station:* the chief place of earth, the Cow being the altar. Mahīdhara explains it as the station of the Bull, that is, the disc of the Sun: 'I beheld thy form in the disc of the Sun.' *Most greedy eater:* regarded as an earthly horse.

20 *His horns:* according to Sāyaṇa his mane is intended. There may be a reference also to the rays of the Sun. *Him who mounted:* Indra, as is said in verse 13.

21 The horses of the Sun are spoken of. The exact meaning of two of the epithets is uncertain.

22 *Thy horns:* here, perhaps, meaning hoofs.

23 The strong Steed hath come forward to the slaughter, pondering with a mind directed God-ward.
The goat who is his kin is led before him: the sages and the singers follow after.

24 The Steed is come unto the noblest mansion, is come unto his Father and his Mother.
This day shall he approach the Gods, most welcome: then he declares good gifts to him who worships.

25 Thou in the house of man this day enkindled worshippest Gods, a God, O Jâtavedas.
Wealthy in friends! observant, bring them hither. Thou art a sapient envoy, full of wisdom.

26 Tanûnapât, fair-tongued, with sweet mead balming the paths and ways of Order, make them pleasant.
Convey our sacrifice to heaven, exalting with holy thoughts our hymns of praise and worship.

27 With sacrifice to these we with laudations will honour holy Narâṣaṃsa's greatness—
To these the pure, most wise, the thought-inspirers, Gods who enjoy both sorts of our oblations.

28 Invoked, deserving laud and adoration, O Agni, come accordant with the Vasus.
Thou art, O vigorous One, the Gods' Invoker, so, best of Sacrificers, bring them quickly.

29 By rule the Sacred Grass is scattered eastward, a robe to clothe the earth when dawns are breaking.
Widely it spreads around and far extended, fair for the Gods and bringing peace and freedom.

30 Let the expansive Doors be widely opened, like wives who deck their beauty for their husbands.
Lofty, celestial, all-impelling Portals, admit the Gods and give them easy access.

---

23 *The goat:* to be attached to the Horse at the sacrificial stake.

24 *Noblest mansion:* heaven, to which he goes by sacrifice. *His Father and his Mother:* Heaven and Earth.

25 This and the following verse are taken from R. V. X. 110. 1, 2.

26 *Order:* sacrifice.

27 *Both sorts:* libations of Soma juice and offerings of clarified butter, rice-cakes, etc.

28 This and the eight following verses are taken from R. V. X. 110. 3—11, forming, with verses 25 and 26, a complete Âprî or Propitiatory Hymn.

31 Pouring sweet dews, let holy Night and Morning, each close to each, be seated at their station—
Lofty, celestial Dames, with gold to deck them, assuming all their fair and radiant beauty.

32 Come the two chief celestial sweet-voiced Hotars, arranging sacrifice for man to worship,
As singers who inspire us in assemblies, showing the eastward light with their direction!

33 Let Bhâratî come quickly to our worship, and Iḍâ showing like a human being.
So let Sarasvatî and both her fellows, deft Goddesses, on this fair grass be seated.

34 Hotar more skilled in sacrifice, bring hither with speed to-day God Tvashṭar, thou who knowest,
Even him who framed these two, the Earth and Heaven, the Parents, with their forms, and every creature.

35 Send to our offerings which thyself thou balmest the Companies of Gods in ordered season.
Agni, Vanaspati, the Immolator sweeten our offered gift with mead and butter.

36 Agni as soon as he was born made ready the sacrifice and was the Gods' preceder.
May the Gods eat our offering consecrated according to the true Priest's voice and guidance.

37 Thou, making light where no light was, and form, O men! where form was not,
Wast born together with the Dawns.

38 The warrior's look is like a thunderous rain-cloud's when, armed with mail, he seeks the lap of battle.
Be thou victorious with unwounded body: so let the thickness of thine armour save thee.

39 With Bow let us win kine, with Bow the battle, with Bow be victors in our hot encounters.
The Bow brings grief and sorrow to the foeman: armed with the Bow may we subdue all regions.

---

32 *Eastern light:* the Âhavanîya fire: cf. verse 7.

37 Taken from R. V. I. 6. 3, which is addressed to Indra and the Maruts. *Thou:* the Sun, with whom Agni is identified. *O men!:* perhaps merely an exclamation expressive of admiration. If the Maruts be meant, the words *thou, making, wast born* may apply to these Gods as one company.

38 In connexion with the Horse, who plays a most important part in raids and battles, the bow and various implements of war are eulogized in fourteen verses taken from R. V. VI. 75 and six from R. V. VI. 47. 26—31.

40 Close to his ear, as fain to speak, She presses, holding her well-loved Friend in her embraces.
Strained on the Bow, She whispers like a woman—this Bowstring that preserves us in the combat.

41 These, meeting like a woman and her lover, bear, motherlike, their child upon their bosom.
May the two Bow-ends, starting swift asunder scatter, in unison, the foes who hate us.

42 With many a son, father of many daughters, He clangs and clashes as he goes to battle.
Slung on the back, pouring his brood, the Quiver vanquishes all opposing bands and armies.

43 Upstanding in the Car the skilful Charioteer guides his strong Horses on whitherso'er he will.
See and admire the strength of those controlling Reins which from behind declare the will of him who drives.

44 Horses whose hoofs rain dust are neighing loudly, yoked to the Chariots, showing forth their vigour.
With their forefeet descending on the foemen, they, never flinching, trample and destroy them.

45 Car-bearer is the name of his oblation, whereon are laid his Weapons and his Armour.
So let us here, each day that passes, honour the helpful Car with hearts exceeding joyful.

46 In sweet association lived the fathers who gave us life, profound and strong in trouble,
Unwearied, armed with shafts and wondrous weapons, free, real heroes, conquerors of armies.

---

40 *She:* the bowstring. *well-loved friend:* the arrow. *Whispers like a woman:* 'twangs like the scream of a woman.'—Muir. But the faint sound made by the string while it is being drawn to the ear is intended. Homer likens the sound to the voice of a swallow.

41 *These:* the two ends of the bow. *Like a woman and her lover:* or, 'drawing close like two women to their lovers.' *Their child:* the arrow.

42 *With many a son:* the quiver is called the father of sons and daughters, it is said, because the words signifying arrow are both masculine and feminine.

45 *Car-bearer: rathavâhanam:* a platform, stand, or truck on which the chariot is placed when not in use. The word seems in this place to mean also the oblation offered by the warrior to the ideal war-chariot personified, or to a tutelary deity of chariots.

46 There is no verb in this stanza, and the only substantive, *pitaraḥ*, fathers, is explained by both Commentators as *pâlayitâraḥ*, guards, defenders, that is, apparently, those who attend the chariot of the chief. Professor Wilson, following Sâyana, translates: 'The guards (of the chariot), revelling in the savoury (spoil), distributors of food, protectors in calamity, armed with spears, resolute, beautifully arranged, strong in arrows, invincible, of heroic valour, robust, and conquerors of numerous hosts.'

47 The Brâhmans, and the Fathers meet for Soma draughts, and, graciously inclined, unequalled Heaven and Earth.
Guard us from evil, Pûshan! guard us strengtheners of Law! let not the evil-wisher master us.

48 Her tooth a deer, dressed in an eagle's feathers, bound with cow-hide, launched forth, She flieth onward.
There where the heroes speed hither and thither, there may the arrows shelter and protect us.

49 Avoid us thou whose flight is straight, and let our bodies be as stone.
May Soma kindly speak to us, and Aditi protect us well.

50 He lays his blows upon their backs, He deals his strokes upon their thighs.
Thou Whip who urgest horses, drive sagacious chargers in the fray.

51 It compasses the arm with serpent windings, fending away the friction of the bowstring:
So may the Brace, well skilled in all its duties, guard manfully the man from every quarter.

52 Lord of the Wood, be firm and strong in body: be, bearing us, a brave victorious hero.
Show forth thy strength, compact with straps of leather, and let thy rider win all spoils of battle.

53 Its mighty strength was borrowed from the heaven and earth: its conquering force was brought from sovrans of the wood.
Honour with holy gifts the Car like Indra's bolt, the Car bound round with straps, the vigour of the floods.

54 Thou bolt of Indra, Vanguard of the Maruts, close knit to Varuṇa and Child of Mitra,—
As such, accepting gifts which here we offer, receive, O God-like Chariot, these oblations.

55 Send forth thy voice aloud through earth and heaven, and let the world in all its breadth regard thee;
O Drum, accordant with the Gods and Indra, drive thou afar, yea, very far, our foemen.

---

47 *The Brâhmans and the Fathers:* or, perhaps, the sacerdotal Fathers. The stanza, which is grammatically difficult, seems out of place.

48 *Her tooth a deer:* the point of the arrow is made of a piece of deer's horn attached to the shaft with leather strings. The butt of the arrow is feathered.

50 *He:* the whip.

51 *It:* the brace or guard worn on the archer's left arm, fastened on with leather straps.

52 Here follow six verses from R. V. VI. 47. 26—31 in praise of the Chariot and the Drum. *Lord of the Wood:* tall tree, the timber of which the Car is made.

55 *O Drum:* the *dundubhi* here addressed and glorified was a sort of loud kettle-drum like those which are still used.

56 Thunder out strength and fill us full of vigour: yea, thunder forth and drive away all dangers.
Drive hence, O War-drum, drive away misfortune: thou art the Fist of Indra: show thy firmness.
57 Drive hither those, and these again bring hither: the War-drum speaks aloud as battle's signal.
Our heroes, winged with horses, come together. Let our car-warriors, Indra, be triumphant.
58 The black-necked victim belongs to Agni; the ewe to Sarasvatî; the brown victim is Soma's; the dusky Pûshan's; the white-backed is Bṛihaspati's; the dappled belongs to the All-Gods; the red to Indra; the spotted to the Maruts; the strong-bodied to Indra-Agni; one with white marks below to Savitar; to Varuṇa a black ram with one white foot.
59 To Agni Anîkavân is sacrificed a red-marked ox; two with white spots below are for Savitar; two with silvery navels for Pûshan; two yellow hornless he-goats for the All-Gods; a spotted one for the Maruts; the black-faced he-goat is Agni's; the ewe is Sarasvatî's; the ram is Varuṇa's.
60 To Agni of the Gâyatrî, of the Trivṛit hymn and of the Rathantara Sâman is to be offered a rice-cake on eight potsherds; to Indra of the Trishṭup, the Pañchadaṣa hymn and the Bṛihat Sâman one on eleven potsherds; to the All-Gods of the Jagatî, the Seventeenfold hymn and the Vairûpa Sâman, one on twelve potsherds; to Mitra-Varuṇa of the Anushṭup, the Ekaviṃṣa hymn, and the Vairâja Sâman, a mess of curdled milk; to Bṛihaspati of the Paṅkti metre, the Triṇava hymn, and the Ṣâkvara Sâman, an oblation of rice boiled in milk; to Savitar of the Ushṇih, the Thirty-threefold hymn, and the Raivata Sâman, a rice-cake on eight potsherds; a mess of boiled rice is to be made for Prajâpati; the same for Vishṇu's Consort Aditi; to Agni Vaiṣvânara is to be offered a rice-cake on twelve potsherds, and to Anumati one on eight.

---

57 Drive to us the cows of the enemy and send our own home in safety. Or, as Mahîdhara explains, understanding *senâḥ*, troops, instead of cows, with the feminine pronoun: Drive thither away the troops of the enemy, and rally ours and lead them to victory.

58—60 These verses are supplementary to the list of sacrificial animals in Book XXIV.

59 *Anîkavân:* having a face or an army (of pointed rays); perhaps, set in the front or van of the army. See Sacred Books of the East, XII. p. 408, note.

60 *Of the Gâyatrî, etc.:* praised in the metres, hymns, and Sâmans named in the verse. *Anumati:* divine Grace or Favour shown in the Gods' acceptance of oblations, personified as a female deity. *Vishṇu's Consort Aditi:* only in this place and in a passage of the Taittirîya-Saṃhitâ is Aditi said to be the wife of Vishṇu. In the Epic and Purâṇic mythology she is the wife of Kaṣyapa and the mother of Vishṇu in his Dwarf Incarnation.

# BOOK THE THIRTIETH.

OUR sacrifice, God Savitar! speed onward: speed to his share the sacrifice's patron.
May the Celestial Gandharva, cleanser of thought and will, make clean our thoughts and wishes.
The Lord of Speech sweeten the words we utter!

2 May we attain that excellent glory of Savitar the God:
So may he stimulate our prayers.

3 Savitar, God, send far away all troubles and calamities,
And send us only what is good.

4 We call on him distributer of wondrous bounty and of wealth,
On Savitar who looks on men.

5 For Brahman (Priesthood) he binds a Brâhman to the
stake; for Kshatra (Royalty) a Râjanya; for the Maruts
a Vaisya; for Penance a Sûdra; for Darkness a robber;
for Hell a homicide or a man who has lost his consecrated
fire; for Misfortune a eunuch; for Venality an Ayogû;
for Kâma a harlot; for Excessive Noise a Mâgadha;

---

Books XXX. and XXXI. treat of the Purushanedha or Human Sacrifice, an old-established custom among almost all nations of antiquity. The ceremony was to be performed by a Brâhman or a Râjanya, and was expected to obtain for the Sacrificer universal preëminence and every blessing which the Horse-sacrifice might have failed to secure. The ritual resembles in many respects that of the Asvamedha; man, the noblest victim, being actually or symbolically sacrificed instead of the Horse, and men and women of various tribes, figures, complexions, characters, and professions being attached to the sacrificial stakes in place of the tame and wild animals enumerated in Book XXIV. These nominal victims were afterwards released uninjured, and, so far as the text of the White Yajurveda goes, the whole ceremony was merely emblematical, a type of the allegorical self-immolation of Purusha, Embodied Spirit or the Cosmic Man. See Colebrooke, Miscellaneous Essays, II.; Weber, Indische Streifen, I. 54 seq.; Wilson, Selected Works, II. 247 seq.; Muir, Original Sanskrit Texts, IV. 289, note; Oldenberg, Religion des Veda, p. 365; Romesh Chunder Dutt, Civilization in Ancient India, I. 274, 275 (first edition); Max Müller, Ancient Sanskrit Literature, 419 seq.; Vedic India (Story of the Nations Series), pp. 406—413; A. Hillebrandt, Ritual-Litteratur, p. 153.

1 The verse is repeated from XI. 7.

2 Repeated from III. 35 and XXII. 9.

3 Taken from R. V. V. 82. 5.

4 Taken from R. V. I. 22. 7.

5 *Lost:* that is, allowed to go out. *Ayogû:* the meaning is uncertain; perhaps 'a gambler,' or 'an unchaste woman,' as Prof. Weber translates in Indische Streifen, I. 76, where, and in the following pages, Prof. W. has given a version, with explanatory notes, of the whole list of victims and objects to which they are dedicated *Mâgadha:* the word meaning originally 'belonging to the Magadha country (South Bahâr)' means a professional bard, minstrel, or panegyrist, the son of a Vaisya and a Kshatriyâ.

6 For Dance a stable-master; for Song a public dancer; for Duty one who attends court; for Pastime a timid man; for Sport a chatterer; for Laughter an artist; for Pleasure a woman-lover; for Desire a damsel's son; for Dexterity a car-builder; for Firmness a carpenter;

7 For Trouble a potter's son; for Device an artificer; for Beauty a jeweller; for Welfare a sower; for the Arrow-deity a maker of shafts; for Injury a bowyer; for Action a bowstring-maker; for Fate a rope-maker; for Death a hunter; for the Finisher a dog-leader;

8 For Rivers a fisherman; for Ṛikshîkâs a Nishâda's son; for the Man-tiger a madman; for the Gandharvas and Apsarases a Vrâtya; for Motives one demented; for Serpents and Genii an untrustworthy man; for Dice a gambler; for Excitement a non-gambler; for Piṣâchas a woman who splits cane; for Yâtudhânas a woman who works in thorns;

9 For Rendezvous a lover; for Homestead a paramour; for Trouble an unmarried elder brother; for Nirṛiti a younger brother who has married before his elder; for Misfortune the husband of a younger sister whose elder sister has not been married; for Representation a woman who embroiders; for Agreement a woman who deals in love-charms; for Garrulity a by-sitter; for Colour an obstinate man; for Strength a yielding man;

10 For Interruptions a hunch-back; for Delight a dwarf; for Doors a blear-eyed man; for Sleep a blind man; for Unrighteousness a deaf man; for Purifying Medium a physician; for Insight an astrologer; for Craving for Knowledge an inquisitive man; for Desire of extra Knowledge an extra-inquisitive man; for Moral Law a question-solver;

11 For Eye-diseases an elephant-keeper; for Speed a horse-keeper; for Nourishment a cowherd; for Manliness a shepherd; for Keenness a goatherd; for Refreshment a ploughman; for Sweet Beverage a preparer of Surâ; for Weal a house-guard; for Well-being a possessor of wealth; for Supervision a doorkeeper's attendant;

---

7 *The Finisher:* Antaka, another name of Death.

8 *Ṛikshîkâs:* a class of evil spirits, mentioned in A. V. XII. 1. 49 in connexion with lions, tigers, hyenas, and wolves. *Vrâtya:* the chief of a band of nomad Nonconformists of Âryan extraction, but absolutely independent and not following the Âryan or Brâhmanist way of life. See A. V. XV. *Piṣâchas:* a class of fierce and malignant imps or goblins. *Yâtudhânas:* fiendish sorcerers.

9 *Nirṛiti:* or Destruction.

11 *Sweet Beverage:* kilâla; see II. 34; III. 43; XX. 65.

12 For Light a wood-bringer; for Brightness a fire-kindler; for the Sun's Station a besprinkler; for Highest Heaven a high steward; for the World of Gods a carver; for the World of Men a distributer; for All-Worlds a pourer-out: for Poverty, Affliction a stirrer-up of strife; for Sacrifice a washerwoman; for Delight a female dyer;

13 For Assault a thievish-hearted man; for Homicide a slanderer; for Discrimination a door-keeper; for Inspection a door-keeper's attendant; for Strength a servant; for Plenty a running footman; for the Beloved a sweet speaker; for Safety the rider of a horse; for the World of Svarga a dealer-out of portions; for Highest Heaven a high steward;

14 For Passion an iron-smelter; for Anger a remover; for Yoking a yoker; for Pain an assailant; for Quiet an unyoker; for Up-hill and Down-hill one who stands on three legs; for Form a conceited man; for Virtue a female ointment-maker; for Nirṛiti a female scabbard-maker; for Yama a barren woman;

15 For Yama a mother of twins; for the Atharvans a woman who has miscarried; for the First Year a gad-about; for the Parivatsara one who has not borne a child; for the Idâvatsara one who exceeds; for the Idvatsara one who transgresses; for the Vatsara one who is worn out; for the Saṃvatsara one with grey hair; for the Ṛibhus a hide-dresser; for the Sâdhyas a currier;

16 For Lakes a fisherman; for Standing Waters a fisher; for Tank-waters a Nishâda; for Reed-beds a fish-vender; for the Opposite Bank one who gropes for fish; for This Bank a fish-catcher; for Fords an Ânda; for shallows a Mainâla;

---

12 *Besprinkler:* a priest who consecrates a king by aspersion. *High steward:* chief attendant at meals. *Distributer:* of portions of food.

14 *Remover: nisaram;* the meaning is uncertain: Niedergehender:—Weber; perhaps a sort of 'chucker-out.' *Three legs:* with a staff to make his footing surer.

15 *Twins:* the word Yama meaning originally one of twins. *The Atharvans:* spells and charms, such as are contained in the Atharva-veda. *First Year:* of the Five-year Cycle. Parivatsara, Idâvatsara, Idvatsara, Vatsara are names of the other years. See XXVII. 45. *Saṃvatsa:* the first year of the cycle mentioned again. *Ribhus:* three artificers, raised to Godhead for their merits. *A hide-dresser:* alluding to the re-animation of the dead cow's skin by the Ṛibhus, that is, the refreshment and restoration of the parched earth by the Rains, the Ṛibhus being Seasonal deities. See R. V. I. 110. 8. *Sâdhyas:* see XXIV. 27; XXIX. 11.

16 *Ânda:* said to mean one who catches fish by damming up water. *Mainâla:* a netter of fish. *Bhilla:* a Bheel. 'The Bheel is a black man, only hairier. He carries bows and arches in his hands. When he meets you he shoots you and throws your body in a ditch. By this you may know the Bheel.' —Indian Examinee's Answer-paper. *Kirâta:* a savage who lives by hunting.

for Sounds a Bhilla; for Caverns a Kirâta; for Mountain-heights a destructive savage; for Mountains a wild man;

17 For Abhorrence a Paulkasa; for Colour a goldsmith; for Balance a merchant; for Repentance a sluggard; for All Spirits a leper; for Prosperity a watchful man; for Failure a sleepy man; for Mischief a chatterer; for Misfortune a shameless man; for Undoing one who cuts up into small pieces;

18 For the Dice-king a gambler; for the die Kṛita one who contemplates his adversary's ill luck; for the Tretâ a gamble-manager; for the Dvâpara a chief manager; for Âskanda one who will not leave the gambling-hall; for Mṛityu one who approaches cows; for Antaka a Cow-killer; for Hunger one who goes begging to a man who is cutting up a cow; for Misdeed a leader of the Charakas; for Misery a robber;

19 For Echo a reviler; for Noise a snarler; for End a very talkative man; for Endless a mute; for Sound a drummer; for Might a lute-player; for Cry a flute-blower; for Confused Tone a Conch-blower; for the Wood a wood-ranger; for Partly-wooded Land a forest fire guard;

20 For Pastime a harlot; for Laughter a jester; for Lust a woman with spotty skin; for Might these, the head-man of a village, an astrologer, and a watchman; a lute-player; a hand-clapper, a flutist, these for Dance; for Pleasure a musician;

21 For Fire a fat man; for Earth a cripple; for Wind a Châṇḍâla; for Mid-Air a pole-dancer; for Sky a bald-head; for the Sun a green-eyed man; for Stars a spotty man; for the Moon a leper; for Day a white yellow-eyed man; for Night a black man with yellow eyes.

---

17 *Paulkasa:* a man of very low birth, son of a Nishâda and a Kshatriyâ.

18 *Dice-king:* the ace, the die called Kali; Kṛita, Tretâ, Dvâpara, Âskanda being the names of the other four in general use. *Who will not leave:* etc.: *sabhâsthâṇum:* literally a gambling-saloon pillar or post. *Mṛityu:* Death. *Antaka:* the Finisher. Death. *Who approaches cows:* a cow-knacker (Kuhschinder):—Weber. *Charakas:* followers of one of the principal schools of the Black Yajurveda, regarded as opponents.

19 *Forest fire guard:* forest conflagrations, caused by the inter-friction of dry branches and other accidents, are not uncommon in the hot weather.

20 *Lust:* an aquatic monster, according to Sâyaṇa.

21 *Châṇḍâla:* a man of an impure or degraded tribe, an outcast. *Pole-dancer:* an acrobat. See The Hymns of the Rigveda, I. 10. 1, note.

22 Now he ties up the eight following variform men: one too tall, one too short, one too stout, one too thin, one too white, one too black, one too bald, one too hairy. These must be neither Śûdras nor Brâhmans, and must be dedicated to Prajâpati.

A minstrel, a harlot, a gambler, and a eunuch—neither of Śûdra nor Brâhman caste—are to be dedicated to Prajâpati.

---

22 *Minstrel*: Mâgadha; see verse 5.

## BOOK THE THIRTY-FIRST.

PURUSHA hath a thousand heads, a thousand eyes, a thousand feet.
Pervading earth on every side he fills a space ten fingers broad.

2 Purusha is in truth this All, what hath been and what yet shall be;
Lord, too, of immortality which waxes greater still by food.

3 So mighty in his grandeur; yea, greater than this is Pûrusha.
All creatures are one fourth of him, three fourths eternal life in heaven.

---

The ceremony is continued and concluded. The Brahman priest recites to the assembled human victims the famous Purusha Hymn (verse 1—16), taken, with transpositions and variations, from R. V. X. 90 (A. V. XIX. 6), which celebrates the mystical immolation of Purusha, the origin of all creation, of which the Purushamedha or Human Sacrifice is an emblematical representation.

1 *Purusha:* the Person, embodied spirit, or Man personified and regarded as the soul and original source of the universe, the personal and life-giving principle in all animated beings, is said to have *a thousand*, that is, innumerable, *heads, eyes*, and *feet*. as being one with all created life. In the A. V. version *arms* has been substituted for *heads*, to agree, apparently, with the numbers of eyes and feet. *A space ten fingers broad:* the region of the heart of man wherein the soul was supposed to reside. Although, as the Universal Soul, Purusha pervades the universe, as the Individual Soul he is enclosed in a space of narrow dimensions. Cf. A. V. IV. 16. 3. 'The loins of Varuṇa are both the oceans, and this small drop of water, too, contains him'; one of the recently discovered Logia or Sayings of Jesus is to the same effect: 'cleave the wood, and thou wilt find me; lift the stone, and I am there.'

2 The second line is variously explained. The meaning of the words seems to be: he is lord of immortality or the immortal world of the Gods, which grows greater by food, that is, by the sacrificial offerings of men. According to Sâyaṇa: he is the lord or distributer of immortality because he becomes the visible world in order that living beings may obtain the fruits of their actions and gain *moksha* or final liberation from their bonds; 'he is also the lord of immortality; for he mounts beyond (his own condition) for the food (of living beings).'—Wilson. Colebroke translates the line: 'he is that which grows by nourishment, and he is the distributer of immortality.' Muir renders it by:—'He is also the lord of immortality since by food he expands.' According to the paraphrase in the *Bhâgavata Purâṇa*, the meaning of the last clause is: 'since he hath transcended mortal nutriment.' Prof. Ludwig's version is: 'auch uber die unsterblichkeit gebietend, [da er,] was durch speise [ist,] weit überragt, ruling also over immortality, [since he] far transcends what [exists] through food; but in his Commentary a somewhat different explanation is given. 'Ruling over immortality, he was all that grows by food.'—Peterson.

3 *Eternal life: amṛitam:* immortality, or the immortal Gods.

4 With three fourths Purusha rose up: one fourth of him again was here.
Thence he moved forth to every side over what eats not and what eats.

5 From him Virâj was born; again Purusha from Virâj was born.
When born, he spread to west and east beyond the boundaries of earth.

6 From that great General Sacrifice the dripping fat was gathered up.
He formed the creatures of the air and animals both wild and tame.

7 From that great General Sacrifice Ṛichas and Sâma hymns were born:
Therefrom were spells and charms produced; the Yajus had its birth from it.

8 From it were horses born, from it all cattle with two rows of teeth:
From it were generated kine, from it were goats and sheep produced.

9 They balmed as victim on the grass Purusha born in earliest time.
With him the Deities and all Sâdhyas and Ṛishis sacrificed.

10 When they divided Purusha how many portions did they make?

---

4 *Over what eats not and what eats:* over animate and inanimate creation. According to Sâyaṇa and Mahîdhara, over both classes of created things, those capable of enjoyment, that is, who can taste the reward and punishment of good and evil actions, such as Gods, men, and lower animals, and those who are incapable thereof, such as mountains and rivers—*chetanam*, or conscious, *achetanam*, or unconscious, creation.

5 *From him:* or, from that, the 'one-fourth' mentioned in stanzas 3 and 4. *Virâj*, or, in the nominative form, Virâṭ, is said to have come, in the form of the mundane egg, from Âdi-Purusha, the primeval Purusha, or presiding Male or Spirit, 'who then entered into this egg, which he animates as its vital soul or divine principle.' Or Virâj may 'be the female counterpart of Purusha as Aditi of Daksha in X. 72. 4, 5.' See Muir's exhaustive Note on this passage, *O. S. Texts*, V. pp. 369, 370; and Wallis, *Cosmology of the Rigveda*, p. 87.

6 *Dripping fat:* 'the mixture of curds and butter.'—Wilson. *He:* or, It; the sacrificial victim Purusha, or the sacred clarified butter.

7 *Ṛichas:* verses of praise and prayer for recitation. *Sâma hymns:* psalms for chanting. *Spells and charms:* magical incantations; probably those of the later collection of the Atharva-veda. *The Yajus:* the Collection of Sacrificial formulas.

9 *Sâdhyas:* see XXIV. 27; XXIX. 11; XXX. 15.

What was his mouth? what were his arms? what are the names of thighs and feet?

11 The Brâhman was his mouth, of both his arms was the Râjanya made.
His thighs became the Vaiṣya, from his feet the Ṣûdra was produced.

12 The Moon was gendered from his mind, and from his eye the Sun had birth;
Vâyu and Prâṇa from his ear, and from his mouth was Agni born.

13 Forth from his navel came mid-air; the sky was fashioned from his head;
Earth from his feet, and from his ear the Quarters. Thus they formed the worlds.

14 When Gods performed the sacrifice with Purusha as offering
Spring was the butter, Autumn the oblation, Summer was the wood.

15 Then seven were his enclosing-sticks, his kindling-brands were three times seven,
When Gods, performing sacrifice, bound as their victim Purusha.

16 Gods, sacrificing, sacrificed the victim: these were the earliest holy ordinances.
The Mighty Ones attained the height of heaven, there where the Sâdhyas, Gods of old, are dwelling.

---

11 The Brâhman is called the mouth of Purusha as having the special privilege as a priest of addressing the Gods in prayer. The arms of Purusha became the Râjanya, the prince and soldier who wields the sword and spear. His thighs, the strongest part of his body, became the agriculturist and tradesman, the chief supporters of society; and his feet, the emblems of vigour and activity, became the Ṣûdra or labouring man on whose toil and industry all prosperity ultimately rests. This is the only passage in the Rigveda which enumerates the four castes.

13 Cf. the creation-myth of the world-giant Ymir in Old Northern poetry. The hills are his bones, the sky his skull, the sea his blood, and the clouds his brains. See Corpus Poeticum Boreale, II. 468.

15 *Enclosing-sticks:* See II. 3. *Kindling-brands:* See II. 4. Sâyaṇa explains *paridhayaḥ* here as the seven sacred metres, or as six shallow trenches dug round the fire and an imaginary one round the Sun. According to Mahîdhara, the twenty-one kindling-brands are the twelve months, five seasons, the three worlds of earth, air, and heaven, and the Sun.

This pantheistic hymn, which is generally called the Purushasûkta, is of comparatively recent origin, and appears to be an attempt to harmonise the two ideas of sacrifice and creation. For further information regarding it, see Muir, O. S. Texts, I. pp. 6—11, and V. 368—377, Prof. Max Müller, Ancient Sanskrit Literature, pp. 570f, and Dr. Scherman, Philosophische Hymnen

17 In the beginning he was formed, collected from waters, earth, and Viṣvakarman's essence.
Fixing the form thereof Tvashṭar proceedeth. This was at first the mortal's birth and godhead.

18 I know this mighty Purusha whose colour is like the Sun, beyond the reach of darkness.
He only who knows him leaves Death behind him. There is no path save this alone to travel.

19 In the womb moves Prajâpati: he, never becoming born, is born in sundry figures.
The wise discern the womb from which he springeth. In him alone stand all existing creatures.

20 He who gives light and heat to Gods, first, foremost Agent of the Gods,
Born ere the Gods—to him the bright, the holy One, be reverence!

21 Thus spake the Gods at first, as they begat the bright and holy One:
The Brâhman who may know thee thus shall have the Gods in his control.

22 Beauty and Fortune are thy wives: each side of thee are Day and Night.
The constellations are thy form: the Aṣvins are thine open jaws.
Wishing, wish yonder world for me, wish that the Universe be mine.

---

aus der Rig-und Atharva-veda-Sanhitâ, pp. 11—23. The hymn has also been translated by Colebrooke, Miscellaneous Essays, pp. 167, 168; by Wallis, Cosmology of the Rigveda, pp. 87, 88; and by Peterson, Hymns from the Rigveda, pp. 289, 290; also by Burnouf, Bhâgavata Purâṇa, Preface to Vol. I., and by Weber, Indische Studien, IX. p. 5. Grassmann's Translation in his Appendix to Vol. II., and Ludwig's Translation and Commentary should be consulted. See also The Hymns of the Atharva-veda, XIX. 6, which is a reproduction of this hymn with transpositions and variations.

17 The earliest performer of the Purushamedha, who gained thereby the form of the Sun, is glorified. *He:* there is no noun in the text. Mahîdhara supplies *yo rasaḥ*, the essence which. *Tvashṭar:* the Sun. *Proceedeth:* on his daily course. *Godhead:* gained by Sacrifice.

19 The first line is taken, with a variation, from A. V. X. 8. 13. *Sundry places:* every birth that occurs being in reality a re-birth of the Creative Power Prajâpati.

20 *He:* Prajâpati in the form of the Sun. *Foremost Agent: purohitaḥ.*

22 *Beauty and Fortune:* Ṣrî and Lakshmî. *Thy:* the Sun is addressed. *Constellations:* or stars in general. *The Aṣvins:* here according to Mahîdhara, meaning Heaven and Earth. *The Universe:* he wishes for liberation from the bonds of this world and absorption into Brahma, the All.

## BOOK THE THIRTY-SECOND.

AGNI is That; the Sun is That; Vâyu and Chandramâs are That.
The Bright is That; Brahma is That, those Waters, that Prajâpati.

2 All twinklings of the eyelid sprang from Purusha, resplendent One.
No one hath comprehended him above, across, or in the midst.

3 There is no counterpart of him whose glory verily is great.
In the beginning rose Hiraṇyagarbha, etc. Let not him harm me, etc. Than whom there is no other born, etc.

4 This very God pervadeth all the regions; yea, born aforetime, in the womb he dwelleth.
He verily born and to be born hereafter meeteth his offspring, facing all directions.

5 Before whom naught whatever sprang to being; who with his presence aids all living creatures,
Prajâpati, rejoicing in his offspring, he, Shoḍaṣî, maintains the Three great Lustres.

6 By whom the heavens are strong and earth stands firmly, by whom light's realm and sky-vault are supported;
By whom the regions in mid-air were measured. What God shall we adore with our oblation?

---

This and the two following Books contain texts and formulas to be used at the performance of a Sarvamedha or Sacrifice for Universal Success and Prosperity, a ten-day ceremony that ranks higher and is considered to be more important than even the Purushamedha. After performing this ceremony the Sacrificer has to leave his home and retire to the wilderness for the rest of his life. This Book is considered to be an Upanishad, entitled Tadeva from the first two words.

1 *That: tad;* the Supreme Self. *Chandramâs:* the Moon. *Those:* the celebrated.

2 *Twinklings:* moments and measures of time. *Comprehended:* as an object of perception.

3 *In the beginning, etc.:* three passages are referred to, which have occurred, respectively, in XXV. 10—13; XII. 103; VIII. 36, all celebrating the greatness of Prajâpati or Purusha.

4 *Aforetime:* or, the first. Cf. XXXI. 19.

5 The second line is repeated from VIII. 36. *Three ...... Lustres:* Agni, Vâyu, Sûrya, or the Sun, the Moon, and Agni.

6 Taken from R. V. X. 121. 5. *What God, etc.:* or, Worship we Ka the God. See XIII. 4.

7 To whom, supported by his help, two armies embattled look while trembling in their spirit,
Where over them the risen Sun is shining. What God shall we adore with our oblation ?
What time the mighty waters, etc. He in his might surveyed, etc.

8 The Sage beholdeth That mysterious Being wherein this All hath found one only dwelling.
Therein unites the Whole, and thence it issues: far-spread it is the warp and woof in creatures.

9 Knowing Eternity, may the Gandharva declare that station, parted, kept in secret.
Three steps thereof in mystery are hidden : he who knows these shall be the father's father.

10 He is our kin, our Father and Begetter : he knows all beings and all Ordinances,
In whom the Gods obtaining life eternal have risen upward to the third high station.

11 Having encompassed round existing creatures, the worlds and all the Quarters and Mid-quarters,
Having aproached the first-born Child of Order he with his Self into The Self hath entered.

---

7 *Two armies embattled look :* or perhaps better : To whom, supported by his favour, Heaven and Earth look up. See M. Müller, Vedic Hymns, Part I. pp. 2, 9. *What time, etc. :* repeated from XXVII. 25. *He in his might :* repeated from XXVII. 26.

8 *Mysterious Being :* Brahma, the Absolute. *Unites :* is absorbed, at the periodical destruction of the universe at the end of a Kalpa or day of Brahmâ, an eon of four hundred and thirty-two million years of mortals. *Issues :* at the time of a new creation.

9 Taken, with a variation, from A. V. II. 1. 2. *The Gandharva :* meaning here, according to Mahîdhara, Colebrooke, and Weber, the sage, the learned theologian ; or, it may be, the Sun. *Parted :* in the absorption and the re creation of the universe. The A. V. reading is *paramam*, highest. *Three steps :* according to Mahîdhara, the three *padâni*, steps, or conditions, are creation, continuance, and disappearance, or the Absolute (Brahma), the Demiurgus or Creator, and the individual Self. Prof. Weber suggests that the reference is to the Purusha Sûkta, 3, 4, of Book XXXI. *Father's father:* wiser than and able to teach, his elders.

10 *He :* the Almighty Creator. *Obtaining life immortal :* Agni alone who is here identified with the Creator was originally immortal and the other Gods obtained immortality through him. *Third high station :* highest heaven. The first line is taken from A. V. II. 1. 3. Cf. R. V. X. 82. 3.

11 The performer of the Universal Sacrifice is liberated from the bonds of human life. *Encompassed round :* with the glance of his enlightened mind which shows the universe to be Brahma. *Order :* the eternal Law of the universe, whose *first-born Child* is apparently Prajâpati ; or, according to Mahîdhara, Vâk the Sacred Word connoting religious ceremonies performed therewith. *He :* the performer of the Universal Sacrifice.

12 Having gone swiftly round the earth and heaven, around the worlds, around the sky, the Quarters,
Having spread out the lengthened thread of Order, he views, and he becomes and is That Being.

13 To the Assembly's wondrous Lord, to Indra's lovely Friend who gives
Wisdom, have I drawn near in prayer.

14 That wisdom which the Companies of Gods, and Fathers, recognize.
Even with that intelligence, O Agni, make me wise to-day. All-hail!

15 Varuṇa grant me wisdom! grant it Agni and Prajâpati!
Wisdom may Indra, Vâyu grant. May the Creator grant it me. All-hail!

16 Let these the Priests and Nobles both enjoy the splendour that is mine.
Best splendour may the Gods bestow on me. To thee, that splendour, hail!

---

12 *Thread of Order:* sacrifice, which is a line reaching down from ancient times and uniting men and Gods.

13 *The Assembly's wondrous Lord:* Agni, called Sadasaspati, Lord or Guardian of the congregation of priests and worshippers. The verse is taken from R. V. I. 18. 6.

## BOOK THE THIRTY-THIRD.

His be the fires, eternal, purifying, protectors of our homes, whose smoke is shining,
White, waxing in their strength, for ever stirring, and seated in the wood : like winds are Somas.

2 Gold-coloured, bannered with the smoke, urged by the wind, aloft to heaven
Rise, lightly borne, the flames of fire.

3 Bring to us Mitra-Varuṇa, bring the Gods to the great sacrifice ;
Bring them, O Agni, to thine home.

4 Yoke, Agni, as a charioteer, thy steeds who best invoke the Gods :
As ancient Hotar take thy seat.

5 To fair goals travel Two unlike in semblance : each in succession nourishes an infant.
One bears a Godlike Babe of golden colour : bright and fair-shining is he with the other.

6 Here by ordainers was this God appointed first Invoker, best at worship, to be praised at rites,
Whom Apnavâna and the Bhṛigus caused to shine, bright-coloured in the wood, spreading to every house.

7 Three times a hundred Gods, and thrice a thousand, and three times ten, and nine have worshipped Agni,
For him spread sacred grass, balmed him with butter, and stablished him as Priest and Sacrificer.

---

The formulas for the Universal Sacrifice are continued.

1 The first seventeen verses constitute a litany to Agni. The first verse is taken from R. V. X. 46. 7. *Protectors:* this is Mahîdhara's explanation of *aritrâ*, as though the word came from *ari*, an enemy, and *trâ*, to protect from. The literal meaning is oars, rudders, or propellers. *Like winds:* as winds fan flame, so Soma libations increase the might of Agni.

2 Taken from R. V. VIII. 43. 4.

3 R. V. I. 75. 5.

4 Repeated from XIII. 37,

5 R. V. I 95. 1. *Two:* Day and Night. *Infant:* Agni as the Sun by day, and Fire, or the Moon, by night.

6 Repeated from III. 15 ; taken from R. V. IV. 7. 1.

7 R. V. III. 9. 9. In the Vaisvadeva Nivid or Formula of Invitation to the All-Gods, the number of the Gods is said to be 3 times 11, then 33, then 303, then 3003. By adding together 33 + 303 + 3000 the number 3339 is obtained. See Haug's Aitareya Brâhmaṇam, II. p, 212, note.

8 Him, messenger of earth and head of heaven, Agni Vaiśvânara, born in holy Order,
The Sage, the King, the Guest of men, a vessel fit for their mouths, the Gods have generated.

9 May Agni slay the foemen,—fain for riches, through the love of song
Kindled, bright, served with sacrifice.

10 With the All-Gods, with Indra and with Vâyu drink the Soma mead,
O Agni, after Mitra's laws.

11 When splendour reached the Lord of men to speed him, down from the heaven was shed the brilliant moisture.
Agni brought forth to light and filled with spirit the youthful host benevolent and blameless.

12 Show thyself strong for mighty bliss, O Agni; most excellent be thine effulgent splendours.
Make easy to maintain our household lordship and trample down the might of those who hate us.

13 We have elected thee as most delightful for thy beams' glow: hear our great laud, O Agni.
The best men praise thee as the peer of Indra in strength, mid Gods, like Vâyu in thy bounty.

14 O Agni who art worshipped well, dear let our princes be to thee,
Our wealthy patrons who are governors of men, who part in gifts their stalls of kine.

---

8 Repeated from VII. 24; taken from R. V. VI, 7. 1. *A vessel:* through whom they receive sacrificial offerings.

9 R. V. VI. 16. 34.

10 *After Mitra's laws: mitrasya dhâmabhiḥ;* according to Mahîdhara, (praised) by the names of Mitra.

11 R. V. I. 71. 8. *The Lord of men*: the protector of the sacrificer, according to Mahîdhara, that is, Agni. *From the heaven:* the text has *dyauḥ*. which, Mahîdhara says, is used in the sense of the genitive *dyoḥ*. into which probably, it may be corrected. See Oldemberg, Vedic Hymns, Part II. p. 80, note. *Youthful host:* probably the Maruts, the verse being here a Nivid formulary used on drawing the Marutvatîyagraha or cup for Indra attended by the Maruts.

12 R. V. V. 28. 3. *Make easy to maintain:* or, to follow Sâyaṇa and Mahîdhara: Perfect the well-knit bond of wife and husband.

13 R. V. VI. 4. 7.

14 R. V. VII. 16. 7. *Gifts:* sacrificial offerings of milk, curds, and clarified butter as well as honoraria to the priests.

15 Hear, Agni who hast ears to hear, with all thy train of escort Gods.
Let Mitra, Aryaman, seeking betimes our rite, seat them upon the sacred grass.

16 The Freedom of all Gods who merit worship, freely received as Guest in all men's houses,
Agni who hath secured the Gods' high favour, may he be gracious to us, Jâtavedas.

17 In great enkindled Agni's keeping and, for bliss, free from all sin before Mitra and Varuṇa,
May we share Savitar's best animating help. We crave this gracious favour of the Gods to-day.

18 Like barren cows, moreover, swelled the waters: singers approched thy holy cult, O Indra.
Come thou to us as to his team comes Vâyu. Thou through our solemn hymns bestowest bounty.

19 Ye Cows, protect the fount. The two mighty Ones bless the sacrifice.
The handles twain are wrought of gold.

20 Now when the Sun hath risen to-day may sinless Mitra, Aryaman,
Bhaga, and Savitar speed us forth.

21 Pour on the juice the ornament which reaches both the heaven and earth:

---

15 R V. I. 44. 13. *Let Mitra, Aryaman:* and Varuṇa, implied and understood.

16 R. V. IV. 1. 20. *Freedom:* or, Aditi, meaning the freest, most independent. There is a play on the words *aditiḥ* and *atithiḥ*, guest.

17 R. V. X. 36. 12. The verse is a Nivid formula used when the Sâvitragraha, or cup for Savitar, is drawn.

18 Verses 18–29 constitute a service of praise addressed to Indra. Verse 18 is taken from R. V. VII. 23 4. *Barren cows:* supposed to be fatter than others. *The waters:* used for swelling the stalks of the Soma plant.

19 R. V. VIII. 61. 12. *The fount:* the caldron called *gharma* or *mahâvîra* in which libations of milk are heated. According to Mahîdhara, the *Chât-vâla* or pit (see VII. 26; VIII. 23) is intended, which the cows are to approach. *The two Mighty Ones:* Heaven and Earth. *Bless:* conjecturally translated, the meaning of *rapsudâ* being uncertain. 'The two kinds of milk in the sacrifice are plentiful and fruit-giving':—Wilson, according to Sâyaṇa. *The handles:* of the caldron; but this too is doubtful.

20 R. V. VII. 66. 4. *Sinless: anâgâḥ:* taken by Sâyaṇa as = *anâgasaḥ:* may Savitar, Mitra, Aryaman, And Bhaga send us sinless forth.

21 R. V. VIII. 61. 13. *The ornament:* the milk which is mingled with Soma. *The Bull:* the mighty Soma. I take *rasâ* (as Prof. Ludwig has done) as an instrumental case. According to Mahîdhara the translation should be: The river nourishes the Bull; i. e. the Soma which grows near it. *Thou: See:* the beginnings of two Nivid formulas repeated, respectively, from VII. 12 and 16.

Supply the liquid to the Bull.
Thou in the first old time. See, Vena.

22 As he was rising up they all revered him: self-luminous he travels, clothed in splendour.
That is the Bull's, the Asura's lofty nature: he, Omniform, hath reached the eternal waters.

23 I laud your Mighty One who joyeth in the juice, him who is good to all men, who pervadeth all;
Indra whose conquering strength is powerful in war, whose fame and manly vigour Heaven and Earth revere.

24 Great is their fuel, strong their laud, wide is their sacrificial post
Whose Friend is Indra, ever young.

25 Come, Indra, and delight thee with the juice at all the Soma feasts,
Conqueror, mighty in thy strength.

26 Leading his band, Indra encompassed Vṛitra; weak grew the wily leader of enchanters.
He who burns fierce in forests slaughtered Vyaṃsa, and made the milch-kine of the nights apparent.

27 Whence comest thou alone, thou who art mighty, Indra, Lord of the Brave? What is thy purpose?
Thou greetest us, encountering us the Bright Ones. Lord of Bay Steeds, say what thou hast against us.
Indra, great in his power and might. Ne'er art thou fruitless. Never art thou neglectful.

---

22 R. V. III. 38. 4. *He:* Indra as the Sun. *Eternal waters: amṛitâni; jalâni*, waters, being understood; 'the forces of eternity,' according to von Roth. *Nature:* or, title, such as Vritra-slayer, etc.

23 R. V. X. 50. 1.

24 R. V. VIII. 45. 2. Well provided with the materials of sacrifice, and consequently successful, are those whom Indra favours.

25 R. V. I. 9. 1.

26 R. V. III. 34. 3. *His band:* the Maruts. *Encompassed Vṛitra: vṛitramavṛiṇot;* a play upon the words, both from *vṛi*, to encompass; Vṛitra the drought demon being the encompasser or obstructer of the seasonal rains. *He who burns fierce:* perhaps the thunderbolt. *Vyaṃsa:* the name of one of the demons of drought. See R. V. I. 101. 2; 103. 2. *Milch-kine of the nights:* according to Sâyaṇa, the (stolen) cows (that had been hidden) in the night; that is, he recovered the vanished rays of light. Mahîdhara's interpretation, 'and made the lauds of devotees apparent,' seems very far-fetched.

27 R. V. I. 165. 3. The Maruts address Indra whom they meet alone, unattended by them as usual, in consequence of some ill-feeling that has arisen. See M. Müller. Vedic Hymns, Part I. (Sacred Books of the East, XXXII. pp. 179—203). The verse ends with 'against us.' Then follow the beginnings of three Nivid formulas repeated respectively, from VII. 40, VIII. 2 and 3.

28 Those men extolled that deed of thine, O Indra, those who would fain burst through the stall of cattle,
Fain to milk her who bare but once, great, lofty, whose sons are many and her streams a thousand.

29 To thee the Mighty One I bring this mighty hymn, for thy desire hath been gratified by my laud.
In Indra, yea, in him victorious through his might, the Gods have joyed at feast and when the Soma flowed.

30 May the Bright God drink glorious Soma-mingled mead, giving the sacrifice's lord uninjured life;
He who, wind-urged, in person guards our offspring well, hath nourished them with food and shone o'er many a land.

31 His bright rays bear him up aloft, the God who knoweth all that lives,
Sûrya, that all may look on him.

32 Pure Varuṇa, with that same eye wherewith thou lookest upon one
Actively stirring mid the folk—

33 Ye two divine Adhvaryus, come hither upon a sun-bright car:
Bedew our sacrifice with mead.
Thou in the first old time. See, Vena. The brilliant presence.

34 Loved of all men, may Savitar through praises offered as sacred food come to our synod,
That ye too, through our hymns, ye ever youthful, may gladden at your visit all our people.

---

28 R. V. X. 74. 4. *Those men:* the Angirases. *Burst through the stall of cattle:* to recover the stolen cows, the rays of light that had been carried away by the demons of darkness. *Her who bare but once:* Heaven, according to Sâyaṇa; Earth, according to Mahîdhara. Pṛiśni, the mother of the Maruts, must be meant.—Ludwig. See R. V. VI. 48. 22.

29 R. V. I. 102. 1.

30 R. V. X 170. 1. Verses 30—43 are formulas in praise of Sûrya, accompanying libations to that deity on the third day of the ceremony. *Wind-urged:* the disc of the Sun deriving its motion from the wind.

31 R. V. I. 50. 1. See VII. 41.

32 R. V. I. 50. 6. *Varuṇa:* the word is, as Sâyaṇa points out, used as an appellative (encompasser) and applied to Sûrya. Sâyaṇa explains it as *anishṭanivâraka*, averter of evils. *Actively stirring:* in the performance of sacrifice. In the original hymn the sense is completed in the following verse, 'thou metest with thy beams our days.' Mahîdhara supplies, 'look upon us who are similarly busied here.'

33 *Two divine Adhvaryus:* the Asvins, the Adhvaryus of the Gods, the heralds of the Sun's approach, are addressed. *Thou etc.:* see verse 21, and VII. 42.

34 R. V. I. 186. 1. *Savitar:* the Sun, especially regarded as the vivifier and generator. *Ye too:* the Visvedevas or All-Gods.

35 Whatever, Vṛitra-slayer! thou Sûrya hast risen on to-day,
That, Indra, all is in thy power.

36 Swift, visible to all art thou, O Sûrya, maker of the light,
Illuming all the radiant realm.

37 This is the Godhead, this the might of Sûrya: he hath withdrawn what spread o'er work unfinished.
When he hath loosed his horses from their station, straight over all Night spreadeth out her garment.

38 In the sky's lap the Sun this form assumeth that Varuṇa and Mitra may behold it.
His Bay Steeds well maintain their power eternal, at one time bright, and darksome at another.

39 Verily, Sûrya, thou art great; truly, Âditya, thou art great.
As thou art great indeed thy greatness is admired: yea, verily thou, God, art great.

40 Yea, Sûrya, thou art great in fame: thou, evermore, O God, art great.
Thou by thy greatness art the Gods' Home-Priest, divine, far-spread, unconquerable light.

41 Turning, as 'twere, to meet the Sun, enjoy from Indra all good things.
When he who will be born is born with power we look to treasures as our heritage.

42 To-day, ye Gods, when Sûrya hath ascended, deliver us from trouble and dishonour.
This boon may Varuṇa and Mitra grant us, and Aditi and Sindhu, Earth and Heaven.

---

35 R. V. VIII. 82. 4. *Indra:* as identified with Sûrya.

36 R. V. I. 50. 4.

37 R. V. I. 115. 4. *He hath withdrawn:* 'The cultivator or artisan desists from his labour, although unfinished, upon the setting of the Sun'; when the sun 'has withdrawn (into himself) the diffused (light which has been shed) upon the unfinished task':—Wilson. The stanza is difficult, and no thoroughly satisfactory explanation of it has yet been offered. See Ludwig, Der Rigveda, IV. 131, 132.

38 R. V. I. 115. 5. *This form:* of might and Godhead. *Varuṇa:* as God of the Night. *Mitra:* as God of the Day.

39 R. V. VIII. 90. 11.

40 R. V. VIII. 90. 12.

41 R. V. VIII. 88. 3. This stanza is difficult and obscure. Mahîdhara's explanation is: The gathering (rays) proceeding to the sun distribute all Indra's treasures (to living beings, as rain, corn, etc.): may we too by our power leave those treasures as an inheritance to him who has been or will be born'—See Prof. Cowell's note in Wilson's Translation.

42 The second line is the stock conclusion of many Ṛigveda hymns. *Sindhu:* is the deity presiding over, or identified with, water, and it may mean the Sea, or the Indus.

43 Throughout the dusky firmament advancing, laying to rest the immortal and the mortal,
Borne on his golden chariot he cometh, Savitar, God, beholding living creatures.

44 Soft to the tread the sacred grass is scattered: these go like Kings amid the band around them,
At the folk's early call on Night and Morning,—Vâyu, and Pûshan with his team to bless us.

45 Indra, Vâyu, Bṛihaspati, Mitra, Agni, Pûshan, Bhaga, Âdityas, and the Marut host.

46 Be Varuṇa our chief defence, let Mitra guard us with all aids:
Both make us rich exceedingly!

47 Regard us, Indra, Vishṇu, here, ye Aṣvins, and the Marut host, us who are kith and kin to you.
Thou in the first old time. See, Vena. O ye eleven Gods. Loved of all men, may Savitar. With the All-Gods. Ye Viṣvedevas who protect.

48 O Agni, Indra, Varuṇa, and Mitra, give, O ye Gods, and Marut host, and Vishṇu.
May both Nâsatyas, Rudra, heavenly Matrons, Pûshan, Sarasvatî, Bhaga accept us.

49 Indra, Agni, Mitra, Varuṇa, Aditi, the Waters, Mountains, Maruts, Sky, and Earth and Heaven,
Vishṇu I call, Pûshan and Brahmaṇaspati, and Bhaga, Ṣaṃsa, Savitar that they may help.

50 With us are raining Rudras, clouds accordant in call to battle at the death of Vṛitra,
The strong, assigned to him who sings and praises. May Gods with Indra as their chief protect us.

---

43 R. V. I. 35. 2.

44—54 celebrate the Viṣvedevas or All-Gods. Verse 44 is taken from R. V. VII. 39. 2.

45 R. V. I. 14. 3.

46 R. V. I. 23. 6.

47 The Gâyatrî verse is taken from VIII. 72. 7. *Kith and kin:* as common children of Aditi the General Mother of all living beings. The six unconnected Pratîkas or Verse-beginnings are repeated from (1, 2) XXXIII. 21; (3) VII. 19; (4) XXXIII. 34; (5) XXXIII. 10: (6) VII. 33.

48 R. V. V. 46. 2.

49 R. V. V. 46. 3. *Ṣaṃsa:* Praise or Prayer, personified. According to Mahîdhara, praiseworthy, qualifying Savitar.

50 R. V. VIII. 52, 12. *Raining:* pouring down riches; bounteous. *The strong:* perhaps the thunderbolt, with which Indra aids the worshipper.

51 Turn yourselves hitherward this day, ye Holy, that fearing in my heart I may approach you.
Protect us, Gods, let not the wolf destroy us. Save us, ye Holy, from the pit and falling.

52 This day come all the Maruts, etc., as in XVIII. 31.

53 Listen, All-Gods, to this mine invocation, ye who inhabit heaven and air's mid-region.
All ye, O Holy Ones, whose tongue is Agni, seated upon this sacred grass be joyful.

54 For thou at first producest for the holy Gods the noblest of all portions, immortality.
Thereafter as a gift to men, O Savitar, thou openest existence, life succeeding life.

55 I with a lofty song call hither Vâyu all-bounteous, filler of his car, most wealthy.
Thou, Sage, with bright path, Lord of harnessed horses, impetuous, promptly honourest the prudent.

56 These, Indra-Vâyu, have been shed, etc., as in VII. 8.

57 Mitra of holy strength I call, and foe-destroying Varuṇa,
Who make the oil-fed rite complete.

58 Nâsatyas, Wonder-workers, yours are these libations with clipt grass.
Come ye whose paths are bright with glow.

59 When Saramâ had found the mountain's fissure, that vast and ancient place she plundered throughly.
In the floods' van she led them forth, light-footed: she who well knew came first unto their lowing.

---

51 R. V. II. 29. 6.

52 Repeated from XVIII. 31.

53 R. V. VI. 52. 13. *Whose tongue is Agni:* who enjoy oblations offered in the sacrificial fire.

54 R. V. IV. 54. 2.

55—69 Here follows a compilation of unconnected verses in praise of various deities. Verse 55 is taken from R. V. VI. 49. 4. *Filler of his car:* with wealth to reward his servants. *The prudent:* the wise worshipper.

57 R. V. I. 2. 7. *Oil-fed:* performed with *ghṛitam, ghî*, or clarified butter. *Complete:* by granting the worshipper's prayer.

58 R. V. I. 3. 3. *Nâsatyas:* Aṣvins; see XIX. 83, note.

59 R. V. III. 31. 6. *Saramâ:* the messenger and scout of Indra, variously explained as Dawn, Stormcloud, Wind, etc. See R. V. X. 108; and Mme. Zénaïde Ragozin, Vedic India (Story of the Nations Series), pp. 256—260. In later Vedic literature Saramâ is regarded as the hound of the Gods. *In the floods' van:* hastening out of the mountain cavern, that is, the massive [illegible]d, in advance of the liberated waters. *Them:* the cows, the waters.

60 For nowhere did they find another envoy to lead the way than this Vaiṣvânara Agni.
The Gods immortal strengthened the immortal Vaiṣvânara to win the land in battle.

61 The strong, dispellers of the foe, Indra and Agni, we invoke:
May they be kind to one like me.

62 Sing forth to Indu, O ye men, to him as he is purified,
Fain to pay worship to the Gods.

63 Drink Soma, Indra, banded with the Maruts who, Boon Lord! strengthened thee at Ahi's slaughter,
'Gainst Ṣambara, Lord of Bays! in winning cattle, and now rejoice in thee, the holy singers.

64 Thou wast born mighty for victorious valour, exulting, strongest, full of pride and courage.
There, even there the Maruts strengthened Indra when his most rapid Mother stirred the Hero.

65 O thou who slewest Vṛitra, come, O Indra, hither to our side,
Mighty One with thy mighty aids.

66 Thou in thy battles, Indra, art subduer of all hostile bands.
Father art thou, all-conquering, cancelling the curse: vanquish the men who fight with us.

67 Heaven and Earth cling close to thy victorious might
As sire and mother to their child.

68 The sacrifice obtains the Gods' acceptance, etc., as in VIII. 4.

69 Protect our habitation, Savitar, this day with guardian aids around, propitious, ne'er beguiled.
God of the golden tongue, keep us for newest bliss: let not the evil-wisher have us in his power.

---

60 *They*: the Gods. *To win the land*: from the original inhabitants for the new Âryan settlers.

61 R. V. VI. 60. 5.

62 R. V. IX. 11. 1. *Indu*: Soma.

63 R. V. III. 47. 4. *Ahi*: the Serpent; a demon of drought. *Ṣambara*: another drought-fiend. *In winning cattle*: in recovering the stolen kine, the rays of light carried off by the demons of darkness, or, generally, in battle with the demons who withhold the rain.

64 R. V. X. 73. 1. *Thou*: Indra. *Mother*: Aditi. *Stirred the Hero*: incited him to action by telling him of his future opponents. See R. V. VIII. 45. 5, and 66. 2.

65 R. V. IV. 32. 1.

66, 67 R. V. VIII. 88. 5, 6.

69 R. V. VI. 71. 3. *Of the golden tongue*: ever-truthful (Solem quis dicere falsum Audeat?); or, having tongues or rays of golden light.

70 For you have flowed, through noble ministration, pressed by Adhvaryus, bright sweet-flavoured juices.
Drive on thy team and come thou hither, Vâyu: drink for thy rapture of the sap of Soma.

71 Ye Cows, protect, etc., as in verse 14.

72 Come ye foe-slayers to the place of meeting, to the birth-places of the two great Sages,
With force of intellect unto the dwelling.

73 Ye two divine Adhvaryus, etc., as in verse 33. Thou in the time of old. See, Vena.

74 Transversely was the severing line extended: was it above, or was it, haply, under?
There were begetters, there were mighty forces, free action here and energy up yonder.

75 He hath filled heaven and earth and the great realm of light, when at his birth the skilful held him in their hold.
He like a steed is led forth to the sacrifice, Sage, graciously inclined, that he may win us wealth.

76 Call hither with the song and lauds the two best slayers of the foe,
Delighting even in our hymn.

77 All Sons of Immortality shall listen to the songs we sing,
And be exceeding good to us.

78 Mine are devotions, hymns, sweet are libations. Strength stirs, and hurled forth is my rocky weapon.
They call for me, for me their lauds are longing. To their libations these my Bay Steeds bear me.

---

70 Vâyu is the deity addressed. *For you:* the Sacrificer and his wife.

72 *Come ye:* Mitra and Varuṇa are addressed. *Two great Sages:* the two Gods who are addressed. The stanza is difficult and obscure.

73 The two Pratîkas are repeated from VII. 12 and 16.

74 R. V. X. 129. 5. *Line:* drawn by the ancient creative Rishis or Demiurgi to make a division between the upper world and the lower, and to bring duality out of unity. *Begetters:* the Fathers may be meant. *Free action:* the happiness of the Fathers. The verse is one of the obscurest of a very obscure hymn on Creation.

75 R. V. III. 2. 7. *He:* Agni Vaisvânara. *The skilful:* the priests who kindle the fire.

76 R. V. VII. 94. 11. *Call hither:* I follow Prof. Ludwig in reading *divâsata* instead of *divivâsataḥ* which involves a harsh construction. The deities invoked are Indra and Agni.

77 R. V. VI. 52. 9. *Of Immortality:* or, of the Immortal One, Prajâpati, the progenitor of gods and men.

78 R. V. I. 165. 4. Indra addresses the Maruts in reply to their question in verse 27.

79 Nothing, O Bounteous Lord, stands firm before thee: among the Gods not one is found thine equal.
None born or springing into life comes near thee. Do what thou hast to do, exceeding mighty!

80 In all the worlds That was the Best and Highest whence sprang the mighty God of splendid valour.
Quickly when born he overcomes his foemen, he in whom all who lend him aid are joyful.

81 May these my songs of praise exalt thee, Lord, who hast abundant wealth.
Men skilled in holy hymns, pure, with the hues of fire, have sung them with their lauds to thee.

82 Good Lord of wealth is he to whom all Âryas, Dâsas here belong.
E'en over unto thee, the pious Ruṣama Pavîru, is that wealth brought nigh.

83 He, with his might advanced by Ṛishis thousandfold, hath like an ocean spread himself.
His majesty is praised as true at solemn rites, his power where holy singers rule.

84 Protect our habitation, Savitar, etc., as in verse 69.

85 Come, Vâyu, drawn by fair hymns, to our sacrifice that reaches heaven.
Poured on the middle of the straining-cloth and dressed, this bright drink hath been offered thee.

86 Indra and Vâyu, fair to see and swift to hear, we call to us,
That in assembly all, yea, all the folk may be benevolent to us and free from malady.

---

79 R. V. I. 165. 9. The Maruts address Indra in continuation of the dialogue.

80 R. V. X. 120. 1. *That:* Brahma, the original Cause of the universe. *The Mighty God:* Indra.

81 R. V. VIII. 3. 3. Indra is addressed. *With the hues of fire:* or, radiant as Agni.

82 Vâlakhilya 3. 9. *He:* the prince named in the following line. *Dâsas:* aboriginal inhabitants. *Ruṣama Pavîru:* the people called Rusamas are mentioned in R. V. V. 30. 13—15. The name of Pavîru, apparently their prince, does not occur again.

83 R. V. VIII. 3. 4. *He:* Indra.

85 R. V. VIII. 90. 9.

86 Taken, with variations and additions, from R. V. X. 141. 4.

87 Yea, specially that mortal man hath toiled for service of the Gods,
Who quickly hath brought near Mitra and Varuṇa to share his sacrificial gifts.

88 Approach ye, and be near to us. Drink, O ye Aṣvins, of the mead.
Draw forth the milk, ye mighty, rich in genuine wealth! Injure us not, and come to us.

89 May Brahmaṇaspati draw nigh, may Sûnṛitâ the Goddess come,
And Gods bring to our rite which gives the fivefold gift the Hero, lover of mankind.

90 Within the Waters runs the Moon, he with the beauteous wings, in heaven.
To yellow-hued abundant wealth, object of many a man's desire, loud-neighing goes the tawny Steed.

91 Singing their praise with godlike hymn let us invoke each God for grace,
Each God to bring you help, each God to strengthen you.

92 Agni Vaiṣvânara, set in heaven, with mighty splendour hath shone forth.
Increasing in his power on earth, benevolent, he quells the darkness with his light.

93 First, Indra-Agni! hath this Maid come footless unto those with feet.
Stretching her head and speaking loudly with her tongue, she hath gone downward thirty steps.

---

87 R. V. VIII. 90. 1.

88 R. V. VII. 74. 3.

89 R. V. I. 40. 3. *Sûnṛitâ:* Pleasantness; according to the Commentators, Vâk the Goddess of Speech as lover of truth. *Fivefold gift:* oblations of grain, gruel, curdled milk, rice-cake, and curds, offered, respectively, to various deities.

90 The first line is taken from R. V. I. 105. 1. *The waters:* the ocean of air. *He with the beauteous wings:* or, the eagle; the Sun. *Yellow-hued:* in the form of gold, or golden-coloured grain. *The tawny Steed:* Soma. Mahîdhara explains the whole stanza sacrificially, as referring to Soma identified in the first line with the Moon.

91 R. V. VIII. 27. 13. *Their:* the Viṣvedevas'.

92 Attributed to a Ṛishi named Medha.

93 R. V. VI. 59. 6. *This Maid:* the text has only the feminine pronoun *iyam* (haec); Ushas or Dawn is intended. *Footless:* moving unsupported in the sky. *Thirty steps:* the thirty divisions of the Indian day and night through which Dawn passes before she reappears.

94 For of one spirit are the Gods with mortal man, co-sharers all of gracious gifts.
May they increase our strength hereafter and to-day, providing ease and ample room.

95 Indra who quells the curse blew curses far away, and then in splendour came to us.
Indra, refulgent with the Marut host! the Gods eagerly strove to win thy love.

96 To Indra, to your mighty Chief, Maruts, sing forth a mighty prayer.
Let Ṣatakratu, Vṛitra-slayer, kill the fiend with hundred-knotted thunderbolt.

97 Indra increased his manly strength at sacrifice, in the wild rapture of this juice;
And living men to-day, even as of old, sing forth their praises to his majesty.
May these. Good Lord of wealth. He with his might. Stand up erect.

---

94 R. V. VIII. 27. 14.

95 R. V. VIII. 78. 2.

96 R. V. VIII. 78. 3. *Ṣatakratu*: Lord of a Hundred Powers; Indra. *The fiend*: Vṛitra.

97 R. V. VIII. 3. 8. The four Pratīkas, May these, etc., are repeated from verses 81—83 of this Book and XI. 42.

## BOOK THE THIRTY-FOURTH.

THAT which, divine, mounts far when man is waking, that which returns to him when he is sleeping,
The lights' one light that goeth to a distance, may that, my mind, be moved by right intention.

2 Whereby the wise and thoughtful in assemblies, active in sacrifice, perform their duties,
The peerless spirit stored in living creatures, may that, my mind, be moved by right intention.

3 That which is wisdom, intellect, and firmness, immortal light which creatures have within them,
That without which men do no single action, may that, my mind, be moved by right intention.

4 Whereby, immortal, all is comprehended, the world which is, and what shall be hereafter,
Whereby spreads sacrifice with seven Hotars, may that, my mind, be moved by right intention.

5 Wherein the Richas, Sâmans, Yajur-verses, like spokes within a car's nave, are included,
And all the thought of creatures is inwoven, may that, my mind, be moved by right intention.

6 Controlling men, as, with the reins that guide them, a skilful charioteer drives fleet-foot horses,
Which dwells within the heart, agile, most rapid, may that, my mind, be moved by right intention.

7 Now will I glorify great strength's upholder, Food,
By whose invigorating might Trita rent Vritra limb from limb.

---

The first six verses of this supplementary Book constitute a hymn regarded as an Upanishad and called the Sivasankalpa, Right-intentioned, from the concluding words in each stanza. The rest is a compilation of miscellaneous texts which may be used in the performance of the General Sacrifice.

1 *Moved by right intention:* or, having an auspicious resolve; *sivasankalpam. The lights' one light:* the illuminator of all the perceptive senses.

4 *Seven Hotars:* the chief Hotar and six assistant priests, the Maitrâ-Varuna, Achchhâvâka, Grâvastut and others.

7 The first verse of R. V. I. 187, entitled Annastuti, the Praise of Food, (in the shape of Soma). *Trita:* (see I. 23, note) a mysterious ancient deity frequently mentioned in the Rigveda, principally in connexion with Indra, Vâyu, and the Maruts. His home is in the remotest part of heaven, and he is called Âptya, the Watery, that is, sprung from, or dwelling in, the sea of cloud and vapour. By Sâyana he is identified sometimes with Vâyu, sometimes with Indra as the pervader of the three worlds and sometimes with Agni stationed in the three fire-receptacles. Mahîdhara identifies him, without explanation, with Indra who is generally regarded as the slayer of Vritra. See Macdonell, Vedic Mythology, pp. 67—69.

8 Do thou, in truth, Anumati, assent and grant us happiness.
Urge us to strength and energy: prolong the days we have to live.

9 Anumati this day approve our sacrifice among the Gods!
Oblation-bearing Agni be, and thou, bliss to the worshipper!

10 O broad-tressed Sinîvâlî, thou who art the sister of the Gods,
Accept the offered sacrifice, and, Goddess, grant us progeny.

11 Five rivers flowing on their way speed onward to Sarasvatî,
But then became Sarasvatî a fivefold river in the land.

12 O Agni, thou the earliest Angiras, the Seer, hast, God thyself, become the Gods' auspicious Friend.
After thy holy ordinance the Maruts, sage, active through wisdom, with their glittering spears, were born.

13 Worthy to be revered, O Agni, God, preserve our wealthy patrons with thy succours, and ourselves.
Guard art thou of our seed and progeny and cows, incessantly protecting in thy holy law.

14 Lay this with care on her who lies extended: straight, when impregned, hath she brought forth the Hero.
With his bright pillar—radiant is his lustre—in our skilled task is born the Son of Iḍâ.

15 In Iḍâ's place, the centre of the earth, will we deposit thee,
That, Agni Jâtavedas, thou mayst bear our offerings to the Gods.

16 Like Angiras a gladdening laud we ponder to him who loveth song, exceeding mighty.
Let us sing glory to the far-famed Hero who must be praised with fair hymns by the singer.

---

8 *Anumati:* Divine Favour, shown especially in the acceptance of sacrifice, personified. See XXIX. 60.

10 R. V. II. 32. 6. *Sinîvâlî:* a Lunar Goddess, associated with childbirth. See XI. 55.

11 *Sarasvatî:* here, apparently, meaning the Indus. See Vedic India, (Story of the Nations Series) pp. 267, 268.

12 R. V. I. 31. 1. *Glittering spears:* the lightning flashes that accompany the Storm-Gods.

13 R. V. I. 31. 12.

14, 15 R. V. III. 29. 3, 4. The two texts accompany the production of sacrificial fire by means of the fire-drill. *Lay this:* place the upper fire-stick, which is to be turned rapidly round, on the lower piece of wood which is prepared to receive it. *The Son of Iḍâ:* Agni. *Iḍâ's place:* the northern altar, the place of worship and libation, or prayer and praise.

16, 17 R. V. I. 62 1. 2. The two verses are in honour of Indra. *Found the cattle:* recovered the rays of light that had been carried away by the fiends of darkness.

17 Unto the Great One bring great adoration, a chant of praise to him the very potent,
Through whom our sires, Angirases, singing praises, and knowing well the places, found the cattle.

18 The friends who offer Soma long to find thee: they pour forth Soma and present their viands.
They bear, unmoved, the cursing of the people, for all our wisdom comes from thee, O Indra.

19 Not far for thee are mid-air's loftiest regions: start hither, Lord of Bays, with both Bay Horses.
Pressed for the Firm and Strong are these libations. The pressing-stones are set, the fire is kindled.

20 Invincible in fight, saviour in battles, guard of our camp, winner of light and water,
Born amid hymns, well-housed, exceeding famous, victor, in thee may we rejoice, O Soma.

21 To him who worships Soma gives a milch-cow, a fleet steed, and a man of active knowledge,
Skilled in home duties, competent in council, meet for the court, the glory of his father.

22 These herbs, these milch-kine, and these running waters, all these, O Soma, thou hast generated.
The spacious firmament hast thou expanded, and with the light thou hast dispelled the darkness.

23 Do thou, God Soma, with thy God-like spirit, victorious, win for us a share of riches.
Let none prevent thee: thou art Lord of valour. Provide for these and those in fight for cattle.

24 The earth's eight points his brightness hath illumined, three desert regions, and the Seven Rivers.

---

18, 19 R. V. III. 30. 1, 2. *Of the people:* who oppose the worship of Indra.
20–23 R. V. I. 91. 21, 20, 23. The God Soma, identified with the Moon, is addressed.
21 *A man:* a manly son.
22 *These milch-kine*: referring to the milk which is to be mingled with the Soma juice.
23 *For these and those:* for the priests and their patrons. The text has only *ubhayebhyaḥ*, for both; for our gain of both worlds, according to Mahîdhara.
24–27 R. V. I. 35. 8–11. *Three desert regions:* the meaning is not clear; heaven, firmament, and earth, according to Sâyaṇa and Mahîdhara. *The Seven Rivers:* according to Prof. Max Müller, the Indus, the five rivers of the Panjâb (Vitastâ, Asiknî, Parushṇî, Vipâs, Ṣutudrî), and Sarasvatî. Lassen and Ludwig put the Kubhâ in the place of Sarasvatî. See Zimmer, Altindisches Leben, pp. 3 sqq.

God Savitar the gold-eyed hath come hither, giving choice treasures to the man who worships.

25 Savitar, golden-handed, swiftly moving, goes on his way between the earth and heaven,
Drives away sickness, bids the Sun approach us, and spreads the bright sky through the darksome region.

26 May he, gold-handed Asura, kind leader, come hitherward to us with help and favour.
Driving off Râkshasas and Yâtudhânas, the God is present, praised in hymns at evening.

27 O Savitar, thine ancient dustless pathways are well established in the air's mid-region.
O God, come by those paths so fair to travel: preserve thou us from harm this day and bless us.

28 Drink our libations, Aṣvins twain, grant us protection, both of you,
With aids which none may interrupt.

29 Make ye our speech effectual, O Aṣvins, and this our hymn, ye mighty Wonder-workers.
In luckless game I call on you for succour: strengthen us also on the field of battle.

30 With undiminished blessings, O ye Aṣvins, through days and nights on every side protect us.
This prayer of ours may Varuṇa grant, and Mitra, and Aditi and Sindhu, Earth and Heaven.

31 Throughout the dusky firmament, etc., as in XXXIII. 43.

32 Night! the terrestrial realm hath been filled with the Father's power and might.
Thou spreadest thee on high unto the seats of heaven: terrific darkness cometh nigh.

---

25 *Bids the Sun approach us:* approaches the Sun, according to Sâyaṇa 'ho observes that although Savitar and the Sun (Sûrya) are the same as egards their divinity, yet they are two different forms, and therefore one nay be said to go to the other.

26 *Asura:* mighty Lord. *Yâtudhânas*: a class of demons, sorcerers or oblins.

28 R. V. I. 46. 15.

29, 30 R. V. I. 112. 24, 25. *In luckless game*: a metaphorical expression orrowed from dicing; that is, in a time of difficulty, perhaps the eve of a esperate battle. Sâyaṇa, following a different derivation of the word, explains it, in the absence of light, or in the last watch of night just before lawn, when the Aṣvins are especially to be worshipped.

32 A. V. XIX. 47. 1. *Terrestrial realm*: the atmosphere immediately bove the earth. *With the Father's power and might:* or mighty laws. According to Mahîdhara, together with the places of the mid-world.

33 O Dawn enriched with ample wealth, bestow on us that wondrous gift
Wherewith we may support children and children's sons.

34 Agni at dawn, and Indra we invoke at dawn, and Varuṇa and Mitra and the Asvins twain,
Bhaga at dawn, Pûshan and Brahmaṇaspati, Soma at dawn, Rudra may we invoke at dawn.

35 May we invoke strong early-conquering Bhaga, the Son of Aditi, the great Arranger,
Thinking of whom the poor, yea, even the mighty, even the King says, Let me share in Bhaga.

36 Bhaga our guide, Bhaga whose gifts are faithful, favour this prayer and give us wealth, O Bhaga.
Bhaga, increase our store of kine and horses: Bhaga, may we be rich in men and heroes.

37 So may felicity be ours at present, and when the day approaches, and at noontide;
And may we still, O Bounteous One, at sunset be happy in the Deities' loving-kindness.

38 May Bhaga verily be Bliss-bestower, and through him, Gods! may happiness attend us.
As such, O Bhaga, all with might invoke thee: as such be thou our Champion here, O Bhaga.

39 To this our worship may the Dawns incline them, and come to the pure place like Dadhikrâvan.
As strong steeds draw a chariot may they bring us hitherward Bhaga who discovers treasure.

40 May friendly Mornings dawn on us for ever, with wealth of kine, of horses, and of heroes,
Streaming with all abundance, pouring fatness. Preserve us evermore, ye Gods, with blessings.

---

33 R. V. I. 92. 13. *Wondrous gift:* of riches.

34–40 R. V. VII. 41. The hymn is addressed chiefly to Bhaga, the Bountiful, whose name, slightly corrupted, survives in Slavic languages as the name of the God of monotheistic Christianity.

35 *Early-conquering:* in his character of the morning Sun overpowering Ushas or Dawn who in Ṛigveda I. 23. 5 is called his sister. *Let me share in Bhaga:* or, Give me my portion. The meaning is that every one, poor and weak, strong and mighty, looks to Bhaga as the giver of his allotted fortune.

38 *Bliss-bestower: bhagavân*; originally, possessing a happylot, fortunate, blessed, adorable; now generally meaning Almighty God.

39 *The Dawns:* the lights of morning, personified. *The pure place:* where sacrifice is performed. *Like Dadhikrâvan:* with the swiftness of the famous mythical horse, the type and model of racers. See IX. 14, note.

41 Secure in thy protecting care, O Pûshan, never may we fail:
We here are singers of thy praise.

42 I praise with eloquence him who guards all pathways. He, when his love impelled him, went to Arka.
May he vouchsafe us gear with gold to grace it: may Pûshan make each prayer of ours effective.

43 Vishṇu the undeceivable Protector strode three steps, thenceforth
Establishing his high decrees.

44 This, Vishṇu's station most sublime, the singers ever vigilant,
Lovers of holy song, light up.

45 Filled full of fatness, compassing all things that be, wide, spacious, dropping meath, beautiful in their form,
The Heaven and the Earth by Varuṇa's decree, unwasting, rich in seed, stand parted each from each.

46 Let those who are our foemen stand afar from us: with Indra and with Agni we will drive them off.
Vasus, Âdityas, Rudras have exalted me, made me preëminent, mighty, thinker, sovran lord.

47 Come, O Nâsatyas, with the thrice eleven Gods; come, O ye Asvins, to the drinking of the meath.
Prolong our days of life, and wipe out all our sins: ward off our enemies; be with us evermore.

48 May this your praise, may this your song, O Maruts, sung by the poet, Mâna's son, Mândârya,

---

41 R. V. VI. 44. 9.

42 R. V. VI. 49. 8. *Who guards all pathways:* Pûshan the special protector of travellers and guardian of roads and paths. *Arka:* the Sun, to whom Pûshan appears to have gone, both as an envoy on behalf of the other Gods when Sûryâ or Sunlight was to be given in marriage, and as a suitor on his own account.

43, 44 R. V. I. 22. 18, 21. *Three steps:* as the Sun, over earth and through firmament and heaven. See X. 19. *Light up:* glorify with praise.

45 R. V. VI. 70 1. *Parted each from each:* heaven and earth were, it is said, originally in close juxtaposition, and were subsequently separated and held apart by Indra, Agni, Soma, or, as in this place, Varuṇa.

46 R. V. X. 128. *Have exalted . . . made:* that is, may they do so.

47 R. V. I. 34. 11, *Thrice eleven:* the number of the Gods is said to have been originally three thousand three hundred and thirty-nine, then reduced to 33, to 6, to 3, to 2, to 1½, and at last to one, which one is the breath of life, the Self, and his name is That. See Max Müller, Three Lectures on the Vedânta Philosophy, p. 26.

48 R. V. I. 165. 15. I borrow three-fourths of this verse from Prof. Max Müller, Vedic Hymns, Part I.

Bring offspring for ourselves with food to feed us. May we find strengthening food in full abundance.

49 They who were versed in ritual and metre, in hymns and rules, were the Seven godlike Rishis.
Viewing the path of those of old, the sages have taken up the reins like chariot-drivers.

50 Bestowing splendour, length of life, increase of wealth, and conquering power,
This brightly shining gold shall be attached to me for victory.

51 This gold no demons injure, no Piśâchas; for this is might of Gods, their primal offspring.
Whoever wears the gold of Daksha's children lives a long life among the Gods, lives a long life among mankind.

52 This ornament of gold which Daksha's children bound, with benevolent thoughts, on Śatânîka,
I bind on me for life through hundred autumns, that I may live till ripe old age o'ertakes me.

53 Let Ahibudhnya also hear our calling, and Aja-Ekapâd and Earth and Ocean.

---

49 R. V. X. 130. 7. *Seven godlike Rishis:* Bharadvâja, Kaśyapa, Gotama, Atri, Vasishṭha, Viśvâmitra, and Jamadagni. 'The knowledge of the ritual is derived from the divine priests; the sages or Rishis have followed them in sacrificing, and modern priests are only imitators of those who preceded them.'—Ludwig.

50 *Gold:* worn as an amulet.

51, 52 Taken, with variations, from A. V. I. 35. 2, 1. *Daksha's children:* Daksha is in the Veda a Creative Power associated with Aditi (Infinity or Eternity), the mother of the Âdityas. In post-Vedic literature he is generally regarded as the son of Brahmâ, and placed at the head of the Prajâpatis or Lords of Created Beings. The Dâkshâyaṇas, or descendants of Daksha, are mentioned also in the Śatapatha-Brâhmaṇa, II. 4. 4. 6. *Piśâchas:* see XXX. 3.

The investiture of *Śatânîka* must be an occurrence of ancient times, of which no particulars have been preserved. *Hundred autumns:* regarded as the natural duration of human life; an expression frequently occurring in the Rigveda, alternating with 'hundred winters.' Cf. Isaiah LXV. 20: There shall be no more thence an infant of days, nor an old man that hath not filled his days: for the child shall die a hundred years old.

53 R. V. VI. 50. 14. *Ahibudhnya:* the Serpent or Dragon of the Deep; a mysterious atmospheric deity, regent of the depths of the firmament. *Aja-Ekapâd:* according to von Roth, probably a genius of the storm, 'the stormer of one foot.' But *aja* signifies also unborn, birthless, and the Sun may be intended. Aja-Ekapâd is called, in R. V. X. 65. 13, the bearer of heaven, 'and the ascription of one foot to the Sun might be due to his appearance alone in the sky as opposed to the Dawns and the Aśvins.'—Wallis, Cosmology of the Rigveda, p 54. Other conjectural explanations have been proposed. See Macdonell, Vedic Mythology, pp. 73, 74.

All Gods Law-strengtheners, invoked and landed, and Texts recited by the sages, help us !

54 These hymns that drop down fatness, with the ladle I ever offer to the Kings Âdityas.

May Mitra, Aryaman, and Bhaga hear us, the mighty Varuṇa, Daksha, and Aṃ a.

55 Seven Ṛishis are established in the body: seven guard it evermore with care unceasing.

Seven waters seek the world of him who lies asleep: two sleepless Gods are feast-fellows of him who wakes.

56 O Brahmaṇaspati, arise. God-fearing men, we pray to thee.

May they who give good gifts, the Maruts, come to us. Indra, be thou most swift with them.

57 Now Brahmaṇaspati speaks forth aloud the solemn hymn of praise,

Wherein Indra and Varuṇa, Mitra, Aryaman, the Gods have made their dwelling-place.

58 O Brahmaṇaspati, be thou controller of this our hymn, and prosper thou our children.

All that the Gods regard with love is blessèd. Loud may we speak, with brave sons, in assembly.

He who sate down. Mighty in mind. Father who made us. A share of good, O Lord of Food.

---

54 R. V. II. 27. 1. *Aṃṣa:* the Distributer ; one of the Âdityas.

55 *Seven Ṛishis:* here meaning the vital breathings. *Seven guard it:* touch, sight, hearing, taste, smell, mind, and intellect. *Waters:* pervaders, according to Mahîdhara ; meaning the vital airs. *World:* the soul or self. *Two sleepless Gods:* Inbreath and Outbreath.

56, 57 R. V. I. 40. 1, 5.

58 R. V. II. 23. 19. *With heroes:* with brave sons about us who will give us confidence. The four Pratîkas that follow are taken, respectively, from XVII. 17, 26, 27, and XI. 83.

# BOOK THE THIRTY-FIFTH.

BEGONE the Paṇis, hence away, rebellious, scorners of the Gods!
The place is his who poured the juice.

2 Let Savitar approve a spot upon the earth for thy remains:
And let the bulls be yoked for it.

3 Let Vâyu purify. Let Savitar purify. With Agni's glitter. With Savitar's lustre. Let the bulls be unyoked.

4 The Holy Fig Tree is your home, your mansion is the Parṇa Tree:
Winners of cattle shall ye be if ye regain for me this man.

5 Let Savitar lay down thy bones committed to the Mother's lap.
Be pleasant to this man, O Earth.

6 Here in the God Prajâpati, near water, Man, I lay thee down:
May his light drive mishap from us.

7 Go hence, O Death, pursue thy special pathway apart from that which Gods are wont to travel.
To thee I say it who hast eyes and hearest: Touch not our offspring, injure not our heroes.

---

This Book is connected with the Pitriyajña or Sacrifice to the Fathers or Ancestral Manes (II. 29. 34), containing chiefly formulas to be used at funeral ceremonies. See R. V. X. 14; 16; 18; and Muir, Original Sanskrit Texts, V. pp. 291—297.

1 *Begone:* addressed to the Paṇis, Piśâchas and other evil spirits that haunt the ground prepared for the cremation of the corpse. Cf. R. V. X. 14. 9. *His:* the deceased householder's who in his life time duly worshipped the Gods with libations of Soma juice.

2 *Remains:* the bones and ashes which are to be buried. *Let the bulls be yoked:* six in number, to a plough with which furrows are driven from the south or north side of the ground, to keep evil spirits at a distance.

3 Four furrows are drawn, with a formula for each.

4 Addressed to the various plants whose seeds he sows. The formula, taken from R. V X. 97. 5, is repeated from XII. 79. Sacrificial vessels and implements are made of the Asvattha or Ficus Religiosa and the Parṇa, Palâśa, or Butea Frondosa, which are therefore said to be the *home* of plants used in religious ceremonies.

5 The collected bones and ashes are laid down in the middle of the prepared ground.

6 *Man:* the name of the deceased is to be supplied. The last line of the formula is the burden of R. V. I. 97, 1—8. *Mishap from us:* our sin, according to Mahîdhara.

7 R. V. X. 18. 1. *Death:* Mrityu, distinct from Yama the judge and ruler of the departed. *Our offspring;* meaning here, says Sâyaṇa, female offspring. *Our heroes:* our sons and grandsons.

8 Pleasant to thee be wind and sun, and pleasant be the bricks to thee.
Pleasant to thee be the terrestrial fires: let them not scorch thee in their flames.

9 Prosper for thee the regions and the waters, and let the seas for thee be most propitious.
Auspicious unto thee be Air. Prosper all Quarters well for thee!

10 On flows the stony flood: hold fast each other, keep yourselves up, my friends, and pass the river.
Here let us leave the powers that brought no profit, and cross the flood to Powers that are auspicious.

11 Drive away evil, drive away fault, sorcery, and guiltiness.
Do thou, O Apâmârga, drive the evil dream away from us.

12 To us let waters and the plants be friendly, to him who hates us, whom we hate, unfriendly.

13 For our prosperity we touch the ox the son of Surabhi.
Be bearer and deliverer to us as Indra to the Gods.

14 Looking upon the loftiest light, etc., as in XX. 21.

15 Here I erect this rampart for the living: let none of these, none other, reach this limit.
May they survive a hundred lengthened autumns, and may they bury Death beneath this mountain.

16 Agni, thou pourest life, etc., as in XIX. 38.

---

8 The deceased householder is addressed. *The bricks:* three of which are laid down towards each quarter of the sky. *Let them not scorch thee:* cf. R. V. X. 16. 1:—Burn him not up, nor quite consume him, Agni: let not his body or his skin be scattered.

10 R. V. X. 53. 8. The original verse contains words of encouragement to the bearers who with the funeral procession are crossing a stream. Here the natural stream is represented by a ditch cut for the purpose, filled with water and covered with aquatic plants and Kuṣa grass, into which stones are cast.

11 Purificatory and benedictive formulas follow. *Apâmârga:* (from *mṛij,* to cleanse or wipe, with *apa + â*) Achyranthes Aspera. a biennial plant frequently used in medicine, in incantations or countercharms, and in sacrifices. See The Hymns of the Atharva-veda, Index.

12 Repeated from VI. 22 and XX. 19.

13 *Surabhi:* the Cow of Plenty, regarded as the mother of all bovine cattle. See The Râmâyaṇa, II. 74.

15 *This rampart:* a mound of earth (or, according to some, a brand or enclosing-stick from the Southern Fire) raised by the Adhvaryu as a line of demarcation between the dead and the living, limiting, as it were, the jurisdiction of Death until the natural time for his approach. *This mountain:* the mound or ridge so raised.

17 Waxing with sacrifice live long, O Agni, with butter on thy face and homed in fatness.
When thou hast drunk the cows' fair savoury butter, guard, as a father guards his son, these people.

18 These men have led about the ox, have duly carried Agni round,
And raised their glory to the Gods. Who will attack them with success?

19 I drive Corpse-eating Agni to a distance: sin-laden let him go to Yama's kingdom.
Here let this other, Jâtavedas, carry oblation to the Deities, foreknowing.

20 Carry the fat to Fathers, Jâtavedas, where, far away, thou knowest them established.
Let rivulets of marrow flow to meet them, and let their truthful wishes be accomplished. All-hail!

21 Pleasant be thou to us, O Earth, without a thorn, our resting-place.
Vouchsafe us shelter reaching far. May thy light drive mishap from us.

22 Born art thou, Agni, from this man: let him again be born from thee,
For Svarga's world, the man I name. All-hail!

---

18 *The ox:* see verse 13. The text, taken from R. V. X. 16. 5, is a giving over or recommendation of the people to divine protection.

19 A. V. XII. 2. *Corpse-eating Agni:* Agni Kravyâd, the fire that consumes the bodies of the dead, to be extinguished as soon as the cremation is completed. *This other:* the friendly sacrificial fire.

21 R. V. I. 22. 15. The additional concluding line is repeated from verse 6.

22 *Born . . . . from this man:* generated or produced by the deceased householder at the Agnyâdhâna or ceremonial establishment of his own sacrificial fires. See I. 1, note; III. 1, note. *Born from thee:* reproduced from the funeral fire for new life in Svarga or heaven.

A full and excellent account of the old Indian funeral ritual will be found in Madame Ragozin's Vedic India (Story of the Nations Series) pp. 349 – 359. See also Max Müller, India, What can it Teach us? pp. 231 – 342.

## BOOK THE THIRTY-SIXTH.

Refuge I take in Speech as Ṛich; refuge in Mind as Yajus-text; refuge in Breath as Sâma-chant; refuge in Hearing and in Sight.

Speech-energy endowed with strength, inbreath and out-breath are in me.

2 Whatever deeply-sunk defect I have of eye, or mind, or heart, that may Bṛihaspati amend!
Gracious to us be he, Protector of the world.

3 Earth! Ether! Heaven! May we attain that excellent, etc., as in III. 35.

4 With what help will he come to us etc., as in XXVII. 39.

5 What genuine, etc., as in XXVII. 40.

6 Do thou who art, etc., as in XXVII. 41.

7 O Hero, with what aid dost thou delight us, with what succour bring
Riches to those who worship thee?

8 Indra is king of all that is: may weal attend our bipeds and our quadrupeds.

9 Gracious be Mitra unto us, and Varuṇa and Aryaman;
Indra, Bṛihaspati be kind, and Vishṇu of the mighty stride.

10 Pleasantly blow the wind for us, may Sûrya warm us pleasantly.
Pleasantly, with a roar, the God Parjanya send the rain on us.

11 May days pass pleasantly for us, may nights draw near delightfully.
Befriend us with their aids Indra and Agni, Indra and Varuṇa who taste oblations.
Indra and Pûshan be our help in battle, Indra and Soma give health, strength, and comfort.

12 May the celestial Waters, our helpers, be sweet for us to drink,
And flow with health and strength to us.

---

This Book contains preliminary formulas—chiefly prayers for long life, unimpaired faculties, health, strength, prosperity, security, tranquillity, and contentment—of the Pravargya ceremony which is a preparatory rite of the Soma sacrifice. See Sacred Books of the East, XII. 44; XXVI. 104.

7 R. V. VIII. 82. 19. *O Hero:* Indra is addressed.

9 R. V. I. 90. 9.

10 The first line is taken from A. V. VII. 69. 1, as is also the first line of the following verse.

11 *Befriend us:* taken from R. V. VII. 35. 1.

13 Pleasant be thou to us, O Earth, etc., as in XXXV. 21.

14 Ye, Waters, are, etc., as in XI. 50.

15 Give us a portion, etc., as in XI. 51.

16 To you we gladly come, etc., as in XI. 52.

17 Sky alleviation, Air alleviation, Earth alleviation, Plants alleviation,
Trees alleviation, All-Gods alleviation, Brahma alleviation, Universe alleviation, just Alleviation alleviation—may that alleviation come to me!

18 Caldron, strengthen me. May all beings regard me with the eye of a friend. May I regard all beings with the eye of a friend.
With the eye of a friend do we regard one another.

19 Do thou, O Caldron, strengthen me. Long may I live to look on thee. Long may I live to look on thee.

20 Obeisance to thy wrath and glow, etc., as in XXII. 11.

21 Homage to thee the lightning flash, homage to thee the thunder's roar!
Homage, O Bounteous Lord, to thee whereas thou fain wouldst win to heaven!

22 From whatsoever trouble thou desirest, give us safety thence.
Give to our children happiness and to our beasts security.

23 To us let Waters and let Plants be friendly, etc., as in VI. 22.

24 Through hundred autumns may we see that bright Eye, God-appointed, rise,
A hundred autumns may we live.
Through hundred autumns may we hear; through hundred autumns clearly speak: through hundred autumns live content; a hundred autumns, yea, beyond a hundred autumns may we see.

---

17 Cf. the nearly similar verse in A. V. XIX. 9. 14 which ends differently: 'By these alleviations, these universal alleviations, I allay all that is terrific here, all that is cruel, all that is wicked. This hath been calmed, this is now auspicious. Let all be favourable to us.'

18 *Caldron:* he addresses the chief earthen vessel, the Gharma or Mahâvîra (see XIX. 14) in which the offering of heated milk is prepared. This Caldron is glorified in A. V. IV. 11. 1—6. See also Muir, O. S. Texts, V. 399.

21 The first line, addressed originally to Lightning personified, is taken from A. V. I. 13. 1.

24 The first two lines are taken from R. V. VII. 66. 16. *Bright Eye:* of the universe, the Sun; here meaning the glorified Caldron. *Hundred autumns:* alternating with 'a hundred winters' and 'a hundred years' regarded as the natural duration of human life.

## BOOK THE THIRTY-SEVENTH.

By impulse of God Savitar I take thee, etc. Spade art thou. Woman art thou, etc., as in XI. 9, 10.

2 The priests of him the lofty Priest, etc., as in V. 14.

3 O Heaven and Earth divine, may I duly prepare for you this day the head of Makha on the place of earth where the Gods sacrificed.

For Makha thee, thee for the head of Makha!

4 Ye who were born the earliest of creation, Ants divine, may I duly prepare for you this day the head of Makha on the place of earth where the Gods sacrificed.

For Makha thee, thee for the head of Makha!

---

This Book and the two that follow contain the formulas to be used at the actual performance of the Pravargya ceremony, when the necessary animals, vessels, and implements have been brought to the sacrificial ground, and the propitiatory texts (Book XXXVI) have been recited by the priests.

1 *I take thee:* the wooden sacrificial spade, with which earth is to be dug to form two square beds for the chief Caldron, called Mahâvîra and Gharma, to rest on. *Woman: abhri*, spade, being feminine: see V. 22. note.

3 *Heaven and Earth:* the Adhvaryu takes up a lump of clay, the moisture of which represents the vapoury heaven, and the earthy portion the earth. *The head of Makha:* according to the legend related in the Śatapatha and Pañchavimsa Brâhmaṇas, Makha (who appears as a malignant demon in R. V. IX. 101. 13 and perhaps X. 171. 2) was attending a sacrificial session with Agni, Indra and other Gods who agreed to share among them any glory that should accrue from it. The glory came to Makha who took it and was going to depart, but the Gods surrounded him and claimed their shares. He stood leaning on his bow when the string (gnawed through by confederate ants, according to the Ś. Brâhmaṇa) gave way, and the bow-end, springing upwards, cut off his head. This head, replaced by the Aśvins, became the Pravargya, and when men offer this sacrifice they replace the head of Makha. See Muir, O. Sanskrit Texts, IV. pp. 124–129. Mahîdhara, however, without allusion to this legend (which is somewhat differently related in the two Brâhmaṇas), explains *makha* by *yajña*, sacrifice, the *head*, or main essential of which is the Mahâvîra or chief caldron containing the heated milk.

4 *Ants:* meaning termites (Hindî *dîmak* or *dîwak*, corrupted from *upajihvikâ*, an older form of *upajîka* or *upadîka*, and found in the Rigveda), here erroneously called *vamryaḥ*, ants or emmets, and white ants in English. Earth thrown up by them, a nest or hill containing some of the insects, is taken up and placed on a black-antelope skin. They are addressed as *divine* on account of the wonderful power, bestowed upon them by the Gods, of producing water wherever they dig. See The Hymns of the Atharva-veda, Vol. I. pp. 44 and 300, notes. A lump from a white ants' nest is used in the Atharva-veda ritual in connexion with a charm for diarrhœa, and as an antidote against poison. See Bloomfield, American Journal of Philology, Vol. VII. pp. 482–484. An ant-hill has been employed also in the ritual of this Veda. See XI. 17, note. These white ants are addressed as 'the earliest of creation,' and it seems to be a fact that these Corrodentia of Pseudo-Neuroptera have been in existence from Carboniferous ages, while ants, which are Hymenopterous insects, do not occur before Tertiary times. See Chambers's Encyclopædia, Termites. Mahîdhara explains the antiquity of their origin by their close connexion with the 'first-born' earth. *Thee:* the lump of earth.

5 Only so large was it at first. Duly may I prepare for you this day the head of Makha on earth's place where the Gods sacrificed.
For Makha thee, thee for the head of Makha !

6 Indra's effective might are ye. Duly may I prepare for you this day the head of Makha on earth's place where the Gods sacrificed.
For Makha thee, thee for the head of Makha ! For Makha thee, thee for the head of Makha ! For Makha thee, thee for the head of Makha !

7 May Brahmaṇaspati draw nigh, etc., as in XXXIII. 89.
For Makha thee, thee for the head of Makha, etc., as in verse 6.

8 Thou art the head of Makha. Thee for Makha, thee for Makha's head ! Thou art the head of Makha. Thee for Makha, thee for Makha's head ! Thou art the head of Makha, thee for Makha, thee for Makha's head !
For Makha thee, thee for the head of Makha, etc., as in verse 6.

9 Thee on Gods' sacrificial ground with stallion's dung I fumigate.
For Makha thee, thee for the head of Makha !
For Makha thee, thee for the head of Makha ! For Makha thee, thee for the head of Makha ! For Makha thee, thee for the head of Makha !

10 Thee for the True. Thee for the Good. Thee for the place of happy rest.

---

5 *It:* the earth. *At first:* when raised up by Vishṇu in his Boar-incarnation.

6 *Ye:* he addresses the Pîtîkas, plants used to expedite the curdling of the sacrificial milk, and as substitutes for Soma plants when these are not at hand ; a kind of grass, according to Mahîdhara. *Thee:* the milk which he lays down on the antelope skin.

7 Murmuring the text from the Ṛigveda, the Adhvaryu and his assistants go to the Parivṛit, an enclosed shed or shrine, where he deposits the sacrificial apparatus, the most important of which is the Mahâvîra or chief caldron, two inferior caldrons being kept in reserve. *Thee:* he addresses the chief Mahâvîra.

8 He touches and addresses each of the three caldrons.

9 He fumigates each caldron with horse-dung, addressing each in turn with the formula.

10 The heated vessels are lifted up, each being addressed. *Thee for the True:* I raise thee, the first Mahâvîra, to gratify the truthful Sun. *Thee for the Good:* the second to please Vâyu. *Thee for the place of happy rest:* the third to please Earth. *For Makha, etc.:* he sprinkles the three Mahâvîras with goat's milk, addressing a formula to each.

For Makha thee, thee for the head of Makha! For Makha thee, thee for the head of Makha! For Makha thee, thee for the head of Makha!

11 For Yama thee. For Makha thee. For Sûrya's fervent ardour thee.

May Savitar the God with balm anoint thee. Guard thou the touches of the earth

Flame art thou; thou art radiance; thou art heat.

12 Unconquerable, eastward, in Agni's overlordship, give me life.

Rich in sons, southward, in Indra's overlordship give me offspring.

Fair-seated, westward, in God Savitar's overlordship, give me sight.

Range of hearing, northward, in Dhâtar's overlordship, give me increase of wealth.

Arrangement, upward, in Bṛihaspati's overlordship, give me energy.

From all destructive spirits guard us. Thou art Manu's mare.

13 All-hail! By Maruts be thou compassed round.

Guard the sky's touches. Mead, mead, mead.

14 Germ of the Gods, Father of hymns, all living creatures' guardian Lord,

Radiant, with radiant Savitar united, with the Sun he shines.

15 Agni combined with flaming fire, combined with Savitar divine, hath shone together with the Sun.

---

11 Directed by the Brahman priest, the Adhvaryu besprinkles the chief Mahâvîra three times, consecrating it to Yama, here said to mean the Sun, to Makha or Sacrifice, also meaning the Sun, and to the Sun's heat, the Mahâvîra being regarded as the representative of the Sun in these three forms. *May Savitar, etc.:* he anoints the Mahâvîra with sacrificial butter. *Guard thou, etc.:* he addresses a silver plate which has been put under the Mahâvîra to protect it from the evil spirits that infest the earth. It has also been covered with a plate of gold.

12 The Adhvaryu makes the Sacrificer recite the seven following formulas addressed to Earth. *Dhâtar:* the Ordainer; Creator. *Manu's mare:* bearer of the representative man and father of the human race, here represented by the Mahâvîra.

13 He surrounds the Mahâvîra with ashes and coals, and above them lays thirteen pieces of Vikaṅkata wood, representing the thirteen months, the Pravargya being the year. *By Maruts:* that is, by us thy people. *Guard, etc.:* he addresses the plate of gold with which he covers the Mahâvîra. *The sky's touches:* meaning the Gods, according to Mahîdhara, those who touch the sky. *Mead, etc.:* the three breathings which the Adhvaryu establishes in the Mahâvîra.

14 They fan the fire, walk reverentially round the Mahâvîra, and do obeisance to it as the representative of the Sun.

15 *Agni:* represented by the Mahâvîra.

16 He shines on earth upholder of the sky and heat, the Gods' upholder, God, immortal, born of heat.
To him address a speech devoted to the Gods.

17 I saw the Herdsman, him who never stumbles, approaching by his pathways and departing.
He, clothed with gathered and diffusive splendour, within the worlds continually travels.

18 Lord of all earths, Lord of all mind, Lord of all speech, thou Lord of speech entire.
Heard by the Gods, Caldron divine, do thou, a God, protect the Gods.
Here, after, let it speed you twain on to the banquet of the Gods.
Sweetness for both the sweetness-lovers! Sweetness for those the twain who take delight in sweetness!

19 Thee for the heart, thee for the mind, thee for the sky, for Sûrya thee.
Standing erect lay thou the sacrifice in heaven among the Gods.

20 Thou art our Father, father-like regard us. Obeisance be to thee. Do not thou harm us.
May we, accompanied by Tvashṭar, win thee. Vouchsafe me sons and cattle. Grant us offspring. Safe may I be together with my husband.

21 May Day together with his sheen, fair-lighted with his light, accept. All-hail!
May Night together with her sheen, fair lighted with her light, accept. All-hail!

---

16 *He:* the Caldron identified with and sprung from the Sun.

17 R. V. I. 164. 31. *The Herdsman:* the Sun who surveys and guards the world; here represented by the Mahâvîra.

18 *You twain:* the Asvins. *Sweetness:* according to Sâyaṇa and Mahîdhara, *madhu* here means Madhuvidyâ, the knowledge of sweetness or mead; that is, the esoteric lore of Soma which was unlawfully revealed to the Asvins by Dadhyach the son of Atharvan. See The Hymns of the Rigveda, I. 116. 12; V. 75. 1, notes.

19 *Thee:* the Caldron. *For the heart, for the mind:* for their purification. *For the sky:* that we may obtain a home in heaven. We praise, is understood.

20 *Accompanied by Tvashṭar:* favoured by the God who presides over procreation and the bestowing of children. This formula is spoken by the Sacrificer's wife.

21 He offers a burnt oblation of Rauhiṇa, a special kind of rice-cake, so called, it is said, because the Sacrificer thereby ascends (*rohati*) to heaven.

# BOOK THE THIRTY-EIGHTH.

By impulse of God Savitar I take thee with arms of Asvins, with the hands of Púshan.

A zone for Aditi art thou.

2 Idâ, come hither. Aditi, come hither. Sarasvatî, come hither.

Come hither, So-and-So. Come hither, So-and-So. Come hither, So-and-So.

3 Thou art a zone for Aditi, a diadem for Indrâṇî. Pûshan art thou. Spare some for the Gharma.

4 Overflow for the Asvins. Overflow for Sarasvatî. Overflow for Indra.

All-hail, what belongs to Indra! All-hail, what belongs to Indra! All-hail, what belongs to Indra!

5 That breast of thine, exhaustless, fount of pleasure, wealth-giver, treasure-finder, free-bestower,

Wherewith thou rearest all things that are choicest,—bring that, Sarasvatî, that we may drain it.

Throughout the spacious middle air I travel.

6 Thou art Gâyatra metre. Thou art Trishṭup metre. With Heaven and Earth I grasp thee. With the Firmament I raise thee up.

Indra and Asvins, drink ye the hot draught of sweet honey: sacrifice, ye Vasus. Vâṭ! All-hail to the rain-winning beam of the Sun!

---

The Pravargya formulas are continued.

1 The Adhvaryu takes the rope that is to tie the cow for milking. *Thee*: the rope. The formula has been used in XI. 9 and elsewhere. *A zone*: cf. I. 30; XI. 59.

2 In the first line he calls the cow by her three sacrificial names. Cf. III. 27; VIII. 43, note. In the second line he calls her three times by her ordinary name, White, Dapple, or whatever it may be, which is to be supplied accordingly.

3 *A zone for Aditi*: he ties the cow to a post. *Pûshan art thou*: he looses and addresses the calf. *Some*: of the milk. *The Gharma*: the heated caldron.

4 He milks the cow, addressing the milk. *What belongs to Indra*: milk that drops on the ground, regarded as a sacrificial offering.

5 Taken from R. V. I. 164. 49, addressed originally to the Goddess, here to the cow also. *Throughout, etc.*: repeated from I. 7.

6 He addresses the Parisâsa, a duplex implement, probably like a pair of tongs, with which the caldron is lifted from the fire. One leg is said to be Gâyatra metre, and the other Trishṭup. *Thee*: the Mahâvîra, representing the Sun.

7 Thee with Svâhâ to Vâta the sea. Thee with Svâhâ to Vâta the flood.
Thee with Svâhâ to Vâta the unconquerable. Thee with Svâhâ to Vâta the irresistible.
Thee with Svâhâ to Vâta the protection-seeker. Thee with Svâhâ to Vâta the non-destructive.

8 Thee with Svâhâ to Indra Lord of Vasus. Thee with Svâhâ to Indra Lord of Rudras.
Thee with Svâhâ to Indra killer of foes. Thee with Svâhâ to Savitar attended by Ṛibhu, Vibhu, and Vâja. Thee with Svâhâ to Bṛihaspati beloved of all the Gods.

9 Svâhâ to Yama attended by the Angirases, attended by the Fathers!
Svâhâ to the Gharma! The Gharma for the Father!

10 Here hath he worshipped, seated south, all the sky-regions, all the Gods.
Drink, Aṣvins, of the heated draught, the Svâhâ-consecrated mead.

11 In heaven lay thou this sacrifice; lay thou this sacrifice in heaven.
To sacrificial Agni hail! May bliss be ours from Yajus texts.

12 Drink, Aṣvins, with your daily helps, the Gharma, strengthener of hearts.
To him who draweth out the thread be homage, and to Heaven and Earth.

13 The Gharma have the Aṣvins drunk: with Heaven and Earth have they agreed.
Here, verily, be their boons bestowed.

14 Overflow for food. Overflow for energy. Overflow for the Priesthood. Overflow for the Nobility. Overflow for Heaven and Earth. Thou, O duteous one, art Duty. Innocent one, in us establish manly powers; establish the People.

---

7 *Thee*: the Mahâvîra; 'I consecrate,' understood, to Vâta the Wind God under various appellations. *Protection-seeker*: protection-giver, would be more suitable, but the word does not seem to bear this meaning.

8 *Ṛibhu, Vibhu* (more commonly Vibhvan), *and Vâja*: the Ṛibhus, sons of Sudhanvan, raised to heaven and Godhead for their merits. See XXX. 15. note, and The Hymns of the Rigveda, Index.

11 *Lay thou*: the Mahâvîra is addressed.

12 *Him who draweth out the thread*: or web, of time, the Sun, according to Mahîdhara.

14 *Innocent one*: here the Caldron is placed on the *khara* or bed of earth prepared to receive it.

15 All-hail to Pûshan, to the milk's skin! All-hail to the press-stones!
All-hail to their echoes! All-hail to the Fathers who are above the grass, who drink the Gharma! All-hail to Heaven and Earth! All-hail to the All-Gods!

16 All-hail to Rudra invoked by worshippers! All-hail! Let light combine with light.
May Day together with his sheen, fair-lighted with his light, accept. All-hail!
May Night together with her sheen, fair-lighted with her light, accept. All-hail!
May we enjoy the mead offered in most Indra-like Agni. Homage to thee, divine Gharma! Do not thou injure me.

17 Thy far-spread majesty, instinct with wisdom, hath surpassed this heaven,
And, with its glorious fame, the earth.
Seat thee, for thou art mighty: shine, best entertainer of the Gods.
Worthy of sacred food, praised Agni! loose the smoke ruddy and beautiful to see.

18 Gharma, that heavenly light of thine in Gâyatrî, in the Soma-store,—
May it increase and be confirmed for thee, that light.
Gharma, that light of thine in air, in Trishṭup, in the sacred hearth,—
May it increase and be confirmed for thee, that light.
Gharma, that light of thine on earth, in Jagatî, of the priest's shed,—
May that increase and be confirmed for thee, that light.

19 Thee for the sure protection of the Nobles. Guard thou from injury the Brahman's body.
We follow thee in interest of the People, for the renewal of our peace and comfort.

---

15 He anoints the Mahâvîra with sacrificial butter, and offers oblation. *Pûshan:* represented by the Mahâvîra. *The milk's skin:* raised by boiling on the contents of the Mahâvîra. Cf. XXXIX. 5.

16 *Let light, etc.:* he pours some of the milk into the Upayamanî, a large wooden spoon from which the Sacrificer drinks, the two lights being the milk and the butter. *May Day, etc.:* these two lines are repeated from XXXVII. 21. *Most Indra-like:* most mighty.

17 The Mahâvîra is placed on the Âsandî or stool, the seat of which is made of muñja grass. Agni represented by the Mahâvîra, is addressed. *Seat thee etc.:* repeated from XI. 37.

19 *Thee:* the Gharma or Mahâvîra; we follow, being understood. The Sacrificer's wife is brought in and stationed in front of the Gharma.

20 Square, far-spread is the sacrifice's navel: it spreads for us wide, full of all existence, spreads wide for us full of complete existence.
We turn against the hate and guiles of him who keeps an alien law.

21 This, Gharma! is thy liquid store. Swell out and wax in strength thereby.
May we too grow in strength and wax to greatness

22 Loudly the tawny Stallion neighed, mighty, like Mitra fair to see.
Together with the Sun the sea, the store shone out with flashing light.

23 To us let Waters and let Plants be friendly; to him who hates us, whom we hate, unfriendly.

24 Looking upon the loftier light above the darkness we have come
To Sûrya, God among the Gods, the light that is most excellent.

25 A brand art thou, fain would we thrive. Fuel art thou, and splendour: Give me splendour.

26 Far as the heaven and earth are spread in compass, far as the Seven Rivers are extended,
So vast thy cup which I with strength am taking, Indra, unharmed in me, uninjured ever.

27 In me be that great hero power, in me be strength and mental force.
The Gharma shines with triple light, with lustre fulgent far away, with holy lore, with brilliancy.

28 Brought hither is the seed of milk. Through each succeeding year may we enjoy the bliss of draining it.
Invited, I enjoy a share of that which hath been offered me, the savoury draught by Indra drunk and tasted by Prajâpati.

---

20 *Square:* or four cornered; the Gharma which is placed on the High Altar. *Navel:* the central and chief point. *Keeps an alien law:* follows other than Vedic observances. Cf. R. V. V. 20. 2.

21 Repeated, with variation, from II. 14.

22 *The tawny Stallion*: the Caldron representing the Sun. *Together with*: equally with; as brilliantly as. *The sea:* the Caldron with its liquid contents. *The store:* of blessings.

23 The priests and the Sacrificer perform ablutions at the Châtvâla or pit. The formula is repeated from VI. 22.

24 The Sacrificer returns from the Châtvâla and goes towards the north-east. The formula, taken from R. V. I. 50. 10, has been used in XX. 21; XXVII 10; XXXV. 14.

25 The Sacrificer lays a kindling-stick on the Âhavanîya fire. The formula is repeated from XX. 23.

26 *Seven Rivers:* the five rivers of the Panjâb, the Indus, and the Sarasvatî or the Kubhâ. *Thy cup:* the draught from the caldron which the Sacrificer drinks. *Unharmed:* may it be unharmed, according to Mahîdhara.

27 The Sacrificer and the priests drink the remains of the contents of the caldron.

## BOOK THE THIRTY-NINTH.

SVÂHÂ to the Vital Breathings with their Controlling Lord! To Earth Svâhâ! To Agni Svâhâ! To Firmament Svâhâ! To Vâyu Svâhâ! To Sky Svâhâ! To Sûrya Svâhâ!

2 To the Quarters Svâhâ! To the Moon Svâhâ! To the Stars Svâhâ! To the Waters Svâhâ! To Varuna Svâhâ! To the Navel Svâhâ! To the Purified Svâhâ!

3 To Speech Svâhâ! To Breath Svâhâ! To Breath Svâhâ! To Sight Svâhâ! To Sight Svâhâ! To Hearing Svâhâ! To Hearing Svâhâ!

4 The wish and purpose of the mind and truth of speech may I obtain.

Bestowed on me be cattle's form, sweet taste of food, and fame and grace. Svâhâ!

5 Prajâpati while in preparation; Samrâj when prepared; All-Gods' when seated; Gharma when heated with fire; Splendour when lifted up; the Asvins' while milk is poured in; Pûshan's when the butter trickles down it; the Maruts' when the milk is clotting; Mitra's when the milk's skin is spreading; Vâyu's when it is carried off; Agni's while offered as oblation; Vâk when it has been offered.

6 Savitar on the first day; Agni on the second; Vâyu on the third; Âditya (the Sun) on the fourth; Chandramâs (the Moon) on the fifth; Ritu on the sixth; the Maruts on the seventh; Brihaspati on the eighth; Mitra on the ninth; Varuna on the tenth; Indra on the eleventh; the All-Gods on the twelfth.

---

This Book contains expiatory formulas intended to remedy and atone for any failure or defect in the performance of the Pravargya ceremony; in case, for instance, the caldron should break, or the contents be allowed to boil over, or the cow give sour or bloody milk. Oblations of butter, accompanied with the formulas, are offered to various deities and deified objects.

1 *Svâhâ!* the sacrificial exclamation on making an offering; May the oblation be properly made! *Their Controlling Lord:* Hiranyagarbha or Prajâpati.

2 *Navel:* the central point; the High Altar may be meant. *The Purified:* according to Mahîdhara, the God who purifies.

3 *Speech, etc.:* meaning the deities who preside over these faculties. *Cattle's form:* beauty or splendour connected with cattle, says Mahîdhara.

5, 6 The Mahâvîra represents or belongs to various deities at different stages of the ceremony, and expiatory oblations, if required, are to be offered accordingly. *Milk's skin:* Cf. XXXVIII. 15.

6 *Ritu:* the Season, personified.

7 Fierce; Terrible; The Resonant; The Roarer; Victorious; Assailant; and Dispeller. Svâhâ.

8 Agni with the heart; Lightning with the heart's point; Paṣupati with the whole heart; Bhava with the liver.

Ṣarva with the two cardiac bones; Îṣâna with Passion; Mahâdeva with the intercostal flesh; the Fierce God with the rectum; Vasishṭha-hanuḥ, Ṣiṅgis with two lumps of flesh near the heart.

9 The Fierce with blood; Mitra with obedience, Rudra with disobedience; Indra with pastime; the Maruts with strength; the Sâdhyas with enjoyment.

Bhava's is what is on the throat; Rudra's what is between the ribs; Mahâdeva's is the liver; Ṣarva's the rectum; Paṣupati's the pericardium.

10 To the hair Svâhâ! To the hair Svâhâ! To the skin Svâhâ! To the skin Svâhâ! To the blood Svâhâ! To the blood Svâhâ! To the fats Svâhâ! To the fats Svâhâ! To the fleshy parts Svâhâ! To the fleshy parts Svâhâ! To the sinews Svâhâ! To the sinews Svâhâ! Svâhâ to the bones! Svâhâ to the bones! To the marrows Svâhâ! To the marrows Svâhâ! To the seed Svâhâ! To the anus Svâhâ!

---

7 This formula, called technically *araṇye' nûchyam*, To be recited in the forest, contains the names of seven of the fiercest Maruts. See XVII. 81–85, from the last line of which the formula is repeated.

8 *With the heart:* I propitiate or gratify, understood. *Paṣupati:* Lord of Beasts or Cattle, a title of Rudra who is called also Bhava and Ṣarva. See XVI. 28. *Cardiac bones:* or, according to some, kidneys See XIX. 85; XXV. 8. *Iṣâna:* Lord; Ruler; also one of the older names of Rudra. See A. V. XV. 5. *Mahâdeva:* the Great God; Rudra, *Vasiṣtha-hanuḥ, Ṣiṅgis:* nothing can be made out of the text which appears to be corrupt.

9 *The Fierce:* Rudra in his terrible manifestations; I propitiate, being understood. *Sâdhyas:* a class of ancient deities; Blessed Gods: Eggeling.

10 The object of the Pravargya, which is a purificatory and introductory ceremony like Dîkshâ or Consecration (IV. 2; V. 6) is the bodily regeneration of the Sacrificer, the provision of a heavenly body with which alone he is permitted to enter the residence of the Gods (Haug, Aitareya Brâhmaṇam, II. 42, note). At the conclusion of the ceremony, therefore, the sacrificial materials are so arranged as to form the semblance of a human figure. The Mahâvîras represent the head; the Prastara or sacrificial bunch of grass the hair; the two milk-vessels are his ears; the plates of gold and silver his eyes; the Rauhiṇa-cake potsherds represent the heels; the contents of the caldron are the blood, and so on (see Hillebrandt, Ritual-Litteratur, p. 135). The formulas contained in this verse provide the Pravargya-man with the bodily parts enumerated, and the regeneration of the Sacrificer is thus completed. Faculties and feelings are imparted by the formulas which follow.

11 To Effort Svâhâ! To Exertion Svâhâ! To Endeavour Svâhâ! To Viyâsa Svâhâ! To Attempt Svâhâ!

12 To Grief Svâhâ! To the Grieving Svâhâ! To the Sorrowing Svâhâ! To Sorrow Svâhâ!

To Heat Svâhâ! To him who grows hot Svâhâ! To him who is being heated Svâhâ! To him who has been heated Svâhâ! To Gharma Svâhâ!

To Atonement Svâhâ! To Expiation Svâhâ! To Remedy Svâhâ!

13 To Yama Svâhâ! To the Finisher Svâhâ! To Death Svâhâ! To the Priesthood Svâhâ! To Brâhmanicide Svâhâ! To the All-Gods Svâhâ! To Heaven and Earth Svâhâ!

---

11 *Viyâsa:* the meaning of the word is not clear, and Mahîdhara offers no explanation: 'a tormenting spirit of Yama's world, according to the Commentators' :—S. P. Lexicon. Formed from *vi+yas*, as the other words in the line are from *â*, *pra-â*, *sum*, and *ud+yas*, it might, perhaps, be rendered by Distraction or Distraint.

12 *To Gharma:* the word means (1) heat (2) the heated caldron (3) its heated contents. *Atonement: Expiation:* for defects in the sacrifice. See first note. *Remedy:* the putting together of the Pravargya-man and the bodily regeneration of the Sacrificer.

The Pravargya, which was originally, probably, a milk-offering to the Sun and his heralds the Aṣvins, is alluded to in the Ṛigveda (V. 30. 15; VII. 103. 8), and the ritual (with formulas different from those of the Yajurveda) is described in the Aitareya-Brâhmaṇa which belongs to that Veda. See Haug, Ai. Br. II. 41—51. The Caldron is also glorified in A. V. IV. 11. 1—6. More details of the performance of the rite may be found in Prof. A. Hillebrandt's Ritual-Litteratur, and in Sacred Books of the East, Vol. XLV. See also Oldenberg, Die Religion des Veda, under Pravargya.

## BOOK THE FORTIETH.

ENVELOPED by the Lord must be This All—each thing that moves on earth.
With that renounced enjoy thyself. Covet no wealth of any man.

2 One, only doing Karma here, should wish to live a hundred years.
No way is there for thee but this. So Karma cleaveth not to man.

3 Aye, to the Asuras belong those worlds enwrapt in blinding gloom.
To them, when life on earth is done, depart the men who kill the Self.

---

This, the last Adhyâya or Book of the White Yajurveda Saṃhitâ, is an Upanishad or religious and philosophical treatise, not directly connected with any sacrificial ceremonial. It 'is professedly designed', says Professor Weber, 'to fix the proper mean between those exclusively engaged in sacrificial acts and those entirely neglecting them. It belongs at all events to a very advanced stage of speculation as it assumes a Lord (îś) of the universe. According to Mahîdhara's commentary, its polemic is directed partially against the Bauddhas, that is, probably, against the doctrines which afterwards were called Sâṃkhya'.—History of Indian Literature, p. 108.

1 *Enveloped:* or covered *The Lord:* Îś, the Soul of All, and thy inmost Self—the only Absolute Reality. *This All:* the phenomenal universe. *On earth:* in the three worlds; in the whole imaginary Cosmos. *With that renounced:* after absolute renunciation of the world and all the vain desires connected with it. *Enjoy thyself:* delight in the bliss of the Beatific Vision. According to Śrî Śaṅkara, save or protect the Self. *Covet no wealth:* and set not thy heart upon what thou callest thine. The seeming existence of the world is to be covered by the all-embracing, all-absorbing, all-satisfying thought of the Deity.

2 Of the two courses, Sannyâsa or Renunciation and Karma or Religious Action, the former, consequent on right knowledge of the Self, is the better way. *Only doing Karma:* he who desires life is not fitted to follow the higher path and in order to avoid sin he must perform the religious works, such as Agnihotra (III. 9) and the like, ordained by the Śâstras. Thus, and thus only, will he be untainted by evil action, and by a gradual purification of the heart he will attain to Renunciation and its direct goal of Mukti, Liberation, or Final Beatitude, that is, the reabsorption of the individual Self into the Supreme Self or Soul of the Universe.

3 This text condemns those who perform Karma with a view to future advantages in this world or sensual enjoyments in Svarga, and who kill the Self by ignorance of its eternal nature. *To the Asuras:* as compared with the nature of the Supreme Spirit who is without a second, even the Gods and other beings are spoken of as Asuras or demons. The worlds of Asuras include Gods, human beings, the lower animals, and even plants and minerals.

4 Motionless, one, swifter than Mind—the Devas failed to o'ertake it speeding on before them.
It, standing still, outstrips the others running. Herein doth Mâtariṣvan stablish Action.
5 It moveth; it is motionless. It is far distant; it is near.
It is within This All; and it surrounds This All externally.
6 The man who in his Self beholds all creatures and all things that be,
And in all beings sees his Self, thence doubts no longer, ponders not.
7 When, in the man who clearly knows, Self hath become all things that are,

---

4 As ignorance of the Âtmâ or Self leads to repeated mundane transmigrations, some explanation of its nature is now given. *Motionless:* in its unconditioned state, free from the obstructions of the body, its organs of perception, conception, etc., and of the objective or external world. *One:* all-pervading, and really only one, although appearing to the ignorant to be encased separately in every body. *Swifter than Mind:* seeming, as it is all-pervading, to travel faster than even the Mind (Manas, Mens, 'the *sensorium commune*, the rallying-point of the senses'—Max Müller). The Mind, says Srî Saṅkara, by its power of imagination is known to travel to the world of Brahmâ even in a second, and the Self—Âtmâ—seems to arrive there previously. Because Âtmâ or Brahma—Intelligence Absolute—which is the basis of all perception, imagination and thought, and as such reflects itself in all the conscious functions of the senses of the Mind, cannot but be considered as going before; otherwise how can the Mind function at all? *The Devas:* here meaning the organs of sense, sight, etc. *It:* the entity of the Âtmâ. *The others:* the senses. *Herein:* on by it, the entity of the Âtmâ which pervades all existence. *Mâtariṣvan:* Vâyu, Air; the special supporter of all life, which allots their respective functions to the forces of Nature, urging fire to burn, the Sun to give his light, and the clouds to pour their rain. *Action:* the manifestations of all activity; the actions of human beings as well as natural phenomena.

5 *It moveth; it is motionless:* substantially a repetition, to add force to the assertion, from verse 4. *It:* the entity of the Âtmâ. Although constant and unmoving in itself, it seems to the ignorant to move. Or, physically, it is stationary in plants and minerals and moving in animated creatures. *Far distant:* far beyond the reach of the ignorant. *Near:* close to those who know its nature. Or, Mahîdhara says, it is far away in the sun and the stars and close at hand in the earth. *Within This All:* being all-pervading and extremely subtile it is at the same time within and without the Universe.

6 *The man:* he who has renounced the world and wishes for final release from transmigration. *In his Self:* as not distinct from his own Âtmâ or Self. *Thence:* consequently. *Doubts no longer;* this interpretation of *na vichikitsati* is given by Mahîdhara who quotes a Sûtra from Pâṇini (3. 1. 5) implying that the affix *san* is used in the root's own sense—*svârthe san pratyayaḥ*—i. e. not in the desiderative sense. The reading of the Kâṇva recension is *na vijugupsate,* that is, does not shrink away from them as alien and inferior to his own Self.

7 As ignorance, the source of grief and delusion, has been destroyed in the man who beholds the one, all-pervading, pure Self, free from duality, his condition is one of uninterrupted bliss.

What wilderment, what grief is there in him who sees the One alone?

8 He hath attained unto the Bright, Bodiless, Woundless, Sinewless, the Pure which evil hath not pierced.
Far-sighted, wise, encompassing, he self-existent hath prescribed aims, as propriety demands, unto the everlasting Years.

9 Deep into shade of blinding gloom fall Asambhûti's worshippers.
They sink to darkness deeper yet who on Sambhûti are intent.

10 One fruit, they say, from Sambhava, another from Asambhava.
Thus from the sages have we heard who have declared this lore to us.

11 The man who knows Sambhûti and Vinâşa simultaneously,
He, by Vinâşa passing death, gains by Sambhûti endless life.

---

8 *He:* the man who has this right knowledge of the Self. *The Bright, etc.:* Brahma. the Highest Essence, the Supreme Being. Şrî Şankara explains differently: He (the Âtmâ) encompassed or pervaded all, being bright, etc., thus putting these neuter adjectives in apposition to the masculine pronoun *saḥ* (he). Mahîdhara also gives this alternative explanation. *Far-sighted, etc.:* referring either to the man who knows, or to the Âtmâ, according to the preferred interpretation of the first line of the verse. *As propriety demands:* so that every living being might receive the proper fruit of his action. *Years:* Prajâpatis or Creative Powers, Prajâpati being identified with the Year, of which he is the Presiding Genius. See IX. 20; XXVII. 45.

9 In order to enjoin the combined worship of Asambhûti and Sambhûti, their separate worship is condemned. *Asambhûti* is, according to Şrî Şankara. undeveloped Prakriti, Nature in its causal or germinal state when it has not evolved as the universe which is the effect. It is also called *tamas*, darkness or chaos. This worship is mere blindness and ignorance, and its adherents fall into corresponding darkness. *Sambhûti:* explained by Şrî Şankara as the manifestation of Brahma as Brahmâ the phenomenal creator, called Hiraṇyagarbha the Golden Germ, or Prajâpati. See R. V. X. 121. According to Mahîdhara's first explanation, Asambhûti is the denial of a new birth or existence after death, and Sambhûti is the exclusive assertion of that belief, devotion to which will produce excess in the practice of Karma.

10 The text now declares the separate fruit of each element of the combined worship of Undeveloped Nature and Hiraṇyagarbha in order to teach their combination, having first condemned the cults practised separately. *From Sambhava:* from the cult of Sambhava which is the same as Sambhûti in verse 9, or Hiraṇyagarbha. *Asambhava:* Undeveloped Nature or Asambhûti. The result of the former cult is the attainment of certain supernatural powers called Siddhis which enable their possessor to increase or reduce his size and weight to any extent at his pleasure, etc. Eight of these faculties are usually enumerated. The worship of Prakriti results in absorption into Prakriti. Each, therefore, fails to attain the object to be desired, redintegration in the Supreme Self.

11 *Sambhûti:* standing for Asambhûti, say the Commentators, by aphaeresis, and so meaning Undeveloped Nature. *Vinâşa:* (Destruction) that is,

12 To blinding darkness go the men who make a cult of Nescience.
The devotees of Science enter darkness that is darker still.

13 Different is the fruit, they say, of Science and of Nescience.
Thus from the sages have we heard who have declared this lore to us.

14 The man who knoweth well these two, Science and Nescience, combined,
O'ercoming death by Nescience by Science gaineth endless life.

15 My breath reach everlasting Air! In ashes let my body end.
Om! Mind, remember thou; remember thou my sphere; remember thou my deeds.

---

Hiraṇyagarbha. The combination of the two cults is now expressly enjoined, since the fruits can be obtained only by one and the same person successively, and not by different persons practising each cult independently. *Passing death:* that is, overcoming death in the shape of the absence of supernatural powers and of vice and desire by means of the faculties obtained by the worship of Hiraṇyagarbha (verse 10). *Sambhûti:* here again meaning Asambhûti or Undeveloped Nature. *Endless life:* that is, conditioned or limited immortality by absorption into Prakṛiti.

12 *Nescience:* Avidyâ, the opposite of Vidyâ or true Science; including ignorance of the real nature of the Âtmâ and belief in the phenomenal and transient objective world. See Professor Max Müller's Three Lectures on the Vedânta Philosophy, pp. 97—100. Here the word is used as equivalent to Karma (verse 2), one of its results, the constant performers of which, exclusively, fall into darkness which prevents their knowing the truth. *Science:* Vidyâ; meaning, here, only knowledge of the Devatâs or Deities, not of the Paramâtmâ or Supreme Self. This Science, alone, is insufficient.

13 *Different is the fruit:* Science (knowledge of the Deities) leads a man after death to the Devaloka, the world of the Devas or Gods. Nescience, that is, Karma, leads to the Pitṛiloka, the world of the Fathers, Manes or Ancestral Spirits.

14 The person who practises the sacred rites and conjointly cultivates the Science of the Deities successively attains the fruits of both, obtaining, in the end, the union with the Gods called immortality in a limited sense.

15 This and the two succeeding verses are addressed to Brahma, the True, typified by Fire, and designated Om the Sacred Symbol of the Deity. The Solar Fire, the Supreme Deity, and the Self manifested in the Mind are here addressed in identity by the dying devotee, meditating upon the Supreme Light in the Sun as no other than his own Inner Light. The meaning of this verse is:—May my breath—the life-principle in me (called the *liṅga-śarîra*, and consisting of the five organs of action, the five organs of sense, the five Airs, the Mind and the Intellect), leaving its bodily limitation, reach, or be united with, the immortal Hiraṇyagarbha or Sûtrâtman, the Soul-thread, the Divine, all-pervading, Cosmic Life; and may this gross body consumed on the funeral pile end in ashes. *My sphere: klibe,* which is not in the Kâṇva text, is explained by the Commentators as 'the region allotted to, or intended (kalpita) for, me'.

16 By goodly path lead us to riches, Agni, thou God who knowest all our works and wisdom.
Remove the sin that makes us stray and wander: most ample adoration will we bring thee.

17 The Real's face is hidden by a vessel formed of golden light.
The Spirit yonder in the Sun, the Spirit dwelling there am I.
Oм! Heaven! Brahma!

---

16 This verse, repeated from V. 36, and taken from R. V. I. 89. 6, is a continuation of the dying devotee's prayer. *Goodly path:* not by the path that leads to the abode of the Manes and subsequent transmigration, but by the fair road travelled by the Gods, on which there is no returning. *To riches:* that is, according to the Commentators, enjoyment of the reward of our Karma.

17 *The Real's face:* the face or real form of that True Being—Brahma—the indwelling Spirit of all beings, animate or inanimate,—the Inward Ruler (antaryâmin), the Purusha who dwells in the Sun yonder and in the body. In the Kâṇva recension a verse numbered 16 follows: O Nourisher, Sole Mover (or Sole Seer), Yama (Controller), O Sun, Prajâpati's Son, remove thy rays and draw together or contract thy burning energy, so that I may behold thy most blessed Form. That Spirit (Purusha) who dwelleth in the Sun yonder, I am He (the immaterial eternal Soul). 'Thy most blessed Form' implies that True Spiritual Light which is, as it were, veiled by the golden orb of physical material light which typifies it.

In both recensions, Mâdhyandina and Kâṇva, the order of verses 1—8 is the same. In the Kâṇva recension verse 9 corresponds with 12 of the Mâdhyandina; 10 with 13; 11 with 14; 12 with 9; 13 with 10; 14 with 11; 15 (varied) with 17; 16 has no corresponding verse; 17 with 15; 18 with 16.

This Upanishad of the Vâjasaneya-Saṃhitâ, called also the Îśâvâsyam from its initial words, Îśâdhyâya, and Îśopanishad, Îśâ Book and Îśâ Upanishad, has been translated by Sir William Jones (Posthumous Works); by Râjâ Ram Mohan Roy; by Dr. Röer in Vol. XV. of the Bibliotheca Indica; by Professor Max Müller in Vol. I. of the Sacred Books of the East, and recently, together with the Commentary of Srî Sañkara, by S. Sitarama Sastri, B. A. (published by V. C. Seshachari, B.A., B.L., through G. A. Natesan & Co., Madras). I am indebted to my old pupil and valued friend Babu Pramadâ Dâsa Mitra of Benares, completer of Dr. Ballantyne's translation of the Sâhitya-darpaṇa and author of an admirable English version of the Bhagavad-Gîtâ, for kind revision of my translation of, and notes on, this Upanishad, and for many corrections and improvements therein. The following Excursus from this scholar's pen, mainly in defence and justification of the Commentator Srî Sañkara, is, I think, a valuable addition to my annotations.

---

"Simple in language as this Upanishad is, it presents difficulties in the shape of apparently conflicting sentiments which it has taxed the ingenuity of ancient and modern commentators to reconcile; yet a doubt sometimes arises whether the real sense has been actually discovered.

"This translation is generally in accordance with the Commentary of Srî Sañkarâchârya who is followed by the great majority of commentators and is recognized as the greatest authority on the Vedânta Philosophy as expounded in its *prasthâna-traya* or triple course, *viz.* the Upanishads, the Vedânta Sûtras, and the Bhagavad-Gîtâ.

"The chief paradox is contained in verse 12 which declares that ignorance (avidyâ) leads to blind darkness, and knowledge (vidyâ) to darkness blinder still.* Srî Sankara explains vidyâ to mean knowledge of the inferior Deities and not the knowledge of the Supreme Brahma. For, according to him, the true knowledge of the Supreme Brahma being the highest object of all religious duties and the sole end of the Upanishads, it cannot be said, under any circumstances, to result in darkness. Whilst a knowledge of the Divinities and certain forms of their worship, also termed vidyâ in the Upanishads, may bring a man into darkness or an unhappy region if he neglects the duties ordained by the Sruti and Smriti. Srî Sankara, in all his Vedântic Commentaries, has urged repeatedly and forcibly that true knowledge of Brahma cannot be combined with Karma, for it removes the notion of duality and fills the devotee's mind with an ever-abiding consciousness of the Eternal Spirit, the Sole Reality. His mental and bodily acts are almost automatical, not being caused by any strong desire or passion. They are results of the residual avidyâ the source of his present and last birth. Exception is made only in the case of Divine Incarnations and those who work solely for the good of the world without any selfish motive or passion.

"The fourth Chapter of the third Book of the Vedânta-Sûtras opens with the Sûtra: 'The end of man (is attained) by this (the independent knowledge of the Self ordained in the Vedânta): such being the word of the Veda. So says Bâdarâyana. In refuting the opponent's arguments Srî Sankara explains that verse 2 of this Upanishad refers to men in general and not specially to one who knows Brahma (III. 4. 13), and that even if it be conceded by virtue of the context that it refers to such a person it implies only a permission and not an injunction to perform works, for the purpose of praising knowledge, as is shown by the words *na karma lipyate nare*, 'work does not taint the man'. That is to say, even if a man who knows Brahma performs work as long as he lives it has no tainting effect upon him: such is the power of knowledge (III. 4 14).† This discussion about the connection of work with wisdom is concluded by explanations summed up in the following words:—'Knowledge, when produced, does not require anything else for the attainment of its fruit (salvation): but for its production it does require (the help of sacrifices, etc). So says the Sruti: 'Him (the Supreme Spirit) do the Brâhmans desire to know by study of the Veda, by sacrifice, by gift, by austerities, and by fasting‡ (Com. on Vedânta S III. 4 26). 'Thefore, thus knowing, serene and self-subdued, retiring (from the world), enduring (every pain and self-concentrated, one sees the Self in his own self' (Brih. Up. VI. 4 23). 'Whereas the qualifications serenity, etc. are directly connected with knowledge as is implied in the epithet *evam-vit*, 'thus knowing,' they are the intimate or immediate (pratyâsanna) means of gaining knowledge; whilst sacrifice, etc., being connected with the *desire* of knowledge, are its outward and remote means. Such is their distinction.' (Com. Ved. S. III. 4. 27)

"It will be seen from the above that there is no inconsistency, as Professor Max Müller (Sacred Books of the East, Vol. I. p. 319) supposes, in the

* This verse occurs also in the Brihadâranyaka Upanishad (IV. 40. 10), where vidyâ is explained as that portion of the Veda which treats of Karma only.

† Vâchaspati Misra says: 'One only doing, etc., verse 2, refers to a person who has no knowledge. Even if it should refer to one who knows there would be no contradiction, glorification of knowledge being intended.'—Bhâmatî. a gloss on Sankara, p. 675. S. 13.

‡ Brihadâranyaka Upanishad IV. 4. 22. Fasting (anâsaka) is explained as moral fasting, abstaining from sensual gratifications.

explanations given by Sri Sankara of verse 2 in his Commentaries on this Upanishad and the Vedânta-Sûtras. The Professor rightly remarks: 'Our Upanishad seems to have dreaded libertinism, knowledge without works, more even than ritualism, works without knowledge, and its true object was to show that orthodoxy and sacrifice, though useless in themselves, must always form the preparation for higher enlightenment.' It would seem that it did not strike the Professor that Sri Sankara's contention is not that work should not precede the highest knowledge, but that when it has been attained, there is no necessity for going back to the preparatory stage, seeing that the goal has already been reached for which the preparation was previously undergone. It cannot be too carefully borne in mind that this knowledge to which the great Sannyâsî attaches so much value is not a verbal or even a speculative knowledge of the Supreme Brahma, which, as the Professor justly fears, may lead to libertinism. Far from being the highest knowledge as understood by Sri Sankara, the latter knowledge may indeed be lower than that of the Gods who are manifestations of Brahma as Wind, Fire, Sun, etc. Brahma so manifested is worshipped in verses 15—17 of our Upanishad. So Sankarânanda, the preceptor of Sâyanâchârya, following as he does Sri Sankara, adds an alternative explanation of vidyâ in verse 12, *viz.* a knowledge of Brahma that lies only on the lip or in the mouth (mukhato Brahmavâdino vâ), and not in the actual realization of Brahma, shown in a life altogether free from desires and affections, doubts and fears, grief and delusion (see verse 7). Certainly it would be a contradiction to connect such knowledge with libertinism, and so after all Sri Sankara must be pronounced to be right.

"It may not be out of place to remark here that Sri Sankara's view of the relation of wisdom to work accords also with the teaching of the Bhagavad-Gîtâ which sets forth so prominently the importance of duty done unselfishly, without expectation of reward. The Gîtâ says: 'But the man who delighteth in Spirit (the Inner Self), is satisfied in Spirit, and is contented in Spirit alone, he (indeed) hath no work to do.' III. 17.

"I feel tempted to give here an interpretation of verse 12, being the expansion of an idea hinted at by a Pandit. It is not, however, found in any of the published Commentaries. It removes the apparent contradiction of the verse, and at the same time restores the force of *iva* rendered meaningless in all the other interpretations, and gives to *vidyâ* its highest sense:—

"Those who are devoted to knowledge (the highest knowledge of Brahma) enter into darkness, as if blinder still, i. e. a darkness devoid of all forms and colours—of all this phenomenal world—darkness indeed as being beyond the light of the sun, the moon, the stars, fire and lightning, for the Sruti says: There the Sun shines not, nor the Moon, nor the Stars, nor do these lightnings shine, far less does fire (Katha Up. 5. 15). Sri Sankara in his Ânandalaharî, a hymn to the Primeval Power or Sakti, sings: 'I adore the Supreme Sambhu, seated in the lotus, named Âjñâ-chakra, between the eyebrows (termed Avimukta or Kâsî in the Jâvâla Upanishad), bearing the brilliance of a hundred millions of suns and moons, united on one side with the Supreme Intelligence (Para Chit, the power of universal consciousness); whom to worship with devotion, man dwelleth in the lightless house of his own Light, unapproached by the Sun and Moon and fire'. The Bhagavad-Gîtâ also gives expression to a similar idea when it says: 'What is night to all creation—therein waketh the self-concentrated' (II. 69). Milton's 'Dark with excessive light' might perhaps be explained in a like spiritual sense.

"Lastly in favour of Sri Sankara it may be observed that he avoids the tautology which other Commentators make of verses 9—11 by explaining Sambhûti and Asambhûti in the same sense almost as vidyâ and avidyâ."

# I.—INDEX OF HYMNS AND VERSES TAKEN FROM THE ṚIGVEDA AND THE ATHARVA-VEDA.

## ṚIGVEDA.

### BOOK I.

## BOOK II.



## BOOK III.

## BOOK IV.



## BOOK V.



## BOOK VI.

## BOOK VII.



## BOOK VIII.



## VÂLAKHILYA.

## BOOK IX.



## BOOK X.

# ATHARVA-VEDA.

# II.—INDEX OF NAMES, ETC.

# CORRIGENDA.

Page 3 line 5 *read* harms *for* harm
" 17 " 15 of notes read *Sky!* for *Sky*
" 23 " 11 *read* merchandise *for* merchandize
" 32 " 9 of notes *read* text *for* texts
" 34 " 4 from below read *Ones* for *One*
" 36 " 7 of notes *read* the *for* he
" 38 " 19 *read* Savitar *for* Savitars
" 41 " 2 of notes *read* Achchhâvâka *for* Achhâvâka
" 55 " 5 of notes *read* Brâhmaṇâchchhamsî *for* Brâhmaṇachhamsi
" 61 " 7 from below *read* 32 *for* 31
" 66 " 6 from below *read* Âgnîdhra *for* Agnîdhra
" 75 " 1 of notes *read* recite *for* recites
" 78 " 11 of notes *read* title *for* little
" 80 " 11 of notes read *dhishṇya* for *dhishṇyâ*
" 91 " 16 *read* Ye *for* Yea
" 91 " 5 of notes *read* addresses *for* address
" 92 " 3 of notes *read* Vrishan *for* Vrishan
" 96 " 9 of notes read *Varûtrîs* for *Varutrîs*
" 133 " 1 of notes read *Praüga* for *Praüg*
" 134 " 1 *read* Viṣvakarman *for* the Omnific
" 139 " 6 from below read *Âyu's* for *Ayu's*
" 143 " 3 from below read *Ṣitikaṇṭha* for *Ṣitikanṭha*
" 156 " 13 *read* bliss-invoking for bless-invoking
" 157 " 1 of notes read *mid-region* for *mid-regiver*
" 158 " 10 *read* strengthening *for* strengthing
" 159 " 15 *read* thou *for* those
" 159 " 24 *read* declare *for* Declare
" 159 " 4 *read* hold for held
" 159 " 25 from below *read* Mythologie *for* Mythologic
" 164 " 14 *read* Marutvatîya *for* Marutvatiya
" 172 " 14 *read* doth *for* may.
" 172 " 3 from below *after* IX *insert* 1. 6
" 176 " 23 *read* Sautrâmaṇî for Santrâmaṇi
" 194 " 1 of notes *read* rain-withholding *for* rain-with-holding
" 199 " 3 from below *read* turns *for* turns.
" 233 " 13 *read* flow *for* flow
" 290 " 3 of notes *after* XII. *insert* 8
" 305 " 8 of notes read *sorium* for *serium*
" 307 " last of notes *read* allotted *for* alloted